ALLE ZEIT WACH
1842

E. Kube · H.U. Störzer (Eds.)

Police Research in the Federal Republic of Germany

15 Years Research Within the "Bundeskriminalamt"

R.V. Clarke (Consulting Editor)

Foreword by H.-L. Zachert

Springer-Verlag
Berlin Heidelberg New York
London Paris Tokyo
Hong Kong Barcelona
Budapest

Prof. Dr. Edwin Kube
Hans Udo Störzer
Bundeskriminalamt
Postfach 1820, W-6200 Wiesbaden
Federal Republic of Germany

Prof. Dr. Ronald V. Clarke
Rutgers University
School of Criminal Justice
S.I. Newhouse Center for Law und Justice
15 Washington Street
Newark, NJ 07102, USA

With 28 Figures

ISBN-13:978-3-642-74178-4 e-ISBN-13:978-3-642-74176-0
DOI: 10.1007/978-3-642-74176-0

Library of Congress Cataloging-in-Publication Data. Police research in the Federal Republik of Germany : 15 years research within the „Bundeskriminalamt" / E. Kube, H.U. Störzer (eds.). p. cm. Includes bibliographical references and index. ISBN-13:978-3-642-74178-4

1. Germany (West) Bundeskriminalamt 2. Criminology--Germany (West) 3. Crime--Germany (West) 4. Police--Germany (West) I. Kube, Edwin. II. Störzer, Hans Udo. HV6022.G3P65 1991 364.943--dc20.

Softcover reprint of the hardcover 1st edition 1991

19/3130-543210 – Printed on acid-free paper

Foreword

Practice, if left to itself, tends to develop makeshift solutions to new problems. Science helps practice to find more lasting solutions to existing problems and may even serve to anticipate and prevent potential ones.

The practice of criminal law requires science. This means more than forensic specialists visiting the scene of the crime. It also means that criminology has relevance for the entire spectrum of the work of the police and criminal justice system. Recognition of this fact led to the setting up of criminological research institutes in the Federal Republic of Germany over the last 15 years. More recently, it has been the *Bundeskriminalamt* (BKA), in particular, which has taken the lead in promoting investigative and forensic science.

Policy-making also requires science. Crime policies should be based on the findings of criminology and forensic science. It is a pleasure to report that in the last few years criminologists and forensic scientists – many of them from the BKA – have been invited to submit evidence to legislative bodies.

Existing criminological knowledge is, of course, far from complete. Not enough light has been cast, for example, on unreported, and thus hidden, crime. This is why criminology so far has been able only in a few cases to give direct support to the police and the criminal justice system in the form of concrete instructions, and why for practical policy-making it cannot have more than an advisory function. This means that criminological research is necessary on a larger scale and that the international exchange of information should be encouraged. Science thrives on discussion. The more comprehensive the discussion, the faster science will advance. At a time when borders between countries are about to be removed – as will be the case in Europe in 1992 – a dialogue must also be sought with both neighboring and more distant countries. The BKA is taking a first important step in this direction by publishing the present volume.

We are glad that Springer-Verlag, an internationally renowned publisher, is publishing this book. Both Ronald V. Clarke, as scientific adviser, and Virginia Sonntag-O'Brien, as translator, have taken care that the concept, language, and style of the book are in a form that will arouse the interest of readers and stimulate scientific discussion.

Hans-Ludwig Zachert
President of the *Bundeskriminalamt*

Preface

This book has its origins in a letter I wrote in 1986 to Edwin Kube, Head of the Research and Training Institute at the *Bundeskriminalamt*. As his onetime British counterpart in the Home Office, I had known of his Institute's existence for some years and had even participated in a conference he organized in 1978 at Wiesbaden on crime and the built environment. I also knew something of the Institute's research through being in regular receipt of its maroon and yellow research reports, written in German, but which sometimes carried two or three page summaries in English. These short summaries had whetted my appetite for more information, but the difficulty of arranging translations had always deterred me.

I was eventually moved to write to Professor Kube after reading the summary of a 1986 report by Servay and Rehm[1] which described systematic interviews with a large sample of bank robbers concerning their motives, planning, and modus operandi. These interviews were designed to yield information of practical use in designing preventive measures. The originality of the study and its practical usefulness made a particular impression on me and I felt quite strongly that it deserved to be more widely known. The more important point, however, was that if true of the bank robbery study, this was likely to be true also of other studies, which were now locked away from me and other non-German speakers between those maroon and yellow covers.

My letter therefore suggested to Professor Kube that he might consider publishing a book in English containing extended summaries of a selection of the research undertaken by his Institute. The book would serve some important purposes beyond being a showcase of the Institute's work: (1) It would benefit the scientific community by more widely disseminating the results of some expensive empirical investigations; (2) it would provide further insight into the process of designing and undertaking practically relevant criminological research in a government setting[2]; (3) it would complement some other recent books published in English dealing with university-based criminology in the Federal Republic of Germany[3]. In the long run, however, the Institute itself ought to benefit most from the book's publication because it should provide entry to a much larger community of scholars.

---

[1] Servay W, Rehm J (1986) Bankraub aus Sicht der Täter. BKA-Forschungsreihe vol 19. Wiesbaden, Bundeskriminalamt.

[2] See Clarke RV, Cornish DB (1983) Crime control in Britain – A review of policy research. Albany, New York, State University of New York Press.

[3] e.g., Wegener H, Lösel F, Haisch J (eds) (1989) Criminal behavior and the justice system: Psychological perspectives. New York, Springer.

Membership in this community should benefit the Institute by exposing it to a broader spectrum of research and theory. It also means that the Institute's work would be opened to more critical scrutiny than before, which should have attendant benefits in terms of quality.

Professor Kube had already been thinking along these lines and my letter turned out to be the encouragement he needed. He decided to approach a commercial publisher, Springer-Verlag, because government publication is a further deterrent to securing academic readership, especially abroad. (An example of this, and a particularly sore point with me, is that Home Office Research Studies, of which well over one hundred have now been published, are rarely cited in criminological journals published in the United States.) Springer-Verlag engaged a translator, Virginia Sonntag-O'Brien, and I was invited to join the production team to help ensure that the book would be found understandable and relevant by the average English-speaking criminologist.

We probably all underestimated the difficulties of the undertaking. The various authors were more used to writing for a police readership than for criminologically sophisticated readers who would be the main consumers of the new book. German academic writing tends to be more formal (making use, for example, of elaborate systems of headings and subheadings) than is customary in contemporary American or British writing. Sociological prose, in whatever language, tends to be obscure, which greatly increases the difficulties of translation. My location on the other side of the Atlantic prevented the frequent meetings that considerably assist the progress of joint productions. And my lack of knowledge of the German language meant that I had to wait for chapters to be translated before reading them – and in some cases authors had to wait for my comments to be translated back again.

Most readers of the book will browse through the contents and will read only those chapters of particular interest to them. As I have had to pay sustained attention to the volume as a whole, it may be helpful to record some of my impressions. The clearest of these is that much of the research being undertaken by the *Bundeskriminalamt* uses the same methods and addresses similar problems as policy-relevant research elsewhere. For example, considerable use has been made of victim surveys in the attempt to obtain better measures of crime and a fuller understanding of the consequences of victimization. Detailed crime-specific studies have been carried out in order to provide the information needed for control policies. Dissatisfaction with current criminal policy has led to the exploration of environmental design and other means of crime prevention. In addition, computer technology has been harnessed to improve the effectiveness of crime detection.

Despite these similarities, references to the English-language literature are sparse and the research is firmly located in a German context, both intellectual and political.[4] However, many of the underlying themes are not entirely "foreign". Thus, the Institute must deal with concerns that government sponsorship may compromise the independence of university-based research and that the de-

[4] All references to the Federal Republic of Germany in this book refer to the borders before October 3, 1990.

mand for policy relevance may stifle support for "purer" research endeavors. It must also take into account wide demands for data protection and for limitations on the power of the state. Like any other government criminological enterprise, it has to carve out a role distinct from, but not inferior to, that of university-based research. Furthermore, it has to continually wrestle with the difficulty of communicating results in a form intelligible to the main consumers – in this case the police. (It would be interesting to learn more about the unusual relationship between the police and the *Bundeskriminalamt* social scientists.)

Though much may be familiar, much is also new. For example, the Institute's crime-specific studies include economic and environmental crimes as well as predatory offenses such as bank robbery. The studies of bank robbery, which made unusual use of systematic interviews with large samples of offenders, were mounted not just to improve understanding, but also to yield information for use in prevention and apprehension. A new slant on research into police information systems was given by knowledge of human information processing. Much longer than normal periods of follow-up were employed in the research on the consequences of victimization. And the research on pattern recognition has achieved international recognition for its applications in handwriting analysis and enhancement of low-quality film images.

For these and other reasons, much is to be learned from spending time with this summary of *Bundeskriminalamt* research. I hope that its appearance will help to generate lasting interest among English-speaking criminologists in the work of the Institute.

Ronald V. Clarke
Rutgers, New Jersey, USA

Contents

Part IV Crime-Specific Studies

Part V Enhancing Effectiveness of Detection and Criminal Investigation

Contributors

Bach, Wolfgang, Dipl.-Phys., Dr. rer. nat., Bundeskriminalamt, Postfach 1820, W-6200 Wiesbaden, FRG. In charge of the BKA's Technological Coordination staff section (since February 1990). Studied physics and physical chemistry; from 1971 assistant at the Physical Chemistry Institute of Saar State University. Doctoral thesis on the spectroscopic examination of thin metal films. From 1977 member of the BKA's scientific staff, from 1984 to 1990 in charge of the Operational and Security Technology section within the Research and Training Institute; development and testing of operational equipment for CID use. Publications on issues of operational and security technology related to crime prevention.

Baurmann, Michael C., Dipl.-Psych., Dr. phil., Bundeskriminalamt, Postfach 1820, W-6200 Wiesbaden, FRG. Assistant head of the Criminological Research section within the BKA's Research Unit on Criminology and Criminal Investigation. PhD in psychology. From 1976 responsible for victimology research at the BKA and from 1986 involved in a major research project on violence against persons. From 1978 to 1986 lecturer in social pedagogy at Mainz University (Rhineland-Palatinate). Various publications on the situation and needs of crime victims, senior citizens as victims, sexually deviant behavior, and violence against persons. Author of a longitudinal study on sexuality, violence, and psychological consequences.

Brinkmann, Klaus-Dieter, Dr.-Ing., Hessischer Minister des Innern, Friedrich-Ebert-Allee 12, W-6200 Wiesbaden, FRG. In charge of the Technical Matters in Automatic Information Processing section of the Hesse Ministry of the Interior (since July 1989). Studied electrical engineering at Darmstadt Technical University from 1966 to 1972; served as research assistant at Karlsruhe Technical University and submitted a doctoral thesis on layout procedures for integrated circuits. Since 1979, in charge of digital image processing at the BKA. Author of numerous publications on the theory of electromagnetic waves, aerial design, system theory, computer-aided design, and layout of integrated semiconductor circuits, microprocessor simulation, software engineering, and digital image processing.

Büchler, Heinz, Dipl.-Kfm., Dr. rer. pol., Bundeskriminalamt, Postfach 1820, W-6200 Wiesbaden, FRG. Assistant section head within the BKA's Research Unit on Criminology and Criminal Investigation (since 1982). Doctorate in economics. In 1981–1982 research assistant in business administration at Gießen

University. Since 1982 responsible for organization and planning research within the BKA's Police Working Methods section. Publications on strategic and organizational matters and issues related to criminal investigation and criminology.

Bunge, Ernst, Dr.-Ing., Bundesrechnungshof, Postfach 100433, W-6000 Frankfurt 1, FRG. Head of the Security of Information Processing section in the federal audit Office (since 1988). Doctorate in communications engineering; lecturer at Hamburg University; senior scientist at the Philips research laboratory, Hamburg. Thereafter in charge of technological research at the BKA's Research and Training Institute. Numerous publications, lectures, and patents in the field of scientific computer technology.

Clarke, Ronald V., Prof. Dr., Rutgers University, School of Criminal Justice, S.I. Newhouse Center for Law and Justice, 15 Washington Street, Newark, NJ 07102, USA. Professor, Dean of the School of Criminal Justice, Rutgers University, Newark (since 1987). PhD in psychology. Formerly in charge of the Home Office Research and Planning Unit in London, then Professor of Criminal Justice at Temple University, Philadelphia. Publications on issues related to the theory of crime, police effectiveness, and crime prevention.

Dörmann, Uwe, Dipl. rer. soc., Bundeskriminalamt, Postfach 1820, W-6200 Wiesbaden, FRG. In charge of the Crime Analysis, Crime Statistics section of the BKA's Research Unit on Criminology and Criminal Investigation (since 1980). Chairman of the Police Crime Statistics commission, in which all federal states are represented. Trained and worked in the industrial marketing field. Studied social sciences. Since 1971, member of the BKA's scientific staff. Publications on issues related to crime statistics and criminology.

Dufner, Karl-Heinz, Bundeskriminalamt, Postfach 1820, W-6200 Wiesbaden, FRG. Assistant head of the BKA's Motor Vehicle Crime section. BKA staff member since 1974; from 1977 to 1984 worked in the fields of counterterrorism, computer applications for investigative/analytical purposes, drug enforcement, and others; from 1986 to 1988 assistant head of the Police Working Methods section with special responsibility for drug enforcement matters within the BKA's Research Unit on Criminology and Criminal Investigation.

Koch, Karl-Friedrich, Bundeskriminalamt, Postfach 1820, W-6200 Wiesbaden, FRG. Member of the BKA's Crime Analysis, Crime Statistics section (since 1985). Member of the Hesse police force until 1978. From 1979 in the BKA's Anti-Terrorist Division; from 1983 in the Research and Training Institute. Publications on matters related to the crime situation and crime trends.

Kreuzer, Arthur, Dr. jur., Universität Gießen, Professor für Kriminologie, Jugendstrafrecht, Strafvollzug, Licher Straße 64, W-6300 Gießen, FRG. Professor of criminology, juvenile justice, and correctional matters at Gießen University (since 1976). Doctorate in law. From 1968 magistrate in a juvenile division of the Hamburg regional court and lecturer; in 1975–1976 professor at Hamburg

University. Author of numerous publications, in particular on issues related to criminology (rocker movement, drug problems, unreported crime etc.), juvenile justice, correctional matters, and criminal law relating to the medical profession.

Kube, Edwin, Prof. Dr. jur., Bundeskriminalamt, Postfach 1820, W-6200 Wiesbaden, FRG. Head of the BKA's Research and Training Institute (since 1982), honorary professor at Gießen University (since 1983); member of the managing board of *Neue Kriminologische Gesellschaft* (NKG) (since 1989). Doctorate in law. Until 1974 in the internal administrative service of the state of Baden-Württemberg; from 1975 head of the BKA's Research Unit on Criminology and Criminal Investigation. From 1977 lecturer at Gießen University. Until 1989 vice-president of *Deutsche Kriminologische Gesellschaft*, one of the two predecessors of the NKG. Author of numerous publications, especially on issues related to criminology and criminal investigation.

Kuckuck, Werner, Dipl.-Math., Bundeskriminalamt, Postfach 1820, W-6200 Wiesbaden, FRG. In charge of the Special Information Systems section of the BKA's Research Unit on Technological Development (since 1989). Studied mathematics. From 1977 member of the BKA's technological research staff; from 1986 in charge of the Forensic Information System for Handwritings (FISH) project. Developed methods of pattern recognition and image processing; designed and developed special purpose information systems; publications in the field of computer-assisted handwriting comparison.

Leineweber, Heinz, Bundeskriminalamt, Postfach 1820, W-6200 Wiesbaden, FRG. In charge of the Police Working Methods section of the BKA's Research Unit on Criminology and Criminal Investigation. Lecturer at the Federal College for Public Administration. Studied law. As from 1974 member of the BKA's scientific staff. Author of numerous publications, in particular on issues related to police law and criminal procedure.

Plate, Monika, Dipl.-Soz., Bundeskriminalamt, Postfach 1820, W-6200 Wiesbaden, FRG. Assistant head of the Criminological Research section within the BKA's Research Unit on Criminology and Criminal Investigation. Studied sociology and political science. Since 1972 member of the BKA's scientific staff. Publications on issues related to juvenile delinquency, recent developments in criminology, and the police-social worker relationship.

Poerting, Peter, Dipl.-Kfm., Dr. rer. pol., Bundeskriminalamt, Postfach 1820, W-6200 Wiesbaden, FRG. In charge of the BKA's Situation Monitoring staff section (since December 1989). Doctorate in economics. From 1976 to 1979, research assistant at the Institute for Business Auditing, Cologne University; from 1979 to 1987 assistant section head responsible for research into economic crime within the BKA's Research Unit on Criminology and Criminal Investigation; from 1987 to 1989 in charge of the Fundamentals of Criminology,

Documentation section. Numerous publications, in particular on the subject of business, and criminological aspects of economic crime and its control.

Rebscher, Erich, Dr. jur., Bundeskriminalamt, Postfach 1820, W-6200 Wiesbaden, FRG. Head of the Research Unit on Criminology and Criminal Investigation. Doctorate in law. From 1967 to 1969 in the Hesse state internal administrative service; since 1969 in the senior police service at the BKA. From 1971 to 1974 liaison officer assigned to the General Secretariat of ICPO-Interpol. From 1977 to 1984 in charge of the BKA's Drug Intelligence section. Publications on international police cooperation, drug enforcement, and organized crime.

Risch, Hedwig, Dipl.-Volksw., Bundeskriminalamt, Postfach 1820, W-6200 Wiesbaden, FRG. Assistant head of the BKA's Crime Analysis, Crime Statistics section (since 1985). Studied economics and joined the BKA in 1972; from 1972 to 1974 active in the field of in-house organization; from 1974 to 1983 in the Investigations Division, specializing in economic crime; since 1983 in the Research and Training Institute. Publication on crimes of insolvency.

Römer-Klees, Ruth, Universität Gießen, Professur für Kriminologie, Jugendstrafrecht, Strafvollzug, Licher Straße 64, W-6300 Gießen, FRG. Research assistant in the Department of Criminology, Juvenile Justice, and Correctional Matters, Gießen University (since 1984). Studied law. Since 1987 involved in a project on addict crime (indirect procurement offenses, follow-up offenses) in conjunction with further scientific activity (doctoral thesis).

Rohrer, Franz, Bundeskriminalamt, Postfach 1820, W-6200 Wiesbaden, FRG. Police officer in the BKA's Watch section. With the BKA since 1979; from 1983 to 1988 in the Research and Training Institute; since 1985 in the Research Unit on Criminology and Criminal Investigation.

Seitz, Norbert, Bundesminister des Innern, Postfach 170290, W-5300 Bonn 1, FRG. Assistant head of the Organized Crime, Narcotics, Profit Seizure section, Federal Ministry of the Interior (since 1989). Studied law. From 1984 to 1989 in the BKA, until 1988 assistant section head within the Research Unit on Criminology and Criminal Investigation, with special responsibility for research into environmental crime; thereafter assistant head of the Legal Counsel section. From 1989 in the Federal Interior Ministry's organization section. Publications on issues related to environmental crime and profit seizure.

Störzer, Hans Udo, Bundeskriminalamt, Postfach 1820, W-6200 Wiesbaden, FRG. In charge of the Criminological Research Section within the BKA's Research Unit on Criminology and Criminal Investigation (since 1986). Lecturer at the Federal College for Public Administration. Studied law, administrative science, and history. From 1974 to 1979 research assistant at the Institute of Criminology, Heidelberg University; from 1979 member of the BKA's scientific staff; from 1981 to 1986 in charge of the Fundamentals of Criminology, Documentation section within the Research Unit on Criminology and Criminal Investigation. Author of numerous publications on issues related to criminology, victimology, crime control policy, history, organization of criminological research, training in criminology and criminal investigation, and documentation of criminal science literature; prepared various specialized bibliographies.

Vahlenkamp, Werner, Bundeskriminalamt, Postfach 1820, W-6200 Wiesbaden, FRG. Member of the BKA's Police Working Methods section (since 1989). Entered the BKA as a police officer in 1970; from 1973 to 1983 investigator in the Weapons and Explosives Offenses section; from 1983 in the Research and Training Institute; from 1985 in the Research Unit on Criminology and Criminal Investigation. Publications on organized crime and crime prevention.

Weiß, Rüdiger, Dipl.-Math., Bundeskriminalamt, Postfach 1820, W-6200 Wiesbaden, FRG. Assistant head of the Crime Analysis, Crime Statistics section within the BKA's Research Unit on Criminology and Criminal Investigation. Studied mathematics, computer science, and economics. Positions in university level computer training and in private industry. Since 1979 member of the BKA's scientific staff; work focusing on research into unreported crime, methodology of empirical studies. Publications chiefly on the subject of research into unreported crime.

Wulff-Nienhüser, Marianne, Dr. phil., Magister Artium, Universität Münster, Institut für Politikwissenschaft, Scharnhorststraße 100, W-4400 Münster, FRG. Research assistant at the Political Science Institute of Münster University (since 1985). Studied political science, sociology, and German philology. Scientific works on environmental crime, television research, media policy, and issues related to information and communication technology.

Part I
Introductory Section

CHAPTER 1

The Bundeskriminalamt: The German Federal Criminal Police Office

K.-F. Koch and H. Risch

Contents

1 Fighting Crime in the Federal Republic of Germany: The Provisions of the Federal German Basic Law

The 11 states (resp. 16 states since Oct. 3, 1990) of the Federal Republic of Germany are responsible for policing within their own area. This sovereignity of the states in police matters has its legal anchoring in Article 30 of the federal German Basic Law of May 23, 1949. Correspondingly, there are 11 different state police acts, which resemble each other in many key points. Nonetheless, the individual state police forces differ considerably in terms of their organizational structure.

The Federal Republic of Germany has a total of some 200 000 police officers divided between the state police forces, which include uniformed police, riot police, waterways police, and the criminal investigation department; and the federal police

Kube/Störzer (Eds.)
Police Research in the Federal Republic of Germany

forces, which include the federal border police, the *Bundestag* (Federal Diet) police, full-time officers of the railway police, and the federal criminal police office (*Bundeskriminalamt*).

The increasing mobility of offenders very rapidly made it necessary to introduce regulations to govern cooperation between the state (*Landeskriminalamt*) and the federal criminal police offices and to create the legal prerequisites for combating international crime. These are set down in Article 73, Nos. 10 and 87, Subparagraph 1, of the Basic Law. This article makes provision for central criminal investigation reporting and for information offices to be set up to the state or federal level. It was on the basis of this article of the Constitution that legislation establishing the *Bundeskriminalamt* (BKA) was introduced in March 1951 (see Appendix A).

2 The Historical Development of the BKA

The criminal investigation department of the British zone in Hamburg provided the basis on which the BKA was set up. This authority had been set up by the British military government in 1946 and was taken over by the federal government in 1951. The federal government decreed that the BKA was to be located in Wiesbaden, and the step-by-step move to this city was completed by 1953. A "Security Group" was set up in Bad Godesberg due to its proximity to Bonn, the federal capital. This group was assigned the responsibility of providing protection and security within the federal capital.

Staff members at that time totaled 395, 192 of whom were criminal investigation officers.

During the first 15 years, the crime fighting work of the BKA was restricted virtually without exception to the centralized collection and analysis of information. Social developments then prompted the adoption of a new direction in criminal policy in the mid-1960s and, in the wake of this, the call for a new program for the BKA.

The federal government's action program for the modernization and intensification of crime fighting, which was launched in 1970, marked the first step towards the expansion of the BKA into an up-to-date central office for fighting crime. This expansion has since been completed and, as far as the BKA has been concerned, has involved a significant increase in the number of staff members.

In the period up to 1980, an office building, laboratory complex with forensic facilities, training building, and modern data processing center had been completed. A new sports complex with an underground firing range, which ranks as one of the most modern in the world, marked the temporary culmination of the building program. In 1981, three BKA departments (State Security, the Security Group, and the Technical Services Department) were able to move into new premises at Meckenheim-Merl near Bonn.

In 1955, there were 439 employees at the BKA. In 1971, this number rose above the 1000 mark for the first time and included 545 criminal investigation officers. In 1987 the BKA employed more than 3500 people, including 1572 criminal investigation officers:

	1960	1970	1980	1990
Total staff	597	941	3521	3826
Criminal investigation officers	362	565	1476	1535

The BKA was established in 1951 with a budget of DM 3 million. Personnel expenses totaled DM 2 million. In 1990 the budget reached DM 330 million, with 65% of this spent on personnel:

1960	10.8 million DM
1970	39.0 million DM
1980	282.0 million DM
1990	330.0 million DM

The president and vice president constitute the heads of the BKA. Under them come four organizational units, the planning and coordination staff and the others responsible for cooperation between the federal authorities and the states, domestic and foreign coordination, and public relations. The BKA is further organized into 12 departments, with the three departments located in Meckenheim forming a principal department. Each department is made up of two to four groups or specialist groups. These, in turn, are divided into three to six sections or specialist units (see Appendix B).

3 The Duties of the BKA Under the Terms of the BKA Act

The 1951 act sees the BKA first and foremost as an instrument of cooperation and coordination between the federal authorities and the individual states. To this end, it works closely together with state criminal investigation departments. As the central information collection and analysis point and the central information retrieval office of the criminal investigation police of the Federal Republic of Germany, the BKA has the task of collecting all information and documents that are of relevance in combating crime and of notifying federal and state criminal prosecution authorities without delay of any findings of interest to them. Over and above this, the BKA maintains identification and forensic facilities. It is the sole official channel for conducting dealings with foreign police and judicial authorities in matters relating to the search for international offenders.

On the basis of this comprehensive mandate, the BKA conducted police investigations under its own responsibility only in a very small number of cases up to the mid-1960s. This it did when so instructed by the Federal Minister of the Interior or at the request of an appropriate state authority.

The features of the BKA's work that have been outlined above make it clear why the BKA remained virtually unnoticed by the public during the initial years of its existence.

Under the terms of the 1969 amendment, the Federal Prosecutor General can commission the BKA to carry out investigations within the framework of his responsibility. A further innovation was the "right of assignation" – in certain cases, the BKA can assign the responsibility of the search for criminals operating in more than one region to an individual state. This ruling was designed to ensure that the fight against crimes which transgressed regional boundaries could be organized more efficiently. A large number of formal prerequisites, however, prevented the BKA from exhausting the full range of possibilities open to it. It was only with the advent of the spectacular crimes of politically motivated terrorism, which spread uncertainty among the population at the start of the 1970s, that the expansion of the BKA's responsibilities was spurred on at an unprecedented rate.

A further amendment to the BKA Act was passed as part of the Program for Internal Security within the Federal Republic of Germany, dated June 1972. This amendment contained the above-mentioned expansion of responsibilities.

In the 1973 amendment to the BKA Act (see Appendix A), the BKA was not only deemed to be responsible in those cases where it was commissioned or requested to act, but was also allocated new criminal investigation duties in its own right, in cases where specific, internationally organized crimes had been committed and where there were matters to be cleared up abroad. The investigation of crimes committed against persons in political life as well as crimes involving political motives or touching on federal or foreign policy was also brought under the competence of the BKA at that time. The amendment further specified that the BKA shall serve as the central office for the electronic data network that links the federal level with the state level in police matters. Over and above this, the activities of the security group in the area of the protection of persons were placed on a legal footing (Appendix C).

4 Fulfilling the Function of a Central Office

4.1 Tracing Persons and Property: Identification

As the central office for the collection and analysis of all information and documents of relevance to the police in combating crime, the BKA is required to notify the federal and state criminal prosecution authorities without delay of all findings of interest to them. Its round-the-clock operations ensure that the office can be contacted at all times when requests are made for arrests, for establishing the whereabouts of persons, or when it comes to establishing the identities of dangerous individuals or obtaining information on the modus operandi, criminals, and accomplices.

Criminal records are an indispensable tool for police work. In the ideal case, these records make it possible to reconstruct the entire criminal career of an offender. This, together with the personal information on the individual concerned, provides important points of reference for the measures to be taken when investigating a case. A computerized index is used at the BKA to establish whether records, fingerprints, or any other documents exist for a particular person. More than 1.5 million personal data with their sources were maintained, as of 1987, in the computer files. Almost 2 million records of these persons were maintained.

In line with the legal provisions governing the protection of data, criminal records are regularly removed to respect the specified deletion deadlines.

With the electronic police information system (INPOL) set up in 1972, an information system was created for all the police forces within the Federal Republic of Germany. The system is run jointly by the federal government and the states, who divide the work between them, and with the BKA acting as the central office. The input, modification, and retrieval of information is carried out on a decentralized basis. INPOL is a passive information system. This means that information is only supplied in response to a specific inquiry. Within the BKA, it is the data processing department that is responsible for work involving electronic data processing.

Until the introduction of the INPOL system, the police used lists and card indexes of wanted persons and lists of stolen property in their on-the-spot checks. These are now only used for specific purposes, such as in foreign offices of the Federal Republic of Germany.

Tracing persons and property constitutes the central task of the INPOL system today. The wanted persons files contain the particulars of persons who the police or judicial authorities wish to have arrested, whose whereabouts they wish to have established, or who they wish to have expelled. At present, some 170 000 requests for arrest have been registered (including some 103 000 nonappealable expulsion orders against foreigners) together with more than 59 000 requests regarding persons whose whereabouts need to be established.

The INPOL property tracing files can be used to register numbered articles which are connected to a crime, such as motor vehicles, equipment, identity documents, and bank notes. More than 3.3 million articles are currently listed in the property register.

Video display units are installed in police stations, at border crossings, and at airports. Beyond that, there are telex machines connected to the INPOL system. In addition to these fixed installations, mobile data radio units are used for direct dialogues with the computer via a radio link.

A large number of data protection and data security measures reliably ensure that unauthorized access to the INPOL system is prevented. The use to which the BKA puts the wide range of data available to it is subject to control by the Federal Commissioner for Data Protection.

A further important aid in conducting investigations is the *Bundeskriminalblatt* (Federal German Criminal Investigation Bulletin), published by the BKA. This has a daily circulation of some 9200 and contains information on the search for known and unknown offenders, unidentified corpses, and stolen and found goods as well as general police information. It publishes personal data, photographs, and descriptions of persons, modus operandi, and property.

The tasks of the identification service are the identification of persons and unidentified corpses, the establishment of the circumstances of a crime, the determination of the person or persons involved, and the submission of expert opinions regarding fingerprints. The fingerprint is the central point of focus here, constituting an individual, unalterable, and hence absolutely reliable identification feature.

As the central office, the BKA collects the ten-fingerprint sheets that are obtained in the course of police identification service work. The chief features of the fingerprints are "translated" into a special alphanumerical code to enable new entries to be compared, by means of the computer, with the sheets that are already on file. This permits existing fingerprints to be allocated within a short period of time. At present, some 3.2 million fingerprint sheets, relating to approximately 1.6 million persons, are held in the archives. An average of some 20000 fingerprint sheets reach the BKA every month.

Photographs of persons constitute an essential part of identification work and are archived in a central photograph collection. This currently holds some 4 million photographs of 2 million persons. These are likewise available to all police stations. Photographs are removed from the central collection at regular intervals in line with the provisions of the legislation on data protection.

Scientific and technical findings are indispensable when it comes to solving crimes and ensuring that there is evidence that can subsequently be used in court. The task of present-day forensic departments is to find, secure, and analyze relevant evidence and clues based on research findings and using the latest in technical equipment. This often makes a decisive contribution towards establishing the objective facts of a case.

As specified in the legal provisions, the BKA is responsible for maintaining the facilities required in all areas of forensic investigation and forensic research and for coordinating cooperation among the police departments throughout the country in these fields. Moreover, the BKA is responsible for organizing advanced training courses in special fields of criminal investigation and for submitting expert forensic opinions when so requested by the police, public prosecutor's offices, and the courts. The six specialist groups of the Forensic Institute perform these tasks within the BKA.

4.2 Research and Teaching

Responsibility for research and teaching within the BKA lies with the Research and Training Institute (see Chap. 2). The aim of the research work is to improve the fight against crime with both research findings which can be put directly into practice and through the development of information systems, in the broad sense of the term. A prerequisite for the effective prevention and efficient deterrence of crime is precise knowledge of the motives, structural conditions, and laws of cause and effect that govern criminality. Over and above this, methods of counteracting crime need to be optimized. Only with the aid of systematic criminological and technical research will it be possible to obtain the necessary knowledge and develop the right concepts.

The Research Unit on Criminology and Criminal Investigation conducts investigations, based on scientific principles and methods, which are designed to produce findings on subjects and problems that are of relevance to the police and are topical and fundamental in nature. The findings established in this way are passed on for practical implementation through a wide variety of publications, through training and advanced training courses, and through seminars, conferences, and lectures.

The research work is guided primarily by the needs and concerns of practical police work, which, in some investigations, include visiting the scene of the crime, the course of events during the crime, a description of the persons involved, interrogation of the offender, and the specific search and investigation strategies employed by the police officer in charge. Other concerns deal, for example, with the role of the police officer in the preliminary proceedings, in specific cases, or in court. Other work covers selective forms of investigation into specific kinds of crime or modus operandi. Areas of special interest include violent crime, economic crime, environmental crime, drug-related crime, and certain aspects of victimology.

A further important task of the Research Unit on Criminology and Criminal Investigation is to compile and publish the annual *Polizeiliche Kriminalstatistik* (police crime statistics, PCS) for the Federal Republic of Germany. All the crime data collected in the individual states are summarized here. The PCS gives an overview of the crime registered in the police files and also highlight trends and developments. At the same time, they are an essential source of data for research.

In order to represent the interests of the police in the area of criminal policy, expert statements and opinions are drawn up on proposed new legislation, proposed reforms, and general legal matters of relevance to the police.

A practical contribution towards improving the combating of crime has been made by the development and trial of special equipment and instruments in the fields of operational and security techniques. Support is provided for individual police stations that are engaged in ongoing operations.

The computer-aided documentation system is designed to ensure that the police have access to and can retrieve criminological literature and expert forensic opinions. It is intended that the system should include the full range of knowledgte from the fields of criminology and forensic science and should be kept up to date, indicating the sources of practical police work, theory, and research. All police stations and public authorities are entitled to access the system.

The task of the Research Unit on Technological Development is to establish the need for new technical equipment and processes, working in cooperation with those who use this equipment within the police force. Research and development projects are then drawn up on this basis and the corresponding projects carried out. A further task involves the acquisition of as much information as possible on the latest scientific and technical developments to emerge from industry, universities, and other research establishments. In this way, the police keep abreast of technological trends that have an impact on their practical work. Focal points of this technical research to date have included the development of new processes for speaker recognition, the handwriting recognition service, linguistic text analysis, and image enhancement.

The Research Unit on Technological Development is supported in its work by a computer center equipped with a comprehensive range of special periphery for the input, output, and processing of measured data, voices, images, and texts related to criminal investigation work.

The duties of the Research and Training Institute cover not only the wide field of research, but also training and continuing education. This includes both the training of criminal investigation officers for the BKA and the training of federal and state police officers to become forensic and fingerprint experts. This guarantees a uniform, specialized training focused on current central issues and problems of combating crime. The program is rounded off by further training in scientific and technical fields, foreign language courses, and task-related operational training. Apart from these duties, the BKA also provides practical assistance in the forensic training of police officers from other countries.

5 Fulfilling the Task of a Police Investigating Authority

5.1 Investigative Responsibilities

The BKA departments that conduct investigations are the Drug Squad, the Investigation and Analysis Department, the Anti-Terrorist Unit, and the State Security Department. This work covers the fields of drug offenses, organized crime, economic crime, and other crimes involving financial assets, violent crime, and offenses against porperty, terrorism, treason, and threats to state security. In addition, the BKA conducts police investigations in criminal cases:

- When it is so requested by a competent state authority
- When it is given express orders to this end by the Federal Minister of the Interior
- In serious cases
- When it is so requested or instructed by the federal prosecutor general (No. 5, Subparagraph 3 of the BKA Act).

In special cases, the BKA conducts autonomous investigations without having been instructed or requested to do so (Article 5, Subparagraph 2 of the BKA Act). These are cases which bear the stamp "internationally organized" and cover offenses relating to illegal dealing in arms, ammunition, and explosives; illegal drug trafficking; and illegal production and distribution of counterfeit currency.

Over and above this, the BKA is responsible for investigating, in its own right, offenses committed against persons in political life where it can be assumed that the offense was politically motivated and where the offense has bearing on federal or foreign policy matters.

The competence of the BKA also covers the field of police protection of state. This work is carried out by the State Protection Department or the Anti-Terrorist

Unit, as appropriate. The State Protection Department, alongside the state protection units maintained by the state police forces, is responsible for the police tasks of counterespionage, combating offenses involving threats to peace and high treason, threats to the democratic constitutional state (extremism), and politically motivated crimes committed by foreigners.

The Anti-Terrorist Unit was set up in May 1975 as a result of the increased criminal activity of terrorist groups in the Federal Republic of Germany and the increasingly international nature of terrorism. This unit has the task of effectively combating this type of criminality throughout the Federal Republic of Germany and in cooperation with other countries. The success of the fight against terrorism is not only reflected by the large number of arrested and convicted violent terrorists and their supporters, it is also a matter or preventing planned murders, assassinations, and kidnappings. Considerable importance is attached to the latest forensic methods, such as the analysis of microclues and the handwriting recognition service.

Apart from the support functions already mentioned, the BKA is also responsible for providing personnel and material support to the state police forces in cases which involve particularly extensive investigations. The operational and criminological knowledge available within the BKA is thus placed at the service of the state police forces.

5.2 The Protection of Persons

The Security Group has been responsible for the protection of persons since 1951. It makes use of the latest technical operational equipment and facilities in its work, including armored escort vehicles, an extensive range of arms, and special radio and telecommunications facilities, such as programmable video monitoring units for the protection of objects.

Since the BKA Act stipulates that the reponsibility of other police forces should continue to stand, all the necessary measures are worked out and implemented in close cooperation with the state police forces, the federal border police, or the parliament police. The same applies in cases in which the Security Group carries out security duties abroad and cooperates with the security authorities of the country in question.

5.3 The Identification Commission

Ever since the start of the 1970s, there has been a steady increase in international mass tourism. In the event of serious accidents, either at home or abroad, the BKA provides support in identifying the accident victims. As many as 60 experts from different BKA departments make up the identification commission, and the commission is sent to the location of the accident without delay (with the approval of the country involved, where necessary).

In parallel with on-the-spot investigations, a central office within the BKA obtains documents on potential victims, which can then be compared with the findings at the scene of the accident.

The work of the identification commission has been much acclaimed worldwide, and others have studied modus operandi, equipment, and experience of this commission when planning similar commissions in their countries.

5.4 Cooperation in the National and International Fight Against Crime

The BKA has been the national central office for the Federal Republic of Germany since 1952, as is provided for in Article 1, Subparagraph 2 of the BKA Act. Article 10 specifies that the BKA shall be the sole official channel for communicating with foreign police and judicial authorities when this is necessary for pursuing international, nonpolitical offenders. Exceptions may be permitted to this rule in border regions. When working together with other national Interpol central offices, the BKA has to observe not only national laws and the legal aid provisions (Federal German Extradition Act, guidelines for dealings with other countries in criminal matters), but also international treaties and agreements. In terms of the Interpol statutes, the chief function of the national central office is to support police investigation work by supplying information of relevance to criminal investigations; by conducting identification work, searches, interrogations, confiscations, and seizures; and also by making arrests for purposes of extradition. Political offenses are excluded here. A total of 154 countries currently belong to Interpol.

The increase in internationally organized crime, in general, and in terrorism that crosses international borders, in particular, calls for cooperation between the countries involved both on an administrative level and in the practical and legal fields. In those areas in which the BKA conducts independent investigations, it thus cooperates closely with police, customs, border control, and judicial authorities abroad. Various working groups have been formed to promote these joint endeavors; the BKA is a member of these working groups.

In the fields of terrorism and drug offenses, in particular, the working groups draw up guidelines for international policy, conclude agreements on the alignment of legislation, and coordinate and improve international cooperation. Methods of combating crime are proposed, agreed upon, and then jointly implemented; the exchange of information and experience is intensified, and mutual training and retraining further advanced.

On the national level the AG Kripo (*Arbeitsgemeinschaft der Leiter der Landeskriminalämter mit dem Bundeskriminalamt*) is the most senior expert group within the federal criminal police that is entrusted with coordination tasks. The work of the group is intended to help overcome difficulties that arise through the different areas of responsibility and organizational rulings that apply to the police at the federal level and in the different states. Membership of AG Kripo comprises the heads of the state criminal police offices (*Landeskriminalämter*) and the president of the BKA, who holds the chair. The BKA is likewise responsible for conducting the business of the group. Meetings of the working group are also attended by representatives from the police staff college and, where appropriate, advisers from other authorities.

It is the intention that the conceptual approaches presented at these meetings and the discussion of criminal strategy provide solutions to promote cooperation between police forces at the federal and state levels. In order to achieve this aim, the AG Kripo consults subcommittees from the state criminal investigation departments and the BKA.

6 A Comparison of the BKA with the Federal Bureau of Investigation (FBI) and New Scotland Yard

6.1 FBI and BKA

In the Federal Republic of Germany the main responsibility for police work lies with the states, whereas in the USA it lies with the municipal authorities. The constitutional situation differs in so far as that, under the federal German Basic Law, responsibility for combating crime is borne jointly by the federal and the state governments. In the USA, by contrast, general policing comes under the jurisdiction of the states and other territorial authorities (municipalities, etc.). These have created their own police forces and enacted laws in their areas of responsibility, and the police are responsible for pursuing any violation of these laws.

In the Federal Republic of Germany, the penal code defines statutory offenses on a uniform basis for the whole of the country and, hence, state legislation does not contain any significant penal norms. In theory, therefore, executive control of the BKA in criminal investigations cannot be confined a priori to specific types of offenses. The FBI, by contrast, has to be satisfied with a role that is likewise theoretically restricted by a catalogue of federal laws. The extensive field of state penal law in the USA remains largely closed to the FBI.

In the USA, however, federal laws extended the field of responsiblity of the FBI, supplementing the laws of the states and closing existing gaps. Over the years, federal laws have also been passed which have produced parallel responsibilities for the FBI and the state police. An extension of the BKA's responsibilities on this scale is not possible in the Federal Republic of Germany under the terms of the Basic Law.

Under the terms of the BKA Act, the BKA is allowed to conduct investigations in its own right only for very specific crimes. Over and above this, the BKA can act on an executive basis within specified limits and then only when so requested or instructed. This has virtually the same effect of creating a limited catalogue of responsibility for the BKA, as does the federal penal legislation limiting the responsibilities of the FBI. The offenses pursued by the BKA and the FBI are of a similar nature, however, being primarily either those that transgress state boundaries or serious crimes.

The constitutions of the USA and the Federal Republic of Germany have a different organizational structure, and this has led to the development of different legislation and subsequent responsibilities. In both countries, however, criminal investigation authorities have developed at the federal level which closely resemble each other on many points. The problems of close cooperation between the federal, state, and municipal criminal investigation departments are also similar. All in all, it can be seen that solutions worked out by the FBI in the USA can basically be adopted by the BKA in Federal Republic of Germany.

6.2 New Scotland Yard and the BKA

In Great Britain, "the police" comprises a network of 52 separate police forces: 43 in England and Wales, 8 in Scotland, and the Royal Ulster Constabulary in Northern Ireland. There is no national police force. A considerable amount of coordination and cooperation takes place in all fields of police activity, albeit in different committees.

The police of the capital city are the premier police force. They are responsible to the Home Office and not to the local police authorities as are the other police forces. Two police organizations work in Greater London – the Metropolitan Police and, in the city center, the City of London Police. New Scotland Yard is the name that has been given to the headquarters of the Metropolitan Police. In this capacity, New Scotland Yard houses offices for the work conducted by the Metropolitan Police in its own area of responsibility. Criminal investigation work is carried out, in principle, by police officers of the individual police districts. New Scotland Yard, however, also provides accommodations for criminal investigation experts. These experts take over investigations into serious offenses. Their work can extend over the whole of the country (with the exception of Scotland); this also applies, moreover, to all police officers in Great Britain.

Alongside this, departments with central responsibility have also developed in New Scotland Yard over the years. Parts of New Scotland Yard can thus rank as national criminal investigation departments and are, in fact, frequently regarded as such. Central tasks of this type include:

- The National Central Office for the Suppression of Counterfeit Currency
- The Extradition, Illegal Immigration, and Passport Squad
- The Metropolitan and City Police Company Fraud Department (Fraud Squad) whose national responsibility is keeping records on corruption in public life
- The Special Branch, which provides personal protection and is involved in matters of national security
- The National Drugs Intelligence Unit.

Beyond this, further facilities that are typical for a central office are maintained at New Scotland Yard. These are: the National Central Bureau of Interpol; the National Identification Bureau, including the National Fingerprint Office and the

National Criminal Records Office; and the Forensic Science Laboratory, which works basically for the Metropolitan Police but also for county police forces.

There are many parallels to the work carried out by the departments of the German BKA, even if the legal system and police organization in Great Britain and the Federal Republic of Germany can otherwise only be compared with great difficulty.

6.3 Conclusion

A comparison can be drawn between the BKA and the FBI and – with limitations – between the BKA and New Scotland Yard only if consideration is given to the different historical development that has taken place for each one. This has given rise to a different constitutional basis for police work, even though the three authorities do display a certain degree of similarity in practice. Common features include the importance of cooperation with other police forces and offices in the country, responsibility for similar offenses, and the maintenance of central facilities for fighting crime.

Appendix A: Nonofficial Translation of the Law Concerning the Establishment of a Federal Criminal Police Office (Bundeskriminalamt)

As proclaimed on 29th June 1973 (Federal Law Gazette I, p. 704), amended by laws dated 2nd March 1974 (Federal Law Gazette I, p. 469) and 9th December 1974 (Federal Law Gazette I, p. 3393).

Article 1

(1) The Federation shall establish a Federal Criminal Police Office for the cooperation between the Federation and the States in CID matters. Its task shall be to counteract the activities of criminal offenders whose activities extend, or are likely to extend, to an international level or beyond the borders of a State.

(2) The Bundeskriminalamt shall be at the same time the National Central Bureau of the International Criminal Police Organization (Interpol) for the Federal Republic of Germany.

Article 2

(1) In its capacity as central office the functions of the Bundeskriminalamt shall be:

1. To collect and analyze all information and records relevant for crime control by the police. In this respect, it shall also be the central office for the electronic data network jointly operated by the Federation and the States;
2. To advise Federal, and State, criminal justice authorities promptly of any information concerning them and of any connections between crimes that have been revealed;
3. To maintain identification facilities;
4. To maintain the necessary facilities for all fields of analysis and research in forensic science and to coordinate police cooperation in these areas;
5. To monitor crime trends and compile analytical reports and statistics on this basis;
6. To conduct research with a view to developing police methods and procedures for crime control;
7. To support State police forces in their crime-prevention work;
8. To provide advanced training in specialized fields of criminal investigation.

(2) At the request of police authorities, public prosecutors, and the courts, the Bundeskriminalamt shall prepare expert opinions in the fields of identification and forensic science for use in criminal proceedings.

Article 3

(1) To ensure cooperation between the Federation and the States, the latter shall be obliged to maintain central criminal investigation services (State Criminal Police Offices) for their respective territories. These offices shall pass on to the Bundeskriminalamt all information and records necessary for the discharge of its tasks.

(2) Several States may maintain a joint State Criminal Police Office within the terms of Paragraph 1.

Article 4

(1) The State Criminal Police Offices shall inform the Bundeskriminalamt promptly of the commencement, interruption, and termination, of any judge-ordered custody.
(2) The justice and administrative authorities shall have the same reporting obligation towards the State Criminal Police Offices.

Article 5

(1) The prevention and prosecution of crime shall remain a matter of State responsibility, except where otherwise provided for by law.
(2) The Bundeskriminalamt itself shall discharge the police tasks relating to criminal prosecution (Articles 161, 163 of the Code of Criminal Procedure)

1. In cases of internationally organized illegal traffic in arms, ammunition, explosives, or narcotics, and of internationally organized manufacture or distribution of counterfeit currency which require investigation abroad, as well as in the case of offences committed in connection with any of these; in cases of minor importance the public prosecutor may, in agreement with the Bundeskriminalamt, refer the investigation to another police authority of competent jurisdiction;
2. In the case of offences against the lives (Sections 211, 212 Penal Code) or the freedom (234, 234a, 239, 239b Penal Code) of the Federal President, members of the Federal Government, the Federal Parliament, and the Federal Constitutional Court, or of guests of the federal constitutional bodies from foreign countries, or the heads and members of diplomatic missions accredited to the Federal Republic of Germany, when it appears that the offender has acted for political motives and the offence affects any federal, or foreign, policy interests.

For the execution of the tasks laid down in Sentence 1 (No. 2), the consent of the Federal Minister of the Interior shall be required; in case of imminent danger, the Bundeskriminalamt may act before such consent is given.
(3) Furthermore, the Bundeskriminalamt itself shall discharge the police tasks relating to criminal prosecution where

1. An appropriate State authority so requests, or
2. The Federal Minister of the Interior so orders for grave reasons, or
3. The Federal Prosecutor General so requests or orders.

(4) The supreme State authorities responsible for criminal justice and police matters shall be informed without delay when the Bundeskriminalamt discharges police tasks in the field of crime control; furthermore, information shall be forwarded without delay to the Federal Prosecutor General in cases where he is responsible for the direction of the investigation and, in the remaining cases, to the prosecutors general in whose areas jurisdiction lies. This shall apply without prejudice to the obligation of other police authorities to take initial action and to carry out any necessary measures which must not be delayed, as well as the powers of public prosecutors under Articles 161 and 189 of the Code of Criminal procedure.
(5) In the cases of Paragraphs 2 and 3, the Bundeskriminalamt may give the appropriate State Criminal Police Offices [Article 3 (1)] directions as to cooperation. The supreme State authority shall be informed promptly.

Article 6

(1) The Bundeskriminalamt may send members of its staff to State police authorities to support police action in the field of criminal prosecution if the appropriate State authority so requests, or where this may be useful for the investigation. This shall apply without prejudice to the responsibilities of the State police authorities.

(2) The supreme State authority shall be informed promptly.

Article 7

(1) Where an offence concerns the area of more than one State or is related to an offence committed in another State, and it is deemed appropriate for police tasks in the field of criminal prosecution to be coordinated, the Bundeskriminalamt shall inform the supreme State authorities and the prosecutors general in whose areas jurisdiction lies. In agreement with a prosecutor general and a supreme State authority of a State, the Bundeskriminalamt shall assign the discharge of police tasks in the field of criminal prosecution to that State asking it to assume overall responsibility for these tasks.

(2) The responsibility for the discharge of the tasks assigned to a State under Paragraph 1 shall be incumbent upon the appropriate State Criminal Police Office; the supreme State authority may assign responsibility to a police authority within the State other than the State Criminal Police Office.

Article 8

(1) In the cases mentioned in Articles 5 (2 and 3) and 7 (1), Federal, and State, law enforcement officers may perform official functions within the extent of this law; in this respect, they are auxiliary officials of the appropriate prosecutors. They shall inform the local police in a timely fashion of any investigations they conduct within the latter's jurisdiction, unless there are serious reasons for acting to the contrary. Whenever possible, officers of the appropriate local police services shall be called in to attend such investigative activities.

(2) In such cases where it is responsible, State police services shall give information and record access to the Bundeskriminalamt and its officers sent under Article 5 (2 and 3). The same shall apply to State police officers performing tasks under Article 7 (1).

(3) The appropriate local police services shall lend personnel and material support to investigating officers of the Bundeskriminalamt, or, in the case of an assignment under Article 7 (1), of another State.

Article 9

(1) Without prejudice to the rights of the President of the Federal Parliament and the responsibilities of the Federal Border Guard and of State police forces, the Bundeskriminalamt shall be responsible for

1. The necessary immediate personal protection of members of the constitutional bodies of the Federation and, in special cases, of guests of these constitutional bodies from other countries;

2. The internal protection of the offices and residences of the Federal President, the members of the Federal Government, and, in special cases, their guests from foreign countries and of any premises where they may be staying.

(2) Where officers of the Bundeskriminalamt and other police personnel are deployed simultaneously for any tasks under Paragraph 1, the decision theron shall be taken by the Federal Minister of the Interior and the supreme State authority in mutual agreement.

(3) For the discharge of its tasks under Paragraph 1, the Bundeskriminalamt shall have the powers mentioned in Articles 10 to 32 of the Law on the Federal Border Guard. The basic rights to freedom from injury [Article 2 (2) (Sentence 1) of the Constitution], personal freedom [Article 2 (2) (Sentence 2) of the Constitution], freedom of movement [Article 11 (1) of the Constitution], and inviolability of the residence (Article 13 of the Constitution) shall be restricted within the terms of those provisions.

(4) If any person suffers injury or damage during the discharge of the tasks of the Bundeskriminalamt under Paragraph 1, Articles 34 to 41 of the Law on the Federal Borders Guard shall apply accordingly.

Article 10

Official relations with foreign police and justice authorities necessary in combatting international common criminals shall be the exclusive responsibility of the Bundeskriminalamt. Exceptions may be made for border areas by agreement between the Federal Minister of the Interior and the supreme State authorities.

Article 11

The general administrative regulations required for the implementation of this law shall be enacted by the Federal Government with the approval of the Bundesrat.

Article 12

This law shall also apply to Berlin as soon as the State of Berlin decides to implement this law under Article 87 of its constitution.

Article 13

The Reichskriminalpolizeigesetz (Reich Criminal Police Law) dated 21st July 1922 (Reich Law Gazette I, p. 593) is hereby repealed.

Appendix B: Organizational Structure of the BKA

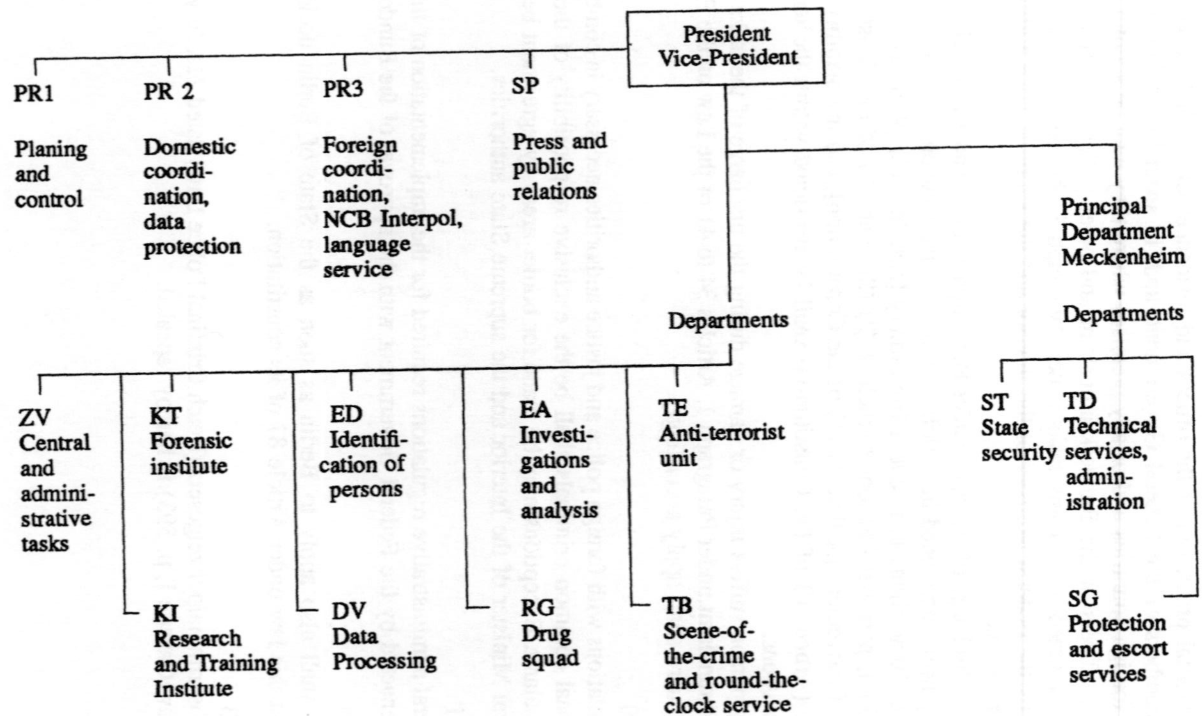

Appendix C: Functions of the Bundeskriminalamt

Federal Minister of the Interior

Federal Criminal Police Office (Bundeskriminalamt)

Crime Investigation in cases of:	**Central Agency for:**	**Crime Prevention**	**Interpol National Central Bureau** (Art. 1 of the BKA law)	**Other**
– Jurisdictional authority under Art. 5 of the BKA Law: - Drugs offences - Weapons/explosives offences - Currency counterfeiting - Offenses against the life or freedom of the Federal President, members of the Government, the Bundestag (Federal Diet), the Federal Constitutional Court or of guests of the constitutional organs – At the request of an appropriate State authority – By order of the Federal Ministry of the Interior – By order of the Federal Prosecutor General – Assignment of criminal proceedings to a *Land* (Art. 7 of the BKA Law) – Assistance to *Länder* (Art. 6 of BKA Law)	– Electronic data processing – Collection and analysis of police intelligence – Conveyance of information to appropriate agencies – Identification service – Forensic science laboratories – Statistics – Research – Continuation courses in special police fields, i.e. identification, forensic science	– Assistance to *Länder* for protection of VIPs, members of constitutional organs and their guest	– Combating international criminals – Official relations with foreign police and judicial authorities (mutual judicial assistance)	– Gaming clearance certificates – Exemption permits for weapons

References

Ahlf E-H (1985) Das Bundeskriminalamt als Zentralstelle. Wiesbaden (BKA-Forschungsreihe Special volume)

Albrecht H (1988) Im Dienst der Inneren Sicherheit. Die Geschichte des Bundeskriminalamtes. Wiesbaden

Bundeskriminalamt (ed) Das Bundeskriminalamt. Seine Aufgaben und Funktionen im föderalistischen Sicherheitssystem der Bundesrepublik Deutschland. Wiesbaden o.J.

Bundeskriminalamt (ed) (1987) Das BKA in Zahlen. Eine Beilage zu der Broschüre „Das Bundeskriminalamt". Wiesbaden

Hessel H-J (1979) Gesetz über die Einrichtung eines Bundeskriminalpolizeiamtes (BKA-Gesetz). Commentary, Wiesbaden

Mergen A (1987) Die BKA Story. München, Berlin

Policing and Justice in Europe. Police and justice systems, in the United Kingdom, France, the Federal Republic of Germany, Spain, and Denmark (1987) In: International Criminal Police Review 42, no 407, pp 2–17 (The Federal Republic of Germany, pp 9–12)

Riegel R (1985) Bundespolizeirecht: Bundeskriminalamtsgesetz, Bundesgrenzschutzgesetz, Gesetz über den unmittelbaren Zwang. München (Beck'sche Kurz-Kommentare vol 42)

Schweppe R (1974) FBI und BKA. Federal Bureau of Investigation und Bundeskriminalamt. Ein Vergleich von Organisation und Kompetenzen. Stuttgart (Kriminologie. Abhandlungen über abwegiges Sozialverhalten no 12)

CHAPTER 2

Police Research and Its Significance for Policing and Criminal Policy

E. Kube and E. Rebscher

Contents

1 Historical Development

Until the beginning of the 1970s, criminological research in the Federal Republic of Germany focused primarily on enhancing knowledge regarding the causes and manifestations of crime. Research was chiefly conducted by universities and private scientific institutes. The results obtained augmented scientific theories and literature. In addition, they provided information for criminal policy, particularly in the area of legislation.

The police reacted to this kind of criminological research with skepticism or, at most, indifference. The primary response to new problems in everyday policing was an increase in personnel or funding. Once the federal and state budget situation no longer allowed unlimited new resources, many police chiefs finally realized that the only appropriate response to the increasingly complex problems they were facing was to elicit the support of practice-oriented research. As a result, in the 1970s and 1980s, research facilities were created within police forces. These were assigned the task of conducting practice-related criminological studies. The objective of this research work was to analyze specific types of crime and to improve policing methods and procedures. Special efforts were made to raise problem consciousness.

Kube/Störzer (Eds.)
Police Research in the Federal Republic of Germany

2 The Main Facilities and Their Jurisdictions

There are essentially three police agencies that deal with police research:

1. *Polizei-Führungsakademie* (police staff college): The *Polizei-Führungsakademie* is a training and research institute which is financed by both the federal government and the *Bundesländer* (states). The main task of the college is to train police officers; in addition, it must conduct criminological research. Unfortunately, the lack of personnel and funding has held up the research, which is why only smaller studies have been carried out thus far. The college also has a bureau for the development and testing of police equipment.
2. *Landeskriminalämter* (state criminal police offices): While possessing a mandate for research, the central criminal police agencies in the 11 old states of the Federal Republic of Germany have undertaken only a few studies. This is mainly due to the pressures of everyday policing. An exception to this is the research group of the Bavarian *Landeskriminalamt*, which has conducted studies on subjects such as the efficiency of policing, conflict management by the police, and violence against women.
3. *Bundeskriminalamt* (federal criminal police office): The Bundeskriminalamt (BKA) is the center of information and communication for the German police. Among other things, the BKA Act gives the responsibility to the BKA "to observe the development of crime and to provide, based on these observations, crime analyses and statistics; to undertake research on the development of police methods and modes of operandi for fighting crime."

Within the Research and Training Institute of the BKA an interdisciplinary team has been assigned responsibility to undertake research since 1973. At present, two research units (which have been recognized as national research institutions) are comprised of about 40 researchers, representing criminology, physics, mathematics, and data processing, and about 10 police practitioners. The Research and Training Institute also employs engineers and technicians who develop and test police equipment and other material. In addition, there are administrative personnel and staff for the library and documentation services.

The research projects are either executed by the BKA itself or are farmed out to universities or other research institutes. Programs that are conducted at an outside institute are monitored by the BKA staff from the planning stage to publication.

Each member of the two research groups is responsible for a particular area. The objective is to cover the entire spectrum of research interests of the police. Each member can initiate research projects. All of the findings are published in the *BKA-Forschungsreihe*, a series of edited research reports which are distributed free of charge to police agencies, universities, and other institutions or individual persons interested in police research.

This chapter presents summaries of research studies falling under four main headings: the picture of crime, urban planning and crime prevention, crime-specific studies, and enhancing the effectiveness of detection and criminal investigation.

3 The Picture of Crime

One of the most important tasks of research addressing the needs of criminal policy and the police is to provide an accurate and detailed picture of crime. This is a prerequisite for the development of effective preventive or law enforcement measures. The researchers of the BKA have carried out numerous crime analysis projects in the last 15 years, many employing innovative methods.

In addition to continuous crime analyses (see Chap. 4), victimization surveys have been performed. One was repeated 11 years after it was originally conducted in the same town by the same research team using the same method (see Chap. 5). The purpose of the follow-up survey was to detect any changes in unrecorded crime and in the population's attitude toward reporting crime to the police. In another survey the method of interviewing victims by telephone was successfully tested (see Chap. 6). At short intervals, opinion polls were repeated to obtain information on respondents' attitudes toward the police and police work and data on their fear of crime (see Chap. 7). Victims of crime were questioned about their victimization to obtain additional information which could be useful for establishing measures to prevent crime and which could help the police learn how to assist victims (see Chap. 8).

Finally, on the basis of interviewing police and other experts and following analysis of survey and statistical data, attempts were made to produce forecasts of trends in certain kinds of crime. These forecasts were attached more importance, the less experience the police had with fighting the specific type of crime. In this respect, predicting the development of environmental crime was of particular relevance in the Federal Republic of Germany (see Chap. 15). By its analyses and forecasts the BKA was able to supply important research findings for use in developing criminal policy and police strategy.

4 Urban Planning and Crime Prevention

Another topic studied was situational crime prevention, which aims at making it more difficult for the potential offender to commit a crime. An attempt was made to demonstrate the geographical structures most likely to be involved in crime and to analyze the significance of urban planning and defensible space for crime prevention (see Chap. 9). Valuable findings were obtained with regard to the importance of (informal) social control (see Chap. 10).

5 Crime-Specific Studies

A major portion of the research is made up of crime-specific studies. One of these is a large, in-house project designed to shed light on the interaction between offender and victim in violent crimes (see Chap. 11). Depth interviews of 50–100 offender-victim "pairs" are planned concerning this interaction in what the police consider to be a major area of violence against persons. The phenomenon of violence will therefore be investigated and described not as an isolated incident, but as a total and complex continuum. The dangers of escalation and possibilities of de-escalation will be identified as will the background and causes responsible for the individual act of violence.

The interviewing of "pairs" of offenders and victims represents a useful mix of victim and offender surveys, because it takes into consideration the interaction between persons involved in the crime. Such an interview is costly and time-consuming, so that limits have to be placed on the number of respondents and on the types of violence addressed.

Organized crime was the topic of another special study carried out by the BKA research unit (see Chap. 14). Police experts in various parts of the Federal Republic of Germany were asked for their opinion regarding trends in organized crime. In addition, they were asked to make suggestions for improving and intensifying the fight against this dangerous form of crime. The results of this investigation, published in 1988, revealed that the "criminal networks" existing in the Federal Republic of Germany can be best combatted by a law enforcement network of offender-oriented and case-oriented police divisions. The importance of the offender-oriented investigation at the local level became very evident. The study also showed that violence as a guarantor of the cohesion of the organization does not have the same significance for organized criminals in Germany as it does in the traditional forms of organized crime found in the USA or in Italy.

Another important crime-specific study undertaken was on environmental crime with focus on its present status and – as was mentioned above – the forecast for the near future (see Chap. 15).

Further crime-specific studies conducted in the last few years covered, among other topics, drug-related crime (see Chap. 12), economic crime (see Chap. 13), and bank robbery (see Chaps. 16, 17).

6 Enhancing the Effectiveness of Detection and Criminal Investigation

A series of further research projects focused on ways to improve criminal investigation, for example, concerning economic crime (see Chap. 18). Special emphasis was placed on the employment of electronic data processing (see Chap. 21). The computer-aided analysis of handwriting, for instance, has replaced the more time-consuming manual technique. A pattern recognition system provides the handwriting experts with a "hit list" of handwriting samples that resemble the one being investigated. This rapid means of identifying offenders by their handwriting has become particularly advantageous in the fight against terrorism, for which purpose the BKA has already tried out the method (see Chap. 22). Another technique that has been developed is that of digital image enhancement, which is used to improve the frequently poor quality of photographs, films, and video films taken of criminal activities, such as bank robberies. By means of this process the quality of such pictures can be enhanced so that persons and objects unrecognizable on the originals can be identified (see Chap. 23).

One empirical project evaluated the information retrieval system and use of computer systems for criminal intelligence (see Chap. 20). Among the findings which were obtained, the following two were of particular importance: (1) When a police officer translates his perceptions into a written text, an unconscious distortion often takes place caused by the intention to give "objective" depictions that fit in with criminal law or with the type of language used in the forms or in the data processing systems. (2) The criterion for feeding case data into a central electronic file should thus not be the legal or criminological definition of the offense, but rather only the value of the data in allowing patterns of offenses to be identified and analyzed.

Numerous studies have been conducted in order to improve security measures. This research has resulted in the development of highly sensitive and reliable methods for detection of illegal drugs (see Chap. 19) and provided reliable knowledge about the impact of technical security measures on bank robbery (see Chap. 17).

Besides the immediate practical goals of the research projects described above, a further purpose of these studies was to find applications for new research methods or methods that had previously been used to address criminological issues. One example is the so-called objective hermeneutic method, which was used in the research on information retrieval systems (see Chap. 20). In addition, methods developed in other countries – such as offender surveys – are being employed with the goal of improving the prevention of crime (see Chap. 17) with respect to bank robbery and recently theft as well. Not only were imprisoned criminals interviewed, but a successful attempt was made to interview people immediately after they had been interrogated by the police.

Experience has shown that by using a wide range of methodologies in research the police can be offered practical help in their everyday work.

7 Implementation of Research Findings

The practice-oriented nature of police-related research necessarily entails a certain amount of cooperation between theoreticians and practitioners, for theoretical findings and research results in themselves do not have any influence on practice. Criminological research must therefore be subject of communication. Communication in this context means the two-way transfer of knowledge: the flow of information from the researchers to the police and the feedback of experience and findings from the police to the researchers.

One way to guarantee the translation of research findings into practice and to get the necessary feedback is to engage police experts in the planning, execution, and evaluation of research projects. Familiarizing young police officers with the research process right from the start of their training will encourage their willingness to accept the help provided by such research. An effective way to disseminate police-related criminological research is to include it in the scope of special advanced training courses and to publish the findings in publications usually read by the police rather than in academic journals.

Efforts to translate research into practice are primarily directed to the police during training, either in initial training or subsequently. This is when they are most open to new ideas and knowledge. The routine work of policing does not leave much time for such "education". Therefore, police research and training institutions such as the Research and Training Institute of the BKA and the *Polizei-Führungsakademie* in the Federal Republic of Germany are assuming the role of catalysts between science and the police by integrating police-related research findings into their curricula.

If research is to be implemented, it is also important for research findings to be published in condensed and intelligible reports. For example, the BKA publishes a *Research and Development* newsletter supplementing the *Criminal Police Bulletin*. This supplement, which appears three to four times a year, contains abstracts of systematically evaluated research reports which might be useful for everyday police work.

It goes without saying that procedures and results should be documented carefully in research reports, if only for reasons of scientific communication and methodological clarity. A further point is that the cataloguing of ongoing justice-related and police-related research projects is far from satisfactory. This is all the more reason for encouraging initiatives such as the International Crime Prevention Information Network (ICPIN) created under the aegis of the Council of Europe. This network maintains a secretariat in the Hague at the Research and Documentation Centre of the Dutch Ministry of Justice. The objectives of ICPIN are to promote and facilitate the computer-aided exchange of information on crime prevention, victim assistance, and other criminological topics of interest to government agencies and international bodies.

8 Summary

In order for law enforcement agencies to fulfill their task, they need ongoing support in the form of financial resources and practice-related research. Internal police research is able to provide this support by in-house and contract research projects. In the Federal Republic of Germany police research institutes exist both on the federal and state levels.

The research undertaken by the BKA concentrates on the crime picture, crime prevention, crime-specific studies, and the enhancement and effectiveness of detection and criminal investigation. The findings of the studies have been implemented and, above all, have been integrated into programs for police training.

CHAPTER 3

"State Criminology": An Old Phenomenon – A New Problem

H.U. Störzer

"While the Germans are torturing themselves
trying to solve philosophical problems,
the English, with their practical way of thinking,
are laughing at us and winning the world."

Johann Peter Eckermann, Conversations with Goethe towards the end of his life (Sept. 1, 1829)

Contents

1 The Institutionalization of Criminology at Universities[1]

Criminology, the study of crime, its causes, and manifestations, has grown into a highly organized discipline in the Federal Republic of Germany. This development had its origins in the universities. After a number of chairs and institutes for criminology had been established in universities in Italy, Austria-Hungary, and Switzerland between 1905 and 1912, criminology departments were set up in the law schools of the universitites of Hamburg (1920), Cologne (1923), Freiburg

[1] For a thorough discussion see Störzer 1984 pp 327–390; overview in Störzer 1976 pp 85–86, 1983 pp 80–81.

Kube/Störzer (Eds.)
Police Research in the Federal Republic of Germany

(1930), Bonn (1943), Saarbrücken (1953), and Kiel 1957).[2] These departments, however, were headed by professors who specialized in subjects such as penal law and criminal procedure and who therefore could only be involved in criminology more or less on the side.[3]

This began to change in 1959 when the first department dealing exclusively with criminology was established at the University of Heidelberg Law School (in the state of Baden-Württemberg). The head of the department was Heinz Leferenz. This "innovation in the history of German universities"[4] was followed in 1962 by the founding of an institute solely for criminology at the University of Tübingen Law School. A second department in Tübingen and the Institute for Criminology at the University of Heidelberg were then established.[5]

In 1971, criminology was included in the law curriculum and in state law examinations.[6] This led to an increase in departments which were obliged to conduct criminological research.[7] Along with members of the fields of law and medicine[8], people from other disciplines, particularly social scientists, turned their attention to criminological matters.[9]

Today, the relevance of criminology in the first of the two state law examinations has been reduced – in some states drastically.[10] Thus, when hiring, law school faculties are once again beginning to give preference to instructors offering several subjects, rather than "pure" criminologists. In this respect, the University of Hamburg is an exception. The *Gemeinsame Kommission für das Aufbau- und Kontaktstudium Kriminologie* (roughly: the Joint Committee for Studies of Criminology for Graduates and Practitioners) was linked to the Law School II as a special unit, in which Fritz Sack and Sebastian Scheerer are currently active. In its studies for graduates, research is even a part of the curriculum.[11]

---

[2] See Würtenberger 1964/65 p 154; 1977 p 270.

[3] Brauneck 1966 p 222; also Radzinowicz 1961 p 25; Kaiser 1988a p 105.

[4] Göppinger 1980 p 34; also Kürzinger 1974 p 128.

[5] Kürzinger 1974 p 129; Göppinger 1980 p 34; Kaiser 1988a p 105.

[6] In accordance with the decisions of the 38th Conference of the Ministers of Justice in 1969. See also Wolff 1971 p 266.

[7] Kürzinger 1974 p 128; Sack 1978 p 220; Steinhilper and Berckhauer 1980 p 139, footnote 35; Kaiser 1988a p 111.

[8] See Leferenz 1959 p 119; Kürzinger 1974 p 128.

[9] See Kürzinger 1974 p 128; Kaiser 1988a pp 106, 111, 113.

[10] See Störzer 1984 pp 409–411; Jung 1988 pp 13–17.

[11] For more information on Aufbau- und Kontaktstudium Kriminologie at the University of Hamburg, see Störzer 1984 pp 358–359; Deichsel, Hufeland, Kunstreich, and Löschper 1985 pp 69–76; Sack 1986 pp 6–18.

2 The Establishment of Criminology Outside of the Universities

The idea of establishing criminological research outside the university dates far back and was initiated by eminent university instructors. Hans Groß considered establishing a public criminological central institute when, in 1913, he called for the founding of a *Reichskriminalinstitut;* in contrast, Franz von Liszt suggested that research facilities be created within police departments in larger cities.[12] In 1961, Leon Radzinowicz proposed setting up a purely criminological national institute or regional institutes.[13] In 1969, Thomas Würtenberger suggested a central research institute for criminology and criminalistics "as part of the criminal police."[14]

2.1 In-House Government Research Facilities

Corrections was the first topic to be addressed by non-university criminological research, when, in 1921, the state of Bavaria was inspired by the Criminal Anthropological Laboratory in Brussels. Other states soon followed suit. After World War II, criminological services for the prison administration were set up, such as the Department of Criminal Psychology in Hamburg in 1947, and the Criminological Investigation Office in Berlin in 1955.[15] A starting point for crime research within the police was the task of the *Reichskriminalpolizei* to gather findings from both criminal policing and research and evaluate them for the purpose of criminal policymaking.[16] Since its founding in 1951, the BKA has also had a division which deals with criminological and criminal investigation research (Research and Training Institute), though initially only on a small scale.[17]

Since the beginning of the 1970s, the institutionalization of criminological research among the police and the criminal justice administration has increased. On the one hand, such facilities were directly linked to state agencies. In 1972, on a mandate by the Permanent Conference of the Ministers and Senators of the Interior of the Federation and of the States, in the Program for Internal Security in the Federal Republic of Germany, the BKA in Wiesbaden set up and began to develop its Research Unit on Criminology and Criminal Investigation.[18] In 1973, a special criminological research unit was established in the Federal Department of Justice in Bonn.[19] In 1979, a Planning and Research Unit was set up in the

---

[12] See Radzinowicz 1961 pp 24, 30; Würtenberger 1969 p 237.

[13] Radzinowicz 1961 p 30.

[14] Würtenberger 1969 p 237.

[15] See Kaiser, Kerner, and Schöch 1982 p 277.

[16] See Zirpins 1955 p 286.

[17] See Heinl 1969 p 10; Gemmer 1969 p 245.

[18] Most recently Kube 1988 pp 249–262; Störzer 1990 pp 205–211.

[19] See Hobe 1988 pp 215–221; 1990 pp 165–172.

Lower Saxony Department of Justice in Hanover;[20] in Munich, the Criminological Research Unit of the Bavarian Police was founded in the state criminal police office of Bavaria.[21] A Criminological Research Unit in the state criminal police office in Hamburg was installed at the beginning of 1989. On the other hand, legal bases for police-related criminological and criminal investigation research by the *Polizei-Führungsakademie* (police staff college) in Münster (1972)[22] and for research within the prison administration by criminological services in the states of the Federal Republic were created[23].

2.2 Independent Research Facilities

Along with the in-house government research institutes, facilities were founded that were independent of both universities and the government. In 1970, the *Max-Planck-Gesellschaft zur Förderung der Wissenschaften e.V.* approved the establishment of a criminological research group within the Max Planck Institute for Foreign and International Criminal Law, in Freiburg.[24] In 1979, the Criminological Research Institute of Lower Saxony was set up in Hanover as an *eingetragener Verein* (registered organization). This was a result of initiatives taken by the Justice Department of Lower Saxony and passed by the state government.[25] On October 2, 1981, after a decision passed at the 38th conference of the ministers of justice, in October 1969, the Central Institute of Criminology was established by the federal government and the States; it was also in the form of a registered organization.[26]

3 The Problem of State Criminology

As late as 1978, for Sack[27], a leading supporter of critical (university-based) criminology, criminological research being carried out by a government authority, viz. the BKA, was a good example of the fact that criminology, despite its scientific theoretical problems, "was showing success in trying to acquire the social resources every science needs for its own survival". However, 2 years later critical criminologists took a firm stand against *Staatskriminologie* (state criminology).

What exactly the new term *Staatskriminologie* denoted was difficult to determine. Manfred Brusten, in his many lectures held at home and abroad in Ger-

[20] For a thorough discussion see Steinhilper and Berckhauer 1980 pp 127–137; Berckhauer, Hasenpusch, and Steinhilper 1988 pp 223–248; Hasenpusch 1990 pp 197–198.

[21] For more details see Steffen 1988a pp 151–162; 1988b pp 263–276; 1990 pp 217–219.

[22] See Matthes 1974 pp 35, 37–38.

[23] See Steinhilper 1986 pp 62–67; Dolde 1988 pp 187–206; Hasenpusch 1990 pp 195–196.

[24] Most recently Kaiser 1988b pp 165–174.

[25] For a more detailed analysis see Kury 1981 pp 33–79; Pfeiffer 1988 pp 175–197.

[26] See Egg and Feuerhelm 1988 pp 117–142; Jehle 1988 pp 199–214; 1990 pp 176–183.

[27] Sack 1978 p 221.

man, English, and French[28], offered some thoughts which helped to elucidate the meaning. First, the *Staat* was not the subject of scientific efforts, but rather the originator. Second, the *Staat*, in this case, did not refer to the overall complex of state-affiliated organizations and facilities under which the universities would also be subsumed since nearly all German universities are public. Instead, *Staat* referred only to government authorities, offices, agencies, etc., and made a clear distinction between these and the universities. Furthermore, university members to whom research projects were assigned by a government authority as well as criminological research facilities in the private sector which were somehow affiliated with a government authority (for instance, if their founding was initiated by a government authority) were felt to be in the neighborhood of *Staatskriminologie*. Thus, *Staatskriminologie* referred to criminology conducted by government authorities, on commission from them, or in institutions affiliated with them in the broadest sense.

This chapter is not intended to present a comprehensive and detailed discussion of the objections to *Staatskriminologie* and its representatives. The statements made by the critics derive their viability, similar to branches on a tree, from a "root" argument. They present "state-run" research and "independent" research as opposites and this polarization will be used as a basis for discussion. The conclusion, that "the police... due to their scientific resources are in a good position to get criminology under their control – at least in part"[29], suggests that advocates of *Staatskriminologie* are preparing a counterattack against critical university-based criminology, which is only feasible as an independent form.[30] At the end of this chain of thoughts is inevitably the nightmare of a "state-run system of change" in the area of criminology.[31]

Brusten found agreement with his philosophy, particularly in the *Kriminologisches Journal* published by the *Arbeitskreis Junger Kriminologen* (Working Group of Young Criminologists).[32]

4 Discussion

The criticism that *Staatskriminologie* works against freedom of research was refuted not only by representatives of the prison administration (Rotthaus[33]), crim-

---

[28] Brusten 1980a pp 69–72; 1980b pp 17–47; 1981a pp 135–182; 1981b pp 177–186; 1981c pp 58–77; 1986a pp 25–38; 1986b pp 194–212; Brusten and van Outrive 1981 pp 7–51.

[29] Brusten 1980b p 39, footnote 4.

[30] Brusten 1980a p 70.

[31] Brusten 1980a p 70; 1981a p 161.

[32] See, in particular, Gipser and Klein-Schonnefeld 1980 pp 199–208 and Kreissl 1983 pp 110–121.

[33] Rotthaus 1980 pp 208–209.

inal justice administration (Berckhauer[34], Schwind[35], G. Steinhilper[36]), the police (Schreiber[37], Steffen[38], Störzer[39], Wehner[40]), and private research institutions (Kaiser[41], Pfeiffer[42]), but also by members of the university itself (Jäger[43], Kreuzer[44], Schwind[45]).

4.1 On the Term "State Criminology"

As the devil in Goethe's *Faust* said, you can argue splendidly with words.[46] The term "state criminology" does not correctly describe criminology conducted outside the universitites. It does, however, give rise to conceptual associations with state enterprise, state monopoly, and state-controlled research. Thus, *Staatskriminologie* is inevitably distinguished from independent research conducted under the sole responsibility of the scientist. Furthermore, it is incorrect to subsume in-house government research, private research institutes with government affiliation, and university members working on a government research project under one and the same heading. Though there are naturally some common elements, lumping all of them together conceals specific problems. The use of language as ammunition does nothing more than add polemics to the discussion.[47]

In sharp contrast to traditional university research, which sees itself as being free of any personal interest, is the research conducted in ministeries and government offices, which is oriented toward particular tasks. Since the university researcher and the private research institute conduct *Staatskriminologie* only because of their affiliation with some authority, this can be referred to as only "derivative" *Staatskriminologie* , a label they can get rid of, for instance, by turning down the affiliation. The research conducted by government authorities implies "original" *Staatskriminologie* . This type of organization is the basis for the rest of this discussion. The term "in-house government research" coined by Steinhilper

---

34 Berckhauer 1985 p 154; 1986 pp 39–50; Steinhilper and Berckhauer 1980 pp 137–143.
35 Schwind 1981 pp 81–82.
36 Steinhilper 1982 pp 16–18; 1987 pp 351–366; Steinhilper and Berckhauer 1980 pp 137–143.
37 Schreiber 1986 p 349.
38 Steffen 1984 pp 70–76; 1986 pp 51–60.
39 Störzer 1983 pp 69–90; 1990 pp 204–205, 211.
40 Wehner 1985 p 18.
41 Kaiser 1983 pp 58–63; 1988a pp 28–30.
42 Pfeiffer 1986 pp 215–224.
43 Jäger 1980 pp 228–231.
44 Kreuzer 1986 p 571.
45 Schwind 1986 pp 145–146.
46 Goethe: Faust. Ein Fragment. 1790, Schülerszene.
47 Compare Störzer 1983 pp 70, 75, 76–77, 78–79; Berckhauer 1986 pp 39, 41.

and Berckhauer[48] seems to me to be the most suitable, as it is purely descriptive and does not unnecessarily tinge the discussion right from the start.

4.2 On the Scope of In-House Government Research

The portent was alarming: "Police and administration of criminal justice are taking criminological research more and more into their own hands."[49] A closer look, however, showed that the "gigantic research potential"[50] that allegedly was to be installed to combat critical criminology in universities was shrinking back to normal. A study by Berckhauer at the end of 1982 revealed that 28 scientists were employed in government facilities, as opposed to 113 criminologists working at universities. The budget plans for 1983 earmarked a total of DM 10 225 000 for university departments and DM 3 000 000 for government facilities.[51]

In the government institutes referred to above[52] the following must be considered[53]: As the name Research Unit on Criminology and Criminal Investigation indicates, in the BKA a part of the research activity is in the area of criminal investigation; other research projects are often farmed out to universitites. In the Criminology Unit of the Federal Department of Justice, more research is farmed out than is done within the unit. In 1986, the Planning and Research Unit of the Lower Saxony Department of Justice, whose sphere of responsibility was temporarily extended in 1982 to include social services, was incorporated into the Corrections Division.[54] Prior to that, research was only one of many tasks. In the Criminological Research Unit of the state criminal police office in Hamburg, only two of the five positions authorized are occupied. The *Polizei-Führungsakademie* conducted only one criminological research project and issued only two such research assignments. The criminological services departments within the prison administration have been assigned many other tasks besides research. Only 3 of the 11 states of the Federal Republic of Germany have set up such departments (Baden-Württemberg, Lower Saxony, North Rhine-Westphalia).

Since in this connection still further facilities will be listed[55], it should be mentioned that not all government units that have the word "research" in their titles actually undertake research. The CID Prevention, Planning and Research Unit of the Department of the Interior of Baden-Württemberg and the Criminal

---

[48] Steinhilper and Berckhauer 1980 pp 137–143 passim.

[49] Brusten 1980a p 69.

[50] Brusten 1980a p 70; 1981a p 160.

[51] Berckhauer 1985 p 153; 1986 p 40.

[52] See Sect. 2.1.

[53] For a summary see Berckhauer 1986 pp 39–40; for details see the references in footnotes 18–23.

[54] Compare Steinhilper 1982 p 18; 1987 p 353, footnote 4; Berckhauer 1988 p 105; Berckhauer, Hasenpusch, and Steinhilper 1988 p 227.

[55] See Brusten 1986a p 36, footnote 6; 1986b p 209, footnote 4.

Justice Research and Statistics Unit of the Department of Justice of North Rhine-Westphalia are not able – due to the lack of staff – to conduct research projects. Their responsibility is more to coordinate and promote projects from outside.

4.3 Criticism Expressed by Critical Criminologists of In-House Government Research Facilities

The universities do not have a monopoly on research. This fact is camouflaged by the glib pair of terms "state research" and "independent research". The antinomy behind this reduces everything to black and white and so facilitates argumentation.[56] For example, the research conducted by in-house government criminology research facilities is not top secret, the results are made available to the scientific public[57] either through publications, some of which are in the BKA's own series[58], or through presentations at scientific conferences. Hefty criticism has been aimed at such publishing activity, claiming that, with the help of the state, publications which are usually obtainable free of charge are thus allowed to "get ahead of the open competition"[59]. The critics no doubt have a point. Nonetheless, it should also be kept in mind that disseminating research findings is a way of generating widespread discussion, which can reduce the dangers of the content becoming too one-sided and of the state exerting too much influence. In addition, it cannot be denied that university criminologists love to make use of their own book series[60] as a way to at least alleviate "the constraints of open market competition"[61]. The only positive aspect the critics found in free government research reports is that they make "in-house government criminology transparent", which is necessary "for it to be dealt with more intensively"[62]. This too applies to the presentation of "state-run research" at conferences, and it has even been conceded, that this is a way of keeping state research from becoming "isolated"[63]. It has been pointed out emphatically that scientific conferences, colloquia, and symposia can be so "decisively influenced" and even so severely "infiltrated" by "state researchers"

56 As explicitly stated by Brusten 1981a p 163, footnote 5.

57 See Kaiser 1988a pp 28, 835.

58 The scientific publications of the BKA are listed in the appendix to this volume.

59 Brusten 1981a p 251; also 1986a p 28; 1986b p 200.

60 For example, in the Federal Republic of Germany: Beiträge zur empirischen Kriminologie (Göppinger), Kriminalwissenschaftliche Abhandlungen (Geerds), Kriminologie. Abhandlungen über abwegiges Sozialverhalten (Würtenberger), Kriminologische Forschungen (H. Mayer, Hellmer), Mönchengladbacher Beiträge zur Kriminologie und Sozialarbeit (Kirchhoff), Neue Kriminologische Studien (Schaffstein, Schöch, Schüler-Springorum).

61 Brusten 1981a p 152; 1986a p 28; 1986b p 200.

62 Brusten 1981a p 152.

63 See Brusten 1981a p 151; 1981c pp 65–66; 1986a p 28; 1986b p 200.

that university researchers either "no longer feel free" to present their research or are known to show "opportunistic behavior"[64].

Putting "state-run research" on the one side of the fence and "independent research" on the other is hardly conducive to a fair analysis of the relationship between the two research factions, a relationship which is surely in need of discussion. Such a division is too absolute, since neither is the university research completely independent and nonconforming, nor is in-house government research ipso facto subject to permanent constraints "from above"[65].

Abroad, especially in the USA, but also in Canada, Great Britain, and France, large, in-house government research institutes have existed for some time. In the USA what we consider as huge amounts of financial resources have been made available in the past.[66] Nevertheless the prophecy did not come true: that "independent university research will escape the 'superior might' of police [or judicial] criminology and will finally hand over the field completely to police [or judicial] criminology"[67]. Apparently, such a dreaded development is not as inevitable as one thinks.

Likewise, the accusation that in-house government research is a reaction against critical criminology does not hold up under an examination of the facts. As has been shown[68], the plans to institutionalize criminological research outside the university dates back to times when critical criminology did not even exist.[69] Furthermore, a "counterattack" of this scale presupposes a fear of critical thinking on the part of the state, which in fact does not exist. A better term to describe the feelings towards critical criminology would be (slight) annoyance. Moreover, since there is not just one school of criminological research conducted at universities, it is almost impossible to fight university-based criminology in general.

There was a different reason for establishing in-house government research facilities. Although more and more research was being done[70], university criminological research did not bear much fruit that was translatable into practice.[71] Consequently, the practitioners, who were interested in having their work based on scientific foundations, were forced to delve into the respective problem areas themselves.

---

[64] Brusten 1981a p 173, footnote 34; also 1981a p 151; 1981c p 65; 1986a p 28; 1986b p 200; Brusten and van Outrive 1981 p 17.

[65] See Störzer 1983 pp 78–79; 1990 pp 204–205; Berckhauer 1986 p 41.

[66] See, e.g., Steinhilper and Berckhauer 1980 pp 141–142.

[67] Brusten 1980b p 33; also 1981a p 159; 1986a p 34; 1986b p 206. – Text in brackets is author's addition.

[68] See Sect. 2.

[69] See also Steinhilper and Berckhauer 1980 p 139, footnote 35; Steinhilper 1982 p 17, footnote 16.

[70] See Sect. 1.

[71] See also, e.g., Schwind 1981 p 80; Steinhilper 1982 p 13; Störzer 1983 p 82; Steffen 1986 pp 51–52 (each with further references).

4.4 Assessment of In-House Government Research Facilities

Compared with university institutes, the founding of in-house government research facilities was not only the basis for practice-related research, but was also a particularly advantageous starting point for other planned research activities.

The *advantages* result from the proximity of in-house government research facilities to the subject of the research[72], since "outsiders" have to go through a formidable amount of red tape to gain access to the material they need, with no guarantee of success.[73]

This proximity means easier access to questions concerning practice which require clarification and, at least in part, to pertinent data such as records, statistics, etc. The advantage is also evident in terms of personnel: not only are there both practitioners and scientists working in the in-house government research facilities, but these units also have less difficulty contacting practitioners whose field of work is under study. That does not mean that there is no longer any friction between researchers and practitioners just because they belong to the same organization[74], but there is a kind of compulsion to cooperate as a result of the mutual bond.

The foregoing advantages are important for successful practice-oriented research. In each stage of the project – from the planning through the execution, from the interpretation of the results to their translation into practice – the material, expertise, experience, and needs of practice can be incorporated or at least taken into account. This reduces the danger of researching right past everyday practice.

The proximity of in-house government research facilities to the subjects of their research is not only an advantage, but also a cause of several *disadvantages*.

A host of objections can be listed, which can be subsumed under the slogans "submission to practice" and "routine blindness". In-house government research is often accused of being a legitimization of decisions that have already been made, and suspicion is expressed that the research and, in particular, its findings are influenced "from above".[75]

Such accusations, however, can be countered by the fact that in-house government research institutions have always paid attention to having their work made open to the public.[76] The list of publications presented in the appendix to this volume is evidence of this. Furthermore, reports on planned, ongoing, and completed projects are constantly being published in special periodicals, and open meetings

---

[72] See Steinhilper and Berckhauer 1980 p 140; Steinhilper 1982 p 18; 1987 pp 355–360; Störzer 1983 pp 82–84; Rebscher 1987 pp 367–377.

[73] For more on this problem see Brusten 1986a pp 28–32; 1986b pp 201–204 (each with further references).

[74] On the strained relationship between science and practice see Steinhilper and Berckhauer 1980 pp 137–138; Steinhilper 1982 pp 13–15; Störzer 1983 p 83; 1985 p 248.

[75] See Gipser and Klein-Schonnefeld 1980 p 204; Brusten 1981a pp 144, 156–157, 158–159; 1981c p 62; 1986a pp 33–34; 1986b pp 205–206; Kreissl 1983 p 113.

[76] See Sect. 4.3; also Steinhilper 1982 p 18.

and seminars are held. In addition, interested outsiders have a certain degree of access to the library of the BKA and the computer-aided documentation system for criminal scientific literature.[77]

A more subtle danger arises from the yearly budget negotiations. It is conceivable that an in-house government research institution tries to secure large amounts of funding by gearing its research projects to current political anxieties. Again, this can be counterbalanced by consistent publication of the research work done. To a certain degree, paying attention to what politicians would easily agree to can be regarded as legitimate; but there is scarcely a person in a responsible position in the in-house government research facilities who is unaware of the dangers of scientific opportunism.

There is another internal difficulty associated with in-house government research institutions: the research is supposed to be practice-related. That is easy to say. But how exactly do the institutions interpret the terms "practice-related" or "practice-relevant"? Although the meaning of these terms appears to be obvious, they are not as easy to define as one would think.

The following example confirms this: Before any decision regarding the fight against crime is made, there must be a realistic "assessment of the situation". This applies to both definition of points of emphasis for the prosecution and optimal police deployment in a particular area of a town. Such an assessment, however, is only valid if there is a notion of the total crime picture underlying it. This requires, however, that information on recorded crime has to be supplemented with information on crimes not known to the police. Practitioners recognized this problem some time ago.[78] What was missing were scientifically based examinations shedding light on the "dark figure" (unreported unregistered crime). In the 1970s, the BKA commissioned three research projects on unreported crime, which resulted in three extensive final reports.[79] These reports contain basic findings on the "dark figure", but suggestions for the police on how to use these findings to make their work more efficient and effective do not appear until the third volume. Can such research be considered practice-related or practice-relevant?

Taking these terms as used in essays and discussions, we could come up with the following definition: Criminological research is practice-related/practice-relevant if it aims for results which the criminal justice system can directly apply in executing its work. Of course, this attempt at a definition leaves some questions unanswered, for instance, what exactly does "directly" mean? An expression that says more than the terms "practice-relevant" or "practice-related" is one known from other branches of science and which Kaiser[80], for example, uses: "application oriented."

---

77 See Rebscher 1987 p 376; Störzer 1990 p 208.

78 See Wehner 1957 pp 11–12.

79 Schwind, Ahlborn, Eger, Jany, Pudel, and Weiß 1975; Stephan 1976; Schwind, Ahlborn, and Weiß 1978.

80 Kaiser 1988a pp 829ff passim.

5 Conclusions

The controversy over state criminology vs independent criminology has not been settled, but only shelved. Although new arguments are not to be expected, the standpoints have yet to converge.[81]

In-house government research institutions see their task as being in the area of applied criminology, which has been neglected by the universities and which is indispensable for a complete picture of this science. For this reason it seems to be necessary that the two research factions find a modus vivendi.

An efficient division of labor could be assigning universities with carrying out basic research and in-house government institutions with translating the results into practice.[82] However, such a strict separation will be difficult to execute. The foregoing example concerning research on unreported crime shows that dealing with a practice-related problem can give rise to the necessity of initiating basic research. Conversely, university researchers will not always want to abstain from putting their findings to the test.[83] Moreover, a fixed division of the areas of research presents the danger of too much attention being paid to "overstepping the boundaries", which could produce fuel for new controversies; however, as a rough division this might be practicable. The in-house government research institutions will abide by this because they have a heavy load on their shoulders: Due to their organizational position, they are predestined to be a link between theory and practice and can act as negotiators between practitioners and scientists.[84]

It is now time for criminologists to put an end to their self-absorption and rivalries and to start making concerted efforts in the area of applied criminology. Eckermann's assessment of the Germans, quoted at the beginning, also holds true for criminologists. Some 20 years ago, Leferenz accused German criminologists of spending more time writing about criminology than doing empirical research.[85]

References

Berckhauer F (1985) Institutionen der Kriminologie. In: Kaiser G, Kerner H-J, Sack F, Schellhoss H (eds) Kleines Kriminologisches Wörterbuch, 2nd edn. Heidelberg, pp 152–156 (Uni-Taschenbücher, vol 1274)

Berckhauer F (1986) Hat der Staat einen Bedarf an kriminologischer Forschung? Zur Auseinandersetzung um die „Staatskriminologie". In: Brusten M, Häußling JM, Malinowski P (eds) Kriminologie im Spannungsfeld von Kriminalpolitik und Kriminalpraxis. Stuttgart, pp 39–50 (Kriminologie, vol 22)

[81] See Schreiber 1986 p 349; Steinhilper 1987 p 352.

[82] In this sense, e.g., Steinhilper and Berckhauer 1980 p 143.

[83] Brusten (1986a pp 36–37, footnote 14) rejects this division of labor emphatically.

[84] See Rotthaus 1980 p 209; Steinhilper and Berckhauer 1980 p 139, footnote 35; Steinhilper 1982 p 17, footnotes 16, 18; Störzer 1983 pp 83–84, 89–90; 1985 p 248.

[85] Leferenz 1967 p 5.

Berckhauer F (1988) Praxisforschung in der Referatsgruppe des Niedersächsischen Ministeriums der Justiz. In: Feltes T (ed) Kriminologie und Praxisforschung. Probleme, Erfahrungen und Ergebnisse. Bonn, pp 105–115

Berckhauer F, Hasenpusch B, Steinhilper M (1988) Kriminologie in der Justizpraxis – 10 Jahre Referatsgruppe im niedersächsischen Ministerium der Justiz. In: Kaiser G, Kury H, Albrecht H-J (eds) Kriminologische Forschung in den 80er Jahren. Berichte aus der Bundesrepublik Deutschland, der Deutschen Demokratischen Republik, Österreich und der Schweiz. Freiburg, pp 223–248 (Kriminologische Forschungsberichte aus dem Max-Planck-Institut für ausländisches und internationales Strafrecht, Freiburg i.Br., vol 34)

Brauneck A-E (1966) Der junge Jurist und die Kriminologie. In: Juristische Schulung 6:221–223

Brusten M (1980a) Politik und Praxis der kriminologischen Forschung. Anmerkungen zu einer AJK-Podiumsdiskussion in Bremen. In: Kriminologisches Journal 12:69–72

Brusten M (1980b) Handlungsspielräume der Polizei. Grundlegende Perspektiven der „kritischen Instanzenforschung" und ihre „Überwindung" durch die neue „Polizei-Kriminologie". In: Kriminologisches Bulletin 6, no 1, pp 17–47

Brusten M (1981a) Staatliche Institutionalisierung kriminologischer Forschung – Perspektiven und Probleme. In: Kury H (ed) Perspektiven und Probleme kriminologischer Forschung. Köln Berlin Bonn München, pp 135–182 (Interdisziplinäre Beiträge zur kriminologischen Forschung, vol 1)

Brusten M (1981b) Vers une criminologie sous tutelle étatique? Problematiques en perspective et stratégies des solutions sous l'angle de la recherche universitaire. In: Déviance et Société 5:177–186

Brusten M (1981c) Social control of criminology and criminologists. Descriptions and reflections on some new developments in West Germany. In: State control on information in the field of deviance and social control. Leuven Vienne Wuppertal, pp 58–77 (Working Papers in European Criminology, no 2)

Brusten M (1986a) Kriminologische Forschung unter staatlicher Regie? Probleme und Konsequenzen des Einflusses staatlicher Behörden auf die Struktur und Entwicklung der Kriminologie. In: Brusten M, Häußling JM, Malinowski P (eds) Kriminologie im Spannungsfeld von Kriminalpolitik und Kriminalpraxis. Stuttgart, pp 25–38 (Kriminologie, vol 22)

Brusten M (1986b) Kriminologie und gesellschaftliche Verwertungsinteressen. Die empirische Kriminologie „in den Fängen" staatlicher Verwertungsinteressen – Bekannte Thesen und Fakten erneut zur Diskussion gestellt. In: Löschper G, Manke G, Sack F (eds) Kriminologie als selbständiges, interdisziplinäres Hochschulstudium. Internationales Symposium vom 8.–10. Mai 1986, Universität Hamburg. Pfaffenweiler, pp 194–212 (Hamburger Studien zur Kriminologie, vol 1)

Brusten M (1987) Datenschutz als Vorwand zur Verhinderung institutionenkritischer Forschung? Kritische und destruktive Anmerkungen mit konstruktiver Absicht zu tatsächlichen und potentiellen Folgen des Datenschutzes. In: Jehle J-M (ed) Datenzugang und Datenschutz in der kriminologischen Forschung. Wiesbaden, pp 116–151 (Kriminologie und Praxis, vol 2)

Brusten M, van Outrive L (1981) The relationship between state institutions and the social sciences in the field of deviance and social control. A first step to international comparative research on the institutionalization of criminological knowledge in Western Europe. In: State control on information in the field of deviance and social control. Leuven Vienne Wuppertal, pp 7–51 (Working Papers in European Criminology, no 2)

Deichsel W (1986) Kriminologie und gesellschaftliche Verwertungsinteressen. Diskussionsergebnisse. In: Löschper G, Manke G, Sack F (eds) Kriminologie als selbständiges, interdisziplinäres Hochschulstudium. Internationales Symposium vom 8.–10. Mai 1986, Universität Hamburg. Pfaffenweiler, pp 228–232 (Hamburger Studien zur Kriminologie, vol 1)

Deichsel W, Hufeland J, Kunstreich T, Löschper G (1985) Das Aufbaustudium Kriminologie. Erstens Planung und Programme, zweitens kommt es anders als man denkt. In: Kriminologisches Journal 17:69–76

Dolde G (1988) Praxisforschung zum Strafvollzug unter besonderer Berücksichtigung des Kriminologischen Dienstes. In: Feltes T (ed) Kriminologie und Praxisforschung. Probleme, Erfahrungen und Ergebnisse. Bonn, pp 187–206

Egg R, Feuerhelm W (1988) Praxisforschung in der Kriminologischen Zentralstelle. In: Feltes T (ed) Kriminologie und Praxisforschung. Probleme, Erfahrungen und Ergebnisse. Bonn, pp 117–142

Gemmer K (1969) Die Notwendigkeit und die Möglichkeit einer koordinierten kriminalistischen Forschung. In: Bundeskriminalamt (ed) Grundlagenforschung und Kriminalpolizei. Arbeitstagung im Bundeskriminalamt Wiesbaden vom 21.–25. April 1969. Wiesbaden, pp 243–253 (BKA-Vortragsreihe, vol 18)

Gipser D, Klein-Schonnefeld S (1980) Über die Ergründung des Bösen in der Welt. Fragen an Staatsforschung und staatliche Auftragsforschung. In: Kriminologisches Journal 12:199–208

Göppinger H (1980) Kriminologie, 4th edn. München

Heinl W (1969) Zur Situation der kriminalpolizeilich orientierten Forschung in der Bundesrepublik. In: Bundeskriminalamt (ed) Grundlagenforschung und Kriminalpolizei. Arbeitstagung im Bundeskriminalamt Wiesbaden vom 21.–25. April 1969. Wiesbaden, pp 9–12 (BKA-Vortragsreihe, vol 18)

Hasenpusch B (1990) Criminological research within criminal justice authorities in the Federal Republic of Germany. Lower Saxony Department of Justice, Hannover, FRG. In: Jehle J-M (ed) Criminological research and planning in state and supranational institutions. Wiesbaden, pp 195–202 (Kriminologie und Praxis, vol 5)

Hobe K (1988) Kriminologische Forschung im Bundesministerium der Justiz. In: Kaiser G, Kury H, Albrecht H-J (eds) Kriminologische Forschung in den 80er Jahren. Berichte aus der Bundesrepublik Deutschland, der Deutschen Demokratischen Republik, Österreich und der Schweiz. Freiburg, pp 215–221 (Kriminologische Forschungsberichte aus dem Max-Planck-Institut für ausländisches und internationales Strafrecht, Freiburg i.Br., vol 34)

Hobe K (1990) Criminological research at the Federal Ministry of Justice, Bonn. In: Jehle J-M (ed) Criminological research and planning in state and supranational institutions. Wiesbaden, pp 165–173 (Kriminologie und Praxis, vol 5)

Jäger H (1980) Zur Ambivalenz von Staatsforschung und staatlicher Auftragsforschung in der Kriminologie. In: Kriminologisches Journal 12:228–231

Jehle J-M (1988) Die Kriminologische Zentralstelle – Programm, Organisation, Projekte. In: Kaiser G, Kury H, Albrecht H-J (eds) Kriminologische Forschung in den 80er Jahren. Berichte aus der Bundesrepublik Deutschland, der Deutschen Demokratischen Republik, Österreich und der Schweiz. Freiburg, pp 199–214 (Kriminologische Forschungsberichte aus dem Max-Planck-Institut für ausländisches und internationales Strafrecht, Freiburg i.Br., vol 34)

Jehle J-M (1990) The Central Institute of Criminology. Die Kriminologische Zentralstelle in Wiesbaden. In: Jehle J-M (ed) Criminological research and planning in state and supranational institutions. Wiesbaden, pp 175–184 (Kriminologie und Praxis, vol 5)

Jung H (1988) Einführung in das Studium der Wahlfachgruppe „Kriminologie, Jugendstrafrecht, Strafvollzug". In: Jung H (ed) Fälle zum Wahlfach Kriminologie, Jugendstrafrecht, Strafvollzug, 2nd edn. München, pp 1–28 (JuS-Schriftenreihe, no 31)

Kaiser G (1983) „Biokriminologie", „Staatskriminologie" und die Grenzen kriminologischer Forschungsfreiheit. In: Kerner H-J, Göppinger H, Streng F (eds) Kriminologie – Psychiatrie – Strafrecht. Festschrift für Heinz Leferenz zum 70. Geburtstag. Heidelberg, pp 47–68

Kaiser G (1988a) Kriminologie. Ein Lehrbuch, 2nd edn. Heidelberg

Kaiser G (1988b) Kriminologische Forschung am Max-Planck-Institut. In: Kaiser G, Kury H, Albrecht H-J (eds) Kriminologische Forschung in den 80er Jahren. Berichte aus der Bundesrepublik Deutschland, der Deutschen Demokratischen Republik, Österreich und der Schweiz. Freiburg, pp 165–174 (Kriminologische Forschungsberichte aus dem Max-Planck-Institut für ausländisches und internationales Strafrecht, Freiburg i.Br., vol 34)

Kaiser G, Kerner H-J, Schöch H (1982) Strafvollzug. Ein Lehrbuch, 3rd edn. Heidelberg

Kerner H-J (1988) Probleme des Praxisbegriffs in der Praxisforschung. In: Feltes T (ed) Kriminologie und Praxisforschung. Probleme, Erfahrungen und Ergebnisse. Bonn, pp 17–29

Kreissl R (1983) Staatsforschung und staatstaugliche Forschung in der Kriminologie. Einige Überlegungen zu Tendenzen der Verwissenschaftlichung der Kriminalpolitik in der BRD. In: Kriminologisches Journal 15:110–121

Kreuzer A (1986) Kriminologenschelte in der „Kriminalistik". Eine Erwiderung auf Curt Weinschenk und Manfred Schreiber. In: Kriminalistik 40:568–571

Kube E (1988) Kriminalistisch-kriminologische Forschung im Bundeskriminalamt. In: Kaiser G, Kury H, Albrecht H-J (eds) Kriminologische Forschung in den 80er Jahren. Berichte aus der Bundesrepublik Deutschland, der Deutschen Demokratischen Republik, Österreich und der Schweiz. Freiburg, pp 249–262 (Kriminologische Forschungsberichte aus dem Max-Planck-Institut für ausländisches und internationales Strafrecht, Freiburg i.Br., vol 34)

Kürzinger J (1974) Institutionen der Kriminologie. In: Kaiser G, Sack F, Schellhoss H (eds) Kleines Kriminologisches Wörterbuch. Freiburg i.Br., pp 128–132 (Herderbücherei, vol 479)

Kury H (1981) Das Kriminologische Forschungsinstitut Niedersachsen e.V. und sein Forschungsprogramm. In: Kury H (ed) Perspektiven und Probleme kriminologischer Forschung. Köln Berlin Bonn München, pp 33–79 (Interdisziplinäre Beiträge zur kriminologischen Forschung, vol 1)

Leferenz H (1959) Die Stellung der Kriminologie zwischen Jurisprudenz und Psychiatrie. In: Studium Generale 12:119–126

Leferenz H (1967) Aufgaben einer modernen Kriminologie. Karlsruhe (Juristische Studiengesellschaft Karlsruhe. Schriftenreihe, no 76)

Matthes I (1974) Der Beginn des Forschungsprogramms in der Polizei-Führungsakademie. In: Schriftenreihe der Polizei-Führungsakademie, no 1, pp 35–38

Pfeiffer C (1986) Kriminologie und gesellschaftliche Verwertungsinteressen. Referat. In: Löschper G, Manke G, Sack F (eds) Kriminologie als selbständiges, interdisziplinäres Hochschulstudium. Internationales Symposium vom 8.–10. Mai 1986, Universität Hamburg. Pfaffenweiler, pp 215–224 (Hamburger Studien zur Kriminologie, vol 1)

Pfeiffer C (1988) Institutionen und Entscheidungen. Das neue Forschungsprogramm des kriminologischen Forschungsinstituts Niedersachsen. In: Kaiser G, Kury H, Albrecht H-J (eds) Kriminologische Forschung in den 80er Jahren. Berichte aus der Bundesrepublik Deutschland, der Deutschen Demokratischen Republik, Österreich und der Schweiz. Freiburg, pp 175–197 (Kriminologische Forschungsberichte aus dem Max-Planck-Institut für ausländisches und internationales Strafrecht, Freiburg i.Br., vol 34)

Radzinowicz L (1961) Strafrecht und Kriminologie (unter besonderer Berücksichtigung heutiger Strömungen in der Bundesrepublik Deutschland). In: Bundeskriminalamt (ed) Strafrechtspflege und Strafrechtsreform. Arbeitstagung im Bundeskriminalamt Wiesbaden vom 20.–25. März 1961. Wiesbaden, pp 17–34 (BKA-Vortragsreihe, vol 13)

Rebscher E (1987) Datenschutzprobleme der behördeneigenen Forschung und der Auftragsforschung im Bereich der Polizei. In: Jehle J-M (ed) Datenzugang und Datenschutz in der kriminologischen Forschung. Wiesbaden, pp 367–377 (Kriminologie und Praxis, vol 2)

Rotthaus KP (1980) Kurze Stellungnahme zum Beitrag von Brusten. In: Kriminologisches Journal 12:208–209

Sack F (1978) Probleme der Kriminalsoziologie. In: Rokkan S, Svåsand L, Heberle R, Wolf HE, Sack F Wahlverhalten. Vorurteile. Kriminalität, 2nd edn. Stuttgart, pp 192–492 (Handbuch der empirischen Sozialforschung, vol 12)

Sack F (1986) Kriminologie als selbständiges, interdisziplinäres Hochschulstudium. In: Löschper G, Manke G, Sack F (eds) Kriminologie als selbständiges, interdisziplinäres Hochschulstudium. Internationales Symposium vom 8.–10. Mai 1986, Universität Hamburg. Pfaffenweiler, pp 5–25 (Hamburger Studien zur Kriminologie, vol 1)

Schreiber M (1986) Täterwissen. Zusätzliche Grundlage präventiver Kriminalpolitik. In: Kriminalistik 40:349–351

Schwind H-D (1981) Kriminologische Forschung und Kriminalpolitik. In: Kury H (ed) Perspektiven und Probleme kriminologischer Forschung. Köln Berlin Bonn München, pp 80–94 (Interdisziplinäre Beiträge zur kriminologischen Forschung, vol 1)

Schwind H-D (1986) Kriminologie in der Praxis. Polizei, Justiz, Kriminalpolitik. Heidelberg (Grundlagen, vol 29)

Schwind H-D, Ahlborn W, Eger HJ, Jany U, Pudel V, Weiß R (1975) Dunkelfeldforschung in Göttingen 1973/74. Eine Opferbefragung zur Aufhellung des Dunkelfeldes und zur Erforschung der Bestimmungsgründe für die Unterlassung von Strafanzeigen. Wiesbaden (BKA-Forschungsreihe, vol 2)

Schwind H-D, Ahlborn W, Weiß R (1978) Empirische Kriminalgeographie. Bestandsaufnahme und Weiterführung am Beispiel von Bochum („Kriminalitätsatlas Bochum"). Wiesbaden (BKA-Forschungsreihe, vol 8)

Steffen W (1984) Rückzug in die Schneckenhäuser. Kriminologische Forschung und polizeiliche Praxis in der Bundesrepublik Deutschland. In: Kriminalistik 38:70–76

Steffen W (1986) Kriminologische Forschung und polizeiliche Praxis in der Bundesrepublik Deutschland. In: Brusten M, Häußling JM, Malinowski P (eds) Kriminologie im Spannungsfeld von Kriminalpolitik und Kriminalpraxis. Stuttgart, pp 51–60 (Kriminologie, vol 22)

Steffen W (1988a) Die Kriminologische Forschungsgruppe der Bayerischen Polizei im Bayerischen Landeskriminalamt: Ein Beispiel für Praxisforschung durch Soziologen in Institutionen sozialer Kontrolle. In: Feltes T (ed) Kriminologie und Praxisforschung. Probleme, Erfahrungen und Ergebnisse. Bonn, pp 151–162

Steffen W (1988b) Kriminologische Forschung an Landeskriminalämtern: Die kriminologische Forschungsgruppe der Bayerischen Polizei. In: Kaiser G, Kury H, Albrecht H-J (eds) Kriminologische Forschung in den 80er Jahren. Berichte aus der Bundesrepublik Deutschland, der Deutschen Demokratischen Republik, Österreich und der Schweiz. Freiburg, pp 263–276 (Kriminologische Forschungsberichte aus dem Max-Planck-Institut für ausländisches und internationales Strafrecht, Freiburg i.Br., vol 34)

Steffen W (1990) Experiences of the Kriminologische Forschungsgruppe der Bayerischen Polizei, Criminological Research Unit of the Bavarian Police. In: Jehle J-M (ed) Criminological research and planning in state and supranational institutions. Wiesbaden, pp 217–219 (Kriminologie und Praxis, vol 5)

Steinhilper G (1982) Kriminologische Forschung und Planung im Niedersächsischen Justizministerium. In: Schwind H-D, Steinhilper G (eds) Modelle zur Kriminalitätsvorbeugung und Resozialisierung. Beispiele praktischer Kriminalpolitik in Niedersachsen. Heidelberg, pp 13–33 (Kriminologische Forschung, vol 2)

Steinhilper G (1983) Der Kriminologische Dienst (§166 StVollzG) – Anspruch und Wirklichkeit. In: Kerner H-J, Göppinger H, Streng F (eds) Kriminologie – Psychiatrie – Strafrecht. Festschrift für Heinz Leferenz zum 70. Geburtstag. Heidelberg, pp 91–103

Steinhilper G (1986) Der Kriminologische Dienst: Eine Herausforderung für Wissenschaft und Praxis. In: Brusten M, Häußling JM, Malinowski P (eds) Kriminologie im Spannungsfeld von Kriminalpolitik und Kriminalpraxis. Stuttgart, pp 61–72 (Kriminologie, vol 22)

Steinhilper G (1987) Glanz und Elend justizinterner kriminologischer Forschung. In: Jehle J-M (ed) Datenzugang und Datenschutz in der kriminologischen Forschung. Wiesbaden, pp 351–366 (Kriminologie und Praxis, vol 2)
Steinhilper G, Berckhauer F (1980) Kriminologische Forschung als Beitrag zur Kriminalitätsvorbeugung. Referatsgruppe „Planung und Forschung" des Niedersächsischen Ministeriums der Justiz. In: Schwind H-D, Berckhauer F, Steinhilper G (eds) Präventive Kriminalpolitik. Beiträge zur ressortübergreifenden Kriminalprävention aus Forschung, Praxis und Politik. Heidelberg, pp 127–143 (Kriminologische Forschung, vol 1)
Stephan E (1976) Die Stuttgarter Opferbefragung. Eine kriminologisch-viktimologische Analyse zur Erforschung des Dunkelfeldes unter besonderer Berücksichtigung der Einstellung der Bevölkerung zur Kriminalität. Wiesbaden (BKA-Forschungsreihe, vol 3)
Störzer HU (1976) Die kriminologische Klausur in der Heidelberger Juristenausbildung. Bericht über ein Experiment und seine Hintergründe. In: Ruperto Carola 57:85–89
Störzer HU (1983) „Staatskriminologie". – Subjektive Notizen. In: Kerner H-J, Göppinger H, Streng F (eds) Kriminologie – Psychiatrie – Strafrecht. Festschrift für Heinz Leferenz zum 70. Geburtstag. Heidelberg, pp 69–90
Störzer HU (1984) Kriminologisch-kriminalistische Ausbildung an der Universität. Eine phänomenologische Bestandsaufnahme. In: Kube E, Störzer HU, Brugger S (eds) Wissenschaftliche Kriminalistik. Grundlagen und Perspektiven, Part 2. Wiesbaden, pp 325–412 (BKA-Forschungsreihe, vol 16/2)
Störzer HU (1985) Konzepte der Zusammenarbeit von Wissenschaft und Praxis. In: Bundeskriminalamt (ed) Zweites Symposium: Wissenschaftliche Kriminalistik – „Kriminalitätsprognose" und „Zusammenarbeit von Wissenschaft und Praxis". Referate und Diskussionsbeiträge am 2. und 3. Oktober 1984 im Bundeskriminalamt. Wiesbaden, pp 247–258 (BKA-Forschungsreihe. Special volume)
Störzer HU (1990) The Research Unit on Criminology and Criminal Investigation of the Bundeskriminalamt (BKA) in Wiesbaden. In: Jehle J-M (ed) Criminological research and planning in state and supranational institutions. Wiesbaden, pp 203–216 (Kriminologie und Praxis, vol 5)
Wehner B (1957) Die Latenz der Straftaten (Die nicht entdeckte Kriminalität). Wiesbaden (BKA-Schriftenreihe, vol 7)
Wehner B (1985) Rede des Preisträgers. In: Deutsche Kriminologische Gesellschaft e.V. (ed) Verleihung der Beccaria-Medaille 1984. Frankfurt a.M., pp 11–20
Wolff J (1971) Der Jurist in der Kriminologie. In: Kriminologisches Journal 3:260–276
Würtenberger T (1964/65) Entwicklung und Lage der Kriminologie in Deutschland. In: Juristen-Jahrbuch 5:147–168
Würtenberger T (1969) Notwendigkeit und Möglichkeit einer koordinierten kriminologischen Forschung. In: Bundeskriminalamt (ed) Grundlagenforschung und Kriminalpolizei. Arbeitstagung im Bundeskriminalamt Wiesbaden vom 21.–25. April 1969. Wiesbaden, pp 225–241 (BKA-Vortragsreihe, vol 18)
Würtenberger T (1977) Organisationen und Institute. In: Sieverts R,. Schneider HJ (eds) Handwörterbuch der Kriminologie, vol 2, 2nd edn. Berlin New York, pp 259–279
Zirpins W (1955) Die Entwicklung der polizeilichen Verbrechensbekämpfung in Deutschland. In: Taschenbuch für Kriminalisten 5:250–312

Part II
The Picture of Crime

CHAPTER 4

Crime Analysis

U. Dörmann

Contents

1 Introduction

Effective crime control and crime prevention require considerable knowledge and understanding. Crime must be continuously observed and the social factors influencing it must be analyzed. Research into unreported crime[1] and continuous study of the population, in terms of their attitudes toward the police, crime, etc.[2], are necessary to clarify to what extent police knowledge of criminals and crime reflects reality. The results of this research work are intended to improve crime analyses based on the data provided by official statistics in order to provide a chance to influence crime in its initial stages.

2 Police Crime Statistics

Since 1953, the Bundeskriminalamt (BKA) in cooperation with the 11 *Landeskriminalämter* (state criminal police offices of the 11 old states of the Federal Republic of Germany) has kept crime statistics. These official statistics include cases of felony and misdemeanor in which the police took action against persons suspected of having committed these crimes.[3] This cooperation between the federal government and the individual states (according to the German Constitution, police jurisdiction is vested in the states) was established by voluntary agreement. Since

[1] See Chap. 5 by Weiß, in which these surveys are described in detail.

[2] See Chap. 7 by Dörmann.

[3] On the development of the police crime statistics in Germany see, for example, Dörmann 1983, Graff 1975.

Kube/Störzer (Eds.)
Police Research in the Federal Republic of Germany

1973, a legal base has been in existence: According to the BKA Act, it is now the responsibility of the BKA as a central agency to "observe the trends in crime and to undertake analyses of statistics for the criminal police."

The statistical data are collected according to the following procedure: Cases which have come to the attention of the police are registered with the appropriate local police authorities. The crimes are classified into categories according to a catalogue of offenses based on the German penal code with the addition of criminological elements such as venue (street, home, bank), object of the crime (car, drugs), or method of committing the crime (pickpocketing, computer manipulation). The offenses are statistically recorded after the police inquiries have been completed and before the file is submitted to the public prosecutor. The state criminal police office then forwards the data in tabular form to the BKA, where they are incorporated into the national report entitled *Polizeiliche Kriminalstatistik* (Police Crime Statistics, PCS).

The statistical data are broken down further into tables relating, for example, to:

- Known offenses and attempts; subdivision of the venues by size of community; use of firearms; clearance; list of all suspects[4]
- Damage by amount (for certain offenses only)
- Cleared cases
- Suspects according to age and sex
- Suspects' place of residence
- Further detailed information on the suspects
- German suspects according to age and sex
- Non-German suspects according to age and sex
- Non-German suspects by nature of and reason for their stay in Germany
- Non-German suspects according to nationality
- Victims according to age and sex (for certain offenses only)
- Connections between victims and suspects (for certain offenses only).

The PCS cannot be compared with the prosecution statistics of the justice administration (statistics on convicted persons), as in most cases the time periods covered by the two sets of statistics differ, as do the data collection guidelines and methods.

The PCS at the federal level suffer from considerable limitations. The BKA cannot take full advantage of electronic data processing, since for reasons of data protection it does not have direct access to the original information. Moreover, the tables received by the BKA from the states allow little room for change or interpretation.

This is one of the obstacles in the way of achieving the goals outlined below (taken from the preamble to the *Directives for Keeping Statistics of the Criminal Police*):

"The police crime statistics serve the purpose of observing criminality with respect to various kinds of offenses, the size and composition of the circle of

[4] Suspects are persons whom the police regard as responsible for committing a crime.

suspects, and the change in crime rates, and of gaining knowledge for the fight against crime by prevention and prosecution, for organizational plans and decisions, as well as for criminological and sociological research work and criminal policy measures."

Other obstacles to attaining these goals are found in the criminal statistics themselves. Year after year politicians, the press, researchers, and the police regard the statistics as an indicator of the trends in crime. In this connection the question arises as to how reliably this body of figures reflects the real crime rate.

3 Problems of Interpretation[5]

The PCS provide data on the number and kind of offenses that have become known to the police and on how many and what persons have been identified as suspects. Unreported crime is therefore a major problem associated with analyzing crime on the basis of the PCS. The extent of unreported crime varies with each individual offense. For bank robbery or car theft, for instance, it is small; however, for shoplifting, other minor thefts, fraud, environmental crime, or drug abuse, it is very large.

In analyzing the PCS it must also be kept in mind that statistical crime trends are not necessarily consistent with trends in crimes actually committed. In the last few years, for example, there has been a considerable rise in reported cases of environmental crime as a result of the increased control exercised by the authorities and hence of the increased willingness of the public to report offenses. Similarly, the more intensive control efforts by customs officials and police have led to an increase in recorded cases of smuggling of hard drugs and of trafficking in heroin and cocaine.

A further example is provided by the results of a follow-up survey conducted in Bochum for the years 1975 and 1986. These findings suggest that the strong statistical increase in cases of theft under aggravating circumstances, such as burglary and theft from motor vehicles, seems to be largely caused by an increase in insurance policies which require police reports before damages can be settled.

The foregoing examples demonstrate that possible changes in the public's crime reporting behavior or in the control of crime should be taken into account when assessing statistical crime trends. Other factors which should also be included are any changes in criminal law or in the guidelines for compiling crime statistics.

Superficial interpretations of the PCS can result in false conclusions being drawn, as is shown in the following examples. The percentage of criminal cases solved is not a reliable measure for the quality and quantity of police work. The total number of cases solved depends on what types of crimes these are. In other words, the higher the number of cases that are difficult so solve, the fewer the number of cases that will actually be solved.

---

[5] On the interpretation of criminal statistics see, for example, Heiland 1982, Heinz 1975, 1977, Kerner 1980, Kreuzer 1976, DJ Newman 1965, Pilgram 1980, 1982, and Sack 1985.

Furthermore, it is virtually impossible to make comparisons between crimes committed by Germans and non-Germans. In 1989, non-German nationals in the Federal Republic of Germany constituted 25% of all crime suspects; the percentage of aliens in the total population, however, was only 8%. Such figures with no further explanation are misleading. To begin with, members of the armed forces stationed in Germany, tourists, and persons illegally residing in Germany are included among the number of suspects, but are not included in the total resident population. Moreover, the alien resident population is very different from the German resident population in terms of the breakdown according to age, sex, and social structure. Finally, 20% of all non-German suspects have been registered only because of alien-specific crimes such as illegal entry into the country.

Another objection to the PCS as an indicator of crime frequencies and trends in crime is that criminal charges forwarded by the police may be judged differently by the judicial bodies. As regards public danger, the PCS are a more useful source of information than the prosecution statistics. The PCS are procedurally closer to the original crime and the percentage of undetected crimes is lower because public security is also affected by offenses which have not been cleared (52.8% in 1989), which were committed by minors or other persons who can no longer be convicted (due to escape or death), or where there is no conclusive evidence that one specific person committed the crime.

Many crimes are difficult to reconstruct because they are often so complex and of an ambiguous nature. Distortions and loss of information are inevitable. This applies not only to the PCS, but also to criminological findings obtained through empirical research methods.

Another central problem associated with the PCS is that they do not make recognizable distinctions between the degrees of seriousness of the crimes recorded. If numbers alone were an indication of seriousness, then purse-snatching without using violence would be just as serious as a hold-up involving weapons or injuries; or minor shoplifting would be as serious as embezzling entire carloads of goods.

Crime trends are most affected by the very large quantity of minor offenses. More serious but less frequent crimes disappear among the total number. Using a scale that only measures the total number of registered crimes can result in faulty planning of police deployment and crime prevention measures.

The seriousness of a specific crime cannot be adequately defined by the penalties stipulated in penal provisions, nor by calculating the actual amount of damages. Even determining the costs of the results of a criminal act would pose difficulties, and these difficulties would become insurmountable if subjective criteria were included. Furthermore, social danger and psychological damage cannot be measured in terms of money. Previous attempts to measure the seriousness of crime, such as the Sellin-Wolfgang index[6], neglected crimes directed against groups, institutions, and society in general. General indices should be avoided because the manifold

---

6 Sellin/Wolfgang 1964.

character of the total spectrum of crime cannot be adequately represented by an indicator of averages.[7]

4 International Comparisons of Crime

International comparisons of crime, though indispensable for the assessment of the nature, extent, and trends in crime in any one particular country, pose many problems. International crime statistics are, in fact, published by Interpol. Interpol has established uniform definitions and rules according to which Interpol members should report crimes registered by the police in their own country. However, the very different conditions for collecting crime statistics in each country present major obstacles to such international comparison.[8]

There are various factors that influence the generation of crime statistics. The crime statistics of a given country are governed by that country's penal code, the type of society, and the legal definitions employed. There are differences among the official rules for compiling statistics (e.g., rules for counting cases), as well as differences in the public's attitude toward the police, the degree to which conflicts are settled privately, and the legal principles of police practices.

The figures listed for 1955, 1970, and 1985 in Table 1 convey only a rough picture of the long-term statistical trend in some European countries and, for contrast, Japan. The table shows the frequency (per 100000 inhabitants) of theft including robbery reported in the Interpol statistics. This type of crime seems to be more suitable for comparison than others because the different countries use similar definitions for theft. The table reveals the sharp increase in thefts known to the police in all of the countries listed, with the exception of Japan.

Table 1. Thefts (including robbery)

	1955	1970	1985
Austria	830	1477	2366
Denmark	1925	4557	7454
England and Wales	961	2794	5592
Finland	520	1293	2157
France	445	1343	4134
West Germany	1135	2567	4406
Italy	369	577	1100
Japan	1190	1005	1143
Netherlands	465	1360	5628

Offense rates: cases per 100000 inhabitants.

[7] For more detailed discussions on the basic problems of offense classification and offense rating see Heller 1977, Kerner 1977 and 1980, McClintock 1977, Schindhelm 1972, Törnudd 1977, Villmow 1977.

[8] On the international comparison of crime on the basis of the PCS see, for example, Archer and Gartner 1984, Dörmann 1984, Skogan 1984, van Dijk, Leger, and Shapland 1987.

Kühne and Miyazawa, for example, in their 1979 empirical research project[9] produced more convincing results regarding the international comparison of crime. They also incorporated criminal law, unreported crime, rules of generating the statistics, and social aspects with regard to Japan and Germany.

5 Crime Forecasting[10]

Time-series analysis marks the beginning of making mathematical-statistical crime prognoses. Analysis of current crime is at the same time a prediction of trends in criminal activity. However, can mathematical forecasting methods that are based on questionable data be considered scientific?

In several states attempts have been made to extrapolate long-term crime trends on the basis of predicted demographic and socioeconomic time series.[11] Basically, the comprehensive method seemed promising because criminality is not an isolated factor, nor a factor which can be isolated, but is firmly incorporated in social structures and processes. The problem, however, is the complexity of the correlations.

As with criminological research into causes, it has not been possible with trend forecasts to pick out the various criminological influences in isolation from one another and in a way that can be shown by statistics. This leads to considerable doubt on the validity of any forecasts of future trends. However, even if causal connections for past periods could be established, there is no guarantee that this influence would remain unchanged in the future.

Finally, there is very little usable information to be derived from statistical data from social and economic areas, and what information there is can hardly be correlated with the crime statistical time series, due to the different ways the data are collected. Even the demographic data, which appear to be most reliable, are unsatisfactory. Random checks have revealed that in many cases the laws regulating the registration of residents are not being complied with (in Germany every resident is required to register with the community administration of his place of residence). Furthermore, the size of the alien population is not known.

A basic skepticism toward the possibilities of mathematically forecasting crime would seem to be justified. The BKA, in cooperation with several universities, had a number of different forecasting methods tested, for example, an (unsuccessful)

---

[9] Kühne/Miyazawa 1979. Teske and Arnold (1984) undertook a comparison between the USA (Texas) and Germany with respect to unreported crime and criminal law; Arnold, Teske, and Korinek (1988) a comparison between the USA, Germany, and Hungary.

[10] On the possibilities and limits of crime forecasting in Germany see Dörmann and Beck 1984, Heinz 1985, Kube 1976, 1983, 1984. On the social-scientific prognosis see Popper 1980.

[11] Examples for comprehensive forecasting attempts are offered by Fox 1976 (USA) Hamacher 1973 (FRG), Hasenpusch 1978 (Canada), Nishimura 1972, Kurusu 1974 and Kurusu, Okusawa, Shindo, Sato, Katsurajima and Tokuyama 1975 (Japan). An overview of forecasting attempts up to the beginning of the 1970s in France, Great Britain, and Scandinavia was given by the European Council in the report of the subcommittee No. XV of the CEPC 1973.

econometric model developed using Box-Jenkins techniques in the areas of burglary and bank robbery. The more qualitative "scenario technique"[12] seems to be more promising. For a prognosis of environmental crime the scenario technique was combined with an expert survey (Delphi method).[13]

The foregoing discussion demonstrates that crime analysis in the BKA means the evaluation of data obtained from the PCS in close relationship to the findings of BKA research projects, many of which are described in detail in other chapters in this volume.

References

Allerbeck KR (1978) Meßniveau und Analyseverfahren – Das Problem „strittiger Intervallskalen". Zeitschrift für Soziologie 7:199–214

Archer D, Gartner R (1984) Violence and crime in cross-national perspective. New Haven, CT

Arnold H, Teske RHC, Korinek L (1988) Viktimisierung, Verbrechensfurcht und Einstellungen zur Sozialkontrolle in West und Ost. Ergebnisse vergleichender Opferbefragungen in der Bundesrepublik Deutschland, den Vereinigten Staaten und Ungarn. In: Kaiser G, Kury H, Albrecht H-J (eds) Kriminologische Forschung in den 80er Jahren. Projektberichte aus der Bundesrepublik Deutschland. Freiburg, pp 909–942 (Kriminologische Forschungsberichte aus dem Max-Planck-Institut für ausländisches und internationales Strafrecht, Freiburg i.Br. vol 35, No 2)

Bundeskriminalamt (ed) (1977) "Offence classification and rating, and practical applications thereof". International Symposium organized at the Bundeskriminalamt Wiesbaden (papers). 16–18 February 1977. Wiesbaden (BKA-Forschungsreihe. Special volume)

van Dijk JJM, Leger GJ, Shapland J (1987) Information systems, crime and crime prevention. Strasbourg (Council of Europe: Conference on the Reduction of Urban Insecurity. Barcelona, 17–20 November 1987. Sub-Theme 3: Statistics: Data banks and victimization surveys CPL/ENV/UP (21) 48)

Dörmann U (1983) Die Aussagekraft wesentlich verbessert. Neugestaltung der Polizeilichen Kriminalstatistik. Kriminalistik 37:182–186

Dörmann U (1984) Interpolstatistik: Kein wahrer Spiegel der tatsächlichen Kriminalitätsbelastung. Kriminalistik 38:414–420

Dörmann U (1988) Dunkelfeldforschung im Dunkeln. Zum Problem der statistikbegleitenden Dunkelfeldforschung. Kriminalistik 42:403–405

Dörmann U, Beck H-W (1984) Kriminalitätsanalyse und -prognose. Möglichkeiten und Grenzen. In: Kube E, Störzer HU, Brugger S (eds) Wissenschaftliche Kriminalistik. Grundlagen und Perspektiven. Part 2. Wiesbaden, pp 37–76 (BKA-Forschungsreihe, vol 16/2)

Fox JA (1976) An econometric analysis of crime data. PhD Dissertation University of Pennsylvania

Graff H (1975) Die deutsche Kriminalstatistik. Geschichte und Gegenwart. Stuttgart (Kriminologie. Abhandlungen über abwegiges Sozialverhalten, vol 13)

Hamacher HW (1973) Tatort Deutschland. Bergisch Gladbach

[12] Scenario technique – an analytic technique involving the design of a logical sequence of events starting with a description of current situations and conditions using quantitative data and qualitative judgements to gain information about the probability of future scenarios. Systematic changes in independent variables lead to alternative future models.

[13] For a summary of the results see Chap. 15 by Wulff-Nienhüser and Seitz.

Hasenpusch B (1978) Future trends in crime and policing in Canada. Université de Montréal, Ecole de Criminologie (unpublished paper)

Heinz W (1975) Bekanntgewordene Kriminalität und praktische Erkenntnisinteressen. Erwägungen zur Umsetzung amtlicher Kenntnisse über Kriminalität in numerische Information. Monatsschrift für Kriminologie und Strafrechtsreform 58:225–246

Heinz W (1977) Kriminalstatistiken – Indikatoren der Kriminalität und ihrer Entwicklung? In: Bundeskriminalamt (ed) Polizei und Justiz. Arbeitstagung des Bundeskriminalamtes Wiesbaden vom 12.–15. Oktober 1976. Wiesbaden, pp 93–110 (BKA-Vortragsreihe, vol 23)

Heinz W (1985) Was kann die Kriminologie zur Kriminalitätsprognose beitragen? In: Bundeskriminalamt (ed) Zweites Symposium: Wissenschaftliche Kriminalistik – „Kriminalitätsprognose" und „Zusammenarbeit von Wissenschaft und Praxis" –. Referate und Diskussionsbeiträge am 2. und 3. Oktober 1984 im Bundeskriminalamt. Wiesbaden, pp 31–118 (BKA-Forschungsreihe. Special volume)

Heiland H-G (1982) Kriminalitätsindikatoren und Kriminalpolitik. Zu Arno Pilgrams „Kriminalität in Österreich – Studien zur Kriminalitätsentwicklung". Kriminologisches Journal 14:49–64

Heller NB (1977) The St. Louis, Missouri Police Department's Crime Seriousness Study – Five years later. In: Bundeskriminalamt (ed) "Offence classification and rating, and practical applications thereof". International Symposium organized at the Bundeskriminalamt Wiesbaden (papers). 16–18 February, 1977. Wiesbaden, pp 118–125 (BKA-Forschungsreihe. Special volume)

Kerner H-J (1977) Entwicklung von nach Deliktschwere gewichteten Kriminalitätsindices: Vorstellung eines Forschungsprojekts. In: Bundeskriminalamt (ed) "Offence classification and rating, and practical applications thereof". International Symposium organized at the Bundeskriminalamt Wiesbaden (papers). 16–18 February, 1977. Wiesbaden, pp 84–106 (BKA-Forschungsreihe. Special volume)

Kerner H-J (1980) Kriminalitätseinschätzung und Innere Sicherheit. Eine Untersuchung über die Beurteilung der Sicherheitslage und über das Sicherheitsgefühl in der Bundesrepublik Deutschland, mit vergleichenden Betrachtungen zur Situation im Ausland. Wiesbaden (BKA-Forschungsreihe, vol 11)

Kirchhoff GF (1975) Selbstberichtete Delinquenz. Eine empirische Untersuchung. Göttingen (Kriminologische Studien, vol 22)

Kreuzer A (1976) Über kriminologische Dunkelfeldforschung. Bemerkungen zum Stand, zu Methoden und Problemen dieser Forschung in der Bundesrepublik Deutschland. Kriminalistik 30:145–151

Kube E (1976) Was geschieht auf dem Gebiet der Kriminalitätsprognose? Zugleich ein Bericht über die IKPO-Interpol-Tagung zur Kriminalitätsprognose. Kriminalistik 30:350–355

Kube E (1983) Untersuchung über Möglichkeiten und Grenzen der Vorhersage von Entwicklungen der allgemeinen Kriminalität. Schriftenreihe der Polizei-Führungsakademie, pp 116–127

Kube E (1984) Kriminalitätsprognose. Überlegungen zu Notwendigkeit, Möglichkeiten und Grenzen. Monatsschrift für Kriminologie und Strafrechtsreform 67:1–15

Kühne H-H, Miyazawa K (1979) Kriminalität und Kriminalitätsbekämpfung in Japan. Versuch einer soziokulturell-kriminologischen Analyse. Wiesbaden (BKA-Forschungsreihe. Special volume)

Kürzinger J (1978) Private Strafanzeige und polizeiliche Reaktion. Berlin (Strafrecht und Kriminologie, vol 4)

Kurusu M (1974/75) Estimation of regional crime by the indicator of social change. The Ministry of Justice. Tokyo

Kurusu M, Okusawa Y, Shindo H, Sato T, Katsurajima M, Tokuyama T (1975) Estimation of crime rate based on socio-economic indices – Second interim report: An approach by time-series analysis. Bulletin of the Criminological Research Department, pp 12–18

McClintock FH (1977) Basic problems of offence classification and indexing. In: Bundeskriminalamt (ed) "Offence classification and rating, and practical applications thereof". International Symposium organized at the Bundeskriminalamt Wiesbaden (papers). 16–18 February, 1977. Wiesbaden, 38–48 (BKA-Forschungsreihe. Special volume)
Newman DJ (1965) The effect of accomodation in justice administration on criminal statistics. In: Goulder AW, Miller SM (eds) Applied sociology. New York, pp 163–179
Nishimura (1972) Estimating and forecasting the volume of crime. Tokyo, pp 13–22 (Schriftenreihe des National Research Institute of Police Science)
Pilgram A (1980) Kriminalität in Österreich – Studien zur Kriminalitätsentwicklung. Wien
Pilgram A (1982) Kleine Verteidigung der Kriminalstatistik. Kriminologisches Journal 14:57–65
Plate M, Schwinges U, Weiß R (1985) Strukturen der Kriminalität in Solingen. Eine Untersuchung zu Zusammenhängen zwischen baulichen und sozialen Merkmalen und dem Kriminalitätsaufkommen. Wiesbaden (BKA-Forschungsreihe. Special volume)
Popper KR (1980) Prognose und Prophetie in der Sozialwissenschaft. In: Topitsch E (ed) Logik der Sozialwissenschaft. 10th edn. Königstein/Ts, pp 113–125
Rolinski K (1980) Wohnhausarchitektur und Kriminalität. Wiesbaden (BKA-Forschungsreihe, vol 13)
Sack F (1985) Dunkelfeld. In: Kaiser G, Kerner H-J, Sack F, Schellhoss H (eds) Kleines Kriminologisches Wörterbuch, 2nd edn. Heidelberg, pp 76–84 (Uni-Taschenbücher, vol 1274)
Schindhelm M (1972) Der Sellin-Wolfgang Index – ein ergänzendes Maß der Strafrechtspflegestatistik. Eine Replikationsstudie. Stuttgart (Kriminologie. Abhandlungen über abwegiges Sozialverhalten, vol 9)
Schöch H (1976) Ist Kriminalität normal? Probleme und Ergebnisse der Dunkelfeldforschung. In: Göppinger H, Kaiser G (eds) Kriminologie und Strafverfahren. Neuere Ergebnisse zur Dunkelfeldforschung in Deutschland. Bericht über die XVIII. Tagung der Gesellschaft für die gesamte Kriminologie vom 9. bis 12. Oktober 1975 in Freiburg. Stuttgart, pp 211–228 (Kriminologische Gegenwartsfragen, no 12)
Schwind H-D, Ahlborn W, Eger HJ, Jany U, Pudel V, Weiß R (1975) Dunkelfeldforschung in Göttingen 1973/74. Eine Opferbefragung zur Aufhellung des Dunkelfeldes und zur Erforschung der Bestimmungsgründe für die Unterlassung von Strafanzeigen. Wiesbaden (BKA-Forschungsreihe, vol 2)
Schwind H-D, Ahlborn W, Weiß R (1978) Empirische Kriminalgeographie. Bestandsaufnahme und Weiterführung am Beispiel von Bochum („Kriminalitätsatlas Bochum"). Wiesbaden (BKA-Forschungsreihe, vol 8)
Sellin T, Wolfgang ME (1964) The measurement of delinquency. New York
Stephan E (1976) Die Stuttgarter Opferbefragung. Eine kriminologisch-viktimologische Analyse zur Erforschung des Dunkelfeldes unter besonderer Berücksichtigung der Einstellung der Bevölkerung zur Kriminalität. Wiesbaden (BKA-Forschungsreihe, vol 3)
Stevens SS (1946) On the theory of scales of measurement. Science CIII, no 2684:677–680
Stevens SS (1968) Measurement, statistics and the schemapiric view. Science CLI, no 3844:849–856
Stümper A (1983) Das strukturelle Dunkelfeld. Kriminalistik 37:222–226
Teske RHC, Arnold HR (1982) A comparative investigation of criminal victimization in the United States and the Federal Republic of Germany. In: Criminological Research Unit (ed) Research in criminal justice. Stock-taking of criminological research at the Max-Planck-Institute for foreign and international penal law after a decade. Freiburg, pp 63–83 (Kriminologische Forschungsberichte aus dem Max-Planck-Institut für ausländisches und internationales Strafrecht, Freiburg, vol 2)
Törnudd P (1977) Crime statistics based on damage: experience and plans in Scandinavia. In: Bundeskriminalamt (ed) "Offence classification and rating, and practical applications thereof". International Symposium organized at the Bundeskriminalamt Wiesbaden (pa-

pers). 16–18 Februar, 1977. Wiesbaden, pp 107–117 (BKA-Forschungsreihe. Special volume)
Villmow B (1977) Schwereeinschätzung von Delikten. Zum gegenwärtigen Stand der internationalen Forschung. In: Bundeskriminalamt (ed) "Offence classification and rating, and practical applications thereof". International Symposium organized at the Bundeskriminalamt Wiesbaden (papers). 16–18 Februar, 1977. Wiesbaden, pp 64–83 (BKA-Forschungsreihe. Special volume)
Villmow B (1980) Dunkelfeld und registrierte Kriminalität. In: Forschungsgruppe Kriminologie (ed) Empirische Kriminologie. Ein Jahrzehnt kriminologischer Forschung am Max-Planck-Institut Freiburg i.Brsg. Bestandsaufnahme und Ausblick. Freiburg, pp 59–72 (Kriminologische Forschungsberichte aus dem Max-Planck-Institut für ausländisches und internationales Strafrecht, Freiburg, vol 1)
Weis K, Müller-Bagehl R (1971) Private Strafanzeigen. Kriminologisches Journal 3:185–195
Wittkämper GW, Wulff-Nienhüser M (1987) Umweltkriminalität – Heute und morgen. Eine empirische Untersuchung mit Prognose und Empfehlungen für die Praxis. Wiesbaden (BKA-Forschungsreihe, vol 20)

CHAPTER 5

Research on Hidden Crime

R. Weiß

Contents

1 Introduction

The assessment of trends and patterns in crime in the Federal Republic of Germany is generally based on the *Polizeiliche Kriminalstatistik* (police crime statistics, PCS). It must be kept in mind, however, that the PCS comprise only a portion of the actual crimes committed, namely, crimes that have been reported to and registered by the police. Hidden crime, the unknown number of offenses committed, is not taken into account.[1]

An overriding factor determining the influence of crime control on crime statistics is the public's attitude toward reporting crime to the police. Reporting rates vary not only with region and time, but most certainly with the type of offense. The effect of reporting on recorded crime is seen in the fact that approximately 90% of traditional property crimes, which make up about 75% of all offenses in the police statistics, do not become known until a complaint has been filed.[2] Thus, hidden crime can be regarded as a consequence of public unwillingness to report crime.

[1] See Schwind, Ahlborn, Eger, Jany, Pudel, and Weiß 1975, pp 16ff.

[2] See Steffen 1976, p 158.

Kube/Störzer (Eds.)
Police Research in the Federal Republic of Germany

It is difficult to generalize about crime in the absence of information about reporting behavior, and consequently it is almost impossible to make statements concerning the extent of crime and crime trends. All of the studies on crime reporting conducted in the Federal Republic of Germany thus far have been based on one specific group out of the general population from one specific area at one specific time. Thus, the results of these studies cannot be regarded as providing anything more than hypotheses for further testing.

The BKA has undertaken studies of hidden crime since the middle of the 1970s. These have all been victim surveys. In this chapter only the methodologically comparable studies conducted in the cities of Göttingen 1973–1974)[3], Bochum (1975–1976 and 1986–1987)[4], and Solingen (1981–1982)[5] are discussed.

2 Methods

In victim surveys, respondents are asked whether they have ever been victim to crime. A problem of victim surveys is that not all types of crimes can be addressed. Such crimes include victimless crimes in the strict sense of the word (such as drug taking), those which are not directed against private persons or were not noticed by the victim, and, finally, those where the victim is not able to give any testimony (e.g., murder). Crimes in which the offender and the victim work together are also difficult to detect (such as conjoint arson and insurance fraud).

Other problems associated with victim surveys include: (1) a method must be found that will ensure that the data obtained are reliable and consistent; (2) the questions must be formulated in plain language, easy enough for the respondent to understand; (3) the respondent must be able to remember the crime incident; (4) the respondent must tell the truth.

3 Description of the Individual Studies

Since the data routinely recorded in the PCS were not sufficient for purposes of research, the local police of the cities in which the studies were undertaken completed additional surveys about crime pertaining to one calendar year. In the Göttingen study these covered only the delinquent acts that were later included in the victim survey. This also applied to the first Bochum study, but additional questions were asked concerning suspects. The Solingen survey related to all crimes known to the police and included data regarding suspects. In the second Bochum study only the offenses included in the victim survey were addressed.

---

[3] Schwind, Ahlborn, Eger, Jany, Pudel, and Weiß 1975.

[4] Schwind, Ahlborn, and Weiß 1978; Schwind, Ahlborn, and Weiß 1989.

[5] Plate, Schwinges, and Weiß 1985; see also Chap. 10 in the present volume.

Table 1. Features of the four studies

	Göttingen 1973–1974	Bochum I 1975–1976	Solingen 1981–1982	Bochum II 1986–1987
Residents over the age of 14	126 400	360 000	148 400	358 000
All crimes known to the police	6 780	22 339	9 942	31 794
All crimes based on 100 000 residents (crime rate)	5 691	5 375	6 018	8 344
Planned interviews	1 264	1 980	1 480	1 792
Completed interviews	1 170 (92.6%)	1 680 (84.8%)	1 001 (67.6%)	1 434 (80.0%)
Interview refusals	53 (4.2%)	199 (10.1%)	251 (17.0%)	215 (12.0%)
Other failures	41 (3.2%)	101 (5.1%)	228 (15.4%)	143 (8.0%)

The victim surveys covered theft, robbery, and bodily injury. Property damage was added in the Solingen study. In all four studies, only those offenses were included in which the respondents themselves had been victims.

The samples were obtained from the files of the residents' registration office in each city. All of the residents who had reached the age of 14 years by a particular date were pooled and a random sample was taken which constituted between 0.5% and 1% of the resident population. If names were drawn of persons who had died, moved, or had just recently moved into the city, or if the address was not correct, new names were drawn.

The surveys were conducted in the form of direct interviews using standardized questionnaires. All of the interviewers had received intensive training in evaluating victim reports, which they practiced in test interviews. In the Göttingen and Bochum I studies, the interviewers visited the respondents without having given prior notice. As a result of newly enacted laws, the subjects in the Solingen and Bochum II studies had to be informed in writing and were asked to give their consent in advance.

The reference year for the data in Göttingen was 1973; in Bochum I, 1975; in Solingen, 1981; and in Bochum II, 1986. With the exception of Solingen, the respondents were questioned in January and February as to whether they had been victims of a crime in the previous (i.e., reference) year and whether they had reported the crime. In Solingen the interview had to take place between May and July, which presumably accounts for the high failure rate (32.4%), as many people were away on vacation during these months (Table 1).

The number of reported crimes was extrapolated for the entire population of each city according to the size of the random sample of respondents. These projected figures represent estimates with a degree of error due to the random sample. For this reason, the tables give the limits of the confidence interval in which the true value lies with a 95% probability.

The crimes recorded in the PCS were then compared with those mentioned by respondents but not reported to the police. The ratio 1:6, for instance, means that six nonregistered crimes occurred compared to one registered crime. In other words, only one out of seven delinquent acts were known to the police. For the sake of clarity, all of these unrecorded crime figure ratios have been rounded off to whole numbers.

4 Results

4.1 Theft

The ratios of recorded to unrecorded thefts fluctuated in the four studies between 1:8 (Göttingen) and 1:2 (Solingen and Bochum II) (Table 2). The strikingly high mean value of 1:7 in Göttingen was apparently due to the extremely high number of unrecorded minor thefts (mean value 1:15). As expected, it was found in all the studies that only serious cases of theft were reported to the police (breaking into cars, burglary in a cellar): 50% of such cases were reported to the police, with ratios ranging from 1:1 (Bochum I and II, Solingen) to 1:3 (Göttingen).

In serious cases of theft, the amount of damage (including any property damage) was usually greater than in minor theft. It can be assumed that the likelihood of the victim reporting the crime depended more on the amount of damage than on how the crime was carried out. In Solingen, for example, the mean ratio was 1:15 for theft under DM 25 (interval 1:23–1:6) (Table 3). By contrast, every third case in which the damage was more than DM 100 was reported to the police (mean ratio 1:1). Another factor responsible for the low number of recorded minor thefts was that most insurance companies compensate for stolen property under the value of DM 100 without requiring a police report.[6]

Table 2. Ratios of recorded to unrecorded thefts

	Göttingen 1973–1974	Bochum I 1975–1976	Solingen[a] 1981–1982	Bochum II 1986–1987
Total thefts	1:8 –1:6	1:4–1:3	1:3–1:2	1:3–1:2
Mean value	1:7	1:3	1:2	1:3
Theft without aggravating circumstances	1:17–1:13	1:7–1:5	1:4–1:2	1:9–1:7
Mean value	1:15	1:6	1:3	1:8
Theft under aggravating circumstances	1:3 –1:2	1:2–1:1	1:2–1:1	1:1–1:1
Mean value	1:2	1:2	1:1	1:1

[a] Note that in the Solingen number of recorded crimes the victims were exclusively private persons. This also applies to the next two tables.

[6] The insurance companies have raised the minimum to DM 300.

Table 3. Ratios of recorded to unrecorded thefts as a function of the value of the stolen property

Value of the stolen property	Göttingen 1973–1974	Bochum I 1975–1976	Solingen 1981–1982	Bochum II 1986–1987
Under 25 DM	1:49–1:37	1:28–1:19	1:23–1:6	1:20–1:11
Mean value	1:43	1:23	1:15	1:16
25–100 DM	1:8 –1:5	1:9 –1:6	1:9 –1:3	1:9 –1:5
Mean value	1:6	1:7	1:6	1:7
Over 100 DM	1:2 –1:1	1:1 –1:0.4	1.2 –1:1	1:2 –1:1
Mean value	1:2	1:1	1:1	1:1

Table 4. Ratios of recorded to unrecorded crimes involving bodily injury and property damage

	Göttingen 1973–1974	Bochum I 1975–1976	Solingen 1981–1982	Bochum II 1986–1987
Bodily injury	1:11–1:4	1:10–1:4	1:7 –1:2	1:9–1:4
Mean value	1:8	1:7	1:5	1:6
Property damage	1:36–1:25		1:20–1:12	
Mean value	1:30		1:16	

4.2 Bodily Injury

For crimes of bodily injury the ratios of recorded to unrecorded crimes in the four studies (Table 4) fluctuated between 1:11 (Göttingen) and 1:2 (Solingen). The mean value was between 1:8 and 1:5. Since the intervals overlap, it can be assumed that the unrecorded number remained relatively constant; that is, approximately 13% of the crimes involving bodily injuries were reported to the police. Presumably, these cases were serious incidents of physical injury. The exact number, however, could not be determined. Crimes of physical injury that were not known to the police were almost exclusively the result of fist fights, pushing and shoving, etc., which the victims did not consider serious enough to report.

4.3 Property Damage

The basic problem associated with obtaining data on property damage is that most cases reported involve negligence, which are not prosecuted. In the Göttingen and Solingen studies an attempt was made to filter out these cases by means of control questions. The ratios of recorded to unrecorded crimes in these two cities differed immensely (Table 4). The reason for this is that in the Solingen study only damage to personal property was addressed in the police figures, whereas in Göttingen damage to public property (telepone booths, graffiti on school walls, etc.) was included.

4.4 Robbery

On the average, only four cases of robbery per 1000 respondents were reported. Significant projections therefore could not be made on the basis of this extremely small percentage, since the confidence interval was too broad to permit meaningful conclusions. Thus, much larger random samples are necessary for studies on robbery.

5 Crime Reporting Behavior

Crime reporting behavior is of particular importance in the discussion of hidden crime. Approximately 90% of all recorded crimes were reported to the police by the victims themselves. Thus, encouraging the general public to report crime will help reduce the problem of hidden crime. How this can be achieved and the social consequences of eliminating the problem of unrecorded crime are not the subjects of discussion here. Instead, what will be discussed are the factors that can influence crime reporting behavior in terms of their implications for police strategies and criminal policy.

5.1 Motives for not Reporting the Crime

In all four studies the victims were asked to choose one out of a list of 16 reasons for not reporting a crime. These motives were divided into five groups:

- Lack of effectiveness of law enforcement agencies (group I)
- Personal aversion to dealing with the authorities (group II)
- Consideration for the offender (group III)
- Personal disadvantage resulting from filing a complaint (group IV)
- Minor damage, lack of interest, self-help (group V).

The motives differed according to the type of crime (Table 5). The main reason for failing to report the theft to the police was that the damage was only minimal or there was a lack of interest. The second most common motive was that the victims did not believe the law enforcement agencies would be effective. The remaining three groups of motives played a role in only about 15% of the cases.

5.2 Motives for Reporting the Crime

The second Bochum study was the only one which included the motives for reporting the crime to the police. The victims selected their main motive from a standardized list.[7] In almost 75% of the cases the reason for reporting the crime

[7] Schwind, Ahlborn, and Weiß 1989.

Table 5. Distribution of the groups of motives among nonreported thefts

	Göttingen 1973–1974	Bochum I 1975–1976	Solingen 1981–1982	Bochum II 1986–1987
	%	%	%	%
(I) Ineffectiveness of law enforcement agencies	22.3	21.6	32.0	30.2
(II) Aversion to authorities	5.2	2.6	[a]	2.7
(III) Consideration for the offender	7.4	8.9	[a]	6.7
(IV) Personal disadvantages	3.5	3.2	[a]	4.7
(V) Minor damage or no interest	48.7	61.1	44.0	49.0
Other reasons and no answers	12.9	2.6	10.0	6.7

[a] In the Solingen study, groups II, III, and IV combined make up about 14% of the total.

Table 6. Distribution of motives for reporting theft in the Bochum II study

To get back the stolen goods/ to claim restitution from the offender	30.8%
A police report was necessary in order to receive compensation from the insurance company	43.4%
It was the right thing to do; it was my duty	2.8%
Because I was angry	2.8%
So that the thief would be punished	8.4%
So that something like that does not happen again	7.0%
Other reasons and no answers	4.9%

was to have the material damage replaced, either by the offender or by an insurance company (Table 6). This indicates that the material motive was the overriding factor in both the reporting and nonreporting of crimes. To prevent further crime was apparently not a common motive.

6 Conclusions

To date, the studies on hidden crime in the Federal Republic of Germany have been conducted in geographically limited areas and on relatively small random samples. The projected figures for nonreported crimes fluctuate considerably. Thus, more reliable information can only be supplied by comprehensive data obtained from larger samples from the population extending beyond regional borders. It might be worth considering enlarging the circle of victims to include, for example, department stores and supermarkets for shoplifting, train stations and post offices for graffiti, school authorities for vandalism. Apart from the technical difficulties, this would require considerably more funding than is presently available. It would, however, certainly supply the police and policy-makers with a more reliable picture of criminality which would serve as a basis for future necessary measures.

References

Plate M, Schwinges U, Weiß R (1985) Strukturen der Kriminalität in Solingen. Eine Untersuchung zu Zusammenhängen zwischen baulichen und sozialen Merkmalen und dem Kriminalitätsaufkommen. BKA Forschungsreihe. Special volume. Wiesbaden

Schwind HD, Ahlborn W, Eger HJ, Jany U, Pudel V, Weiß R (1975) Dunkelfeldforschung in Göttingen 1973/74. Eine Opferbefragung zur Aufhellung des Dunkelfeldes und zur Erforschung der Bestimmungsgründe für die Unterlassung von Strafanzeigen. BKA Forschungsreihe vol 2, Wiesbaden

Schwind HD, Ahlborn W, Weiß R (1978) Empirische Kriminalgeographie. Bestandsaufnahme und Weiterführung am Beispiel von Bochum („Kriminalitätsatlas Bochum"). BKA Forschungsreihe vol 8, Wiesbaden

Schwind HD, Ahlborn W, Weiß R (1989) Dunkelfeldforschung in Bochum 1986/87. Eine Replikationsstudie. BKA Forschungsreihe vol 21, Wiesbaden

Steffen W (1976) Analyse polizeilicher Ermittlungstätigkeit aus der Sicht des späteren Strafverfahrens. BKA Forschungsreihe vol 4, Wiesbaden

CHAPTER 6

Unreported Violent Crime: A Victim Telephone Survey in Heidelberg

H.U. Störzer

Contents

1 The Problem

During the course of a comprehensive research project directed by the Research Unit on Criminology and Criminal Investigation of the *Bundeskriminalamt* (BKA) on the problem of violence[1], the question quickly arose as to the extent of violent crime in the Federal Republic of Germany. A look at the statistics does not provide an adequate answer. Since 1971, the annually published *Polizeiliche Kriminalstatistik* (Police Crime Statistics, PCS) has been prefaced with a reference to its limited reliability: The PCS do not "offer a true representation of the criminal reality" because "a portion of the crimes committed are not known to the police".[2] No data are given on the relationship between the crimes actually committed and

[1] For details see the article by Baurmann, Chap. 11. An overview is given by Kube 1986, pp 5–8.
[2] See *Bundeskriminalamt* 1972, p 5, 1987, p 5.

Kube/Störzer (Eds.)
Police Research in the Federal Republic of Germany

those statistically recorded: "The extent of this dark figure [unreported/unregistered crime] is probably dependent on the type of crime and changes in the course of time under the influence of variable factors (e.g., attitude of the population towards reporting crime events, intensity of efforts to control crime)."

There are, in fact, concrete indications of a considerable number of unreported violent crimes. However, they either refer only to certain kinds of crime, such as violence against women, the extent of which is conveyed by the experiences reported by women in safe houses for battered women[3], or, even more particularly, sexual violence, which has been the subject of several scientific investigations[4]. These indications may also apply only to small geographical regions, such as Göttingen, Stuttgart, or Bochum[5], or to a very specific subpopulation, such as students[6]. Basically, little is known to date about unreported violent crime in the Federal Republic of Germany and practically nothing is known about its changes and interactions with the number of reported crimes.[7]

To deal with the problem of unreported violent crime, a joint project was undertaken by the Research Unit on Criminology and Criminal Investigation of the BKA (M.C. Baurmann and H.U. Störzer, investigators) and the Institute for Criminology at the University of Heidelberg (D. Hermann and F. Streng, investigators). Advisory support was provided by the Center for Surveys, Methods, and Analyses in Mannheim (H.J. Hippler and P. Prüfer, consultants).[8]

2 Methodology

2.1 Basic Methodological Considerations

Generally, three different methods are available to measure unreported crime: experiment, (participatory) observation, and *surveys*. For our particular research purposes the survey technique plays a major role to which there are three approaches: offender surveys, victim surveys, and informant surveys[9]. For fairly

[3] Safe houses for battered women (*Frauenhäuser*), which now exist in almost all of the larger cities, offer refuge and protection to abused women and their children at any time of the day or night. On the occasion of the 10-year and 5-year anniversaries of the *Frauenhäuser* in Berlin and Karlsruhe, newspapers made efforts to bring this situation to the attention of the public, even outside these two cities. On the topics violence against women, in general, and the *Frauenhäuser* in Berlin, in particular, see Bendkowski and Rotalsky 1987.

[4] e.g., Kirchhoff and Thelen 1976.

[5] e.g., Schwind et al. 1975, 1978; Stephan 1976.

[6] e.g., Kirchhoff and Thelen 1976.

[7] See Baurmann, Plate, and Störzer 1988, p 117.

[8] An initial report on this study has been completed (Baurmann, Hermann, Störzer, and Streng 1987); the final report is in preparation.

[9] See Schwind 1986, pp 24–32; Kaiser 1988, p 358.

obvious reasons[10], most success can be expected from the *victim survey*, in which the respondent is asked about crimes he or she might have experienced.

Until recently, such information has usually been gathered by means of *personal interviews*,in which the respondent and interviewer meet face-to-face and the interview is conducted orally. The BKA has had considerable experience with this method: in the 1970s such projects were organized in Göttingen[11], Stuttgart[12], and Bochum[13] and in 1985, one in Solingen[14] was completed. In Bochum a duplicate study has just been finished.[15] These studies, however, turned out to be very time and personnel consuming and, consequently, relatively expensive.

Mail surveys, in which researchers mail a questionnaire to be completed and returned by the respondents, enable more respondents to be questioned for the same amount of money and in a shorter time. Victim surveys by mail have also been tried in the Federal Republic of Germany[16], but these, especially the more recent investigations conducted by Arnold and Sessar, did not serve primarily to provide data on unreported crime. An estimate of such crimes can hardly be achieved with a short questionnaire, even if it is confined to one area of crime, e.g., violent crime. On the one hand, crime is extremely varied so that the questionnaire must contain a substantial number of questions to cover all aspects. On the other hand, only a portion of these questions apply to the individual respondent. For this reason, it is necessary to devise a highly complex questionnaire with a number of "filters"; however, for a written survey to be successful the questionnaire must be short and simple[17].

Since it seemed that a personal interview was the only expedient method, but that the topic of the survey required a large number of respondents, the obvious solution for economic reasons was a *telephone survey*. Telephone interviews are 60%–80% cheaper than personal interviews[18], are considered to be reliable and accurate[19], and avoid influences on answers to questions by either a third person or the interviewer[20].

---

[10] See Schwind 1986, p 27.

[11] Schwind et al. 1975.

[12] Stephan 1976.

[13] Schwind, Ahlborn, and Weiß 1978.

[14] Plate, Schwinges, and Weiß 1985.

[15] See also Chap. 5.

[16] e.g., Kirchhoff and Thelen 1976; Arnold 1984; Sessar 1986, and Sessar, Beurskens, and Boers 1986.

[17] See also Killias 1986, p 1.3, 1987a, p 314, 1987b, p 5, 1989, p 31.

[18] See also Dussich 1979, p 102; Waller 1982, pp 180–181; Killias 1986, pp 1.2/1.3, 1987a, p 314, 1987b, p 3, 1989, p 23.

[19] See Dussich 1979, p 102; Waller 1982, p 180; Killias 1987a, pp 314, 315–316, 1987b, p 4, 1989, pp 25–27.

[20] See Killias 1987b, pp 4–5.

2.2 The Feasibility of Victim Telephone Surveys in the Federal Republic of Germany

In North America the telephone interview has been used for some time in conducting victim surveys.[21] Very recently such a survey was successfully carried out in Switzerland.[22] In the Federal Republic of Germany, however, it is not certain that this method can be reliably employed, even if a sufficient telephone density can be assumed[23]. Two of the questions that must be asked are: Is it possible to simply call people up and talk to them about their experience with crime? How does the person called respond and behave when asked about violent crimes which affect a very personal area? To deal with these questions demands consideration of the attitude towards telephone communication in Germany.

Friedrichs and Blasius[24] demonstrated that it is, in fact, possible to conduct a scientific telephone survey in Germany. Moreover, the experience of victim counseling services that do a great deal of work by phone has confirmed that crime victims do cooperate when questioned by telephone. Furthermore, telephone conversations with victims have been conducted for similar research purposes. In 1982, Kurt Weis published a study on rape victims, which was based on telephone interviews with 102 women. The sample was recruited through advertisements on local television, on the radio, and in daily newspapers.[25]

For an unreported crime investigation to obtain usable results it must be based on a representative and randomly selected sample.[26] In other words, the researcher cannot simply wait until the respondents contact him voluntarily, but must select the respondents and personally approach them. This is a delicate point: Germans are very aware of their right to data protection and the interviewer can only promise anonymity and confidentiality, but cannot prove that this promise will be kept. Moreover, telephone interviewing as a method has acquired a bad image due to commercial advertising by telephone.[27] In addition, a regional court of appeal recently decided that "unsolicited telephone calls offend the personal rights of the party called" and deemed it illegal for political parties to campaign by telephone.[28]

In view of this situation we decided that, before attempting a large scale telephone survey to measure unreported violent crime in Germany, we should first investigate the feasibility of such a survey and test the method using a small sample.

---

[21] See Dussich 1979, p 102; Waller 1982, p 181.

[22] Killias 1986, pp 1.1–1.2, 1987a, p 311, 1987b, p 1, 1989, pp 23–24.

[23] About 90%; see also Baurmann 1983, p 102.

[24] Friedrichs and Blasius 1984.

[25] Weis 1982, pp 31, 40–41.

[26] See Schwind 1986, p 27.

[27] See *Der Spiegel*, no 11, March 9, 1987, pp 53–55.

[28] OLG Stuttgart, Decision of March 11, 1988 – 5 W 13/88. See also *Der Spiegel*, no. 16, April 18, 1988, pp 45–48.

3 The Telephone Survey in Heidelberg: Methods

3.1 Interviews

To carry out a feasibility study a random sample was selected from among the adult residents of Heidelberg who could be reached by telephone and interviewed ($n = 523$). The sample was compiled by picking out numbers at random from the Heidelberg telephone directory[29] and then obtaining the corresponding names from the Heidelberg city directory. The persons selected were notified in writing about the telephone survey by the Institute for Criminology.

The interviewers were upper semester law students who were articulate and outgoing. They underwent a training course in interviewing and were instructed on the classification of marginal cases of crime. If the target person could not be reached with the first call, at least four more calls were made at different times of the day and on different days. If the person called was unable to be interviewed (elderly, ill, on vacation), the person who happened to answer the telephone was allowed to substitute.

A standardized questionnaire was used. Half of the interviews began with questions regarding the neutral topic of theft, while the rest immediately addressed more sensitive questions on violent crimes: bodily injury, intimidation and coercion, threat, robbery and blackmail, and crimes involving murder and sexual acts. The sex crimes included rape, sexual coercion, and sexual abuse of children and those unable to defend themselves.

The interviews took place in March, 1987. Twenty persons were given a follow-up interview to provide information about the effect of the interview on the respondents.

Before the notfication letters were sent out, the Heidelberg police headquarters were thoroughly informed about the research project and the procedure (written notification and telephone interview). This information was passed on by headquarters to police stations in the areas where the respondents lived in the event that any of them became suspicious after having received the notification and wanted to contact the police.

3.2 The Number of Known Crimes

In order to derive the amount of unreported crimes from the data given on the telephone it was necessary to obtain the corresponding regional data on crimes recorded by the police. Thus, it had to be determined first whether this was possible for the area in which the survey took place. For this purpose the state criminal police

[29] A person's telephone number not being listed in the telephone directory is the rare exception in the Federal Republic of Germany. Unlisted numbers are usually requested (especially by prominent persons, for instance) to prevent harassment by phone or to protect persons who are in danger. For this reason we felt that we did not have to take unlisted phone numbers into consideration.

office (*Landeskriminalamt*) of Baden-Württemberg provided tables from the PCS which contained those districts included in the Heidelberg telephone directory (the city of Heidelberg and the independent municipalities Dossenheim and Eppelheim). The analysis of the Baden-Württemberg PCS was completed in March, 1988.

4 Results

Since the data obtained in the telephone interviews have not yet been fully analyzed, only preliminary results can be presented.

4.1 Respondents' Acceptance of the Survey Method

Some 73% of the interviews were completed; 12% of those contacted refused to participate or were unable to participate for age or health reasons and 16% could not be reached.

The actual interviewing proved to be less difficult than had been expected. In view of the sensitivity of topics that involve very personal information, not only was there prior speculation about just how the respondents would react[30], but doubt was expressed during the training period as to whether the interviewers would always manage to find the right tone, particularly when asking questions about sexual violence. There was no apparent difference in response when questions concerning theft were asked first. The duration of the interviews ranged from 7 to 30 min, with most interviews lasting 10–15 min.

The results of the follow-up interview were particularly clear. When asked whether the interviewer had been pleasant or unpleasant all of the respondents said "pleasant", even those who had refused to cooperate. All found the questions easy to understand. Only one of the respondents recalled another victimization during the follow-up interview.

Some of the respondents reported that they considered checking with the police about the study and the university institute conducting the interview, but only one such case is known where a person did in fact contact the police.

4.2 Crimes Known to the Police in Relation to Unreported Crimes

Roughly 11% of the respondents reported having been victim of at least one violent crime in 1985 and 1986. Projected to the number of inhabitants in Heidelberg (including Dossenheim and Eppelheim) that means that there were approximately 17400 *victims* of violence in those years. The police, however, had recorded only 1421 *victims* of violent criminal acts (including attempted violent acts) during that period, which represents a ratio of 12:1. The ratio of reported *crimes* to the number

[30] See Sect. 2.2.

of *crimes* committed, i.e., including the projected number of unreported crimes for the Heidelberg area, was 1:8.

The number of unreported crimes varied, however, depending on the particular violent crime. Most were associated with coercion, attempted bodily harm, threats, and attempted sexual offenses. Unreported crimes associated with robbery and blackmail and with completed sex crimes against women were surprisingly low.

5 Discussion

5.1 Comments on the Respondents' Acceptance of the Survey Technique

The victim survey described in this chapter is comparable to the studies carried out by Stephan[31], Villmow and Stephan[32], and Plate, Schwinges and Weiß[33], in that these were not based on a very specific sample population and that they defined a similar refusal rate. In the investigation conducted by Stephan, approximately 68% of all possible interviews were completed; in the two Villmow and Stephan studies 58% and 55%, respectively; in the Plate, Schwinges and Weiß study, about 61%.

These victim surveys used personal interviews. The mail victim surveys conducted by Sessar et al.[34] and by Arnold[35] have not yet been fully reported on. It is evident, however, that mail surveys have a lower response rate than personal interview surveys. Sessar achieved a 44.1% response rate, although this value was corrected to account for interviewees who moved or died. Arnold's two surveys had a response rate of 58.8% and 42.9%.

Our telephone survey had a high response rate, with 73% of the interviews completed. In this respect, therefore, telephone surveys appear to be at least as effective as face-to-face interviews and mail surveys. Furthermore, based on the results of the follow-up interview and the impressions the interviewers gained during the conversations, it appears that there is widespread acceptance of the telephone survey. These findings provide reason for having confidence in this method.

5.2 Comments on the Relationship Between Known Crimes and Unreported Crimes

There are difficulties involved with estimating the relation of the number of known crimes to the number of unreported crimes. First of all, in some areas of crime the PCS include comprehensive information on the number of crimes, not the number of victims – information which is obtained from a victim survey. Another

[31] Stephan 1976.

[32] Villmow and Stephan 1983.

[33] Plate, Schwinges, and Weiß 1985.

[34] Sessar 1986; Sessar, Beurskens, and Boers 1986.

[35] Arnold 1984.

problem in some cases was either that the PCS grouped together several offenses, not all of which were included in the survey, or that offenses were included in the survey which were not specifically stipulated in the PCS. Furthermore, a systematic discrepancy exists between police statistics and the survey results: the police record the number of victims for each year, while the survey could only determine the number of victims who were still living at the time of the study. For example, someone who died in 1986 might be included in the police statistics but not in the survey. Consequently, the projections based on the survey results are systematically underestimated.

A final point is that since the results are based on a small random sample there is a certain amount of error associated with projections of the amount of unreported crime; however, this can be statistically estimated.

In conclusion, the telephone survey has proved to be an efficient and economical way of securing reliable information on the extent of violent crime in the Federal Republic of Germany. A more comprehensive study of this type is currently being planned by the Research Unit on Criminology and Criminal Investigation of the BKA.

References

Arnold H (1984) Verbrechensangst und/oder Furcht vor Viktimisierung – Folgen von Viktimisierung? In: Albrecht H-J, Sieber U (eds) Zwanzig Jahre Südwestdeutsche Kriminologische Kolloquien. Freiburg, pp 185–236 (Kriminologische Forschungsberichte aus dem Max-Planck-Institut für ausländisches und internationales Strafrecht, Freiburg i.Br., vol 18)

Baurmann MC (1983) Sexualität, Gewalt und psychische Folgen. Eine Längsschnittuntersuchung bei Opfern sexueller Gewalt und sexuellen Normverletzungen anhand von angezeigten Sexualkontakten. Wiesbaden (BKA-Forschungsreihe, vol 15)

Baurmann MC, Hermann D, Störzer HU, Streng F (1987) Über die Machbarkeit telefonischer Opferbefragungen. Vortrag, gehalten auf der Konferenz zur schriftlichen und telefonischen Befragungsmethode beim Zentrum für Umfragen, Methoden und Analysen (ZUMA) in Mannheim am 30.4.1987 (unpublished paper)

Baurmann MC, Plate M, Störzer HU (1988) Polizeirelevante Aspekte bei der Auseinandersetzung mit dem Gewaltbegriff. In: Bundeskriminalamt (ed) Was ist Gewalt? Auseinandersetzungen mit einem Begriff, vol 2. Wiesbaden, pp 103–152 (BKA-Forschungsreihe. Special volume)

Bendkowski H, Rotalsky I (eds) (1987) Die alltägliche Wut: Gewalt, Pornografie, Feminismus. Berlin (West) (EP 242: Bilder-Lese-Buch)

Bundeskriminalamt (ed) (1972) Polizeiliche Kriminalstatistik 1971. Wiesbaden

Bundeskriminalamt (ed) (1987) Polizeiliche Kriminalstatistik 1986. Wiesbaden

Dussich JPJ (1979) Lokale und nationale Opferbefragungen in den Vereinigten Staaten. In: Kirchhoff GF, Sessar K (eds) Das Verbrechensopfer. Ein Reader zur Viktimologie. Bochum, pp 95–110

Friedrichs J, Blasius J (1984) Einstellungen zur City – Methodische Ergebnisse einer telefonischen Befragung. Vortrag, gehalten auf dem 22. Deutschen Soziologentag, Sektion „Methoden", in Dortmund am 12.10.84 (unpublished paper)

Kaiser G (1988) Kriminologie. Ein Lehrbuch, 2nd edn. Heidelberg

Killias M (1986) Les Romands face au crime. Crime et insécurité en Suisse romande vus par les victimes et non-victimes. Lausanne (unpublished paper)

Killias M (1987a) Nouvelles perspectives méthodologiques en matière de sondage de victimisation. L'expérience des enquêtes suisses. In: Déviance et Société 11:311–327
Killias M (1987b) New methodological perspectives for victimization surveys. Lessons from Switzerland's National Crime Survey. Presented at the 39th Annual Meeting of the American Society of Criminology (Montreal, November 11–14, 1987) (unpublished paper)
Killias M (1989) Les Suisses face au crime. Leurs expériences et attitudes à la lumière des enquêtes suisses de victimisation. Grüsch (Collection Criminologie, vol 5)
Kirchhoff GF, Thelen C (1976) Hidden victimization by sex offenders in Germany. In: Viano EC (ed) Victims and society. Washington D.C., pp 277–284
Kube E (1986) Vorwort. In: Bundeskriminalamt (ed) Was ist Gewalt? Auseinandersetzungen mit einem Begriff, vol 1. Wiesbaden, pp 5–8 (BKA-Forschungsreihe. Special volume)
Plate M, Schwinges U, Weiß R (1985) Strukturen der Kriminalität in Solingen. Eine Untersuchung zu Zusammenhängen zwischen baulichen und sozialen Merkmalen und dem Kriminalitätsaufkommen. Wiesbaden (BKA-Forschungsreihe. Special volume)
Schwind H-D (1986) Kriminologie. Eine praxisorientierte Einführung mit Beispielen. Heidelberg (Grundlagen, vol 28)
Schwind H-D, Ahlborn W, Eger HJ, Jany U, Pudel V, Weiß R (1975) Dunkelfeldforschung in Göttingen 1973/74. Eine Opferbefragung zur Aufhellung des Dunkelfeldes und zur Erforschung der Bestimmungsgründe für die Unterlassung von Strafanzeigen. Wiesbaden (BKA-Forschungsreihe, vol 2)
Schwind H-D, Ahlborn W, Weiß R (1978) Empirische Kriminalgeographie. Bestandsaufnahme und Weiterführung am Beispiel von Bochum („Kriminalitätsatlas Bochum"). Wiesbaden (BKA-Forschungsreihe, vol 8)
Sessar K (1986) Neue Wege der Kriminologie aus dem Strafrecht. In: Hirsch H-J, Kaiser G, Marquardt H (eds) Gedächtnisschrift für Hilde Kaufmann. Berlin, New York, pp 373–391
Sessar K, Beurskens A, Boers K (1986) Wiedergutmachung als Konfliktregelungsparadigma? In: Kriminologisches Journal 18:86–104
Stephan E (1976) Die Stuttgarter Opferbefragung. Eine kriminologisch-viktimologische Analyse zur Erforschung des Dunkelfeldes unter besonderer Berücksichtigung der Einstellung der Bevölkerung zur Kriminalität. Wiesbaden (BKA-Forschungsreihe, vol 3)
Villmow B, Stephan E (1983) Jugendkriminalität in einer Gemeinde. Eine Analyse erfragter Delinquenz und Viktimisierung sowie amtlicher Registrierung. Freiburg (Kriminologische Forschungsberichte aus dem Max-Planck-Institut für ausländisches und internationales Strafrecht, Freiburg i.Br., vol 6)
Waller I (1982) Victimization studies as guides to action: Some cautions and suggestions. In: Schneider HJ (ed) The victim in international perspective. Papers and essays given at the "Third International Symposium on Victimology" 1979 in Münster/Westfalia. Berlin, New York, pp 166–188
Weis K (1982) Die Vergewaltigung und ihre Opfer. Eine viktimologische Untersuchung zur gesellschaftlichen Bewertung und individuellen Betroffenheit. Stuttgart

CHAPTER 7

Public Opinion Relating to Crime and Police Action

U. Dörmann

Contents

1 Introduction

Criminal statistics and victim surveys supply data on trends and patterns in crime. Another valuable source of information is the population's subjective assessment of criminality and the fight against crime. Formulators of criminal policy are not only concerned with the objective improvement of internal security; people must also *feel* safe.

In 1984, the BKA commissioned EMNID, an opinion research institute, to conduct an opinion poll in which approximately 2000 citizens of the Federal Republic of Germany aged 14 and over were asked to give their opinions about police work and crime. The survey was repeated in 1985 to determine any changes in opinion that may have taken place during the course of a year. The second survey sought to establish whether the death of a demonstrator in Frankfurt in 1985 and the subsequent discussion regarding police behavior would be reflected in the responses. It can be safely assumed, however, that the impact of such events on public thinking cannot be judged on the basis of two rounds of questioning held only 1 year apart. A third survey, which was carried out in 1987 by EMNID, has not yet been completely evaluated, though some of the results are presented below.

In evaluating the results of the surveys, the basic shortcomings of opinion polls must be taken into account. A random sample of interview participants can only

Kube/Störzer (Eds.)
Police Research in the Federal Republic of Germany

approximately reflect the population structure. Distortions are inevitable, as such a sample does not include persons that have no permanent residence, inmates of institutions, and those who refuse to participate. Other possible sources of error are the interviewer's influence on responses and the fact that respondents tend to answer in a way they believe would be socially desirable. Despite long years of empirical experience, such sources of error cannot be totally excluded. However, they are not usually thought to completely undermine the value of surveys as long as the number of refusals is not too high and the questions do not intellectually or emotionally overtax the respondent.

For financial reasons only five topics could be addressed in the surveys, some of which were broken down further. The questions were clear and straightforward and were formulated in a way that would allow comparison of the results with those of previous surveys, in particular, the study conducted by Stephan in Stuttgart for the year 1972 and the one by Kerner for the year 1976.[1]

2 Results

2.1 A High Level of Respect for the Police

In their role as the embodiment of the government's monopoly on power and force, the police are the target of both public attention and criticism. Furthermore, contact between police and citizens often takes place in conflict situations. In an earlier survey, undertaken in 1983–1984 by the Criminal Police Prevention Program of the Federation and the German States, 6000 police officers were questioned concerning the relationship between citizens and the police.[2] Generally speaking, all officers, particularly those of the middle ranks of both the uniformed and criminal investigation branches who have the most contact with the public, tended to rate the relationship between citizens and police as only fair (about 50%) or even poor (about 20%–25%).[3] This was consistent with the results of earlier investigations.[4]

In contrast, the results of the EMNID poll indicated that the police are accepted by a large majority of the population. The first question (Table 1) read: "The citizens of the Federal Republic of Germany have a varied view of the police. What about you? What is your opinion of the police?" Answers were to be given on a scale ranging from -3 ("I have no respect for the police") to $+3$ ("I have high respect for the police"). In the 1984 poll, 21% answered negatively; in 1985, 19% gave negative scores. A clear majority of the persons asked, i.e., four out of every five, held a positive opinion of the police. In comparison with the results of 1984,

[1] For details on the sense of security, on the assessment of crime, and on regard for the police see also Dölling 1986, pp 38ff; Gefeller/Trudewind 1978, pp 309ff; Hough/Mayhew 1985, pp 33ff; Kerner 1980; Murck 1978, pp 202ff; Skogan 1986, pp 167ff; Sporn 1978, pp 293ff; Stephan 1976.

[2] Source: *Landesregierung* Schleswig-Holstein, 1986.

[3] Source: *Landeskriminalamt* Baden-Württemberg 1984, pp 11 and 28ff.

[4] Kerner 1980, pp 231ff.

the positive scores found in the 1985 poll shifted from a relatively weak +1 to a stronger +2 and even to +3. This might be interpreted as a sign of solidarity with the police in reaction to what the respondents perhaps considered to be unjust criticism of the police in connection with the aforementioned demonstration in Frankfurt. In 1987, the percentage of negative attitudes towards the police fell to 16%. The decrease in negative responses among the 30–39 year olds was particularly striking: The percentage of negative attitudes to the police dropped from 26% (1985) to 14% (1987).

2.2 Strong Criticism Among Younger, Better-Educated Respondents

Age seems to be a decisive factor in one's attitude toward the police. Nearly all of those older than 40 years had a positive opinion of the police. This was independent of education, place of residence, or other factors.

Among the younger persons asked, on the other hand, opinions of the police varied depending on age, education, and place of residence. In 1987, the highest percentage of negative attitudes was found among the 21–29 year olds (30%), 7% of whom gave the lowest rating, –3. Among adolescents (14–18 years) and among 30–39 year olds the percentage of negative opinions was markedly lower (21% and 14%, respectively). Regard for the police among the 21–29 year olds was lower in 1985 in comparison with the previous year, probably due to the events of the Frankfurt demonstration. In 1987, it returned to higher levels.

The second important variable was level of education, although only among the younger group. In 1985, 50% of the group under 40 years of age who graduated

Table 1. Results of question 1: view of the police

	Group A: All respondents			Group B: Respondents under 40 years of age with *Abitur* in cities with a population of more than 500 000
Score	1984 (%)	1985 (%)	1987 (%)	1985 (%)
–3	3	4	3	16
–2	5	5	4	30
–1	13	10	9	29
+1	33	25	27	15
+2	29	34	35	8
+3	17	22	23	2

–3: No respect for the police
+3: High respect for the police
Total number of respondents in Group A: 1984, 2012; 1985, 1972; 1987, 2020.
Total number of respondents in Group B: 83.

with *Abitur*[5] gave the police a poor rating. This was twice the percentage of those of the same age group with no *Abitur*. Of the respondents under 40 with *Abitur*, 10% reported having very little regard for the police.

Other surveys also showed that a majority of younger persons with *Abitur*, particularly those from large cities, have value systems that differ from those of the rest of the population.[6] This has an effect on their attitudes towards the police.

2.3 Attitudes of the Population in Large Cities

Along with age and education, the size of place of residence was relevant in the 1984 and 1985 surveys (this analysis has not yet been undertaken for 1987), but again only among those under 40 years of age. In 1985, 60% of this age group living in cities with a population of 500 000 and more had a negative attitude towards the police, which was more than twice as many as those from smaller communities. When age and size of place of residence is combined with level of education, the result becomes even more striking: 75% of those under 40 with *Abitur* who were from large cities rated the police negatively.

A comparison of states revealed that 44% of persons from the city-states (Hamburg, Bremen, and Berlin) had negative opinions of the police. Almost every second respondent rated his or her regard for the police as negative, as compared with every third person in 1984. Frankfurt, where the demonstration fatality occurred, also showed an above-average percentage of negative attitudes, though for some undetermined reason it was lower than in the city-states. The increase over 1984 was also much higher in the city-states (10 percentage points) than in Frankfurt (4 percentage points). As far as the non-city-states were concerned, Hesse (the state in which Frankfurt is located) was the only state with negative police ratings (29%; 1984, 20%) higher than those in the entire Federal Republic (19%).

The events of the Frankfurt demonstration and the subsequent public debate seem to have damaged the police's image only in the eyes of those who had already been critical of the police, namely, younger persons with *Abitur* from the largest cities, especially the city-states, and especially the 21–29 year olds. This was in sharp contrast to the increase in sympathy for the police among the average population in 1985 as compared with 1984.

In 1972, Stephan found that the basically favorable attitude towards the police among the majority of the population was nevertheless marked by ambivalence: Although nine out of ten considered the motto, "The police – your friends and helpers", appropriate, almost as many felt that people would just as soon not have anything to do with the police.[7]

---

[5] The German school system tracks schoolchildren into three kinds of secondary schools, *Hauptschule, Realschule,* and *Gymnasium* for low to high achievers, respectively. *Abitur* is the final exam required for graduation from *Gymnasium*.

[6] Source: *ipos-Institut für praxisorientierte Sozialforschung* 1986.

[7] Stephan 1976, pp 242ff.

Table 2. Results of question 2: success of the fight against crime in the respondents' community

	1984 (%)	1985 (%)	1987 (%)
Crime totally under control	16	13	14
Fairly under control	61	63	62
Less under control	12	15	13
Not under control at all	2	2	3
Don't know	8	7	8

Total number of respondents: 1984, 2012; 1985, 1972; 1987, 2020.

2.4 Success in the Battle Against Crime

The EMNID survey sought to judge the public's perception of whether the police were successful in keeping crime in check in their local community. In 1987, 14% felt that the police had crime in their area completely under control; 62% thought the police had crime fairly under control; 13% were of the opinion that the police had crime less under control; and 3% believed they did not have crime under control at all. As many as 8% answered that they did not know. As can be seen from Table 2, the survey results show a remarkable stability in the appraisals for the years 1984–1987.

The large majority – 75% of the persons asked – positively assessed the success of the police in the battle against crime in their area. Previous research[8], however, has shown that when people are asked about control of crime outside the areas in which they live, they are typically much less satisfied. Also, these results suggest that, even at the local level, 25% of respondents believe that the police do not have crime under control in their community or at least are not sure about this. In cities with populations of 500 000 and more, almost every third person doubts that the police are winning the battle against crime (1985). Accordingly, in a comparison of the federal states, the three city-states had the highest percentage of those who did not believe that crime was being successfully combatted in their place of residence. In contrast, the lowest percentage of doubt was found in the southern states, Baden-Württemberg, Rhineland-Palatinate, Saarland (22% each), and Bavaria (17%). It should be noted that these are the states which, according to police crime statistics, have the lowest relative incidence of crime (cases based on 100 000 residents) and the highest rate of solved crimes.

[8] Kerner 1980, pp 269ff; Gefeller/Trudewind 1978, pp 324ff.

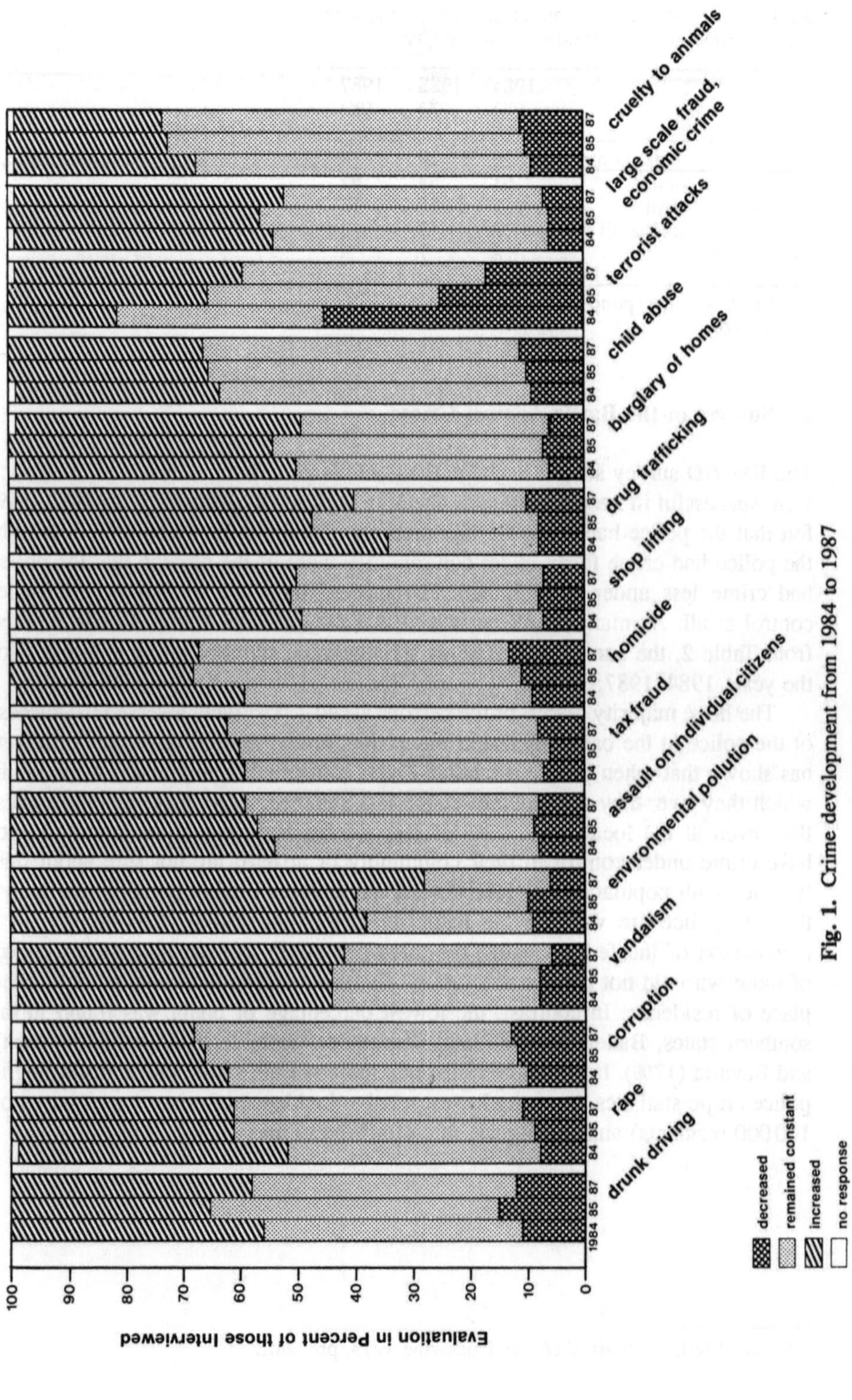

Fig. 1. Crime development from 1984 to 1987

2.5 Perceived Trends in Crime: 1984–1987

In order to obtain information on the public's sense of security and safety, a question was included in the EMNID survey regarding trends in crime. The respondents were presented with 15 very different kinds of criminal offenses and were asked to say whether they thought the incidence of each of these had declined, had remained constant, or had increased in the last few years. Figure 1 shows the percentage of responses according to offense.

In 1987, most of the respondents felt that there had been a rise in environmental pollution (72%), in vandalism such as damage to telephones or parks (58%), and in drug trafficking (59%). Some 50% of respondents assumed there was an increase in burglaries.

The percentage of persons who assumed that the rate of environmental crime had increased was noticeably higher in 1987: Whereas in 1985 59% assumed such crimes had increased, in 1987 this figure rose to 72%. The nuclear reactor catastrophe in Chernobyl and the pollution of the Rhine by chemical accidents that had occurred in the meantime apparently had a strong influence on public opinion.

As for the remaining offenses, most of the persons interviewed assumed they had neither increased nor decreased. In 1984, 46% had assumed that the number of terrorist acts had decreased in previous years. As to the activities of terrorist groups in 1985, about the same number of respondents assumed an increase as assumed a stagnation of such crimes. Only 25% believed terrorism had declined; in 1987 this dropped to 17%.

There is a clear connection between public perceptions of crime and the regard for the police. Persons who had a negative opinion of the police tend to believe that the following crimes are on the rise: bribery of government employees, environmental pollution, tax evasion, economic crime, rape, child abuse, and cruelty to animals. These offenses constitute either white collar crimes or violations against weak or defenseless victims, indicating that such answers may reflect the specific value systems of these respondents.

Another group whose judgment of crime trends deviates from the average are persons who tend to be preoccupied with thoughts of being victimized. They assume that such crimes as murder, rape, assault on individual citizens, burglary, terrorist attacks, and cruelty to animals have increased. This group, mostly made up of elderly persons or housewives, have a disproportionate fear of violence and burglary.

2.6 Judging Crimes by Seriousness

Following the question on crime trends, the respondents were asked to assign a particular degree of seriousness to specific crimes. The purpose of this question

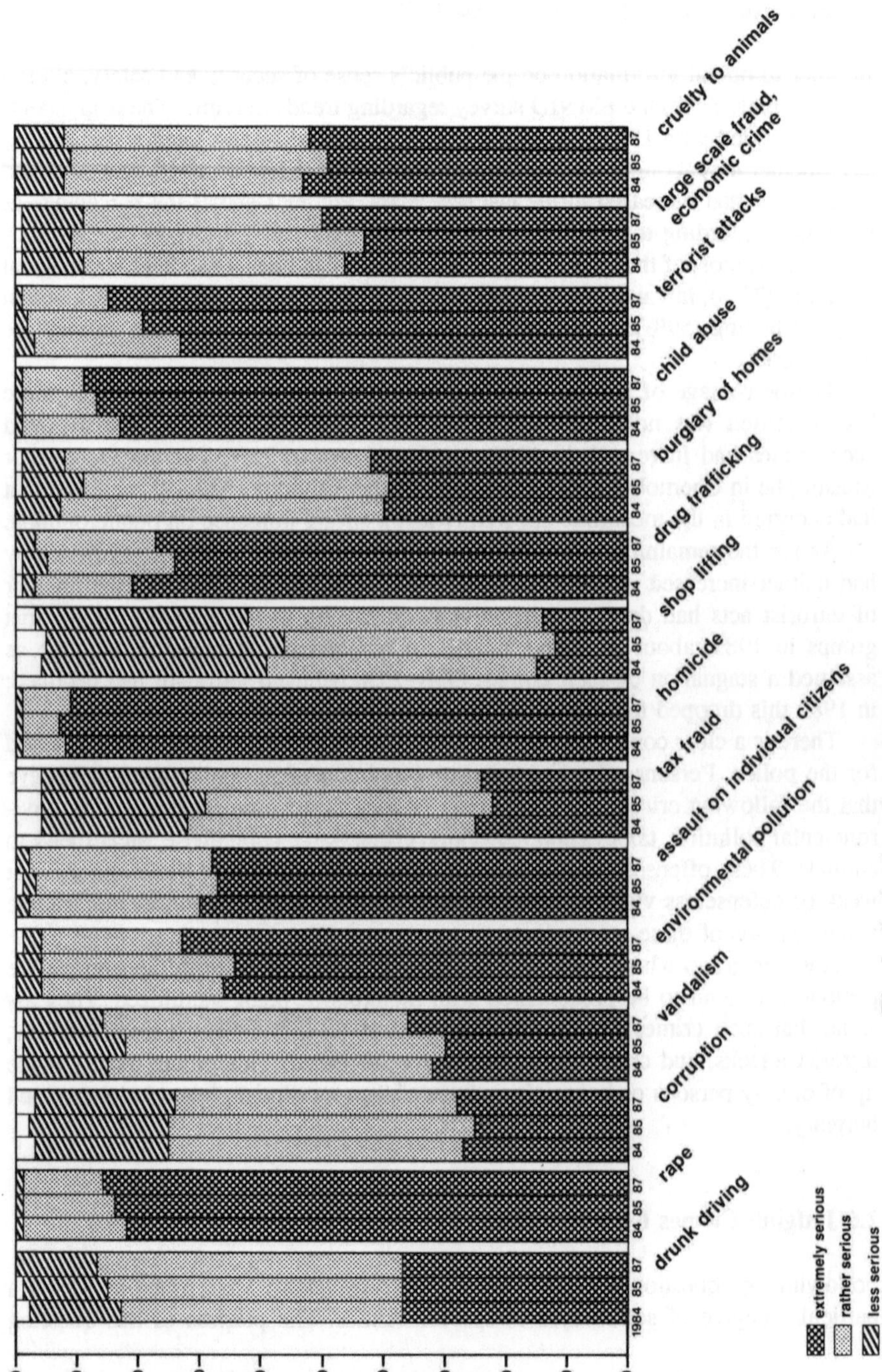

Fig. 2. Evaluation of seriousness of crime

was to ascertain the degree to which the public feels threatened by such crimes.[9] The respondents were presented 15 different types of offenses which they were to classify according to how serious they considered them to be: "extremely serious," "rather serious," "not so serious." "not serious at all." Figure 2 illustrates the responses in percentages for the various crimes.

As was to be expected, a clear majority (91%) rated homicide as being "extremely serious." Other crimes which were labeled "extremely serious" included child abuse (88%), rape (85%), terrorist attacks (84%), drug trafficking (76%), air and water pollution (73%), and attacks on individual citizens (67%).

The least serious offense was shoplifting: 37% placed it in the category of "not so serious" or "not serious at all." Tax fraud and corruption were also ranked in these categories by 28% and 26%, respectively.

There seems to be a relationship between a person's assessment of how serious a particular crime is and his regard for the police. Persons with a negative view of the police judged environmental crime, corruption, tax fraud, and economic crime much more harshly than they did drunk driving, vandalism, drug trafficking, burglary, and terrorist attacks. This again reflects the value systems of these persons, most of whom are younger citizens with *Abitur*. By contrast, persons who are in constant fear of being robbed have a generally rigid attitude towards all kinds of crime. This group rates vandalism, shoplifting, burglary, and cruelty to animals much more harshly than most of the population.

Table 3 shows to what degree the respondents felt threatened by crime.

The results show that the number of respondents who often thought about becoming victims of theft or being attacked was somewhat lower in 1987 than in previous surveys. The fear of theft was almost as common as the fear of being attacked. Thus, what seemed to be measured by the questions was a fear of crime in general, rather than of any particular offense.

This "fear indicator" was highest among persons above 50 years of age and housewives. These are the very groups who, according to statistics on crime victims, have least cause for such fear. The percentage of residents of large cities (over 500000) who never think about becoming victims of theft or being attacked is lower than the average (9% as opposed to 15% in 1985), which is consistent with the crime statistics. Those least concerned with being a victim of crime were adolescents, persons with *Abitur*, and residents of communities of less than 20000.

3 Conclusions

The results of the survey show that, in general, the citizens of the Federal Republic of Germany have a substantial amount of confidence in the police and that this confidence remained stable from 1984 to 1987. At the same time, however, most

[9] On the evaluation of the seriousness of crime see Bundeskriminalamt 1977; Council of Europe 1970; Kerner 1980; Schindhelm 1972; Sellin/Wolfgang 1964; Westermann 1986, pp 125ff.

Table 3. Results of question 5: how often do you have thoughts about being a victim of theft or being attacked?

	Theft			Attack		
	1984 (%)	1985 (%)	1987 (%)	1984 (%)	1985 (%)	1987 (%)
Never	21	15	17	21	15	19
Seldom	35	37	39	36	40	41
Sometimes	28	33	31	28	30	25
Often/constantly	14	13	11	13	14	12
Don't know	2	2	1	2	2	2

Total number of respondents: 1984, 2012; 1985, 1972; 1987, 2020.

of the young people from large cities who have had a formal higher education do not have such a high regard for the police. It will be extremely difficult, although very necessary for the improvement of relations between the public and the police, to improve the image of the police and hence the willingness of this critical group of the population to cooperate.

Similar stability was found in opinions about trends in crime, assessments of the seriousness of crimes, and sense of security. Even when the results of earlier studies are included in the evaluation[10], it can be said that public opinion regarding the police in West Germany has barely changed, at least in the last decade. One area where opinions have dramatically changed, however, is that of environmental crime, partly due to actual incidents and partly to a growing sensitivity to environmental pollution. Public opinion toward acts of terrorism is also strongly dependent on spectacular events.

Opinions about trends in crime were largely consistent with the trend evident in the police crime statistics. A direct influence of the statistical figures on the results of the surveys seems highly unlikely, given the considerable time span between the publication of the statistics and when the surveys were conducted and the sparse coverage by the media. The problem of unreported crime makes it difficult to assess how realistic the appraisal is.

Approximately 20% of respondents ranked tax fraud, corruption, and drunk driving as being not so serious or not serious at all. This suggests that the harm resulting from these victimless crimes may be played down to an alarming degree and that intensive work should be done to make the public aware of the serious economic and social effects of white collar crime.

Fear of crime in the Federal Republic of Germany, as measured by concerns about theft or robbery victimization, is generally rather low. However, it should not be overlooked that persons over 60 years of age and women feel especially threatened by such crimes. This is demonstrated by the results of studies in which the fear of crime outside the home at night was addressed.[11] This fear has serious

[10] See the German (and international) results cited by Kerner 1980, pp 87ff.

[11] See also Gefeller/Trudewind 1978, pp 326ff; Kerner 1980, pp 187ff; Murck 1978, p 206; Stephan 1976, p 398.

behavioral consequences and appropriate measures, such as improving information about the real danger of crime within the local community, should be taken to reduce the risk of older citizens isolating themselves from society out of the fear of crime.

References

Bundeskriminalamt (ed) (1977) "Offence classification and rating, and practical applications thereof." International Symposium organized at the Bundeskriminalamt Wiesbaden (papers), 16–18 February, 1977. Wiesbaden (BKA-Forschungsreihe. Special volume)

Council of Europe (ed) (1970) The index of crime. Some further studies. Strasbourg (Collected studies on criminological research, vol VII)

van Dijk JJM, Steinmetz CHD (1980) The RDC victim surveys, 1974–1979. A report on annual research into the extent and nature of petty crime in the Netherlands, the willingness of the population to report offences to the police, and police policy on official reports. The Hague (Research and documentation centre, Ministry of Justice, vol XXXV)

Dölling D (1986) Kriminalitätseinschätzung und Sicherheitsgefühl der Bevölkerung als Einflußfaktoren auf kriminalpolitische und kriminalstrategische Planung. Schriftenreihe der Polizei-Führungsakademie, pp 38–57

Gefeller I, Trudewind C (1978) Bedrohtheitsgefühl: Erfassung, Verteilung und Beziehungen zu ökologischen Variablen und Persönlichkeitsvariablen. In: Schwind H-D, Ahlborn D, Weiß R (eds) Empirische Kriminalgeographie. Bestandsaufnahme und Weiterführung am Beispiel von Bochum ("Kriminalitätsatlas Bochum"). Wiesbaden, pp 309–337 (BKA-Forschungsreihe, vol 8)

Hough M, Mayhew P (1985) Taking account of crime: key findings from the second British crime survey. London (Home Office Research Study, no 85)

ipos – Institut für praxisorientierte Sozialforschung (1986) Einstellung zu aktuellen Fragen der Innenpolitik 1986. Bericht. Mannheim

Kerner H-J (1980) Kriminalitätseinschätzung und Innere Sicherheit. Eine Untersuchung über die Beurteilung der Sicherheitslage und über das Sicherheitsgefühl in der Bundesrepublik Deutschland, mit vergleichenden Betrachtungen zur Situation im Ausland. Wiesbaden (BKA-Forschungsreihe, vol 11)

Landeskriminalamt Baden-Württemberg/Projektleitung Kriminalpolizeiliches Vorbeugungsprogramm des Bundes und der Länder, Geschäftsstelle (ed) (1984) Polizeiinterne Umfrage Nov 30, 1984. Stuttgart (unpublished paper)

Landesregierung Schleswig-Holstein (1986) Bericht zur inneren Sicherheit in Schleswig-Holstein. Drucksache 10/1546 des Schleswig-Holsteinischen Landtages (10. Wahlperiode; 22.05.1986)

Murck M (1978) Die Angst vor Verbrechen und Einstellungen zu Problemen der öffentlichen Sicherheit. Kriminologisches Journal 10:202–214

Schindhelm M (1972) Der Sellin-Wolfgang-Index – Ein ergänzendes Maß der Strafrechtspflegestatistik. Stuttgart

Sellin T, Wolfgang ME (1964) The measurement of delinquency. New York London Sydney

Skogan WG (1984) Reporting crimes to the police: The status of world research. Journal of Reserach in Crime and Delinqueny 21:113–137

Skogan WG (1986) The fear of crime and its behavioral implications. In: Fattah EA (ed) From crime policy to victim policy. Reorienting the Justice System. Houndmills, London, pp 167–188

Sporn H (1978) Die Einstellung der Bochumer Bürger zur Polizei. In: Schwind H-D, Ahlborn D, Weiß R (eds) Empirische Kriminalgeographie. Bestandsaufnahme und Weiterführung am Beispiel von Bochum ("Kriminalitätsatlas Bochum"). Wiesbaden, pp 293–309 (BKA-Forschungsreihe, vol 8)

Stephan E (1976) Die Stuttgarter Opferbefragung. Eine kriminologisch-viktimologische Analyse zur Erforschung des Dunkelfeldes unter besonderer Berücksichtigung der Einstellung der Bevölkerung zur Kriminalität. Wiesbaden (BKA-Forschungsreihe, vol 3)
Sveri K (1982) Comparative analyses of crime by means of victim surveys – The Scandivanian experience. In: Schneider HJ (ed) The victim in international perspective. Papers and Essays given at the "Third International Symposium on Victimology" 1979 in Münster/Westfalia. Berlin New York, pp 209–219
Westermann R, Hager W (1986) Schwereeinschätzungen von Delikten in verschiedenen Bevölkerungsgruppen. Monatsschrift für Kriminologie und Strafrechtsreform 69:125–130

CHAPTER 8

Asking the Victims

M.C. Baurmann

Contents

1 Introduction

The Research Unit on Criminology and Criminal Investigation of the *Bundeskriminalamt* (BKA) has focused on the topic of victimology for over 13 years now. Comprehensive victimological projects conducted in the last few years have had considerable impact on criminological theory, police training, police work, and on the concepts of victim protection and victim assistance.

Two comprehensive projects are presented below which approach the question of the consquences of victimization not from the point of view of the law en-

Kube/Störzer (Eds.)
Police Research in the Federal Republic of Germany

forcement agencies, nor that of the detatched theorist who speaks over the victims heads, but from the victims' personal experiences during and after the crime.

The outcome of both projects was that common views about victims are often inconsistent with reality. The victim's view often meets with indifference or even hostility.

The first project "Consequences for the Victim of Sexual Assault," was performed during the beginning stages of victimological research at the BKA. The second project, "Perspectives and Expectations of Victims," has just been published in Germany. The two projects convey a good impression of the development of victimological research at the BKA over the last 10 years.

In both projects the BKA dealt with highly topical issues, long before other research institutes in the Federal Republic of Germany (FRG) had even approached these subjects.

The large number of violent sexual assaults committed by persons acquainted with or related to the victim was pointed out in the first study 10 years ago.

The purpose of the second study was to determine the *real* – not the *assumed* – needs and expectations of victims after the crime had been reported. The survey carried out was the first of its kind in the FRG and one of the first internationally.

In the first project, over 8000 declared victims of sex crimes – who either reported the incident themselves to the police or became known as victims by the reporting of others, e.g., parents – were questioned about the sexual attacks they had experienced and about their injuries. It was found that the reports of the victims deviated considerably in some points from the image of sexual crime commonly held by the public and professionals in the field.

In the second project, more than 200 declared victims of various types of crimes were questioned about their injuries, fears, wishes, and needs immediately after the incident had been reported to the police. Here, too, it could be shown that there is much to be learned from simply questioning the victims themselves as to what they actually want, instead of setting up an institutional victim service based on pure speculation.

The results of the two surveys demonstrate that we have long neglected to listen actively and sensitively to the victim and have failed to pose the right questions.

Both projects evolved out of the ethical standpoint that the victim should be given more influence in assessing the crime and in determining the manner in which they cope with its consequences.

In nearly all cases the police initiate criminal proceedings only if a victim, in the role of a witness, reports the crime to the legal authority. Thus, the criminal justice authorities are dependent to a large degree on the victim's willingness to report the crime. Despite this, authorities do not offer adequate services for victim support.

During the course of their development, legal systems have become primarily offender-oriented and have lost sight of the perspective of the victim. This frequently leads to the phenomenon of secondary victimization and may result in unwillingness on the part of victims to report a crime. Thus, the legal system itself is called into question.

Regardless of whether one takes an abolutionist or a reformist standpoint, it must be recognized that we have to listen more attentively to what the victim is saying.

2 Project 1: Consequences for Declared Victims of Sexual Assault. A Longitudinal Investigation[1]

When sexual behavior that deviates from the social norm is being discussed, unconscious fears and ostensibly rational arguments tend to enter the debate. For decades, criminal law experts in the FRG have repeatedly lamented the irrationality of such discussions. The situation of the victims of sex offenses, usually women and girls, has become a central issue and, in the FRG as in other countries, many self-help groups have been founded for victims of forcible rape and sexual abuse.[2] The discussion surrounding legislative changes conducted in the last few years has also focused on victims of sexual assault.

In 1976, the West German parliament passed the Victim Compensation Law for victims of violent crime, which was amended in 1986. In 1987, the first Victim Protection Law was passed. Since 1987, there has been discussion as to whether all cases of violent rape should be handled in the same manner, regardless of whether they were committed in or out of marriage[3], as up to now they have been treated differently. The West German police and several public prosecutors have begun to set up departments specializing in the investigation of sexual violence.[4]

---

[1] The complete report (791 pages) on this reasearch project was published in the BKA Forschungsreihe, vol 15 (Baurmann 1983). This volume contains all of the empirical data, a detailed reference list, and an English summary. A German language summary of the results was published for those who deal professionally with victims of sex crimes (Baurmann 1985). A new edition of the latter, which is currently in preparation, contains a comparison with the most recent research results in the Federal Republic of Germany.

[2] The term "forcible rape" here is defined similar to the definition of the Uniform Crime Reports for the United States, which says: "Forcible rape, as defined in the Program, is the carnal knowledge of a female forcibly and against her will. Assaults or attempts to commit rape by force or threat of force are included; however, statutory rape (without force) and other sex offenses are excluded." (Uniform Crime Reports 1988, p 13).
The German penal code says in § 177 that only attempted or completed forcible coitus with a woman – except when the husband is the offender – is viewed as "forcible rape." Other forcible sexual intercourse is viewed as "sexual assault under duress," also with the exception if the husband is the offender (§ 178 German penal code). Sexual assault on and sexual abuse of children are prosecuted under §§ 173 (incest), 174 (sexual abuse of a dependent person), and 176 (sexual abuse of children) German penal code, if it is not an offense in the sense of §§ 177 or 178. Many of the offenses registered under § 176 of the German penal cose are strictly speaking not violent offenses. In about 30%–35% of these cases a grown-up exhibited his genitals in front of a child.

[3] For more details on this discussion in Germany see Baurmann, Plate, and Störzer 1988, p 127.

[4] In 1981, Baurmann and Störzer proposed a governmental model for the support of victims of violent crimes. Furthermore, the BKA published a study containing the results of a research survey of rape victims performed by police officers (Fehrmann et al. 1986). These

In general, it is apparent that, in dealing with the topic of sexual assault, there is a tendency either to dramatize or to minimize. Even today it is almost impossible to hold a sophisticated discussion on sex crime.

2.1 Design of the Investigation

The entire project consisted of three large and several smaller studies. In the following we will concentrate on the three large surveys of sexual assault victims.

Study of victims of all sex crimes reported in a 4 year period in one state of the FRG (Lower Saxony). The first stage of the investigation consisted of an analysis of special victim-oriented questionnaires, completed by the interrogating police officers, about the sexual offenses (8058 cases) that had been reported to the police in the state of Lower Saxony over a 4 year period (1969–1972). Only some of these cases were later tried before a court. In many cases, for instance those in which there was no identified suspect, police investigations were called off. Since the study was designed to be quantitative, the 29 items of the questionnaire were designed as multiple choice questions.

Follow-up study of a representative sample of reported victims of sexual assault 6–10 years later. In the second stage of the investigation, 112 randomly selected sexual assault victims were requested to participate in a detailed follow-up study. This second survey was performed in 1979 and 1980, i.e., 6–10 years after the crime had been reported (declaration of victimization). It consisted of a partly standardized in-depth interview, integrating established psychodiagnostic tests and victimological items. The face-to-face interviews generally lasted between 2 and 4 h and were held in the home of the victim. In most instances, only the victim and a psychologist (half of whom were male, the other half female) were present.

Analysis of prosecuted cases on the basis of court records containing credibility reports. The court records of 131 sexual offenses belonging to another sample in the state of Rhineland-Palatinate were analyzed. These cases had not only been reported to the police, but had also been tried in court. In this victim-oriented analysis of court records, only those cases were included for which a psychologist had made a written assessment of the truth of the victim's statement. These offenses had been committed approximately at the same time as those in the first survey. The purpose of this third survey was to compare sexual offenses that were merely reported with those that were reported and tried.

---

police officers did a self-critical analysis of how women are treated by the prosecuting authorities. In addition, continous training courses are being run with the support of the author in the states of Baden-Württemberg, Bavaria, Hesse, Lower Saxony, and North-Rhine- Westphalia for police officers who engage in administrative investigation work in sexual assaults. Feminists and critics of the police participate in these training programs.

Nearly all studies published to date have dealt almost exclusively with sexual offenses brought to trial or with selected – in some cases highly selected – groups of victims. Since the distribution of cases of sexual assault in Lower Saxony did not significantly deviate from the distribution in the entire FRG, the following results can be generalized for West Germany.

2.2 Selected Results

Some 89.1% of the victims were girls and women. Approximately two-thirds of the declared victims were between the ages of 7 and 13. The typical age of the victim varied significantly according to the type of sexual offense. Sexually abused children were mostly between 7 and 13 years of age. Victims of rape were predominantly young women between 14 and 20. The ages of those who were the victims of exhibitionism varied greatly, but most of them were younger women.

The crime suspects were almost exclusively men (99.8%), most between 16 and 40 years of age. This contradicts the widely held notion that the majority of sex offenders are old men. Moreover, older crime suspects were seldom charged with threatening or violent behavior; 23.5% of the offenders under 46 years of age had threatened or carried out violence, but this was true of only 7.2% of those over 45 who had committed such acts.

A surprisingly high number of suspects were acquaintenances or relatives of the victim: over one-third in the reported and over 94% in cases brought to trial. One of the most important findings of this study, in addition to the fact that a large number of offenders were known or related to the victim, was that these offenders were also particularly dangerous.[5] This means that warning potential victims about being sexually assaulted by men they do not know is an ineffective protective measure. Through such warnings a feeling of being threatened by strangers is transmitted, while in fact rape is usually committed by a person in the victim's immediate social environment.

In the second survey the so declared sexual victims were asked to report conversations they had held in connection with their victimization. Furthermore, the victims were asked to rate the conversations on a scale ranging from 1 to 5 (1 = "found it pleasant and it helped me"; 3 = "had no effec to me"; 5 = "found it unpleasant and it did harm to me").

The victims questioned had had 12 conversations on the average about the reported sexual offense, including those held within the scope of the criminal investigation. Of course this number varied considerably, depending on the type of offense.

[5] The statistical correlations between the variable "degree of acquaintance between victim and offender", on the one hand, and, on the other hand, the variables "intensity of the sexual act" (CC = 0.58; $p < 0.01$), "number of sexual acts" (CC = 0.58; $p < 0.01$), and "intensity of violent behavior of the offender" (CC = 0.57; $p < 0.01$) were all highly significant. (CC = contingence coefficient for ordinal scales; results comparable to correlations expressed by r.)

These conversations were rated as follows: conversations with boyfriend received an average rating of 2.3; psychologist, also 2.3; teacher, 2.5; sibling, 2.6; physican and own lawyer, 2.7; father, 2.8; peer or colleague, 3.0; mother, 3.1; expert witness, 3.2; police officer, 3.6; representative of youth welfare department, 3.6; judge, 3.9; defendant's layers, 4.5. As can be seen, the conversations with representatives of the authorities did not score favorably (3.2–4.5).

After these results were published in the FRG in 1983, in-service training courses for police officers were introduced with the support of the author and the question of "victim protection" became a topic of much discussion.[6] In 1986 similar ratings of police behavior by victims were taken in one police district (see Sect. 3). The percentage of very negatively evaluated conversations with the police decreased from 21% (1969–1972) to 9% (1986) within about 15 years.

Studying the literature, it was interesting to note that only a few attempts have been made to establish a definition for the term "injury" which can be operationalized for diagnostic purposes. For this investigations, therefore, "injuries caused by sexual offenses" were defined as follows:

Injury as a result of a sexual contact is a reactive, sexual, social, emotional, and/or physical disturbance, which the injured person is subjected to by a guilty party. This disturbance can either be recognized subjectively by the injured person or it can be diagnosed by specific scientific methods. The disturbance can be caused directly by the event itself (primary victimization) as well as indirectly (secondary victimization).

In comparison with other areas of crime, there was a surprisingly large number of victims of sexual offenses (48.2%) who subjectively experienced no injury. This was mainly true for cases involving exhibitionism, some pornographic offenses, superficial sexual contacts, etc., in which the victims did not experience violence or duress and therefore did not perceive themselves as victims (lack of victim perception). In these cases, the incidents usually became known by chance and a third party, such as a parent, reported the crime, sometimes even against the will of the child (heteronomously declared victim).

In contrast, according to the 1986 survey of reported victimizations (see Sect. 3), almost all (96%) of the declared victims of predominantly nonsexual offenses claimed to have felt injured.

The victims of sexual assault who reported some form of injury (51.8) from the total being asked suffered for an average of 4 years and 8 months. Asked in the follow-up study to name their worst injury, most of them reported injuries of a psychological nature: roughly half described disturbances in their social behavior (especially strong fear, distrust, family problems); about one-third described sexual disturbances (difficulties reaching orgasm, abhorrence and fear of sex, fear of pregnancy); and one-fifth described depressive moods (frequent brooding, guilt feelings, insomnia). Thus, the main damage done to the victim of a sexual offense

[6] For further trials to explain possible attitude change on the side of police officers, see Sect. 3.2.2.

is *psychological* harm. (Surprisingly, this also holds true for victims of nonsexual offenses; see Sect. 3.)

The victims were also asked what they thought was the main cause of their injury: half of them named the sexual act itself; one-third, other behavior of the suspect; one-tenth, the behavior of relatives and friends; and one-tenth, the behavior of the police.

While this may be an indication that the police were less often responsible for psychological harm to victims of sexual offenses than had been assumed, the fact that the behavior of police officers was considered as the main cause of psychological trauma in even one-tenth of cases with injured victim is a source of concern.

While many experts in the field have assumed that declared victims with no primary injuries are rare, the results of this investigation indicate that there is a relatively high incidence of declared victims of sexual offenses without primary victimization. To recapitulate, more than half (51.8%) of the declared victims of sexual offenses suffered injuries or even severe trauma. The remainder (48.2%) perceived no harm in connection with the experience. In most of the latter cases the sexual offense was relatively superficial and harmless and/or the "victim" had consented to the act.

Adults who contend that any, even nonviolent, sexual behavior is traumatic for children and young people should consider that in many cases this attitude itself may label a young person as a victim, although the child initially had no such perception of being victimized. In these cases, it is the dramatization behavior by the adults that leads to secondary victimization of the child.

In this study it was neither possible to determine a typology of victims of sexual offenses, nor a typology of sexual offenders. As most sexual offenses, regardless of whether they are violent or nonviolent, are interactions between two or more persons, it is necessary to analyze each case of sexual assault as a single unit of behavior.

To determine whether victimizations could be sorted into groups, a cluster analysis with 38 variables for each individual case was performed (n = 112 cases). Cluster analysis revealed a typology of three major case groups.

- *Group I* (57.1%) is the largest group and includes exhibitionism and comparatively harmless erotic sexual contacts with younger victims. All of the male victims are found here. Injury was very rare.

- *Group II* (11.6%) includes sexual contacts of a more intensive nature. Most of the suspects were known or related to the victim. The victim's family situation could be considered disturbed. A part of these exclusively female victims reported no injury at all; others had injuries within the average range.

- *Group III* (31.3%) comprises sexual assault under duress, forcible rape, and sexual contacts with highly emotional, defensive behavior or attitudes on the part of the victim. The exclusively female victims were older, while the suspects were younger compared with the averages for the entire population studied.

Most of these assaults had been reported immediately to the police. Victims in this cluster had the highest indices of injury.

All 112 cases were then grouped according to the classification defined in the German penal code. Comparison of the three typologies disclosed significanct differences.

The German penal code conforms to the commonly held idea that all offenses involving sexual behavior, including exhibitionism, forcible rape, prostitution, pornography, homosexuality, and sexual abuse of children, belong to the same criminological group. In the 13th section of the German penal code, violent and nonviolent offenses are combined under "Offenses Against Sexual Self Determination" and, especially in the area of sexual abuse of children, very different norm violations are grouped in the same article (such as indecent exposure in front of a child and forcible rape of a child).

According to cluster analysis, cases of exhibitionism and similar offenses (group I) were strictly differentiated from sex-related violent assaults (group III). This is supported by criminological research, which has shown that sexual violence has more in common with criminal violence in general than with nonviolent sexual offenses. Furthermore, prostitution and pornography have much in common with other types of organized crimes, whereas among consenting partners criminal sexual behavior (many homosexual contacts for example) may not lead to primary victimization.

2.3 Final Remarks

Objective and unbiased information on the phenomenon of sexual offenses and the aftereffects would reduce the dangers of dramatization in group I and would elucidate the violent character of the other assaults in groups II and III. It is especially necessary for the protection of potential victims to differentiate between sexual offenses perceived as only unpleasant, on the one hand, and brutal sexual attacks, on the other.

In addition, it should be recognized that there is hardly a criminal career that started out with exposure of the genitals and then progressed to forcible rape and murder. If recidivism on the offenders' side was determined, exhibitionists, pedophiles, and homosexuals showed, often repeatedly, recidivism in *their* field, wereas many of the violent sex offenders showed recidivism in *other* fields of violent crime. The present survey reveals that, contrary to the categories laid down in the German penal code, forcible rape has much in common with other violent offenses and that recidivism is more likely among those who commit forcible rape and sexual coercion than among exhibitionists. If nonviolent child molesters and exhibitionists have relapses, the probability is high that they will resort to their previous form of deviant behavior. It was very rare that a recidivistic exhibitionist displayed violent sexual behavior.

These results should have a strong impact on prevention programs[7], prosecuting strategies, and victim assistance programs.[8] In conclusion, the police should cooperate more with the victim and with victim assistance programs.[9]

3 Project 2: Perspectives and Expectations of Crime Victims. Interviews with Crime Victims Relevant to Victim Protection and Victim Assistance[10]

In Europe, the only studies available dealing with the needs and expectations of crime victims are those conducted by Shapland[11] and Maguire and Corbett.[12] In Germany, no surveys of crime victims have as yet been published. Currently, a comprehensive investigation is being conducted by Sessar et al. at the University of Hamburg, from which excerpts of initial results have already been published.[13] Additional publications are expected in the near future.

In analyzing today's victim support programs, it became clear that little is known about the real concerns and needs of victims and that, in many cases, victim assistance and support programs are built up on what are only presumed to be their wants and expectations.

Moreover, the attitudes of both professional and voluntary helpers often lead to the selective perception of victims' needs. Critical analyses on the helper syndrome (i.e., people providing help sometimes misuse the helplessness of their clients to raise their own self-esteem) from other social, psychological, and educational fields are often disregarded. As too little is known about the real needs of victims, it was considered inappropriate to use a standardized multiple choice questionnaire for this study. Instead, an open, semi-standardized, personal interview was chosen to allow unexpected answers.

Before selecting a sample of crime victims to be interviewed, it was necessary to decide whether only a representative distribution of reported crime should be studied or if cases of unreported victimization would also be of special interest.

---

[7] On the basis of this research project a program to prevent sex crimes was developed in cooperation with the author (see Innenministerium des Landes Baden-Württemberg 1987). In this prevention program, addressed to parents, the impression that the common exhibitionist or pedophile might turn into a violent offender was avoided. Furthermore, it was emphasized that dangerous violent offenders mostly belong to family friends or even to the family itself.

[8] See Baurmann and Störzer 1981. The author is currently consultant to a model facility for victim support in Hanau in the state of Hesse.

[9] See also Sect. 3.

[10] This project was conducted in cooperation with Dr. Wolfram Schädler (Department of Justice in the state of Hesse) to whom I want to express special thanks (see Baurmann and Schädler 1990).

[11] Shapland 1983, 1985, 1986; Shapland, Willmore, and Duff 1985.

[12] Maguire and Corbett 1987.

[13] Sessar, Beurskens, and Boers 1986. (See also Stehr 1988, Hanak, Stehr and Steinert 1989, and Voß 1989).

An important reason for interviewing both groups is that victim assistance programs normally work both with victims of reported and with officially unknown cases. However, since little is known about the distribution of the very important types of violent crimes which are unreported, it is not possible to set up a representative sample of these cases. It is also well-known that unreported cases of criminal violence are several times greater than the number of reported cases.[14] Thus, it would be unreasonable to arrange a representative sample only of reported cases, as such a sample would be too heavily weighted with cases of property crime while cases of criminal violence would be very rare (2.3% of the total). In addition, victims of criminal violence usually seem to need victim assistance the most.

As a representative sample for this investigation was either impossible to select and/or would have provided little information on those victims who seem to need assistance most (victims of violent crime), it was decided instead to interview groups of victims from each of the following:

- Property crimes
- Criminal violence (including sexual violence)
- Other crimes (including nonviolent sexual crimes).

3.1 The Interviews

The interviews were held from November 1985 to July 1986 in the city of Hanau (in the state of Hesse) and in the surrounding area. Hanau (population 100 000) is roughly 15 miles east of Frankfurt and belongs to the Frankfurt metropolitan area. The interviews were conducted chiefly at police headquarters, but, upon request, also in the homes of the victims or at neutral locations, e.g., coffee shops, the local victim support office ("Hanauer Hilfe"), or at the scene of the crime (immediately after the call was made to the police). Participation in the survey was voluntary and the purpose of the project was explained to the victims beforehand.

The 203 interviews were divided up as follows:

1. There were 169 victim interviews immediately after the incident was reported to the police. These took place mostly at police headquarters, but in a separate room. Most of the offenses were against property, more than half of which included theft under aggravating circumstances. Crimes involving theft from motor vehicles were also frequent; however, there were few violent crimes.
2. There were 14 interviews of victims following completion of the prosecution's investigation and after legal proceedings had been initiated, though before sentencing. Most took place at the home of the victim, but sometimes at a neutral location. These were exclusively violent crimes.

[14] See Störzer, Chap. 6 in the present volume.

3. There were 20 interviews of victims after trials in which the offender was convicted. These took place mostly at the home of the victim, but sometimes at a neutral location. These offenses were also exclusively violent crimes.

Interviews with the second and third groups took place on the average 2 1/2 years after the crime event.

3.2 Summary of the Results

The analysis of the results was based on the grouping of victims according to type of crime.

- Victims of criminal violence, including all cases of sexual violence (57; 28.1%).
- Victims of offenses against property (103; 50.7%).
- Victims of other crimes, including nonviolent sexual crimes (43; 21.2%).

The division was important for all further evaluations, as the situations of the victims in each group differed greatly.

3.2.1 Motives for Reporting the Crime and How the Victims Thought Their Case Should be Handled

Of those who reported the offense to the police, there was a substantial group (46.8%) who did so only for insurance reasons. Among the victims of incidents involving property, 76.6% went to the police in order to be able to make an insurance claim to recover the value of the property. This applies especially to the large group of crimes involving motor vehicles, most of which were car radio thefts. In these cases going to the police was considered by the victims a waste of time since the task of the police in these offenses consists primarily of administrative paper work.

For 15.8% of all victims and for 35.9% of the victims of violent crime, punishment of the offender constituted the motive for reporting the offense. (For further details about the wish for punishment, see below.) Some 13.8% of all victims (26.3% of the victims of violent crime) had gone to the police because they wanted to prevent a further crime on the part of the offender. Another 6.4% hoped that by reporting the crime they would be able to recover their losses; 2% of the victims went to the police simply because they were upset.

The victims' motives for reporting the crime to the law enforcement agencies had little to do with satisfying their own emotional needs. An alarming observation is that more than half of the victims interviewed (52.3%) had "no," "low," or "probably low" expectations that reporting the crime would be fruitful, largely because victims of property crimes did not expect to retrieve their losses. Almost three quarters (73.8%) of this latter group did not believe that the offender would be detected. Of the victims of violent crime, 26.3% shared this opinion.

Table 1. Victims' responses to the question, "What do you want to happen after the crime has been reported to the police (regardless of actual possibilities for solving the conflict)?"

Suggestion	Desire (%) Explicit	Desire (%) Possible	Explicit rejection (%)
Victim wants to settle the matter with offender him/herself			
V	22.8	5.3	28.1
P	32.0	10.7	6.8
O	32.6	11.6	11.6
Σ	(39.0)		(13.8)
To make the offender aware of the consequences of this act (e.g., by a third party)			
V	21.1	3.5	1.8
P	10.7	5.8	1.0
O	14.0	2.3	2.3
Σ	(18.7)		(1.5)
Victim willing to forgive			
V	5.3	14.0	31.6
P	5.8	23.3	10.7
O	2.3	18.6	20.9
Σ	(24.6)		(18.7)
Desire for restitution by the offender			
V	24.6	10.5	52.6
P	54.4	24.3	14.6
O	48.8	11.6	37.2
Σ	(62.5)		(30.0)
Desire for legal decision			
V	31.6	1.8	3.5
P	22.3	1.0	2.9
O	9.3	0.0	4.7
Σ	(23.2)		(3.4)
Punishment of the offender (including vague demands for punishment)			
V	75.4	5.3	3.5
P	66.0	11.7	11.7
O	62.8	9.3	20.9
Σ	(77.3)		(11.3)
Desire for offender to undergo treatment measures			
V	19.3	1.8	1.8
P	37.9	2.9	1.0
O	16.3	7.0	2.3
Σ	(31.5)		(1.5)

A total of 725 responses were given by 203 victims.
V, victims of violent crimes; P, victims of property crimes;
O, victims of other crimes; Σ, all victims.

The victims were asked how they thought things should proceed after the offense was reported (Table 1). The question was deliberately formulated so as not to ask what should be done with the offender if he were detected, since the suggestion of offender-oriented solutions was to be avoided. A total of 98.5% of the victims responded to the question, some more concretely, others more vaguely; some responses were inconsistent. Many victims expressed multiple desires. No suggestions were offered by the interviewer. Some victims desired very specific consequences (explicit desires by the victim), some were vaguely in favor (possible desire), and other explicitly rejected certain consequences (explicit rejection; see Table 1).

A closer analysis of the results reveals that victims, especially victims of property crimes, harbor inconsistent feelings with regard to how the offender should be treated. Whereas almost 30% of the victims of property offenses expressed a willingness to forgive the perpetrator and almost 80% were interested in being compensated for their losses, almost 80% of these victims were additionally in favor of some sort of punishment. (Such inconsistent attitudes were even expressed among the victims of violent crimes, albeit to a lesser degree.) The answers indicate that the penalty was frequenlty meant "to teach them a lesson" and that the victims did not experience a feeling of contradiction between their desires for punishment as well as reparation. On the other hand, it became clear during the interviews that many of the victims had only vague notions as to how they thought the offender should be punished and many placed restrictions on their demands for punishment (e.g., "not if it was his first offense, if he is a youth, if he comes from a socially disadvantaged environment").

3.2.2 Victims' Evaluation of Police Response

The victims were asked to rate the attitude of the police when they reported the incident. For this purpose a scale of 5 was used, ranging from "very pleasant" (1) to "very unpleasant" (5). A score of 3 meant that the behavior was regarded as "neither pleasant nor unpleasant."

The police received an average score of 2.5 from victims of property offenses and 2.7 from victims of violent crimes. An average of 2.9 was given by those victims of violent crimes whose cases were under prosecution or had already been tried and had been reported to the police an average of 2 1/2 years previously.

The evaluations of the group of sex crime victims from this study were compared with similar evaluations made by 112 victims of sex crimes from the study described in Sect. 2, which was based on complaints filed in the whole state of Lower Saxony 15 years earlier. A cautious comparison (old score: 3.6; new score: 2.6) suggests that the behavior of the police toward the victim reporting the crime incident (as perceived by the victim) improved in these 15 years. Such reasons could include the victim-oriented impetus supplied by public discussion, an improved personnel structure in the police (a new generation, better hiring criteria, better training, and/or improved in-service courses). It would be worthwhile to look into this working hypothesis further as it seems to contradict the common position held by critics of the police, especially with regard to their work in the area of sex crime.

3.2.3 Material Damage and Emotional Injury to the Victims Interviewed

Of the victims questioned, 94.6% perceived themselves as having been injured. (This was almost twice as high as the comparable results – 51.8% – from the survey in Lower Saxony which delt exclusively with victims of sexual offenses.) Asked to state what damage or injuries they had sustained (multiple answers were allowed), the victims most frequently reported injuries of an emotional nature (emotional injuries specifically named by the victims, 44.8%; very minor or assumed[15] emotional injury, 43.3%; fear of repeated victimization specifically named by the victims, 35.5%; very minor or assumed, 6.4%). Other damages (physical injury, loss of time, other) were more frequent only in very select groups of victims (e.g., loss of time for victims of property crimes, 47.6%). The victims were then asked to name the single most severe injury they had sustained.

Table 2. The most severe injury or damage experienced by the victims ($n = 203$)

Injury/damage stated	%	
Emotional injury	31.0	48.7
Fear of victimization	17.7	
Material damage	21.2	
Bodily injury	3.0	
Loss of time	9.9	
Other damage	5.9	
Assumed or minor damage	4.4	
No damage	3.9	
No answer	3.0	

Table 2 shows that emotional injuries and the fear of repeated victimization were most frequently perceived by the victims as the most severe damage (17.7% + 31.0% = 48.7%). As many as 78.9% of the victims of violent crimes felt they had suffered emotionally, whereas for property offenses the figure was 25.3%.

If we consider that most of the 21.2% with material damages (the most prevalent form of damage among the gorup of "victims of property crimes") were compensated by the insurance companies, there remains only one other important category of trauma: bodily injury, 3.0%. The rest (loss of time, assumed or minor damages, no damages) are more of less superficial.

[15] As the interviews were unstructured, the answers had to be coded afterwards by referring to the interview as a whole. Some answers appeared to be inconsistent, some were stated vaguely, and others had to be assumed from the context of the interview. These unprecise responses are specified as such in the text and tables.

These data indicate that any work on improving the situation of crime victims must emphasize emotional factors rather than focusing on physical injuries. Cases of pure bodily injury are rare. Even in this survey, with an overrepresentation of criminal violence, only 3% stated bodily injury to be their most severe damage.

3.2.4 Desires for Punishment of the Offender

Another purpose of the present study was to determine how many victims wished to have the offender punished and what kind of punishment they wanted. Another point to be clarified was whether victims who had sustained severe damage were more intent on seeing the offender punished than other victims.

Some 12.4% of the victims said they wanted no punishment for "their" offender. These were primarily victims of property crimes and other offenses. In contrast only 6.5% of the violent crime victims demanded no penalty.

The responses of 37.1% of the victims were very general or vague, but nevertheless pointed in the direction of punishment. Almost one-third of the victims requested a more lenient penalty for "their offender" (from "tell him my opinion" to "therapy" – 30.3%). Harsher penalties were called for by 17.4% of the respondents (from "corporal punishment" to "death penalty"). Surprisingly, only 20.9% of the victims of violent crimes called for such severe forms of punishment (Table 3).

Table 3. Kinds of punishment the victims demanded for "their offender" (first answer) ($n = 202$)

Punishment demanded by the victim	No.				%			
	Σ	V	P	O	Σ	V	P	O
No demand for punishment	25	4	12	9	12.4	6.5	12.5	20.5
Expressed generally or vaguely	75	26	39	10	37.1	41.9	40.6	22.7
Victim wants to confront the offender	1	–	–	1	0.5	–	–	2.3
Offender should be admonished by others	6	1	3	2	3.0	1.6	3.1	4.6
Fine	16	2	7	7	7.9	3.2	7.3	15.9
Correctional measures	30	7	19	4	14.9	11.3	18.8	9.1
Therapy	8	4	–	4	4.0	6.5	–	9.1
Corporal punishment	4	2	–	2	2.0	3.2	–	4.6
Most severe punishment possible	4	–	4	–	2.0	–	4.2	–
Imprisonment	21	10	8	3	10.4	16.1	8.3	6.8
Hard labor	5	2	3	–	2.5	1.6	3.1	–
Death penalty	1	–	–	1	0.5	–	–	2.3
Other penalties	5	4	–	1	2.5	6.5	–	2.3
"Don't know"	1	–	1	–	0.5	–	1.0	–
Total	202	62	96	44	100	100	100	100

Σ, all victims; V, victims of violent crimes; P, victims of property crimes; O, victims of other crimes.

These findings suggest that the needs and interests of the victims, including those of victims of violence, do not support arguments for increasing criminal punishment. On the contrary, the victims interviewed in the survey generally tended to demand more moderate punishment. This was underlined, as was mentioned above, by a tendency on the part of many victims to consider mitigating circumstances (e.g., first offense) that would justify reducing the severity of the punishment even further.

No statistically significant correlation was found between the variables "kind of injury" and "kind of punishment called for". There was, however, a correlation between "victim's age" and "kind of punishment called for" in that victims over 30 years of age demanded harsher penalties than younger ones.

3.2.5 Restitution, Compensation, and Mediation

142 victims, questioned directly after having reported the crime to the police, were asked whether they would agree to mediation with the offender for the purpose of negotiating compensation or restitution if such a program were available (Table 4).

Table 4. Willingness of victims to participate in mediation with "their offender" ($n = 142$)

Willingness to mediate	%	
Yes	47.9	
Basically willing	12.7	72.5
Perhaps (vague, assumed)	12.0	
No	27.5	

It was mentioned above (Table 1) that, without having been asked directly by the interviewer, almost two-thirds of all victims in the survey (44.8%) expressed a desire for mediation. Upon direct questioning the percentage was even higher (willing and basically willing, 60.6%; possibly willing, 12.0%; see Table 4), apparently because of the number of victims (17.7%) who had first responded that they would "possibly" agree to restitution (Table 1).

Of all victims questioned directly after having reported the incident to the police, 27.5% rejected the idea of mediation with the offender if such mediation were available; 14.9% of the victims of property crimes and 32.1% of the victims of other crimes rejected the idea. Of all victims of violent crimes, 63.0% were unwilling to consider mediation, whereas, of the victims of violent crimes who were questioned some 2 1/2 years after the assault, only 44.4% rejected the idea.

A careful interpretation of these data may lead to the hypothesis that the more time that elapses after victimization the more willing the victim is to participate in mediation with the offender. In general, however, fewer victims of violence seem to be interested in mediation than victims of other crimes, although it became

Table 5. Victim's demand for punishment and willingness to accept restitution from the offender ($n = 90$)

Demands for punishment	Willingness to accept restitution		Total
	Yes (n)	No (n)	
None	17	1	18
Moderate	32	9	41
Harsh	11	20	31
Total	60	30	90

evident from the conversations that victims of violent crime in particular had little knowledge about ways to arrive at constructive solutions through mediation.

Finally, the victims' demands for punishment (divided into demands for "no punishment," "moderate punishment," and "harsh punishment") were cross-tabulated with the victims' acceptance of possible restitution by the offender (Table 5).

The correlation between the two attitudes is highly significant ($p < 0.001$). Victims who called for moderate or no punishment were more likely to agree to restitution on the part of "their offender".

3.2.6 Victims' Desire for Assistance

The survey shows that an astonishingly low percentage (34.1%) of the respondents either expected to recieve assistance directly after they reported the crime or expected assistance if they were involved in "a more serious case." This excluded those victims whose case proceedings had already been closed. Of the victims of violent crimes, 43.2% said they expected assistance and 10.8% of them "did not know" if they needed victim support. Almost all of the victims questioned (90.2%) had either vague or more concrete ideas about how they or other victims could be helped (Table 6).

Table 6 shows that only half of the victims had concrete ideas about the kind of victim support that could be offered to them in their own case. Nevertheless, this figure was high enough to make it worthwhile to cooperate with victims themselves to reevaluate the current concepts of victim support.

The kind of support victims desired (multiple answers) were not entirely congruent with the injuries described in Table 2. For many of the victims (especially those of property crimes), financial remuneration or return of property seemed obvious (63.1%); the desire for medical treatment constituted a lower priority (3.5%). The victims also expressed an interest in more effective crime prevention (19.8%), legal assistance, and assistance in completing the necessary formalities (together, 57.2%). The desire for psychological assistance constituted a very high priority (56.2%).

Table 6. Victims' ideas about the kind of support they could recieve (in %)

Notion about victim support	All victims	Victims of violence	Victims of property crimes	Victims of other crimes
Concrete ideas in relation to own case	49.8	52.6	42.7	62.8
Vague notion in relation to own case	8.9	10.5	9.7	4.7
Concrete ideas in relation to other cases	26.9	24.6	32.0	16.3
Vague notion in relation to other cases	4.9	3.5	6.8	2.3
No notion	5.4	7.0	2.9	9.3
No answer	4.4	1.8	5.9	4.7

In conclusion it seems that victims have rather vague notions about victim support, which is probably related to the fact that the work done by existing victim assistance programs is not sufficently made known to the general public.

For the most part victims also seem to have accepted their unfortunate situation. Hardly any of them came up with an idea as to how it might be improved. Some indirectly expressed dissatisfaction with the way their "case" was "handled" by the police and the criminal justice system.

3.2.7 How Should Contact Between Victims and Victim Assistance Services be Established?

The victims were asked how, in their opinion, contact should be made between the victim and victim services (Table 7).

The team of evaluators grouped all answers expressing that the initiative should be taken by the victim together because the victims expressed the opinion that they generally should be the ones to contact victim assistance programs.

However, there appeared to be a major difference between those who thought the services should approach crime victims. Those who spoke for others, for example, stated that, while they felt victim services should approach other victims (e.g., those seriously injured), they themselves did not consider this option as applying to them. This response cannot be equated with the answer given by victims who expressed a genuine interest in being approached by victim assistance programs.

Almost two-thirds of the respondents (62.6%) felt that they themselves, as victims, should decide whether or not they wanted to get in touch with victim services. While 14.3% felt that the personnel of such services should approach them, 4.9% were of the opinion that this did not apply to them, but presumably would apply to other victims. Inconsistent answers were given by 8.4% of those questioned and no answer was given by 6.9%.

Table 7. Victims' opinion on how contact should be established between victim and victim services ($n = 203$; in %)

Victims opinion as to who should take the initiative	All victims	Victims of violence	Victims of property crimes	Victims of other crimes
I would like to take the initiative myself / Speaking for other victims: They should take the initiative themselves	62.6	59.9	64.0	62.8
The services should approach me	14.3	19.3	12.6	11.6
Speaking for other victims: the services should approach them	4.9	1.8	5.8	7.0
Unclear/inconsistent	8.4	10.5	4.9	14.0
No answer/not questioned	6.9	5.3	9.7	2.3
Question not relevant for victim	3.0	3.5	2.9	2.3

Most of those interviewed would have liked to have been informed about existing victim services, for instance, by the police officer taking the report. Some of the victims explained that, if someone from such an institution turned up unannounced to offer help, they might feel obliged to accept this help.

Cross-tabulation with the most severe injury perceived by the victim demonstrated that the desire to take the initiative in seeking out victim aid was not related to the seriousness of the injury, but rather seemed to reflect a more general attitude on the part of the victim.

The interviews revealed that many of the crime victims did not wish their personal data, such as name, address, or the details of their victimization, passed on to any other agencies. Some expressed fear of data misuse.

It must be stressed that, depending on the type of crime (Table 7) only a minority (11%–20%) of the victims wanted to be approached. The majority (roughly two-thirds) wanted to take the initiative at their own discretion. This leads to the conclusion that the decision regarding assistance should remain strictly with the victim in order to minimize the danger of secondary damage caused by inappropriate "reaching out" initiatives. Efforts must be made, however, to reach the 14% of "passive victims" by more effective forms of publicity. This would require that an extensive network of victim services be established throughout the country.

The necessity for more effective publicity became clear repeatedly during the interviews, as most of the victims were unaware of the well-established victim assistance facility located in the city of Hanau, where the interviews were being held.

3.3 Summary and Conclusions

Until now we have neglected to question the victims themselves on the type of support needed after victimization; instead, the type of assistance and the structure of victim aid programs has been determined solely by "helpers".

By interviewing crime victims in the city of Hanau, the injured parties were offered the opportunity, for the first time in the FRG, to express what they considered to be appropriate treatment.

Harsh punishment of the offender was of only peripheral interest for the vast majority of victims, whereas recovery of, or compensation for losses had a higher priority. In addition to the demand for compensation, the offender should – from the victim's point of view – receive a rather mild punishment with the purpose of correction, resocialization, or just "to teach them a lesson".

Victims of violent crimes rejected restitution more often than victims of property offenses as they saw no sense in material compensation. Even after a considerable amount of time had passed, most victims of violent crimes refused negotiations with the offender because they feared being reminded of the criminal event. On the other hand, the interviews suggested that some victims of violent acts had a desire to come to terms with the offender, possibly in the presence of a professional mediator, as they wished to learn more about the offender's motives, personality, and social situation.

While the majority of victims claimed that they felt able to cope on their own with the problems resulting from the crime, it was clear that over 30% of them had not, in fact, managed to overcome the situation alone.

The victims expressed a need to talk about their victimization, whether with acquaintances, personal friends, or with representatives of social services. Some of the victims even found being interviewed for this study helpful. It can therefore be assumed that the communication experiences by the victim within his or her immediate social circle was not always satisfying. Victim services should therefore focus on providing assistance not only to the injured parties themselves, but also to their close friends and relatives.

Most victims expressed a desire for more competent advice. Here is where government institutions must play a role in providing consulting services by professionals such as social workers, psychologists, and lawyers.

Victims often feel patronized by representatives of the various authorities or felt that they are treated as routine cases. This tends to incite feelings of helplessness, weakness, and of being at someone else's mercy.

Many of the injured persons did not wish to receive unsolicited help from victim services. The study demonstrates that victims of criminal acts usually choose to decide for themselves whether they need support, what kind of support this should be, and which institution they should contact.

In this connection the police can provide an important service in informing victims about support programs available, as they are usually the first formal contact after victimization.

Victims rarely requested information on the further course of the criminal justice process, but this does not imply any lack of interest. Many of the respondents had no idea of what to expect from the investigation and litigation proceedings. Generally, victims were satisfied with the way they were treated by the police when they reported their victimization. A point to be added, however, is that the injured parties did not have very high expectations of the "service function" of the criminal justice system.

Future victimological research should evolve new and appropriate concepts of victim assistance primarily based on the needs of the victims themselves. Researchers should work in close cooperation with the victims, firstly, to identify victims needs through further pilot studies such as this one; secondly, to engage victims in an evaluation process to develop practical concepts for victim assistance; and thirdly, to set up model programs with constant conceptual renewal.

Victims included in this survey expressed a desire for more government support. As it is the duty of the state to guarantee the protection of its citizens, it should also pay more attention to the needs and wishes of victims and witnesses. Much could be done to establish more governmenal services and to allot more funds for private victim assistance programs.

The most urgent needs and desires of the crime victims interviewed was to overcome their victimization crisis, to be paid restitution for damages with a minimum of hassle and bureaucratic red tape, and to experience empathy from their family, friends, and acquaintances. Many victims also had the vague wish that "something be done with the criminal" in order to prevent future victimization ("he should be taught a lesson", "he shouldn't do it again", "I don't want others to have to go through what I went through"). This was an expression of a more general fear of crime and a need for "insurance" against future victimization – a need which is widely spread among the entire population.

References

Baurmann MC (1983) Sexualität, Gewalt und psychische Folgen. Eine Längsschnittuntersuchung bei Opfern sexueller Gewalt und sexueller Normverletzungen anhand von angezeigten Sexualkontakten. Wiesbaden (BKA-Forschungsreihe, vol 15)

Baurmann MC (1985) Sexualität, Gewalt und die Folgen für das Opfer. Zusammengefaßte Ergebnisse aus einer Längsschnittuntersuchung bei Opfern von angezeigten Sexualkontakten, 4th edn. Wiesbaden (Berichte des Kriminalistischen Instituts)

Baurmann MC (1986) Bundesrepublik Deutschland: Neue Initiativen gegen sexuelle Gewalt. In: Heinrichs J (ed) Vergewaltigung. Die Opfer und die Täter. Braunschweig, pp 162–196

Baurmann MC (1987a) Die offene und die heimliche Gewalt von Männern gegen Frauen, zugleich ein Aufruf gegen Männergewalt. In: Dunde SR (ed) Wenn ich nicht lieben darf, dürfen's andere auch nicht. Vom Umgang der Männer mit sich und anderen. Reinbek bei Hamburg, pp 137–145 (rororo Mann, vol 8227)

Baurmann MC (1987b) Männergewalt. Erscheinungsformen und Dimensionen von Gewalt gegen Frauen und Mädchen. Vorgänge 90, 6:50–60

Baurmann MC, Schädler W (1990) Das Opfer nach der Straftat – seine Erwartungen und Perspektiven. Eine Befragung von Betroffenen zu Opferschutz und Opferunterstützung sowie ein Bericht über vergleichbare Untersuchungen. Mit weiteren Beiträgen von

Margarete Mitscherlich sowie Rolf Guntermann und Inge Möbus. Wiesbaden (BKA-Forschungsreihe, vol 22)
Baurmann MC, Störzer HU (1981) S.O.S. Gewalt. Ein Modell zur Zusammenarbeit verschiedener Institutionen im Bereich sexueller Gewaltdelikte. In: Degler HD (ed) Vergewaltigt. Frauen berichten. Reinbek bei Hamburg, pp 39–56 (SPIEGEL-Buch, vol 13)
Baurmann MC, Plate M, Störzer HU (1988) Polizeirelevante Aspekte bei der Auseinandersetzung mit dem Gewaltbegriff. In: Bundeskriminalamt (ed) Was ist Gewalt? Auseinandersetzungen mit einem Begriff, vol 2. Wiesbaden, pp 103–152 (BKA-Forschungsreihe. Special volume)
Federal Bureau of Investigation (ed) (1989) Crime in the United States: Uniform crime reports. Washington, D.C.
Fehrmann H, Jakobs K, Junker R, Warnke C (1986) Das Mißtrauen gegen vergewaltigte Frauen. Erfahrungen von Vergewaltigungsopfern mit Polizei und Justiz. Eine Untersuchung von Polizeibeamten an der Hochschule für öffentliche Verwaltung in Bremen. Wiesbaden (BKA-Forschungsreihe. Special volume). New edition under the title: Das Mißtrauen gegen vergewaltigte Frauen. Erfahrungen von Vergewaltigungsopfern. Bremen (Kriminalistische Studien. Special volume I)
Hanak, G, Stehr J, Steinert H (1989) Ärgernisse und Lebenskatastrophen. Über den alltäglichen Umgang mit Kriminalität. Bielefeld
Innenministerium des Landes Baden-Württemberg (ed) (1987) Angst lähmt. Aufklärung hilft. Informationen für Eltern und Erzieher über Sexualstraftaten an Kindern. Frankfurt am Main
Maguire M, Corbett C (1987) The effects of crime and the work of victim support schemes. Aldershot (Great Britain), Brookfield (Vermont/USA). (Cambridge Studies in Criminology, vol 56)
Sessar K, Beurskens A, Boers K (1986) Wiedergutmachung als Konfliktregelungsparadigma? Kriminologisches Journal 18:86–104
Shapland J (1983) Victim-witness services and needs of the victim. Victimology 8, 1-2:233–237
Shapland J (1985) The criminal justice system and the victim. In: Viano E (ed) Proceedings of the Third International Institute of Victimology. Lisbon, Portugal, November 11–17, 1984. Arlington, pp 585–599 (Victimology, vol 10, nos 1–4)
Shapland J (1986) Victims and the criminal justice system. In: Fattah EA (ed) From crime policy to victim policy. Reorienting the justice system. London, pp 210–233
Shapland J, Willmore J, Duff P (1985) Victims in the criminal justice system. Aldershot (Great Britain), Brookfield (Vermont/USA). (Cambridge Studies in Criminology, vol 53)
Stehr J (1988) Konfliktverarbeitung im Alltag. Zu den Formen, Strategien und Ressourcen des informellen Konfliktmanagements. Kriminologisches Journal 20:213–227
Voß M (1989) Anzeigemotive, Verfahrenserwartungen und die Bereitschaft von Geschädigten zur informellen Konfliktregelung. Erste Ergebnisse einer Opferbefragung. Monatsschrift für Kriminologie und Strafrechtsreform 72:34–51

Part III
Urban Planning and Crime Prevention

CHAPTER 9

Architecture and Crime Prevention

E. Kube

Contents

1 Residential Planning

The quality of urban living changed dramatically in the 1960s and 1970s. These changes were mainly the result of the growth and concentration of industrial production and of public and private services. Urban residents became aware of such change through the fact that less and less of the inner city was left for their use, the quality of the city-center environment deteriorated, and the residents of heavily populated housing areas had dispersed and moved out to satellite towns.

After having lost the more affluent and upwardly mobile members of the community, city-center residential districts frequently became neglected and fell into decay, reinforcing social segregation. (This trend has been reversed in some places in recent years due to an influx of groups with alternative life-styles and young urban professionals as well as through the deliberate efforts of local authorities to revitalize city-centers.)

City residents, particularly younger people, abandoned the cities and moved to hastily built satellite towns. These areas were regarded and used by their residents as merely a place to eat and sleep. The infrastructure was poor, which made it difficult for residents to make social contacts and for children and teenagers to make creative use of their free time.

Kube/Störzer (Eds.)
Police Research in the Federal Republic of Germany

Many of the highly populated residential areas in the Federal Republic of Germany (which contain a total of at least 400000 state-subsidized apartments) face special problems. Vacant apartments, rapid turnover of tenants, social segregation and interpersonal conflicts, vandalism and burglaries, along with infrastructural weaknesses are symptoms of urban planning defects that have been increasingly noticeable since the late 1970s. For example, 15%–30% of the apartments in Osterholz-Tenever, a section of the city of Bremen, are permanently vacant. A survey revealed deficiencies in roughyl every third major housing project in the Federal Republic of Germany.[1]

The concept underlying these housing projects was that tenants should be able to live their private lives as they wished in a place where they could find refuge from everyday demands. However, this concept was not readily realized. Inadequate insulation against noise, unfriendly surroundings, unimaginative playgrounds, a shortage of part-time jobs for women, and an infrastructure ill-adapted to meet the needs and wishes of teenagers and children are typical of the shortcomings that still exist in such areas.[2] The design of this environment does not encourage the residents to define the environment as belonging to them. There are no gardens or yards for them to use and enjoy, nor is there any space or enough money for community facilities. Facilities created rather recently (indoor swimming pools, athletic grounds, etc.) are being forced to close, as fewer and fewer young families with children are moving into such developments and as the tax revenues of the cities have decreased dramatically, especially in economic crisis areas (such as steel and coal centers).

2 The Environment and Crime

The "geography of crime" often refers to what makes residents turn criminal or what makes criminals take up residence in a particular place. In the interest of crime control it is necessary to analyze the physical design of residential areas in relation to "crime topography." Crime topography is the sum total of systematic knowledge concerning structural features of areas where crimes are committed. It is not so much concerned with the offenders and residents, but more with the location and the immedite vicinity of a crime. Crime topography, however, covers not only the natural and artificial, built environment, but also social aspects.

Questions that are relevant to an investigation of the topography of crime include:

– Where are certain types of crime concentrated? In city centers, slums, redevelopment areas, residential areas? Is the built environment a criminogenic factor? If so, to what extent?

[1] Kube 1988, p 2, with further references.

[2] Jessen 1987, pp 52–65.

- What situational factors pertain to particular instances of crime? Are building design, social factors, or other factors involved? If so, to what extent?

With respect to the home and residential environment, a distinction can be made between private, semiprivate, semipublic, and public space. Semiprivate and semipublic space exists inside and outside residential buildings.[3] The semipublic space outside a residential building is accessible from public areas (in particular, the street), but is set apart as belonging to the building by means of symbolic barriers (such as the public sidewalk and entrance to the apartment building paved in a special color). The space outside a residential building is semiprivate if it is enclosed by physical boundaries (such as a fence around a block of apartments) and is generally only intended to be reached from internal semiprivate or private areas. Entrance halls, staircases, elevators, and landings may be semiprivate, semipublic, or sometimes even public, depending on the building design (e.g., the number of apartments per entrance), formal and informal access control methods (e.g., a doorman in a block of apartments or an intercom system), and the way an environment is actually used by its inhabitants and by strangers. Thus, building design as a possible means of crime prevention pertains to offenses committed in semiprivate and semipublic areas and the adjacent public space. This includes crimes committed in private areas (e.g., apartments, basements) if the perpetrator gains access from nonprivate space.[4]

A point still largely unclarified by criminologists is the extent to which building design can stimulate territorial behavior on the part of tenants and thus actually influence the intensity of informal social control. However, the screening of a building from public view by architectural design apparently can act as an incitement to crime. This point will be dealt with later on in the discussion on defensible space.

The built environment probably has a major influence on socialization, especially for children and teenagers. The home is where a child learns social skills and how to deal with interpersonal relationships. The design of living conditions has a tremendous effect on family life. If these conditions are cramped, it is likely that the child will look to the immediate outside environment for compensation.

The simple design of many new housing developments results in the radius of action of adults in residential districts being effectively confined to a few activities, the major ones being family life, shopping, housecleaning, watching TV, and sleeping. Although there is no denying that anonymity and privacy (and the weak informal social control associated with this) are sometimes appreciated, particularly by the upwardly mobile residents of a district, town planners should pay special attention to the needs of children and teenagers. The design of the immediate surroundings (e.g., play facilities) is a key factor in the socialization process of this group. Whatever the significance of sociocultural factors, urban design can generally foster interpersonal contact and encourage people to remain in their residential environment. In seeking explanations for juvenile delinquency, German criminol-

[3] See Kube 1982, pp 23–27, and Kube 1988, p 4.

[4] Newman 1975, pp 69–100.

ogists have attached great importance to the failure of socialization processes and the lack of informal social control.[5]

To date, however, there has been little progress resulting from criminological research concerning the physical environment of the home and the failure of socialization processes or concerning building design features and the incidence of crime in the Federal Republic of Germany. A study by Rolinski, financed by the *Bundeskriminalamt* (BKA), which evaluated the defensible space theory, determined that the incidence of crime is influenced neither by the building alone nor in combination with social factors.[6]

3 Residential Architecture and Crime

3.1 The Design of the Study

The question addressed in Rolinski's study, carried out in the cities of Munich and Regensburg, was whether different architectural designs in the areas investigated had different effects on the incidence of crime. "Architectural design" was defined in the form of four types of buildings:

1. Residential high-rises (with at least ten stories) that met the architectural criterion of Oscar Newman's concept of "defensible space"[7]
2. High-rises that did not have "defensible space"
3. Multi-family dwellings (with five stories at the most) with "defensible space"
4. Multi-family dwellings without "defensible space".

The concept of defensible space was defined by the structural features of visibility (of entrances to buildings, for example) and by the creation of " zones of influence" for the residents. In deciding whether a building had defensible space features or not, the study attached particular importance to the number of apartments per building entrance, the number of apartments per story, and the ability to see the building entrances from the apartment, particularly from the kitchen.

Klaus Rolinski, a lawyer and psychologist at the University of Regensburg, introduced a further factor into the study, which he called "social strata" and which he based on the formal education, profession, and income of the residents. This increased the number of comparisons to eight, i.e., four building types and a dichotomy of "social strata." Finally, a series of variables were controlled: the "interactional structure" of the building residents (in particular, the type and frequency of communicative contacts), their "satisfaction with their living situation," the "per-

[5] See Kaiser 1989, pp 89–94.

[6] Rolinski 1980. In contrast, the BKA study by Plate, Schwinges, and Weiß 1985, pp 144–146, found significant relationships between architectural factors and the incidence of crime.

[7] Newman 1975, pp 20–28.

ceived presence of the police," "the fear of being victimized," "the willingness to take defensive action," and "avoidance behavior."

Crime was measured by means of a victimization survey, in which 715 households were selected at random from the investigated areas. Based on the expected crime rate, each individual study area was to have around 80 apartments from which the adult resident who spent the most time in the apartment was to be interviewed (80 represents approximately 30%–50% of the total number of apartments in each study area).

3.2 Results

The most important finding was that "architectural design" did not exert a significant influence on the crime rate. This was true also when social strata was taken into account.

The victim survey revealed that 20–30 out of 100 families fell victim to a crime every year. Only a small portion of these offenses were directed against persons and a major portion (47%, 81 cases) represented damage to property (84% involving automobiles). The study showed that with the exception of basements, which were the location for 30% of thefts, almost no crimes were committed in semiprivate building areas such as halls and stairwells – a welcome finding which contrasts with the situation in the USA.

The main location of crimes committed against persons, which were very few, was the area surrounding the apartment building. The two cases of robbery and the one case of rape reported in the study were committed outside the building.

The fear of becoming victim of a crime was generally not pronounced among the residents. This might have to do with the fact that so many offenses involved only damage to property.

Different architectural design and social structures proved to have different influences. The interaction among residents was far more intense in multiple dwellings than in high-rises: among high-rise residents, interaction was greater in buildings with defensible space than in those without. Moreover, in Munich, a city with over a million inhabitants, the residents of high-rises were more afraid of being victimized than those living in multiple dwellings. This suggests that architectural design (including defensible space) plays an important role in fear. Another relevant factor, which Newman increasingly stresses, is "community of interest," in which the tenants share similar interests, professions, family stiuations (e.g., children of the same age).[8] In high-rises in Munich and Regensburg this community of interest had an effect on the feeling of community identity of the residents and on the intensity of the informal social control.

The study showed that residents living with a lack of defensible space tended to be more likely to take defensive action (and, in particular, to install security devices). This willingness to take action tended to be higher in areas with low

[8] Newman 1980.

social strata. However, in such areas the fear of being victim of a criminal act was much stronger than in areas with higher social classes. Thus, the willingness to take defensive action may have been influenced by fear of victimization. On the other hand, no connection between so-called avoidance behavior (evading dangerous situations) and building design could be determined. Again, this behavior was much more pronounced among lower social classes.

3.3 Discussion

Rolinski placed the results of this study into the broader context of an "architecture suited for socialization:" the architecture of the residential building being important for the social and self-confident behavior of the residents. Residential areas (and even the individual apartments) in many cases are not designed with the needs of the residents in mind. Putting too many units in a building can delay and disturb the intellectual developments of small children and can affect their performance in school.

Given the danger of impeding the socialization process, apartments, buildings, and the areas surrounding them should be conceived in such a way that the residents are given a broad field to "shape" their built environment as they see fit. Rolinski feels that residents should ideally be put in a position where they can adapt the use of their environment to whatever needs they may have at a given time.

Nonetheless "crime-deterring architecture," according to Rolinski, should not extend beyond conventional target hardening. Given the crime situation in the Federal Republic of Germany today, he feels that the disadvantages of heavily promoting architectural solutions to the neglect of social elements (with attendant dangers of increasing isolation among the residents) would outnumber the relatively few advantages of such a concept.

4 Urban Design as a Means of Crime Prevention

What is becoming increasingly clear in the Federal Republic of Germany is that refurbishing programs for large housing schemes built in the 1960s and 1970s and redevelopment plans for residential areas within cities should be part of a plan to enhance urban life. Refurbishing strategies for large-scale residential projects are mainly designed to increase their acceptability and attractiveness. A variety of methods are employed, ranging from simple improvements of the surroundings, more tenant-oriented marketing strategies (e.g., geared to people living alone or sharing apartments), repairs of buildings and adjacent areas, decentralization of maintenance functions, better repair services, retroactive rent subsidies, and admission of tenants from income groups above the legal ceiling. Obviously, the expense involved in such projects is overwhelming.

Traffic controls are a central aspect of improving living conditions in downtown residential areas. These are often just as important as housing modernization programs and the increased provision of multifunctional open space in housing estates. Besides reducing noise and air pollution levels, restricting traffic also restores the social function of the street. The concept of the street as simply a thoroughfare for motor vehicles has been held partly responsible for the growing indifference of residents toward the condition and development of their district, the breakdown of social contact in the neighborhood and between generations, and the diminishing level of identification and solidarity with the community. Reducing traffic in residential areas frequently fosters an interest in investing and modernizing. Local retailers benefit. Benches, small shops, and market stands along the street create opportunities for communication. The *Woonerf* project in the Netherlands is an acknowledged trendsetter in this respect.[9]

In addition to local government-financed housing and urban improvement schemes in high density developments or residential areas on busy streets, a wide range of initiatives has been undertaken mainly by building companies or socially comitted architects and social workers.[10] One example is provided by the work of a group of architects in Hamburg-Kirchdorf-Süd, whose slogan is "Women for replanning." The concept reaches from conventional improvements of urban surroundings to motivating residents to run their own maintenance and caretaking services. These approaches often bear a resemblance to the self-help concepts found in connection with the restoration of prewar property, such as providing young unskilled people with training and wages. This is the basis for the concept underlying the *Grohner Düne* housing project in Bremen. Huge building projects often stand in the way of extensive urban environmental improvement by requiring alternations on a scale not feasible for self-help groups.

In the Federal Republic of Germany the initiators of urban environmental improvement – whether public authorities or building companies – seldom see any relation between these improvements on the one hand, and crime prevention and residents' sense of security on the other. Crime prevention is usually only discussed theroretically in connection with town planning and urban environmental design[11], but no communal crime prevention policy has been proposed which could integrate environmental planning recommendations.

5 Fear of Crime

5.1 Fear of Crime and Its Relation to Environmental Design

Fear of crime is often greater than the actual crime risk would suggest. To what degree one is contingent upon the other remains largely unknown. Empirical studies have yet to establish whether violence "imported" by the media, for example, has an impact on the public's sense of security or whether such crime is often subjectively

[9] Monheim 1985, pp 5–20.

[10] See Jessen 1987, p 59.

[11] Flade, for example, 1986, pp 46–55.

assigned the status of mere fantasy. It is the direct fear of victimization in the everyday environment that would normally be expected to have a true relation to the local crime rate.

Research conducted by Schwind et al. and initiated and financed by the Research and Training Institute of the BKA has demonstrated just how complex the feeling of insecurity linked to local conditions can be, particularly with regard to ecological variables.[12] For example, persons who frequently pass through "localities conducive to crime" have a greater fear of becoming the victim of an offense. On the other hand, an awareness of police presence has been shown to have an impact on the subjective sense of security. Persons who felt that the street lighting in the neighborhood was "far too poor" were the same ones who resorted more often to protective measures and were more prone to believing that they would become victims of crime. Several empirical studies have demonstrated that fear exists chiefly with regard to strangers; indeed, this is a constant behavioral stereotype. Special fear is aroused in neighborhoods in which youths and drunkards often "hang around."[13]

5.2 The Physical Environment and Measures to Reduce the Fear of Crime

It is virtually impossible to determine the level of fear that is "functional," that is, the degree of fear which represents the best compromise between exercising caution and taking adequate protective measures, without totally losing trust in the neighborhood. While it would seem that a reduction in fear is necessary in western industrialized countries, it is possible that certain social groups with a marked sense of insecurity, although they are exposed to only a slight risk (e.g., women and elderly persons), are less subject to victimization as a result of their cautious behavior, rather than simply that they are less "attractive" victims for potential offenders.

To alleviate the fear of crime would no doubt be difficult. Police apparently cannot do much, as apprehensive citizens are basically skeptical of the police and generally feel that the police are not up to doing their job.[14] Action to increase security may even backfire and increase fear, since skeptics, in particular, would tend to twist things around and conclude, "If they're making such a big issue about security, my fear must be justified."

Efforts by government authorities to reduce the fear of crime are many and varied, but their impact cannot be predicted. Such efforts include nondramatized crime reports made by the police and the public prosecutor, the supply of appropriate information on crime prevention programs through the media, social efforts in the form of community help (e.g., providing special taxi services for women), intensified police presence or police "reception centers" directly accessible from

---

[12] Schwind, Ahlborn, and Weiß 1978, pp 331ff.

[13] Kerner 1980, p 196.

[14] Kerner 1980, p 155, with further references.

the public highway, and providing citizens with services such as advice on target hardening, etc.

6 Conclusions

As interpreted in the research described in this chapter, the situational perspective on prevention is centered on the theory of defensible space. This concept means designing the immediate residential environment in such a way as to make the residents feel a sense of responsibility for it and to encourage them to exercise informal social control over it. Alice Coleman[15] from Great Britain is now one of the main proponents of this theory and has put it into effect through serving as a consultant to local authorities. However, the effectiveness of this approach in preventing crime in Great Britain is still a subject of debate.[16]

The preventive concept of defensible space – if it works at all – seems to depend on social factors being taken into account, such as the social composition of the tenants and caretaking services.[17] The residents' sense of security, however, is influenced by features such as open access zones, adequate lighting, and well-kept grounds and entrance ways.[18] Excessive fear of crime conceals numerous dangers, from self-isolation to taking the law into one's own hands. Thus, particular importance should be attached to reducing fear in designing preventive programs.

Too little attention has been paid to socialization of children and adolescents. The behavior of older children is greatly influenced by their choice of recreational activities. A person's leisure and recreation time is used to pursue his or her own needs and interests. Local facilities that can be visited at any time and nonrestricted youth clubs (with a specialized staff) are aids to the socialization of young people who do not belong to organized groups such as athletic teams. To reach teenagers who are at a high risk of getting into trouble, youth workers should not put too many demands on socially weak adolescents. Teenagers' abilities should be stimulated by educational recreational activities so that each one can develop his or her own creative talents within the given scope of opportunities. An important preventive goal of recreational facilities should be to draw young people away from commercial entertainment centers, some of which provide a certain degree of crime incentive. The risk of sliding into deviant behavior is not as great for teenagers who are active in recreation groups as for those who do not pursue any purposeful free time activities.[19]

At this point, it should be clear that only complex programs supporting improvements in the local infrastructure can have a lasting preventive effect. Such programs

---

[15] 1985. For a critical analysis see Hope 1986, pp 65–78.

[16] See, for example, Hillier 1986, pp 39–41.

[17] See also Kube 1987, pp 29–55. On the consideration of dynamic aspects, particularly of community crime career, see Bottoms and Wiles 1986, pp 101–162.

[18] Fangohr/Hermann 1987, pp 23ff.

[19] Kube 1982, pp 72–74 with further references.

are directed mainly, if not exclusively, at the residential environment. Incitement to crime should be counteracted by a broad spectrum of measures, ranging from improving living conditions to changing the structure of opportunities for crime in order to hinder potential criminals. Hamburg's program to upgrade the infrastructure of one of its districts is a good example. This program, some points of which are already being implemented, has the following aims:

- Improving recreational opportunities for children and young people by setting up playgrounds, clubhouses, athletic grounds, and workshops run by qualified staff
- Creating places for people to get together (cafés, women's centers, party centers)
- Providing various advisory services for the residents of large developments such as schools for parents, advice on further education, contacts for families of other nationalities, and financial advice from consumer associations
- Changing occupancy structures by modifying tenant stratification (abolishing the income limit stipulated in the Housing Allocation Act for new tenants)
- Improving the standard of target hardening.

Only multidimensional programs will be successful. These must specifically include crime preventive measures. Enhancing the residential environment is an important aim, but not one that can achieve lasting crime prevention on its own.

The need for local crime prevention committees that are assigned initiation and coordination functions is becoming increasingly apparent. Without such bodies, communal crime prevention policies that come anywhere close to meeting the foregoing complex requirements will not stand a chance of achieving success.

In the Federal Republic of Germany, crime prevention is regarded as the duty of the state police. Therefore, it is necessary to make clear via research projects that security and safety can only be guaranteed by joint efforts on the part of the towns, the citizens, and the police.[20]

References

Bottoms AE, Wiles P (1986) Housing tenure and residential community careers in Britain. The University of Chicago Press, Chicago

Coleman A (1985) Utopia on trial. London

Council of Europe (1987) Organization of crime prevention. Summary, draft recommendation, and explanatory memorandum containing guidelines for the organisation of crime prevention. Strasbourg, 10. August 198

Fangohr H, Hermann H (1987) Gebäudekonzeption und Kriminalität Schriftenreihe 04 „Bau- und Wohnforschung" des Bundesministers für Raumordnung, Bauwesen und Städtebau, Bonn

Flade A (1986) Prävention von Kriminalität durch Wohnumweltgestaltung. Monatsschrift für Kriminologie und Strafrechtsreform 69:46–55

Hillier B (1986) City of Alice's dreams. Architects' Journal of 9. July 1986, pp 39–41

[20] Council of Europe 1987, pp 3–41 and Kube 1987, pp 344–346.

Hope T (1986) Crime, community and environment. Journal of Environmental Psychology 6:65–78

Jessen J (1987) Zukunft der Großsiedlungen in schrumpfenden Stadtregionen. Archiv für Kommunalwissenschaften 26, I:52–65

Kaiser G (1989) Kriminologie. Eine Einführung in die Grundlagen, 8th edn. Heidelberg

Kerner HJ (1980) Kriminalitätseinschätzung und Innere Sicherheit. Eine Untersuchung über die Beurteilung der Sicherheitslage und über das Sicherheitsgefühl in der Bundesrepublik Deutschland mit vergleichenden Betrachtungen zur Situation im Ausland. BKA-Forschungsreihe, vol 11. Wiesbaden

Kube E (1982) Städtebau, Wohnungsarchitektur und Kriminalität. Prävention statt Reaktion. Kriminalistik-Wissenschaft und Praxis, vol 15. Heidelberg

Kube E (1987) Systematische Kriminalprävention. Ein strategisches Konzept mit praktischen Beispielen, 2nd ed. BKA-Forschungsreihe. Special volume. Wiesbaden

Kube E (1988) Kriminalitätsverhütung in Wohngebieten durch städtebauliche Maßnahmen. Archiv für Kriminologie 181:1–11

Monheim H (1985) Verkehrsberuhigung und Stadtverkehr Schriftenreihe 03 „Städtebauliche Forschung" des Bundesministers für Raumordnung, Bauwesen und Städtebau, Bonn

Newman O (1975) Design guidelines for creating defensible space. Washington

Newman O (1980) Community of interest. New York

Plate M, Schwinges U, Weiß R (1985) Strukturen der Kriminalität in Solingen. Eine Untersuchung zu Zusammenhängen zwischen baulichen und sozialen Merkmalen und dem Kriminalitätsaufkommen. BKA-Forschungsreihe. Special volume. Wiesbaden

Rolinski K (1980) Wohnhausarchitektur und Kriminalität. BKA-Forschungsreihe, vol 13. Wiesbaden

Schwind HD, Ahlborn W, Weiß R (1978) Empirische Kriminalgeographie. Bestandsaufnahme und Weiterführung am Beispiel von Bochum („Kriminalitätsatlas Bochum"). BKA-Forschungsreihe, vol 8. Wiesbaden

CHAPTER 10

Reflections on Crime Prevention in Areas with a Low Crime Rate

M. Plate

Contents

1 Introduction

There has been increasing discussion in the Federal Republic of Germany over the past few years concerning the relationship between urban design and crime.[1] However, empirically based knowledge about this subject is still lacking. The *Bundeskriminalamt* (BKA) therefore willingly agreed to a suggestion made by the Düsseldorf district administration to include the issue of crime prevention in a comprehensive program on urban renewal in Solingen. The objective of the project was to explore the relationship between crime and building design and infrastructure. The results were to be considered in the plans for urban redevelopment.[2]

2 Social and Building Conditions

The notion of residents exercising "informal social control" over their neighborhoods is comparatively new in connection with crime and the built environment. "Control" in this case does not refer to a formal system of surveillance, but rather to activities of the residents which indicate to the potential criminal that "this neighborhood is under surveillance." The sight of a well-kept front yard, for example, suggests to the potential burglar that the people who live there take an interest in their surroundings and that this interest probably includes a willingness to take defensive action against crime. Informal social control increases the chances of the

[1] Bundeskriminalamt 1979; Rolinski 1980; Kube 1982; Flade 1984.

[2] Published as Plate, Schwinges, and Weiß 1985.

Kube/Störzer (Eds.)
Police Research in the Federal Republic of Germany

potential offender being caught and therefore has a deterrent effect. The results of several studies conducted in the USA have demonstrated the importance of this type of "control."[3] It is assumed that the desire of residents to control their environment is dependent upon such factors as owning property and real estate, but that it is also affected by the design of the built environment.[4]

3 Data Collection and Analysis

The data were collected in Solingen in two stages: First, the police compiled data on reported crime. Second, a victim survey was conducted to analyze unreported crime. The Solingen police carried out an additional comprehensive survey of all offenses reported in 1981. Numerous characteristics of crime relevant to the study were recorded, which were then classified into those pertaining to the offense and those pertaining to the suspect. It was necessary to obtain information concerning preventable cirme and, as the urban section in Solingen was made up of very small residential units, it was possible to pinpoint the locations of crimes and the homes of offenders down to the housing blocks (blocks are geographical units which are usually enclosed on all sides either by streets or by natural or architectural boundaries).

In the summer of 1982, a victim survey was conducted (retrospectively for 1981) in cooperation with the University of Hamburg. The subjects constituted a representative sample of 1% of the resident population over 14 years of age. The offenses chosen were limited to the "classical" unreported crimes of theft and robbery, damage to property, and bodily injury.

All those interviewed, regardless of whether or not they had ever been victimized, were asked questions pertaining to their home and social environment, with specific information requested regarding their apartment, social contacts, family status, level of education, and vocational training. To guarantee confidentiality, the data were processed separately according to reported and unreported crimes. The victim survey data were analyzed at the University of Hamburg; the BKA received only aggregated data which could not be traced back to any one individual. Likewise, the data on reported offenses compiled by the police and analyzed by the BKA were made available to the university, but only in aggregated form.

4 Crime Patterns in Solingen

The crime rate in the city of Solingen is low: Of 40 cities with a population of 100 000–250 000, Solingen is the 16th largest based on population, but was 36th with respect to crime rate based on the number of offenses per 100 000 inhabitants.

[3] Newman 1972; Keim 1981.

[4] Fowler, McCalla, and Mangione 1979.

Table 1. Serious unreported thefts: survey findings projected onto the population

	Residents	Projection of unreported serious thefts
Solingen	158 000	2 816
Göttingen	134 000	7 236
Bochum	390 000	12 214

Similar results are found for particular types of crime: Of these 40 cities, Solingen ranks 31st and 28th in the frequency of robbery and burglary, respectively.[5] To give a concrete example, in 1981 there were only 81 cases of robbery and 336 cases of burglary of dwellings and cellars. Investigations in Solingen on unreported burglaries also produced lower figures in comparison with surveys conducted in Göttingen and Bochum[6] in previous years (Table 1).

As the aim of this study was to examine and analyze the distribution of crime and criminals in Solingen on the basis of small areas (112 so-called city districts and 1000 housing blocks), the small number of reported and unreported crimes constituted a severe restriction. The reason for this is that the offender and/or his residence would have been too easily identifiable.

The findings of the study pertain particularly to the spatial distribution of reported and unreported crimes. A comprehensive comparison of reported and unreported crime was performed as well as a path analysis of the connection between crime and structure data (such as income, population density, contact with neighbors, units per building, etc.).

In Solingen, crime is influenced as much by social factors and building design as it is by informal social control. According to the data obtained in the survey, informal social control is promoted through well thought-out architectural planning and construction. Less crime occurs, for example, in developments in which housing is not so dense. It could be shown that residents tend to have and maintain more contact with their neighbors when they are not living "on top of one another." Obviously, persons with higher incomes seem to prefer, that is, can afford, such types of housing.

Analysis of the spatial distribution of crime density (the number of all offenses per unit area in the city districts) showed only very slight connections between social structure variables (income, social status) and crime density, i.e., the number of all offenses per hectare of area (Fig. 1).

Income and social status negatively correlate with the incidence of crime. In other words, the crime rate is relatively high in areas where there are only a few

[5] This trend apparently continued in the subsequent years. In 1986, Solingen had the 14th highest crime rate among 39 towns with 100 000–200 000 residents based on population; according to frequency it was 26th. In terms of the frequency of break ins into houses and apartments, Solingen was 33rd and 30th, respectlively.

[6] Schwind, Ahlborn, Eger, Jany, Pudel, and Weiß 1975; Schwind, Ahlborn, and Weiß 1978.

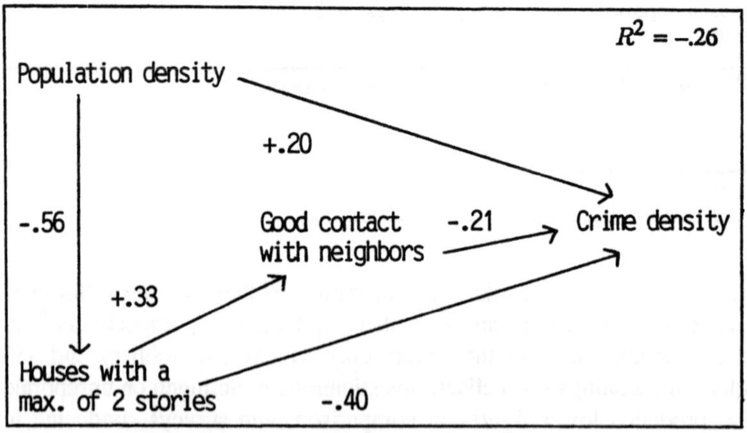

Fig. 1. Model explaining crime density

households with above-average incomes. The type of building seems to be the major influential factor (Beta = –.40): the less the number of two-storied houses, the higher the crime density. Given the close relationship between type of building and population density (Beta = –.56), the population density has an effect on the crime density, both directly and indirectly, so that it can be said that, independent of the type of building, the higher the population density, the higher the crime density. Finally, it was found that the better the contact between neighbors, the lower the crime density (Beta = –.21).

The importance of informal social control as a means of crime prevention has only recently become the subject of criminological research. Empirical findings are still lacking in the Federal Republic of Germany.

5 Measures of Crime Prevention

The low crime rate is an important factor to be considered when deciding on measures to prevent crime. The employment of personnel and material resources should always be kept in proportion to the risk of victimization. Exaggerated security measures, particularly if they are not targeted on certain groups (e.g., the elderly, women), can even increase the fear of crime. Such an effect could have disastrous consequences for a city like Solingen. In recent years, there have been numerous campaigns in the USA to reduce burglaries of private residences. Given the extremely high rate of as many as 22 burglaries per 100 homes a year, such activity is more than justified. However, it is not called for in Solingen, with its 0.46 burglaries per 100 apartments.

Car theft and thefts from cars are a major target of crime prevention. In Solingen, with a total of 75000 registered motor vehicles, there were 2715 vehicle-related offenses in 1982. This amounts to an average of 3.6 offenses per 100 motor vehicles – hardly alarming enough to warrant special preventive action.

Such examples illustrate that, for a town like Solingen, any additional large-scale crime prevention on the part of the police would appear exaggerated (unless, of course, they had a specific reason for doing so, such as a sudden rise in car break-ins in a new parking lot, for example) and would not be justifiable in terms of cost-effectiveness and the probability of victimization. The police should rather concentrate on offering advice and assistance to those requesting it and on reinforcing the individual's subjective sense of security. Such advice, however, must be qualified and should include suggestions on how to achieve effective security using very simple methods. The police have plenty of material available for this purpose. Such help must be easily accessible, such as in a conveniently located "police shop." The police should also invite persons who are fearful or who have been victimized to attend victim support meetings where they can receive help and advice. Alternatively, the police could visit such persons at home, perhaps within the scope of a burglary investigation. Another valuable service would be to reassure and advise the residents of an area where a series of burglaries has caused concern in order to reduce the resultant alarm.

Instead of taking measures to increase the intensity of control in Solingen, emphasis should be put on encouraging members of a neighborhood to identify with their community and to improve contact with one another. Efforts of this kind could directly or indirectly strengthen informal social control. Undesirable side effects of such contact, however, including curiosity, suspicion, interference, and mistrust, must be eliminated. Crime prevention must not be considered solely as a defensive measure against criminal attack – an attitude which necessarily leads to self-righteousness in dealing with crime and which prevents the residents of a community from taking responsibility for the origin and progress of a criminal career.

6 Neighborhood Service Centers

Since Solingen has a decentralized city structure, ideally the social services it offers should also be noncentral and made available in various parts of the city. Neighborhood service centers (NSCs)[7] are an example of such programs. NSCs are an institution that already exist in several towns in the USA. They are social and educational centers conveniently set up in neighborhoods at relatively little expense – usually in a local store. The centers offer services, including in-house programs, for the specific problems of the respective district. The concept underlying the NSC is that residents of problem districts have much less access to help than persons of higher social positions who can afford psychotherapeutic treatment for their personal problems and loans for their financial troubles. The NSC endeavors to offer just the amount of help requested and considered necessary, without trying

[7] For details refer to Palmer 1973, p 135.

to make radical changes in the person and his or her life-style. Help includes information on legal rights, referrals to the appropriate authorities and agencies, and individual and group psychotherapy. The NSC encourages self-organization and self-help and provides supervision of youths in danger of becoming delinquent. It acts as a mediator for conflicts within the community. The police can also be integrated into the center (as an alternative to the aforementioned "police shop"). This not only considerably improves the lack of communication between the police and social services, but more importantly, it takes crime prevention out of isolation and puts it into a more social context.

Solingen's decentralized town structure would require several such centers. A pilot project might be worth considering; for example, a certain district in the north of the city which has a high number of delinquent youths could be selected to try out such a center.

7 Conclusions

The findings show that crime prevention measures undertaken in a particular area have to be determined by the amount of crime that occurs in that region. Crime prevention according to the "watering can" principle is not only costly, its effects are also doubtful. Solingen, as a prototype of a city with a low crime rate, could serve as a site for experimenting with community-oriented crime prevention efforts.

References

Bundeskriminalamt (ed) (1979) Urban planning and crime. Papers presented at the International Symposium held at the Bundeskriminalamt, Wiesbaden, 11–13 December 1978, BKA-Forschungsreihe. Special volume

Flade A (1984) Jugendkriminalität in Neubausiedlungen. Eine empirische Untersuchung. Weinheim and Basel

Fowler FJ, McCalla ME, Mangione TW (1979) Reducing residential crime and fear. The Hartford neighborhood crime prevention program. Washington, D.C.

Keim DK (1981) Stadt und Gewalt. Problemstruktur, Fallstudien, Vorschläge. Berlin

Kube E (1982) Städtebau, Wohnungsarchitektur und Kriminalität. Prävention statt Reaktion. Kriminalistik – Wissenschaft und Praxis, vol 15. Heidelberg

Newman O (1973) Defensible space. Crime prevention through urban design. New York

Palmer S (1973) The prevention of crime. New York

Plate M, Schwinges U, Weiß R (1985) Strukturen der Kriminalität in Solingen. Eine Untersuchung zu Zusammenhängen zwischen baulichen und sozialen Merkmalen und dem Kriminalitätsaufkommen. BKA-Forschungsreihe. Special volume. Wiesbaden

Rolinski K (1980) Wohnhausarchitektur und Kriminalität. BKA-Forschungsreihe, vol 13. Wiesbaden

Schwind HD, Ahlborn W, Eger HJ, Pudel V, Weiß R (1975) Dunkelfeldforschung in Göttingen 1973/74. Eine Opferbefragung zur Aufhellung des Dunkelfeldes und zur Erforschung der Bestimmungsgründe für die Unterlassung von Strafanzeigen. BKA-Forschungsreihe, vol 2. Wiesbaden

Schwind HD, Ahlborn W, Weiß R (1978) Empirische Kriminalgeographie. Bestandsaufnahme und Weiterführung am Beispiel von Bochum („Kriminalitätsatlas Bochum"). BKA-Forschungsreihe, vol 8. Wiesbaden

Part IV
Crime-Specific Studies

CHAPTER 11

Studies on Violence

M.C. Baurmann

Behind the Wall

Last night I heard the screaming
Loud voices behind the wall
Another sleepness night for me
It won't do no good to call
The police
Always come to late
If they come at all

And when they arrive
They say they can't interfere
With domestic affairs
Between a man and his wife
And as they walk out the door
The tears well up in her eyes

Last night I heard the screaming
Then a silence that chilled my soul
I prayed that I was dreaming
When I saw the ambulance in the road

And the police said
"I'm here to keep the peace
Will the crowd disperse
I think we all could use some sleep"

Tracy Chapmann – 1988

Contents

Kube/Störzer (Eds.)
Police Research in the Federal Republic of Germany

1 Introduction

Since 1985, the Research Unit on Criminology and Criminal Investigation of the *Bundeskriminalamt* (BKA) has been engaged in a comprehensive research project on violence against persons. The entire project, entitled "Studies on Violence", is composed of five individual projects analyzing various aspects of the phenomenon of "everyday violence":

1. Analysis of the literature dealing with criminal violence
2. Trends in criminal violence
3. The severity of violent acts evaluated by the population of the Federal Republic of Germany and by the police
4. Survey of police on the major forms of violence
5. Offender-victim interaction in specific areas of violence (analysis of the escalation process).

Independent of this reasearch project, the Research Unit on Criminology and Criminal Investigation has already published other studies on criminal violence: "Violence Against the Police"[1], "Violence as Depicted by the Media"[2], "Vandalism"[3], "Sexual Violence"[4], and "The Needs of Victims of Violence After Their Victimization Has Been Reported".[5]

Before describing the research project which is being done in the BKA itself, a spotlight shall be thrown on the criminological discussion about criminal violence in the Federal Republic of Germany. Furthermore, as it might be of special interest for foreign readers to have more detailed information about the German crime rate in this field, this will also be presented.

2 Public Discussion of Criminal Violence in the Federal Republic of Germany

Although criminal violence comprises only 2.3% of the registered criminality of the Federal Republic of Germany, the general public considers violence to be the most serious form of crime and often thinks of it as a synonym for "crime" in general. Commonly read news items currently are "political violence", "violence in the family", "violence against women and children", "rowdyism", "violence in sports", "violence against property", "vandalism", and "violence as presented in the media".

In recent years, a shift in emphasis has occurred in the presentation of violent crime by the media. While national and international terrorism were once the only

---

[1] Sessar, Baumann, and Müller 1980; Schulze 1986 pp 145–150.

[2] Hefele 1980; Störzer and Hodel 1986 pp 190–209.

[3] Kube and Schuster 1985a, 1985b pp 139–161.

[4] Baurmann 1983. A summary can be found in Chap. 8, Sect. 2 of the present volume.

[5] For a first comprehensive publication, see Chap. 8, Sect. 3 of the present volume.

form of violence to draw public attention – later joined by rowdyism at public functions and violence in connection with squatting in vacant buildings – interest is now centered on:

- International terrorism
- Violence perpetrated by liberation movements
- Politically motivated violence, also in connection with demonstrations
- Group violence among adolescents
- Forcible rape[6]
- Violence in the family
- Telephone harassment
- The portrayal and glorification of violence in the media, especially in video films.

These various manifestations of violence can be grouped into three major types: (1) violence by groups and crowds within the scope of social conflicts; (2) violence, including sexual violence, among acquaintances and relatives; and (3) portrayal of violence with intent to glorify or excite (e.g., sexual stimulation) as well as so-called symbolic acts of violence.

While the first type draws the most attention in the discussion currently taking place at a social and political level in Germany in terms of frequency, the second type must be viewed as the most prevalent form of violent crime. The third type has arisen in the last few years as a product of the technical innovations in the video market.

3 The Victim's Perspective as an Additional Component in the Discussion in Violence

In dealing with crime, criminologists only began to take the victim's perspective into account in the last 30 years, when it finally became evident that the immediate needs of the victim were being neglected by the entire criminal justice establishment. Child protection organizations, women's movements, and, more recently, victim assistance movements deserve the credit for drawing attention to the need for

[6] The term "forcible rape" here is defined similar to the definition of the Uniform Crime Reports for the United States, which says: "Forcible rape, as defined in the Program, is the carnal knowledge of a female forcibly and against her will. Assaults or attempts to commit rape by force or threat of force are included; however, statutory rape (without force) and other sex offenses are excluded." (Uniform Crime Reports 1988, p 13)
The German penal code says in § 177 that only attempted or completed forcible coitus with a woman – except when the husband is the offender – is viewed as "forcible rape". Other forcible sexual intercourse is viewed as "sexual assault under duress", also with the exception if the husband is the offender (§ 178 German penal code). Sexual assault on and sexual abuse of children are procecuted under §§ 173 (incest), 174 (sexual abuse of a dependant person), and 176 (sexual abuse of children) German penal code, if it is not an offense in the sense of §§ 177 and 178. Many of the offenses registered under § 176 of the German penal code are strictly speaking not violent offenses. In about 30%–35% of these cases a grown-up exhibited his genital in front of a child.

changes in regard to assisting victims of violent crimes. Talking about the victims' needs and perspectives, however, is not readily compatible with some long-held notions of legal policy, and the controversial standpoints that have resulted will not be easily resolved unless basic changes in the system of law enforcement are undertaken.

The knowledge that can be obtained from the fields of criminology, sociology, psychology, and social work must be consolidated and used to reconsider the roles of both the victim and the witness of violent crimes.[7] It will not be easy to develop a responsible criminal policy that establishes a balance between the rightful interests of the victim and the legitimate rights of the accused.

Many of the current solutions attempting to improve the treatment of victims are far from perfect and require further modification. In the near future the legal system will most likely be confronted with new tasks in connection with both the protection of victims during legal investigations and prosecution proceedings and the improvement of assistance provided to victims and witnesses.

There are two important reasons for focusing on the victim. Firstly, many victims hope to obtain help from the police as this institution is the first official contact after they have been victimized. Secondly, law enforcement agencies are dependent on victims reporting an offense, as only few legal investigations are initiated by the police themselves.

4 Registration of Violent Crimes by the Police in the Federal Republic of Germany (West Germany)

In countless studies in the past, attempts were made to provide satisfactory definitions of the terms "aggression," "violence," and "violent crime".[8] To date, however, there has been no consensus on the proposed definitions and those commonly in use are of a more pragmatic nature. Thus, it is not surprising that lawyers, politicians, and political organizations have difficulty determining what constitutes a violent

[7] The recent efforts which have led to the first victim protection law and which will probably lead to further legislative measures are also to be understood in this context. It is striking that in the Federal Republic of Germany there have been no empirical studies on the immediate needs of victims (of violence) after they have reported the victimization to the police. (What do the victims themselves actually want?) A survey is presently being conducted in Hamburg (Sessar et al.) and a further study run by the Research Unit on Criminology and Criminal Investigation of the BKA is included in the present volume (see Chap. 8, Sect. 3).

[8] For a thorough discussion of the problems of defining "aggression" and "violence", particularly the police's definition, perception, and registration of "violent crime", see Baurmann 1985, pp IX, 1986a, pp 67, 1986c pp 131. An up to date bibliography pertaining to violence in the family was published by the *Deutsche Jugendinstitut* (Pelz-Schreyögg 1985). A bibliography of the German police literature on violent crime was published in 1985 by the *Bundeskriminalamt* (Göbel and Wallraff 1985). Several interesting reviews and articles on more recent publications on violence in the family can be found in Ostner 1987, pp 189–223.

Table 1. Reported attempted and committed violent crimes in the Federal Republic of Germany (West Germany) based on the Police Crime Statistics (PCS) for 1989

Type of offense	Number	Percentage of total violent crime
Murder, premeditated manslaughter		
Total	2415	0.82
Robbery with murder[a]	(112)[a]	(0.04)[a]
Sexual murder	(52)	(0.02)
Infanticide	(32)	(0.01)
Violent sexual assault[b]		
Forcible rape[c]	4987	1.69
Sexual assault under duress[d]	3406	1.15
Trafficking in human beings[d]	127	0.04
Robbery, armed robbery, and assault on drivers		
Total	30152	10.22
Purse snatching	(5719)	(1.94)
Premeditated assault and battery		
Total	207648	70.38
Bodily injury with fatal outcome	125	0.04
Life-threatening and severe physical injury and poisoning	64840	21.98
Abuse of wards, total[d]	1587	0.54
Child abuse[d]	(1111)	(0.38)
Mild premeditated physical injury[d]	126339	42.82
Offenses against personal liberty		
Total	62090	21.05
Deprivation of personal liberty, duress, threat[d]	60929	20.65
Kidnapping for ransom	54	0.02
Hostage taking	69	0.02
Hijacking	3	0.001
Totals	**Number**	**Percentage of total registered offenses**
Total registered offenses according to PCS[e]	4358573	
Total violent crimes	295033	6.8
Total violent crime according to PCS	(102645)	(2.4)
Total other violent crimes[c]	(192388)	(4.4)

[a] Subtotals in parentheses.
[b] No exact PCS totals are available.
[c] See footnote 6 regarding the term "forcible rape".
[d] Not a violent crime according to the PCS definition.
[e] The subtotals are percentages of total registered offenses.

act. The German police have been inclined to avoid the theoretical and political aspects of the problem. Instead, in accordance with an agreement between the federal and state police forces, they have enumerated crimes on the basis of pragmatic and phenomenological criteria to determine which acts should be classified as "violent crimes" for the police crime statistics (PCS).[9] These are listed, together with numbers registered for 1989, in Table 1 excluding those with the annotation "d". (See footnote d, p. 137).

Violent crimes which could *not* be tabulated include violent cases of incest (§173 German penal code), and of violent sexual abuse of wards (§174 German penal code), of prisoners or persons held in custody by authorities, of patients in institutions (§174a German penal code), and sexual abuse associated with misuse of an official position (§174b German penal code) as these crimes are not listed separately in the PCS as to whether they are violent or nonviolent. On the basis of previous studies[10] it now can be assessed that in an estimated 7000 cases a suspect was charged with actual or threatened sexual violence towards a child.

Besides the above listed sexual attacks, the following groups of offenses are also *not* included in Table 1 under violent acts, as they are not differentiated from other nonviolent crimes in the PCS: (1) violent resistance to authority of the state, for example, resisting arrest (< 14717 cases); (2) violent crimes committed by the police and other officials (< 3130 cases); (3) violent crimes against national security (approximately 1500 cases).

Furthermore, crimes involving explosives and radiation and serious danger caused by the release of poisons could *not* be tabulated as, in the PCS, they are grouped together with cases in which violence was not actually committed.

In 1989, 61989800 persons resided in the Federal Republic of Germany (West Germany). In 1989, the 102645 cases officially registered in the PCS resulted in a frequency rate of 166 violent crimes per 100000 residents, whereas the corrected count[11] (295033 cases, see Table 1) in reality yields a frequency rate of 476 violent crimes per 100000 residents for 1989.

In contrast to the general rise in the total crime rate (annual increase in the last few years from 1% to 3%), the number of violent crimes reported has decreased since 1982. While in 1982 there were 108024 reported cases of violent crime, in 1989 102645 (–5%) were registered. This decrease, however, seems to be related more to demographic shifts in the West German population (the percentage of youths has decreased) than to any decline in the population's propensity to violence.

[9] Enumerative definition see Bundeskriminalamt 1990, pp 7/8. Table 1 has been calculated according to Bundeskriminalamt 1990, Table appendix, Table 01, pp 1–14. Type of offenses follows the federal and state agreement on the definition of the term "violent crime" for the police crime statistics with the exception of those offenses marked with "d". Here a criminologically oriented definition of violence is used as a basis (see Kaiser 1980, p 386). That is, cases of intimidation, sexual intimidation, minor physical injury, child abuse, etc., were included. Steffen very rightly complains (1987, pp 23) that in Germany rape usually is classified as a sexual offense, although it is primarily a violent offense, and adds that in the PCS this criminological error was partly corrected in that these offenses are also listed under the category of "violent crime". It must be added here that this correction was made only half heartedly. Sexual coercion should be viewed just as much a violent offense as forcible rape (for a thorough discussion see Baurmann 1983, pp 285, 307, 484).

[10] Baurmann 1983, pp 394, especially pp 406, as well as Baurmann 1987, pp 52.

[11] Corrected by adding the violent offenses which are not so defined by the German PCS. See Table 1, offenses with annotation "d".

Many of the crimes listed under "robbery" do not represent violence against persons, since, frequently no physical contact between suspect and victim takes place, i.e., many of the cases included in the relatively large group of "purse snatching". This registration is different from the USA crime statistics, where "purse snatching" is registered under "theft". Thus, in the German PCS "robbery" does not comprise a homogeneous group of cases. A similar situation is seen in the registration of "dangerous physical injury." Consequently, these two groups of offenses in the PCS inflate the actual number of violent crimes. By contrast, the relatively frequent cases of sexual assault under duress (§ 178 German penal code) and violent cases of sexual abuse of children (§ 176 of the German penal code, particularly Sect. 3) are not tabulated as violent crimes in the German PCS.[12] Cases of sexual abuse of wards – mostly against children – also could not be designated as violent crimes in Table 1, as they are not tabulated separately in the PCS. An analysis of the offenses of sexual assault on children at the BKA indicated that just as many of them are reported to the police as those of forcible rape and sexual assault under duress directed towards women. It thus becomes clear that the restriction of violent sexual crimes to forcible rape alone in the German PCS (see Table 1) understates the degree of known sexual violence in the Federal Republic by approximately 50%.[13]

In summary, it can be said that, according to a more detailed analysis of the PCS, the attempted and completed violent acts with the highest incidence are: dangerous and severe bodily injury, robbery, and sexual violence.

5 The Design of the BKA Research Project "Studies on Violence"

The project entitled "Studies on Violence" is composed of seven parts that are related to each other in content. Some have already been completed and have appeared in publication.

5.1 Analysis of the Literature Dealing with Criminal Violence

Apart from a bibliographic analysis, a comparative view of the German and American literature is being discussed in cooperation with the National Institute of Justice in Washington, D.C.

---

[12] For more details on the number of unreported violent sexual offenses see Baurmann 1983, pp 90; 1987, pp 52, and for their registration in the PCS, see Baurmann 1983, pp 218, 496, 484; 1987c, p 53.

[13] A thorough analysis of crimes against sexual self-determination, which are initially classified according to the German penal code and later compared to a criminological classification in Baurmann 1983, pp 386, especially pp 406–408. See also Baurmann 1985, p XIV; 1987, pp 52 and Chap. 8, Sect. 2 in this volume.

A computerized documentation of the criminological literature from German speaking countries which exists in the BKA[14] was used to analyze the content of articles dealing with violence against and between persons. All of the articles, which appeared in German language journals and periodicals between 1967 and 1984, particularly in the areas of police work, law, and criminology, were classified according to subject matter and to the criminological case groups they dealt with.

Besides a relatively high proportion of theoretical or methodological articles, dealing with aggression in general (14.1%), methods of criminal investigation (5.1%), youth in connection with violence (7.5%), and with victims of violence in general (2.6%), it became apparent that a large number of the articles dealt chiefly with political violence (14.2%) and hostage-taking (4.2%); another 15.4% dealt with murder, manslaughter, and suicide.[15] Other classifications of violent offenses, which, according to the PCS (see above, Table 1), account for a major portion of total violent criminality, are rarely treated in the journals: physical injury in only 1.2%[16] and violence among close acquaintances and relatives in only 1.4% of the articles. Even articles about robbery (4.9%) and sexual violence (6.4%) are markedly underrepresented. The themes listed here add up to 78.0%. The rest consist of many different themes which are seldom revised.

When the articles on violent criminality are compared with the violent crimes grouped according to type of offenses as defined in the PCS (see Table 2), the impression is conveyed that there is a major discrepancy between the phenomenology

Table 2. Comparison between registered violent crimes in the police crime statistics (PCS) (1984) and the percentage of articles dealing with these crimes in journals specific for police work. (Only the most significant differences are listed)

Crime	Journals [%]	PCS [%]	Difference [%]
Crimes against national security with use of violence	*14.2*	1.2	13.0
Murder, manslaughter, etc.	*9.4*	2.7	6.7
Hostage-taking and hijacking	*4.5*	0.073	4.4
Kidnapping for ransom	2.7	0.07	2.6
Forcible rape and similar sexual violence	*6.4*	5.8	0.6
Physical injury	1.2	*62.6*	61.4
Robbery	4.9	*27.5*	22.6

[14] The computer-aided documentation system for literature of the Bundeskriminalamt (for details about this system see Göbel and Störzer 1989) was used.

[15] Suicide might be viewed as violence against one's own person but naturally not as a violent *crime*.

[16] It is astonishing to note how little has been written in the police literature on the numerically large group of physical injuries. A point that made a comparison between literature and phenomenology difficult was that articles on dangerous and severe physical injury could not be separated from the articles on minor physical injury. In many articles both were dealt with simultaneously. Thus, some of the 1.2% physical injury essays really do not discuss violent crime in the sense of the PCS definition.

of violence as presented in the literature and the phenomenology of violence as seen by the police.

Including the corrections regarding violent sexual offenses (see above) it can be seen that – weighed against the actual number of registered violent crimes – the offenses listed in Table 2 are either overrepresented or underrepresented in the articles published in scientific journals specific for police work (reference year 1984).

Less than half of the articles (43.3%) dealt with the crimes registered in the PCS; the rest dealt with theoretical, methodological, or political aspects of criminal violence.

This comparison not only points out discrepancies, but also demonstrates that rare but apparently spectacular acts of violence are written about much more frequently than "everyday violence". Topics such as "physical injury", "intervening in fights and acts of self-defense", "intervening in family quarrels", etc., which are prevalent in everyday police work, are scarcely treated in the literature.[17] From this it can be assumed that little research is being done into these underprepresented areas of crime and that, consequently, very few new approaches to the solution of these crimes are being published.

5.2 Trends in Criminal Violence

Statements regarding the increase or decrease in violent crime are frequently made by politicians, police, and criminologists. Such statements on the extent of violence frequently omit the fact that very little is known about the number of unreported violent crimes[18] and almost nothing about their changes in relationship to the recorded offense rate. Another factor frequently overlooked is that in evaluating the rate of violence it is necessary to view it in a historical context. Where are the time boundaries to be drawn if one is to determine whether violence has increased or decreased? What significant and thus interpretable changes has it undergone? Are the explanations of increases or decreases oriented more towards scientific analysis or towards so-called common sense? Where can one find scientific studies that incorporate historical, criminological, and statistical knowledge in order to answer this question?

Neidhardt is correct in pointing out[19] that the definition of violence has to be considered over greater historical periods and that it has experienced substantial change in the last few decades. How can violence in ancient times (e.g., slavery), in the Middle Ages (e.g., serfdom, torture, and execution rites), and in modern

---

[17] If cases with minor physical injury were included (as must have been the case in the analysis of the essays), the discrepancy would be even greater. Very few essays deal with the very large group of cases involving severe and dangerous physical injury.

[18] See also Baurmann, Plate, and Störzer 1988, p 117 and Chap. 6, this volume.

[19] Neidhardt (1986, p 125) in his sociological review on violence which he has worked out for the BKA.

times (before and after the penal code used today came into effect) be compared or how can the last 50 years in Germany (e.g., fascism, the first years after World War II, student revolts, terrorist attacks) be related to the years before and after the numerous modifications of the PCS? Criminologists have repeatedly pointed out, particularly with reference to the last few decades, that the concept of violence has become increasingly psychological, that we are increasingly dealing with a broadened definition of violence, and that the term is partly used today in an anigmatic and inconsistent way.[20] However, how can appraisals be compared that are based on such an enigmatic and politicized definition, and one so heavily influenced by professional viewpoints?[21]

Apart from these definitional problems, it must be admitted that only limited empirical data on the number of unreported violent crimes have been available up to now. For this reason the Research Unit on Criminology and Criminal Investigation of the BKA has conducted a feasibility study – the first of its kind – for a victim telephone survey.[22]

5.3 The Severity of Violent Acts Evaluated by the Population of the Federal Republic of Germany and by the Police

It was mentioned above that the definition of the term "violence" is controversial and subject to various interpretations in German criminal law. In this discussion there are basically two factions which, depending on the type of crime and on political motivation, argue either for a more restrictive or for a broader definition of the term. Put somewhat simply, one could say that the label "violent behavior" may be quite readily attached to acts for which the *opposing* political group is responsible. In such political and, accordingly, dogmatic discussions, the opinion of the general population is more or less ignored.

The Research Unit on Criminology and Criminal Investigation of the BKA commissioned an opinion poll of a representative sample of the population in the Federal Republic of Germany in 1985. The survey, which concerned the severity of a variety of violent acts, was repeated 3 years later (November 1988) to determine changes in attitude and, furthermore, to render those attitudes measurable and comparable for the future.

For rating the severity of violent acts, 27 items (brief case reports) were devised. They were to be rated by respondents according to seriousness on a scale from –7 (very serious) through 0 (neither good nor bad) up to +7 (very good). The 3000 respondents were divided into three groups of 1000 persons each, each group receiving nine case reports each describing serious acts of violence (e.g., forcible

[20] Krey who gave a juristic review for the BKA (1986 and 1988) corroborates this impressively.

[21] Neidhardt (1986) makes reference to this on pp 115 and 125.

[22] See Störzer, Chap. 6 in the present volume.

rape or attempted murder), "everyday" acts of violence (e.g., simple assault), and cases involving purely psychological harm (e.g., telephone harassment).

For the second survey, carried out in 1988, one of the groups of nine cases was repeated and, additionally, some items were changed slightly in order to be able to measure the effects on the evaluation of changes in details of the offenses. (Which factors contribute to an incident's being judged as violent?)

Subsequently, in a third stage, a group of nine cases was presented to 225 police officers (uniformed and criminal investigation police) of a representative sample of police departments from all over the Federal Republic.

The initial evaluations revealed that, in comparison to the dogmatic discussion concerning the German penal code, there is a greater sensitivity in the general population toward psychological violence. The population regards psychological force as being more serious than, for example, conflicts between the police and demonstrators, force exerted by the police against two drunks, or simple physical injury (i.e., hitting another person over the head with an umbrella). For this reason the demand that cases involving purely psychological violence be regarded as such in the sense of §250 of the German penal code (compulsion), that is, as coercive violence, seems plausible, since it is consistent with the opinion of a large part of the population.

These studies of attitudes toward violent events among the total population as well as among the police show that the latter are more tolerant of violence than the general population[23], that the common respondent judges the act more harshly when he or she can relate personally to the case described, and that the respondent's sex influences the answer in that women are more sensitive to violence and tend to advocate a broader definition of violence.[24]

Since the criminal justice system is heavily influenced by male attitudes and is composed primarily of male officials, it has to be recognized that in the opinion-forming process of our democracy female attitudes toward violence have been neglected.[25]

---

[23] Initial analyses support working hypotheses, which differ from results of an earlier American study (Toch and Schulte 1961; see Neidhardt 1986, p 117) with respect to the police tolerance of violent acts in comparison with that of the general population.

[24] The results of this survey were published in the series *Studies on Violence* in 1989 (Plate and Schneider 1989).

[25] Steffen (1986, p 143) describes, for example, the minority role held by female police officers in Bavaria by expressing that as long as women are a disappearing minority among the male-run police forces (300 out of 30 000), they will necessarily have to adapt to male modes of behavior and will hardly have a chance to assert their female ways of thinking and acting.

5.4 Survey of Police on the Major Forms of Violence

In 1986 and 1987, a total of 210 police officers from a representative sample of police departments (i.e., ten officers per department) in the entire Federal Republic of Germany were interviewed. Unlike some other surveys, this study sought to inquire about violence in small towns and rural areas as well as in large cities. (In the FRG, only 17% of the population live in large cities with more than 500 000 inhabitants.)

The surveys were undertaken in the form of open interviews covering the following areas:

1. What kind of violent events has the respondent actually dealt with himself? What events has he[26] only heard about indirectly? What percentage of his everyday work is comprised of violent incidents? Can he describe any concrete experiences?
2. What, in the opinion of the respondents, constitutes more harmless and more serious acts of violence (violence between citizens, violence committed by citizens against police officers, violence committed by police officers against citizens)? The respondents were asked to describe concrete experiences they may have had.
3. Does the respondent have any colleagues who are known for contributing to the escalation of conflicts? What conditions are responsible for such escalating behavior?
4. What areas of violence do the police deal with that do not come under the German penal code? (Examples: certain forms of child abuse, other types of family violence, suicide, reckless driving.)
5. What experiences and opinions does the respondent have with regard to traffic violence?
6. What, according to the respondent, are the most significant phenomena of violence, both currently and for the future?
7. How does the respondent view the role of the police in those political conflicts which may become violent?
8. Efficiency of police work in regard to violent crime.
9. Decision processes in solving and/or investigating violent crimes.
10. Adequacy of police training and in-service training dealing with violent crime.
11. What areas of violent crime require further research?
12. (Only for heads of departments, if interviewed)
    What violent acts or effects thereof do the heads of department actually encounter by the time they arrive at the scene of the crime? Is there some sort of selective perception of cirminal violence by the heads of departments?
13. (Only for heads of departments, if interviewed)
    How are subordinates treated after they have participated in solving violent conflicts?

[26] Only three of the respondents were female police officers. Thus, the results give no information about this minority group within the police.

The results of this survey are not yet fully analyzed, but thus far the findings support the working hypothesis that there is a considerable discrepancy between the "everyday violence" the police officer normally has to deal with – for which he would like to receive better training – and the "spectacular violence" which the media prefer to report, but which is rather rare in everyday work.

The police officers questioned considered the following areas of violence as being particularly significant in their everyday work:

- Family conflicts, conflicts in connection with jealousy, child abuse, and neighborhood disputes
- Barroom brawls
- Fights in crowds, conflicts between groups and gangs
- Violence by pimps
- Joint violent behavior against individuals, against policemen
- Telephone harassment and threats
- Violent conflicts resulting from traffic controls, identification, and arrests.

In nearly all of these areas alcohol appears to trigger or intensify the conflict.

5.5 Offender-Victim Interactions in Specific Areas of Violence (Analysis of the Escalation Process)

This part of the project has not yet been started. Based on the results obtained in the project sections described above, the decision will be made as to which topics are particularly relevant for further research, especially regarding offender-victim interactions. Efforts will be made to undertake a qualitative system analysis of the interaction between offender and victim in violent situations. Both the offender and the victim will be interviewed regarding the same case.

6 Future Trends in Criminal Violence

Discussion of the question "what is violence?", as theoretical as it may appear, nevertheless has a considerable impact on everyday police work. Neidhardt has listed consequences for further criminological and political discussion in Germany.[27]

There are social interest groups, says Neidhardt[28], which, like the judiciary and the legislature, tend to use a broader, more psychological definition of violence. Consequently, empirical studies are necessary on the apparent divergence of definitions of "violence" in the various social movements, professional groups, and in individual areas of legal practice. One can assume that, out of the present uncertainty over the definition, the police, too, have developed their own pragmatic "everyday definition." These may be in contrast to the norms held by the general

[27] Neidhardt 1986, pp 128, especially pp 137–141.

[28] 1986, p 128.

population and thus may lead to escalating conflicts between the police and private citizens, which may at first appear incomprehensible.

In the Federal Republic of Germany, social interest groups, on the one hand, and law enforcement agencies, on the other, very clearly demand – and in practice embrace – a widening definition of violence in very opposite areas. In one sense they support each other by providing a body of facts that challenges the other to analogous argumentation and conclusions. Members of both sides must be made aware of the dangers of such an escalation process.

As Neidhardt rightly points out[29], it cannot be in the interest of the police to allow the concept of violence to become too broad. This waters down the taboo, makes it easier to violate norms, and will increasingly put to question government's monopoly on force. For the everyday work of the police it is of consquence to have a precise and explicit definition of violence which is accepted by a majority of the population. A large proportion of the population is presently in favor of a more restrictive definition. That means that the police possibly could resolve relatively harmless violent offenses informally (for instance, in cooperation with other areas of social control) without being bound by the principle of legality, which is very strict in Germany.

Recently, the victim's perspective has taken on a more important role in the discussion on the concept of violence (example: "Whatever hurts mentally or physically can be defined as violence."). The police should be more responsive to the interests of injured victims, not by achieving a broader definition of violence, but by treating the victim with appropriate respect and sympathy. If victims receive such treatment by the police as well as by the entire criminal justice system the demand for a comprehensive definition of violence might become less urgent.

In connection with the broader definition of violence proposed by some social interest groups, the agencies of formal social control are being forced to justify the legitimacy of their practices.[30] The police are increasingly being subjected to public control. Rather than regarding this as burdensome or even inadmissable, however, the police should recognize that well-functioning democratic control of institutions entrusted with the exercise of the government's monopoly on force will increase its chances of being accepted by the public. Consequently, the police should be encouraged to actively participate in designing such controls.

Neidhardt[31] pointed out that one of the dangers of a very broad definition of violence is that the government might use (counter)force more frequently, and, thus, for relatively harmless events. This would almost necessarily lead to a justification and an escalation of force, on the one hand, and, on the other, might limit the amount of leeway granted to political opposition groups, which heretofore have considered themselves to be "nonviolent." Such extreme curtailment of the activities of these opposition groups could drive them underground, or could lead them to define the restrictions themselves as an exercise of force. For this reason it is

[29] 1986, p 139.
[30] Neidhardt 1986, p 139.
[31] 1986, p 140.

mandatory that the police rationally and systematically examine which violent or near-violent actions in fact require specific measures of government counterforce and then determine these measures. Furthermore, the public should be regularly informed of these considerations and direct communication between the police and potential conflict groups should be encouraged to allow each side to clarify its position. In this manner, potential controversies can be made more transparent and, thus, predictable.

In general terms, a broader definition of violence results automatically in more governmental control over the private citizen, as it allows actions and reactions of the police to pervade the private sphere of the family and immediate social environment. In contrast, the political trend today is for the government to avoid involvement in private and social problem areas. It is important that such contradictory tendencies be made known.

For many conflicts in which professional techniques of crisis intervention would be useful, means of intensifying *informal* social control should be sought, whereas the police should be as passive as possible. The police must indicate more clearly than they have up to now where the limits of police intervention lie. Furthermore, the role of the police in resolving family conflicts normally tends to be overestimated, which often leads to exaggerated expectations and an easygoing attitude towards conflicts in general ("I'll simply call the police."). Police intervention should be reserved for the extreme situation.

The results of this continuing discussion have had a considerable impact on police work in the Federal Republic of Germany. For example, one of the tasks of the police is to compile criminal statistics. Up to now it had been almost impossible to conduct a longitudinal comparison of violent crimes over a longer period of time (for instance, from the 1920s to the present) as the definition of violence has undergone several modifications in the course of the last 70 years. Before reliable assertions on the historical or political developments in crime can be made, such as "violence and brutality have increased in the general population", an operable form for recording the relevant types of crime has to be developed, such as an index of violence.

In addition to recorded crimes, it is assumed that the number of unreported violent offenses is roughly seven times higher than the number of offenses officially known. To better assess the current trends of violence, it is mandatory to carry out research on unreported crime at regular intervals.[32] Such analyses, however, can only be conducted if they are based on a precise and explicit definition of violence.

Acknowledgements. This research project is being conducted at the BKA together with Monika Plate and Hans Udo Störzer. I wish to thank both of them for their very effective cooperation. This report gives a picture of this cooperation.

---

[32] See Chap. 6, this volume.

References

Baurmann MC (1983) Sexualität, Gewalt und psychische Folgen. Eine Längsschnittuntersuchung bei Opfern sexueller Gewalt und sexueller Normverletzungen anhand von angezeigten Sexualkontakten. Wiesbaden (BKA-Forschungsreihe, vol 15)

Baurmann MC (1985) Gewalt. Aktuelle Diskussionen und Forschungsergebnisse zu gewaltsam ausgetragenen Konflikten. In: Göbel R, Wallraff F (eds) Gewalt und Kriminalität. Arbeitstagung des Bundeskriminalamtes Wiesbaden vom 17. bis 20. September 1985. Eine Zusammenstellung polizeibezogener Literatur zur Gewaltkriminalität. Wiesbaden, pp VII–XXXVIII (COD-Literatur-Reihe, vol 4)

Baurmann MC (1986a) Gewaltsam ausgetragene Konflikte, wie sie bei der Polizei bekannt werden. In: Haesler WT (ed) Viktimologie. Grüsch, pp 67–79

Baurmann MC (1986b) Konfrontation mit Gewalt im Polizeialltag. Gewaltsam ausgetragene Konflikte, wie sie bei der Polizei bekannt werden. In: Bundeskriminalamt (ed) Gewalt und Kriminalität. Arbeitstagung des Bundeskriminalamtes Wiesbaden vom 17. bis 20. September 1985. Wiesbaden, pp 131–144 (BKA-Vortragsreihe, vol 31)

Baurmann MC (1987) Männergewalt. Erscheinungsformen und Dimensionen von Gewalt gegen Frauen und Mädchen. In: Vorgänge 90, 6:50–60

Baurmann MC, Plate M, Störzer HU (1988) Polizeirelevante Aspekte bei der Auseinandersetzung mit dem Gewaltbegriff. In: Bundeskriminalamt (ed) Was ist Gwalt? Auseinandersetzungen mit einem Begriff, vol 2. Wiesbaden, pp 103–152 (BKA-Forschungsreihe. Special volume)

Bundeskriminalamt (ed) (1985) Gewalt und Kriminalität. Arbeitstagung des Bundeskriminalamtes Wiesbaden vom 17.–20. September 1985. Wiesbaden (BKA-Vortragsreihe, vol 31)

Bundeskriminalamt (ed) (1988) Was ist Gewalt? Auseinandersetzung mit einem Begriff, vol 2. Wiesbaden (BKA-Forschungsreihe. Special volume)

Bundeskriminalamt (ed) (1990) Polizeiliche Kriminalstatistik 1989. Wiesbaden

Federal Bureau of Investigation (ed) (1988) Crime in the United States: Uniform crime reports 1987. Washington, D.C.

Federal Bureau of Investigation (ed) (1989) Crime in the United States: Uniform crime reports 1988. Washington, D.C.

Göbel R, Störzer HU (1987) Das „Computergestützte Dokumentationssystem für Literatur". In: IAI (ed) Rechtsinformationssysteme. Dokumentation des III. Forums Informationswissenschaft und Praxis am 5./6. Juni 1986 in Saarbrücken. München, pp 143–178 (Arbeitspapiere Rechtsinformatik no 22)

Göbel R, Wallraff F (1985) Gewalt und Kriminalität. Arbeitstagung des Bundeskriminalamtes Wiesbaden vom 17.–20. September 1985. Eine Zusammenstellung polizeibezogener Literatur zur Gewaltkriminalität. Wiesbaden (COD-Literatur-Reihe, vol 4)

Hefele B (1980) Gewalt und Kriminalität in den Massenmedien. Eine Auswahlbibliographie des internationalen Schrifttums zur Darstellung von Gewalt, Kriminalität und Polizei in Film, Fernsehen und Literatur. Mit einer Einführung von Henning Haase. Wiesbaden (BKA-Bibliographienreihe, vol 2)

Kaiser G (1980) Kriminologie. Ein Lehrbuch. Heidelberg, Karlsruhe

Krey V (1986) Zum Gewaltbegriff im Strafrecht. Part 1. In: Bundeskriminalamt (ed) Was ist Gewalt? Auseinandersetzungen mit einem Begriff, vol 1. Wiesbaden, pp 11–106 (BKA-Forschungsreihe. Special volume)

Krey V (1988) Zum Gewaltbegriff im Strafrecht. Part 2. In: Bundeskriminalamt (ed) Was ist Gewalt? Auseinandersetzungen mit einem Begriff, vol 2. Wiesbaden, pp 9–100 (BKA-Forschungsreihe. Special volume)

Kube E, Schuster L (1985a) Vandalismus. Erkenntnisstand und Bekämpfungsansätze. Wiesbaden (Berichte des Kriminalistischen Instituts). 1st edn 1983; 3rd edn 1985

Kube E, Schuster L (1985b) Le vandalisme en milieu urbain. Importance, portée et contexte du phénomène; mesures possibles de prévention. In: Revue internationale de criminologie et de police technique 38:139–161

Merten D (1986) Zur Vielschichtigkeit des Gewaltbegriffes. In: Bundeskriminalamt (ed) Gewalt und Kriminalität. Arbeitstagung des Bundeskriminalamtes vom 17.–20. September 1985. Wiesbaden, pp 22–32 (BKA-Vortragsreihe, vol 31)

Neidhardt F (1986) Gewalt – Soziale Bedeutungen und sozialwissenschaftliche Bestimmungen des Begriffs. In: Bundeskriminalamt (ed) Was ist Gewalt? Auseinandersetzungen mit einem Begriff, vol 1. Wiesbaden, pp 109–147 (BKA-Forschungsreihe. Special volume)

Ostner I (ed) (1987) Frauen. Soziologie der Geschlechterverhältnisse. München (Soziologische Revue. Special issue 2)

Pelz-Schreyögg H (1985) Gewalt in Familien. Übersicht über deutsch- und englischsprachige sozialwissenschaftliche Literatur 1975–1983/84. München (DJI-Materialien)

Plate M, Schneider H (1989) Schwereeinschätzung von Gewalthandlungen. Ergebnisse zweier repräsentativer Bevölkerungsbefragungen. Wiesbaden (BKA-Forschungsreihe. Special volume)

Schulze O (1986) Konfrontation mit Gewalt im Polizeialltag. In: Bundeskriminalamt (ed) Gewalt und Kriminalität. Arbeitstagung des Bundeskriminalamtes vom 17.–20. September 1985. Wiesbaden, pp 145–150 (BKA-Vortragsreihe, vol 31)

Sessar K, Baumann U, Müller J (1980) Polizeibeamte als Opfer vorsätzlicher Tötung – Eine Studie zur Eigensicherung. Wiesbaden (BKA-Forschungsreihe, vol 12)

Steffen W (1987) Gewalt von Männern gegenüber Frauen: Befunde und Vorschläge zum polizeilichen Umgang mit weiblichen Opfern von Gewalttaten. München

Störzer HU, Hodel B (1986) Gewaltdarstellungen im Videobereich. In: Bundeskriminalamt (ed) Gewalt und Kriminalität. Arbeitstagung des Bundeskriminalamtes Wiesbaden vom 17.–20. September 1985. Wiesbaden, pp 190–209 (BKA-Vortragsreihe, vol 31)

Toch HT, Schulte R (1961) Readiness to perceive violence as a result of police training. In: British Journal of Psychology 52:389–393

CHAPTER 12

Perspectives on Drug Users

A. Kreuzer, R. Römer-Klees, and K.-H. Dufner

Contents

1 Introduction

The Federal Republic of Germany can be considered as the gateway for the narcotic trade due to its central location in Western Europe. The amount of narcotics seized in the last few years has reached alarming levels.[1] The *Bundeskriminalamt* (BKA) has initiated several research projects dealing with drug-related crime.[2] Their findings should be used to develop more effective policies to combat drug crime.

The studies focused on obtaining an understanding of the behavior of drug users. This could be best achieved by directly approaching drug consumers in the form of interviews. There have been very few investigations, even in the international

[1] See Bundeskriminalamt 1987, pp 3–5.

[2] Apart from the studies described in this chapter, see the two research projects commissioned to the Max Planck Institute for Foreign and International Criminal Law, Freiburg i.Br., "Drug laws in Western Europe" (see Meyer 1987) and "skimming of profits in drug-related crimes" (see Meyer, Dessecker, and Smettan 1989).

Kube/Störzer (Eds.)
Police Research in the Federal Republic of Germany

literature, which include qualitative interviews with drug addicts.[3] In this chapter, BKA projects are described, in which such surveys are undertaken.

2 Drug Dependence and Control[4]

2.1 Aim of the Study

This study was carried out by Arthur Kreuzer and colleagues at the University of Giessen in 1979–1980. The objective of the study was to provide an assessment of the situation concerning drug abuse, drug dependence, and police drug control measures in the Federal Republic of Germany. Emphasis was placed on the use of heroin.

The study was largely based on in-depth interviews with users from selected regions in the Federal Republic of Germany. In addition, a participant observation study of the investigation work done by the police narcotics agencies was undertaken together with interviews with police experts.

2.2 Life History Interviews with Users

2.2.1 Method

Life history interviews with a total of 77 "hard" drug users were conducted between the early summer of 1978 and the summer of 1979. Of the 57 male and 20 female subjects, 20 men and 6 women were from West Berlin; the others were from the Rhein-Main area between Giessen, Hanau, Darmstadt, and Wiesbaden, with most of them being from Frankfurt. Four drug addicts from Munich were also interviewed. The sample was arbitrarily chosen, as emphasis was placed in having a qualitative overview instead of statistical representation. The Rhein-Main area around Frankfurt and Berlin (West) were selected because these two cities are considered to be the center of the black market for heroin.

For convenience, all subjects, with the exception of two, were selected from prisons or rehabilitation facilities. An attempt was made to include as many institutions as possible that deal with the correction and treatment of drug abusers and within these facilities as many departments as possible. The selection procedure varied with each individual institution.

The average age of the subjects at the time of the interview was 24.1 years for the men and 23 years for the women. The interviews lasted an average of 3.7 h, ranging from 90 min to 15 h (standard deviation 1.8 h). The session was divided into two phases: in the first phase the respondent was instructed to relate his or her life story as freely and in as much detail as possible. In the second,

3 e.g., Bennett 1986, pp 85, 93–97.

4 See Kreuzer, Gebhardt, Maassen, and Stein-Hilbers 1981.

more structured phase the interviewer asked specific questions. Most of the addicts asked to participate in the interview were willing, although no remuneration was offered. After a "warming up" phase, which in some cases was quite long, the respondents related their stories openly and with apparent accuracy. The validity was established to a certain extent by a comparison with the person's files and by a psychological analysis of the taped interviews. Only two of the respondents refused to speak on tape; in both cases the interview was transcribed. The tape recordings were first transcribed word for word, but due to their unmanageable length were later put in summary form.

2.2.2 Results

Some 47% of the subjects came from broken homes. Another 29% were from intact but dysfunctional primary families. Some 42% seemed to have been raised by the grandparents, either without or along with parental upbringing. In 22% there was alcoholism in the family, and 23% were raised in institutions. The qualitative evaluation of the interviews did not convey the impression that there was any one family structure responsible for producing later addiction. On the contrary, the structural and familial deficiencies of the primary families were extremely varied.

There was no marked overrepresentation of lower social classes in the survey, which might have been due to the unsystematic selection of the sample. Addicts from higher social levels are possibly more articulate and are thus more willing to take part in such interviews. Of the respondents, 20% had never finished school; of the remaining 70%, 3% had attended and completed special schools, 61% *Hauptschule*, 13% *Realschule*, and 4% *Abitur* (The German school system tracks school children into three kinds of secondary schools: *Hauptschule*, *Realschule*, or *Gymnasium* for low to high achievers, respectively. *Abitur* is the final exam taken to graduate from *Gymnasium*.) Most of them had dropped out of their conventional roles during their work as apprentices; 25% of the men and 40% of the women had completed an apprenticeship. In only a very few cases were school friends and work colleagues instrumental in introducing them to the drug subculture.

Only two of the respondents were employed at the time of the interview. For the others unemployment appeared to be the result and not the cause of their drug career.

The most important drug for all of the respondents was heroin. Almost 90% had experimented with hashish or LSD before advancing to "hard" drugs; the duration and significance of the experimental phase, however, varied from person to person. In 66% heroin had always been the principle injection drug; 8% started out with *"Berliner Tinke"* (a morphine base dissolved in acetic acid, boiled, and injected), 12% with synthetic opiates, and 13% pure opium. These drugs marked the early German hard drug subculture up to the beginning of the 1970s.

Heroin users almost always start out by sniffing powdered heroin. The "sniffers" in the survey switched to the more economical method of injecting the drug after an average of 7.5 months. In most cases the first physical withdrawal signs occurred after about 6 months.

The psychological and social aspects of drug use – such as being integrated into a user group – seem to be more important than the physical effects. The actual physical dependence interacts with psychosocial processes and appears to have a much smaller role than has generally been assumed. Evidence of this is the fact that although all of the subjects had overcome physical withdrawal many times, it was their inability to psychologically "kick the habit" that was responsible for their relapses. The average daily dose of heroin – over the entire drug career including the relatively drug-free periods of imprisonment and therapy – was estimated to be about 100 mg heroin of street quality (approximately 20% purity).

In addition to the "soft" drugs (the alleged "pacemaker function" of which could not be proved), the subjects mainly took "speed," "substitute drugs" (barbiturates, Tilidin, and Methoqualone), and, to a lesser degree and in combination with heroin, cocaine. Cocaine, however, is not likely to become as popular as heroin because of its high price and short-lasting effect.

The interviews give an idea of the history of the hard drug subculture in Germany. The early period was marked by decentralized types of drug procurement – any addict could get drugs cheaply by breaking into a pharmacy, forging prescriptions, or getting hold of them under false pretenses. Later, a unified and complex (but not mafia-controlled) black market formed around the raw substance for the "Berliner Tinke" (heroin #1) and then increasingly for heroin itself. The hard drug black market differs entirely from the older soft drug black market with regard to its channels of communication, dealing practices, and profits. The heroin black market seems to have started in the west and moved to the east between 1972 and 1974. Since then it has remained essentially unchanged and its structure is the same everywhere.

The "scene" is the core of the black market. Scenes are the public markets for the retail sale of heroin and substitute drugs. Examples include the "hash meadow" in Frankfurt, the *Kurfürstendamm* underground station in Berlin, the *Münchener Freiheit* in Munich, and the *Herrengarten* in Darmstadt. Anyone can get hold of drugs at such places, as long as a few rules are observed. The dealers, go-betweens, and customers are subject to certain regulations that are defined by the market (amounts, prices, dealing practices, advertising, protection obligations). The social fabric of the scenes is very elastic and the police appear to have difficulty in penetrating it. Other public venues for drug sales are discotheques and all-night bars. The scene in West Berlin does not differ from that in West Germany.

The subjects tend to be linked to a particular scene; heroin addicts do not seem to be very mobile, except for the travel they have to do when hustling for their fix.

Many of the respondents were able to give a good description of how the drug black market is organized. Most of them had been dealers or at least go-betweens; the women had dealt in hard drugs almost as much as the men. The younger the scene, the less professionally it was organized and the easier it was for the user to gain entry. The subjects' participation in the black market changed constantly; lasting success as a dealer was rare.

Until about the end of 1976, the West German scenes were mainly supplied by imports from Holland which were organized by addicts. After this source dried up in early 1977, dealers from Southeastern Europe and Oriental countries got into the heroin trafficking business, especially in Berlin.

The interviews gave no indication of an existing covert, structurally different subculture of socially conformist heroin users. The respondents knew of very few addicts who were able to control their consumption or who had been able to achieve withdrawal on their own with any lasting success.

The interviews provided information on the sources of money needed for buying drugs. The average cost per day for a junkie is DM 50 (about $ 30; average estimate over the entire heroin career from the beginning of dependence up to and including the period of imprisonment and treatment as well as self-cure attempts). The estimated amount of more than DM 500 per day, which is often cited, is an exaggeration, except for perhaps brief periods in some junkies' careers. Sources of money to pay for drugs include legal income, such as sickpay and social security benefits, and for women, prostitution.

Drug addicts commit a variety of crimes to get money. Most are fast and simple offenses which are repeated regularly. Theft of drugs has decreased considerably since the early 1970s. About one-third of the subjects, and of these twice as many men as women, had had a history of delinquency prior to their drug career. In the other cases either the drug and delinquency careers developed simultaneously or crime was resorted to in order to get money to pay for the drugs. Sooner or later, most users of hard drugs become known to the police. The time that passes before an addict attracts the attention of the police or someone else is surprisingly long – an average of almost 4 years after the first use of drugs (usually soft drugs) and almost 2 years after the consumption of hard drugs.

As concerns police activity, the general opinion of the respondents was that the police have particular difficulties in deciding which one of the many possible suspects to take action against. Police strategy was felt to be virtually unpredictable.

The outcome of prosecution was just as unpredictable. The decision of the court seemed to be contingent upon the amount of drugs found on the defendant; there was plenty of room for negotiating skill and for luck.

The interviews also conveyed a vivid impression of the conditions in prisons and psychiatric hospitals. Although hard drug use is rare in prisons (hashish is more commonly used), a vicious, pathogenic atmosphere prevails in prisons, manifested by the conversations revolving around drugs. Any attempts at therapy in the prison met with hostility from the inmates. In the psychiatric institutions, there seems to be a noticeable difference between hospitals and between the various departments within these hospitals. The practice of admitting drug addicts to rehabilitation facilities was much less common in Berlin than in West Germany.

There seemed to be few differences between the drug subcultures in Berlin and in the Federal Republic of Germany. The Berlin drug scene, however, was fully developed much earlier than in Germany. The careers of the addicts who had used drugs before graduating to heroin on the black market and those of the younger ones who started right out with heroin seemed to have taken the same course.

Table 1. Relationship between drug and delinquency careers – distribution among the various types ($n = 77$)

Type	I	II	III	IV	V
Male	–	20 (35%)	15 (26%)	10 (18%)	12 (21%)
Female	1 (5%)	8 (40%)	8 (40%)	3 (15%)	–
Total	1 (1%)	28 (36%)	23 (30%)	13 (17%)	12 (16%)

The differences between male and female addicts, which still exist with regard to the intensity of drug dealing and other types of crime, appear to lessen as the career with hard drugs progresses. Whereas women use soft drugs far less than men, when it comes to heroin they are just as involved. However, the courts do not seem to be as hard on them as they are on their male counterparts. Significant differences also exist between offenders who had criminal records and those whose criminal activity was precipitated by their drug dependence.

For each respondent an attempt was made to determine the relationship between drug consumption and criminal activity in his or her drug and delinquency career. Kreuzer established five different types of drug and delinquency careers:

Type I is a drug career without previous delinquency and without an accompanying criminal career. There was only one respondent of this type.

Type II denotes a drug career with no previous criminal activity, but which is accompanied by a delinquency career, which in most cases is precipitated by the drug career. As can be seen from Table 1, almost the same percentage of male and female addicts are engaged in this type of career.

Type III refers to a career without previous delinquency in which the drug and delinquency careers have an interactive effect on one another. Most are persons who began using drugs so early in life as to rule out the possibility of prior criminal activity. The women in this group are those who did not begin dealing drugs until they had started using hard drugs and began to engage in crime.

Types IV and V are preceded by a delinquent career. They differ from one another only with regard to the extent of the delinquent career. Whereas in type IV the drug career contributes to expanding and intensifying the criminal activity, the type V addicts have already committed a variety of serious crimes before using drugs. The apparent absence of women in group V is striking.

3 Indirect Drug Procurement, Crime, and Resulting Delinquency of Drug Addicts

3.1 Aim of the Study

This project is also headed by Arthur Kreuzer from the University of Giessen and can be regarded as a follow-up study of the project on "Drug Addiction and Control," which was described above. The data collection phase has been completed and the initial results of the analysis are now available.

In their fight against drug-related crime, the police seem to have a considerable lack of knowledge about "indirect drug procurement crime." An important question that needs answering is what influence the (illegal) financing of drug use by the addict has on the total crime rate, in general, and on the incidence of crimes such as theft and robbery, in particular. Reliable data are also lacking with regard to offenses committed under the influence of narcotics.

The objective of the project is to obtain information about indirect drug procurement and the crimes resulting from it. The project focuses on the following topics:

- Number and types of offenses (recorded and unrecorded crimes)
- Effect on the total crime rate
- Effects of possible changes in drug use and in criminal behavior
- Effect of substitution programs (e.g., methadone)
- Amount of money needed by users of various drugs
- Major procurement patterns.

The project has been carried out in the form of a representative survey of drug addicts.

3.2 Method

There were 100 hard drug addicts, undergoing detoxification treatment, who were interviewed in depth. At the time of the interview 20% were in pretrial detention, 30% in penal custody, and 50% in psychiatric hospitals. Almost all of those asked were willing to be interviewed. With regard to the selection of the sample, it must be pointed out that, due to the requirements of data protection, it was not possible to approach those persons to question them directly; contact persons from the staff of the various institutions had to be used as mediators. Communication with these persons varied; initial difficulties, however, were usually overcome in the course of the contacts with the individual institutions so that any misunderstandings regarding the selection of the drug addicts could be resolved. Nevertheless, this procedure proved to be very time-consuming and it also made it difficult to convince the respondents that there was no exchange of information between the project workers and the contact persons from the institution staff.

It had first been planned to have an initial phase, consisting of priority, high quality, intensive interviews, and then to move over to a shorter, largely standardized form of interviews, but this proved to be impractical. In the course of the interviews, it became evident that the creation of both a sphere of trust and an interest on the part of the interviewer in the person interviewed are absolutely imperative. The degree of willingness to answer questions, especially delicate ones about the kind and extent of undetected crimes, grows in proportion to how much the interviewee feels that his overall personality is being taken into consideration and that he is being taken seriously. For this reason it was decided to waive the largely standardized form of conducting the interviews; only intensive interviews, lasting between 3 and 6 h were carried out, the result of which was that the planned number of 155 sample persons could not be realized. Only 100 interviews, but very informative ones, were conducted.

The sample persons comprised 64 men and 36 women, who were between 17 and 39 years old at the time of the interviews. The average age was 27 years. On the average, the interviewees had been in the respective institution for 3 weeks, which guaranteed that they were able to paint an up-to-date picture of the current drug scene and drug-related crime. They had an average of 8 years' use of hard drugs, in the course of which time 67% of them had experience of in-patient therapy facilities at least once. In the course of their lives, 98% of them had come into contact with the police, 94% had been before a court, which did not mean, however, that they were known as users of hard drugs. Some 80% of them had been under juvenile detention, in pretrial custody, in penal custody, or corrective detention. The trends from these figures, which at first seem very high, correspond to the results of other investigations at home and abroad into the problems of drug abuse, in which other methods of random selection were used; this makes it clear that few drug addicts will manage to go for any length of time without institutional treatment.

3.3 Results

As far as the kind of drug used is concerned, it is to be noted that in addition to heroin (the predominant drug) a multitude of other drugs are taken together with or as a substitute for heroin. The use of cocaine has increased sharply; it has developed from a jet set drug to a street level drug. According to the users questioned here, it is normally not sniffed, but injected intravenously just like heroin. The semilegal sleeping pills, painkillers, and tranquilizers (sometimes prescribed by doctors, but also commonly sold in the drug scene), which are often used in combination with alcohol and heroin (leading to unforeseeable interactions of the individual drugs) are even more significant, especially among women. "Crack" and "designer drugs" have been of no importance so far, at least in the (public) hard drug scene. In certain discotheques it may be different, as some interviews would suggest. "Speed-type" amphetamines, too, play only a subordinate role, at least in the Frankfurt area. This corresponds to the findings of the prosecuting authorities.

According to those questioned, the financial outlay for drug use amounts to an average of 250 DM (approx. $ 140) per day. It must be noted, however, that a drug addict does not use drugs every day (self-withdrawals, bad financial situation, insufficient supplies, periods in hospital, attempts at therapy, or periods in prison make this impossible). Furthermore, drug use is financed largely through dealing and procurement of drugs, that is to say, without the direct outlay of money (Table 2).

As can be seen in Table 2, only 30.8% of the financial outlay for drugs is financed by other crimes, as a rule indirect acquisitive crimes. This is in contrast to the often stated assumptions which are based mainly on information from police sources.

Table 2. Means of financing drug use in 1988 (in %)

	Men	Women	Total
Legal	21.5	17.1	20.2
Prostitution	1.7	27.7	11.2
Drug dealing	37.5	32.4	35.6
Other crimes	39.3	16.0	30.8

Does not add up to 100% because some details are missing.

The main patterns of offenses and how often these were committed last year can be seen in Table 3.

If we compare the levels of delinquency found here with police crime statistics and with the levels of delinquency determined by assessments of unreported or undetected crimes among drug addicts in the USA[5], they first seem very high, both absolutely and relatively. The interpretation of the data, however, is subject to the following restrictions:

- Crime statistics record a crime only once, regardless of the number of accomplices (some of the offenses listed were committed mostly by several accomplices, e.g., burglaries and theft of/from vehicles, among others).
- In the police statistics, attempted crimes are underrepresented, because the victim is often not aware of them or does not report them.
- The method of intensive interviews produces a higher count of delinquency than standardized questioning.
- In self-reported delinquency, petty crimes are generally overrepresented. Especially in intensive interviews, they take on a comparatively large importance, while they are hardly ever addressed in standardized interviews, for example, and in any case are hardly ever remembered or reported.
- Even with intensive interviews, it cannot be ruled out that the respondents estimate the 12 month period with varying degrees of accuracy and tend rather to exceed it.
- Finally, it cannot be ruled out that the levels of delinquency, at least as far as certain offenses are concerned (burglary, theft from vehicles, and others), are higher among the selected respondents because they are located mainly in and around Frankfurt, a high crime area.

When we compare the statistics for known and unknown crimes, it must be said that the rate of the crimes which have been solved recorded here is at most around 1%. There are wide differences between the individual offenses; the rate of solved cases ranges from 0.04% for receiving stolen goods, 0.5% for drug dealing and

[5] See Nurco, Ball, Shaffer, and Hanlon 1985; Inciardi 1986, pp 122–132; Johnson, Anderson, and Wish 1988.

Table 3. Levels of delinquency among drug addicts within the last 12 months (including attempts, complicity, and participation), according to 100 intensive interviews with intravenous drug addicts in Hessen, 1988–1989

	Men ($n = 64$)				Women ($n = 36$)		
	Rank	% Of persons	Average no. of offenses per pers.	Marked devi-ation	Average no. of offenses per pers.	% Of persons	Rank
Drug dealing and procuring	1	100	744		624	92	1
Shoplifting	2	77	234		326	67	3
Prostitution	13	9	5.5	→	386	56	2
Theft from vehicles	3	39	125	←	34	19	4
Receiving stolen goods	4	39	77		11	33	4
Other theft	7	57	25		17	53	5
Fraud involving credit cards, bank cards, loans, etc.	6	30	25		17	19	6
Burglary in houses and other building	5	58	31	←	3	19	13
Other fraud	9	48	17		16	58	7
Living on prostitution	8	14	18		0	0	18
Drug smuggling	11	34	8		5	42	10
Robbery within the drug scene	10	27	9	←	2.7	3	12
Theft from vehicles	12	31	8	←	0	0	17
Theft by decoying	16	8	1.2	→	8.8	31	9
Causing bodily harm	14	52	4.3		0.7	19	14
Prescription forgery	15	14	2.8		3	6	11
Breaking and entering pharmacies, etc.	18	11	1		0.3	8	15
Robbery outside the drug scene	17	23	1.1	←	0.1	11	16

procuring, and 1.2% for theft from vehicles, to 4.4% for burglary, 5.4% for breaking and entering pharmacies, and 15.3% for robbery outside the drug scene.

4 Planned Research Projects in the BKA: Studies on Cocain-Related Crime in the Federal Republic of Germany

4.1 Aim of the Studies

In 1986, for the first time, more cocaine than heroin was confiscated in the Federal Republic of Germany. The amount seized in 1987 was approximately 60% more than in 1986; in 1988, over 60% more drugs were confiscated than in the previous year.[6] Sophisticated organization and stable prices characterize the smuggling and trafficking of cocaine. The number of "first users" and cocaine-related fatalities is increasing. These facts make it necessary to fill the gap of knowledge regarding cocaine trafficking, smuggling, and use.

4.2 Method

Apart from an evaluation (being carried out by the BKA) of police data on first users of cocaine, which aims to provide information on drug addicts (age, sex, occupation) and their consumption of drugs (frequency, kind of drug), another user interview is being planned. Qualitative interviews with cocaine users are expected to produce information on patterns of dealing and procurement. The project was assigned to Wolfram Keup, M.D., in Munich and is expected to be completed in the spring of 1990.

References

Bennett T (1986) A decision-making approach to opioid addiction. In: Cornish DB, Clarke RV (eds) The reasoning criminal. Rational choice perspectives on offending. New York Berlin Heidelberg Tokyo, pp 83–102 (Research in Criminology)

Bundeskriminalamt (1987) Tendenz 1986: Umbruch auf der Drogenszene....? BKA-Rauschgiftkurier 1:1, 3–5

Bundeskriminalamt RG 12 (1988) Lagebericht Rauschgift 1988. Wiesbaden

Inciardi JA (1986) The war on drugs. Heroin, cocaine, crime, and public policy. Palo Alto

Johnson BD, Anderson K, Wish ED (1988) A day in the life of 105 drug addicts and abusers: Crime committed and how the money was spent. Sociology and Social Research 72:185–191

Kreuzer A, Gebhardt C, Maassen M, Stein-Hilbers M (1981) Drogenabhängigkeit und Kontrolle. Kriminologische Untersuchung über Phänomenologie des Heroinkonsums und polizeiliche Drogenkontrolle. Wiesbaden (BKA-Forschungsreihe, vol 14)

---

[6] See BKA – RG 12, 1988, p 2.

Meyer J (ed) (1987) Betäubungsmittelstrafrecht in Westeuropa. Eine rechtsvergleichende Untersuchung im Auftrag des Bundeskriminalamts – with an English comparative analysis. Freiburg i.Br. (Beiträge und Materialien aus dem Max-Planck-Institut für ausländisches und internationales Strafrecht, Freiburg i.Br., vol 5)
Meyer J, Dessecker A, Smettan JR (eds) (1989) Gewinnabschöpfung bei Betäubungsmitteldelikten. Rechtsvergleichende und kriminologische Untersuchung. Wiesbaden (BKA-Forschungsreihe. Special volume)
Nurco DN, Ball JC, Shaffer JW, Hanlon TE (1985) The criminality of narcotic addicts. The Journal of Nervous and Mental Disease 173:94–102

CHAPTER 13

Economic Crime

P. Poerting

Contents

1 Introduction

Economic crime and the means of combating it were two of the very first points on the agenda of criminological research at the *Bundeskriminalamt* (BKA). At their 1974 conference the secretaries of the interior and/or senators from each of the then 11 *Bundesländer*, in a (second) "Program for Domestic Security," called for "an interdisciplinary scientific analysis" with the goal of "conveying knowledge and information to the law enforcement agencies concerning the kinds of economic crime and its spread to be able to establish new means of combating it."[1]

[1] *Programm für Innere Sicherheit* (Program for Domestic Security) 1974, p 22.

Kube/Störzer (Eds.)
Police Research in the Federal Republic of Germany

Accordingly, the research of the BKA into economic crime is designed to cover two large areas: empirical data on the commission of economic crimes and empirically substantiated findings on the appropriateness and effectiveness of crime fighting measures. The first area comprises the perpetrator's motive behind committing the crime, the offender-victim interaction, how the crime was discovered, the amount of damage, etc. The second area includes descriptions and evaluations of the existing measures, especially those of the criminal investigation police, used to solve and prevent economic crimes.

There have been previous studies on certain types of economic crime (balance sheet manipulation, computer crime), but most of them focused on the second area mentioned above. This seems to be typical for German research into economic crime. Geis and Stotland, in a brief analysis of worldwide research into economic crime, maintained that "criminological and legal work in West Germany traditionally has placed great emphasis on *Wirtschaftskriminalität*, but the marked tendency is to concentrate on immediate practical enforcement and prosecutory issues, rather than attempting to gain a more general and theoretical understanding of the class of behavior."[2]

This applies to a great extent to the criminological work of the BKA and is an inevitable result of a stipulation contained in the BKA legislation: "To conduct research for the development of police methods of crime control."

2 The Problem of Definition[3]

A basic dilemma in the scientific and practical treatment of economic crime is one of definition. There exists neither a legal nor any other generally accepted definition. German research originally used the concept of "white collar crime" popularized by Edwin H. Sutherland in 1949. Not until later did German criminologists formulate their own definition, which concentrated on the crime rather than on the criminal.

The German literature on criminology has dealt so much with the definition problem[4] that it is almost impossible to keep track of all the new definitions of economic crime.[5] A leading criminal lawyer and criminologist aptly described the situation by saying that the way things stand now, we do not know exactly what economic crime is, but we are managing to fight it with a fair amount of success.[6]

Economic crime cannot be regarded as a homogeneous group of criminal offenses that can be defined by criteria common for all types. Economic crime is

[2] Geis and Stotland 1980, p 9ff. (underlining in original).

[3] See Poerting 1983, pp 9–18.

[4] Knecht 1971, p 400.

[5] See overview in Poerting 1983, pp 9–15.

[6] Volk 1982, p 86.

therefore more of a working title.[7] In this sense the term can be paraphrased as follows: *Economic crimes are illicit business-related acts committed with the intent of obtaining business or personal advantage.* Business-related can mean that either the offenses are committed against institutions or functions of the business world or they are committed using means derived from the business world. The intent to obtain advantage means that such illegal acts are committed either with the aim of (illegally) gaining money or property or of avoiding having to pay or lose money. Not only short-term goals, but also middle- and long-term strategies constitute this intent to illegally maximize one's gain. Thus, economic crime is not exactly the same as white collar crime, occupational crime, or corporate crime, although to a certain extent these types overlap.[8]

The question regarding the definition of economic crime is certainly not just an academic one. For practical reasons, particularly in terms of developing tactics, it is imperative that a satisfactory definition be found.[9] Since handling economic crimes requires a substantial amount of special knowledge, it became necessary to set up police units and sections under prosecuting authorities specializing in economic crime as well as divisions for matters of economic crime. The range of jurisdiction of these departments was to be established in such a way that it would include the tactical requirements associated with controlling these crimes. If the results of an investigation conducted by the specialized departments turned out to be different from the findings of nonspecialized investigations, the definition of the crime and hence whether it was categorized as economic crime or not would be partly responsible for the outcome of the investigation.

Those researching economic crime thus end up having two tasks: first, they have to adequately and precisely define and describe their own object of research; second, they have to study the definitions themselves, particularly those used by prosecutors. For this reason, the question concerning the content of the term "economic crime" has always played a role in the studies carried out by the BKA.

3 Extent and Nature of Economic Crime in the Federal Republic of Germany

It has proved difficult to determine the exact extent and nature of economic crime. An accurate scientific analysis can only be made on the basis of reported crimes. Since experts claim that most economic crimes go undetected, such analyses are obviously doomed from the start. Furthermore, there is a lack of reliable statistics on the incidence of such crimes, even for registered economic crimes. The police crime statistics (PCS) only began to single out economic crimes in 1984, and they do not include violations of tax and customs laws. The nationwide statistics on

---

[7] Berckhauer 1975, p 137. The term "economic crime" is still not found in German penal code text.

[8] See Poerting 1983, pp 15–17.

[9] See Poerting 1983, p 12 with further references.

Table 1. Economic crime recorded in the PCS: 1984–1987

	1984	1985	1986	1987
Total number of economic crimes	46805	41675	38926	38769
Frauds	30040	28174	23058	25193
Other crimes	15856	13501	15868	13576

economic crime are limited to serious crimes that were already prosecuted between 1974 and 1985. Another problem is that the statistics on court proceedings do not list economic crimes separately, so that these cannot be identified.

In the *Polizeiliche Kriminalstatistik* (PCS), published by the BKA, all crimes known to the police are registered according to:

- The nature of the crime and whether or not it was solved
- Place and time of the crime
- Age, sex, and nationality of the suspect
- Victim and damages (of the individual crimes).

Until recently, the various kinds of economic crimes could also not be identified in the PCS. In 1984, an additional identification code was introduced into the PCS which marked economic crimes, although with no further breakdown by classification. Apparently, however, it was not always easy to categorize a particular reported crime, so that the data of the subsequent 4 years (see Table 1) have to be interpreted with caution.

A large number of economic crimes can be subsumed under the heading "fraud." The PCS, however, do not adequately differentiate among these crimes. Only certain subgroups of fraud (credit fraud, § 265b German penal code, subsidy fraud, § 264 German penal code) are always categorized as economic crimes. Other forms of fraud have to be qualified in terms of whether they constitute an economic crime or not. This, however, calls for discretionary decision making, which can result in statistical errors.

A glance at the figures listed in Table 1 would lead one to believe that economic crime is on the decline. It must be assumed, however, that due to classification uncertainties, at least in the first 2 years of the PCS, certain offenses of fraud were recorded as economic crimes when in fact a closer analysis would prove that they were not. This assumption is supported by the number and percentage of the other offenses labeled as economic crimes, for these are largely offenses that definitely constitute economic crime (e.g., bankruptcy, violations of supplementary statutes relating to economic offenses), in which the possibility of error is ruled out. The percentage of these "definitely economic crimes" rose from 33.9% in 1984 to 40.8% in 1986 – an increase which almost equals that of the "not definitively" economic crimes during the same period. This suggests that a reëvaluation took place in recording those offenses of fraud that would qualify as economic crime. The information obtained by adding the remaining economic crimes to the number of credit and subvention offenses is somewhat more accurate.

Table 2. Specific economic crimes recorded in the PCS 1984–1987

	1984	1985	1986	1987
Credit fraud	1107	713	775	1326
Subsidy fraud	228	280	270	1130
Fraudulent bankruptcy	1904	2241	2411	2485
Other insolvency crimes	1431	1640	1868	1770
Violations of supplementary statutes relating to economic offenses	10947	12455	14848	14788
Profiteering	218	225	163	137
Total	15835	17554	20335	21636

Table 2 reveals a marked increase (36.6%) in these economic crimes, particularly in the areas of bankruptcy (+30.5%) and other insolvency violations of subsidiary penal laws (+23.7%), as well as violations of subsidiary commercial laws (+35.1%).

The PCS report total costs of property crime in 1986 to be 4244000000 billion DM (1985: 4.308 billion DM). Of this amount 1.447 billion DM was a result of economic crimes (1985: 1.917 billion DM). Fraudulent bankruptcy and other violations of subsidiary commercial laws amounted to 1.414 billion DM (1985: 1.182 billion DM). Some 80% of the perpetrators were men and persons older than 30 years of age.

Empirical data provided by the BKA has furnished some additional knowledge regarding the types of economic crime. According to police investigations, the most common types of economic crimes are insolvency crimes, credit fraud, illicit work, and capital investment fraud. The means and modes of perpetration are changing constantly, which supports the hypothesis that economic criminals are skilled in adapting to new economic, legal, and social conditions.

4 Kinds of Economic Crime

4.1 Balance Sheet Offenses

Bookkeeping and annual balance sheets represent an important instrument for informing partners, shareholders, creditors, and other business associates about the company's assets, debts, and earnings. The balance sheet determines the profit sharing of the owners and serves as a basis for tax assessment. Most businesses are obliged under law to keep books and to prepare a balance sheet for each fiscal year. To preserve the foregoing functions the balance sheet must be prepared in accordance with accepted bookkeeping principles. Balance sheet offenses may be defined as significant manipulations or misuse of balance sheets in violation of accepted bookkeeping principles. An offense is considered to be significant if the reader familiar with balance sheets might draw false conclusions about the company's assets and earnings. Balance sheets are used as a tool for carrying out or concealing crimes such as fraudulent bankruptcy, credit fraud, investment fraud, tax fraud, or embezzlement.

In 1973–1974, 34 cases of balance sheet offenses in the Federal Republic of Germany were studied.[10] The results of the study supplied information on the offenders, the victims, the kind of manipulation, and on the conditions that are conducive to the commission of balance sheet offenses. The study also dealt with the prosecution of these types of crimes.

4.1.1 Kinds of Balance Sheet Offenses

An analysis of the cases under study shows that, apart from falsifying figures for certain items on the balance sheet, there are two ways in which economic criminals go about manipulating balance sheets: either they falsify them without even considering the actual bookkeeping figures, or they falsify the bookkeeping figures and then "correctly" draw up the balance sheet on the basis of these fake figures.

The study showed that just about any entry in a balance sheet can be falsified. Figures on "indebtedness for goods and services" were most often manipulated, followed by "stock on hand" and "claims for goods and services." Ordinarily, such figures are sum totals of a large number of different assets and liabilities, making it very difficult to trace the manipulation.

4.1.2 Offenders

In 30 of the 34 cases examined the partners of the firm, acting as general managers, were accused of committing balance sheet offenses. In 19 of the 34 cases general managers who were not owners and thus had no financial interest in the company were found to have committed the balance sheet offenses. Other leading employees such as chief clerks and office managers were accused in only four cases. It could not be determined from the files of the cases whether or not these companies had institutionalized internal auditing sections; thus it should be assumed that such sections in fact did not exist. In the majority of cases (23 out of 34) outsiders had participated in preparing the sheets, but had not done any auditing. The investigations revealed that almost none of them was aware that the balance sheets they had prepared had subsequently been altered by the owners, managers, or others.

A total of 65 persons (58 men and 7 women) were implicated in the balance sheet offenses. In most cases (79.5%) one or two persons were involved. This could indicate that the number of persons involved in carrying out these types of crimes is kept small to reduce the risk of discovery. Age could be established for 51 of the suspects: 30 (58.8%) were more than 30 years old. The results also support the hypothesis that economic crime, and balance sheet offenses in particular, require

[10] Sieben, Matschke, and Neuhäuser 1974.

that the offender have a certain amount of knowledge of the particular business, which can only be acquired through years of training and experience. The police records showed that 36 of the 51 persons had worked almost exclusively in the specific type of business or had had substantial background knowledge of the business; only 15 had no such knowledge.

4.1.3 Victims and Damage

Four groups of victims were distinguished: the first were those associated with the company (owners, shareholders, business associates, private lenders of money); the second group comprised financial institutions that had loaned money to the company; the third group was a combination of the first two; and the fourth group of victims were those who had supplied commodities on credit to the company.

In 6 of the 34 cases the victims were from the first category; in 23 cases from the second group: in 2 cases from the third group; and in 3 cases from the fourth group. The total amount of damages resulting from all economic criminal activities was 87.5 million DM. Of this amount, 65.24 million DM were directly attributed to balance sheet crime.

4.1.4 Conditions Conducive to the Commission of Balance Sheet Offenses

The study presented several model cases typical of balance sheet offenses. These cases also illustrated conditions which act as a deterrent to the commission of balance sheet offenses. This type of offense is probably more likely to be committed:

- The fewer the number of persons in the company who are involved in preparing balance sheets and who could discover the manipulations
- The more closely such persons are connected with the company whose balance sheets are to be falsified and the less closely they are supervised
- The fewer the rights granted by law, contract, or corporate authority to those receiving balance sheets to view the data on which the balance sheets are based or to obtain data to check the accuracy of the balance sheets; or the less use these persons make of such information if given the opportunity
- The less auditing that is done and the less the interested parties make use of opportunities for verification.

4.1.5 Investigation and Prosecution

Those dealing with the investigation and prosecution of economic crime, in general, and balance sheet offenses, in particular, require special training. At the time of the study, only a small number of investigators and prosecutors had undergone such training. Since special knowledge is often lacking, it is conceivable that only a few of the cases in which balance sheet manipulations are involved will be actually recognized as such. Moreover, a lack of expert knowledge results in long investigation times, as unqualified criminal investigation police officials and prosecutors working in this area require more time than those who are adequately trained. The few investigators and prosecutors who are qualified are chronically overloaded with pending cases.

Some 24 of the cases were pending for at least 2 years; more than half of them (18) took longer than 3 years to be settled. Such delays are partly the result of the heavy work load of law enforcement authorities (in more than a third of the cases charges were not brought until after 3 years). However, the more time that passes, the more difficult it is to solve the case.

4.2 Computer Crime

Public attention for some time has focused on crime involving computers, which to a large extent is a result of the mass media exploiting single events to point out the hazards of the "computer era." Although only a few cases of computer-related crime have become publicly known, the actual number of undetected crimes is allegedly very high. For this reason, the BKA initiated a study on computer crime, which consisted of a secondary analysis of previous case studies and a critical analysis of the data on undetected crimes. The study was supplemented by an investigation of computer security.[11]

4.2.1 Extent and Nature of Reported Computer Crime

The objective of the secondary analysis of the studies on computer crime reported in the Federal Republic of Germany was to provide information on the extent and the nature of these crimes. What the term "computer crime" actually covers has not been precisely defined. However, it most frequently encompasses computer fraud, computer espionage (spying and disclosing secrets with the aid of computers, infringing a copyright, embargo violations), computer sabotage, and unauthorized use.

In the Federal Republic of Germany most empirical data on computer crime were compiled only within the scope of scientific studies. An initial study[12] covered 45 cases in the FRG for the period between 1967 and 1973. About 55% of them were cases of computer fraud. In an analysis conducted a few years later, based on prosecution files, a total of 31 cases were evaluated.[13] Computer fraud constituted the majority of the crimes (60%), followed by computer espionage (30%). A further study, based on the investigation of economic crimes, presented 38 proceedings for

[11] Poerting and Pott 1986.
[12] Von zur Mühlen 1973.
[13] Sieber 1977.

the period between 1975 and 1983.[14] Of the 15 closely analyzed cases, almost 60% were attributed to manipulations.

Since 1983, all cases of computer crime known to the police have been registered through a special criminal intelligence service and analyzed by the BKA. Statistics are available from 1980 on (Table 3). Between 10 and 20 cases are registered each year, which are largely cases of computer fraud and computer espionage. In addition, a number of investigations cover software piracy (unauthorized copying of programs for home computers) and, more recently, the misuse of cash dispensing machines.

Table 3. Computer crime reported to the police

	1980–1983		1984		1985		1986	
	n	%	*n*	%	*n*	%	*n*	%
Computer fraud	13	35.1	6	37.5	6	33.3	13	30.2
Computer espionage	20	54.1	6	37.5	8	44.5	26	60.5
Computer sabotage	2	5.4	2	12.5	4	22.2	4	9.3
Unauthorized use	2	5.4	2	12.5	–	–	–	–

Although the statistics show that there has been an increase in the number of computer-related offenses, it cannot be concluded that computer crime is generally on the rise, particularly if such factors are taken into account as the steady rise in the use of computers, the number of persons working with them, and the growing attention paid to computer-related crimes. The analysis of the registered cases showed that, although in many cases a computer had been used, the commission of the crime was not computer-specific; in other words, the manipulation of computer input in these cases is no different from conventional fraud, except that another instrument is used. Therefore, a computer-specific threat cannot be derived from these cases. The results of a parallel survey conducted by a journal for computer security confirmed that the real dangers associated with data processing are presently being seen both in the area of error and carelessness on the part of the persons using the computers and in the area of technical defects and not so much in criminal manipulation.[15]

Thus, in summary it can be said that all of the data on computer crime obtained in the Federal Republic of Germany (Table 4) reveal only a small number of related offenses. There are also certain similarities among the data with regard to the nature of computer crime.

The substantial portion of reported computer crimes fall into the categories of computer fraud and computer espionage. Where computer fraud was the predominant offense until 1984, experts say that today computer espionage is becoming

[14] Liebl 1984.

[15] KES-Sicherheitsenquête 1985.

Table 4. Computer crime case studies

Study	Von zur Mühlen	Sieber	Liebl	BKA
	1967–1973 ($n = 54$)	1963–1974 ($n = 31$)	1975–1983 ($n = 15$)	1980–1986 ($n = 114$)
Computer fraud	55.6%	61.3%	46.7%	33.3%
Computer espionage	16.7%	33.5%	26.7%	52.6%
Computer sabotage	13.0%	–	13.3%	10.5%
Unauthorized use	14.8%	3.2%	6.7%	3.5%
Miscellaneous	–	–	6.7%	–

more and more the problem. This can be seen from the figures in Table 3. These findings agree with the results obtained in other western countries.[16]

4.2.2 Unreported Computer Crime

The fact that there are so few computer crimes on record continues to provide fuel for the hefty debate on unreported computer-related crimes. Every unreported crime is accompanied by a lack of knowledge about it and hence escapes accurate measurement. Rates of 90%, 95%, or even 99%, which are given without any further explanation or justification, are certainly not a respectable basis for discussion. Factors must be found which can be considered responsible for the existence and possibly for the structure of unreported crime. Some plausible indicators include the following:

- The majority of the computer-related offenses known to date were uncovered more or less by chance or by confessions made by the perpetrator. Thus, the probability of discovery is comparatively low.
- The actual standard of computer security achieved and the prevailing philosophy of security create at least potential possibilities for computer crimes to be committed.
- Surveys and collections of data outside the sphere of prosecution reveal that only a small number of the detected computer crimes become known to the prosecuting agencies.
- The steadily increasing use of computers represents a constant growth of the potential threat.

Although these factors may suggest the existence of a considerable amount of unreported crime, they cannot be used to quantify it. They do not even provide information on the nature of these crimes. It is possible that unreported crimes are of a completely different nature than reported crimes, among other things due to the different probability of detection. In this connection it is striking, for example, that virtually no computer crimes in the banking sector have become known.

[16] OECD 1984.

On the other hand, there are also factors that lead to the number of unreported crimes being overstated:

- Frequently, an adequate distinction cannot be made between the acts of computer misuse that have already taken place and those that represent a potential danger.
- A large portion of the population has an irrational fear of techniques they do not understand, such as computers.
- Certain social and economic groups (e.g., some trade unions, the security business) have a real interest in the dangers of computer misuse being brought to light.
- Single events are generalized.
- The media often blow up individual cases into sensations.

The foregoing factors demonstrate the danger of computer misuse being systematically overestimated. Computer crime is undoubtedly a "fashionable" topic with a certain amount of "crime appeal." In such cases the gap resulting from the absence of facts tends to be filled with speculation.

4.2.3 Threats and Countermeasures

To devise effective security measures against computer crime, the potential threat must be thoroughly analyzed. Information on the potential threat can be obtained from the potential circle of offenders and from data about the endangered computer components. Most computer misuse and manipulation to date has been committed internally, that is, by employees of the victim company. However, as more and more electronic data processing (EDP) systems are linked together, the number of crimes being committed from the outside will increase.

The safe operation of an EDP system is determined by the interaction of the computer architecture, the operating systems, teleprocessing, service programs, and network strategies. A weakness of one of these components makes the entire system vulnerable. The circle of offenders and the endangered computer components can be represented in the form of a matrix ("threat matrix"). The matrix shows that offenders can gain access to only certain computer components. Highly privileged users are the only ones who have access to the central hardware components.

Security measures against computer crime must cover several areas: logical, physical, manual, management, and societal. Experience with known cases has shown that the societal and management layers of security have unavoidable weak spots. It therefore seems urgently necessary to shift the focus of security measures to the physical dimension. Such measures must be taken for various components of the system, depending on the nature of the crime. The operating system is particularly important for data safety: a defective operating system can permit a direct attack on the "naked" machine. Conversely, if the operating system is functioning properly, it will keep the entire system strong enough to ward off damages caused by any weaknesses of teleprocessing, service programs, or network components. The structure of the hardware has an effect on all of the software components.

The only way to prevent the threat to a computer system by particularly privileged user programs is to keep a tight control on the design and construction of programs using management systems. Such aids – along with strict requirements for documentation and guidelines for the design – can eliminate the dangers popularly referred to as "Trojan horses" and "virus programs." Attacks against data transmission lines such as telephones, wideband and baseband in local networks, or satellite routes are not difficult for someone who has the know-how and instrumentation necessary for carrying out the attack in the foregoing order. The only sure way to prevent computer abuse is to use new cryptographic symbols to jumble up the information. An attempt to illegally get at a storage medium will be thwarted if the magnetic tapes, drums, and disks contain the data in coded form only.

4.3 Bankruptcy-Related Crime

Apart from certain forms of fraud, crimes related to bankruptcy constitute the largest group of economic crimes registered by the police (see Tables 1 and 2) and they are increasing at a tremendous rate. Estimated costs of bankruptcy-related crime are considerable. Thus, these crimes pose a special problem for the prosecuting authorities. Unfortunately, however, there have been no empirical studies on the phenomena and extent of bankruptcy-related crime nor on the investigation and prosecution of it. At present, only overall statistics are available. The BKA therefore initiated a research project in 1987 with the purpose of systematically analyzing fraudulent bankruptcy and how it is dealt with by the law enforcement agencies. The study comprises several phases of data collection and evaluation under various methods.

The central component of the study is an analysis of the files of closed investigations of bankruptcy crime. The analysis covers approximately 800–900 investigations from the entire Federal Republic of Germany (20% in a random survey). Apart from gaining an insight into the phenomenon of bankruptcy crime, the analysis was aimed at obtaining information on investigation and prosecution procedures and on the legal and actual problems that arose. The initial statistical evaluations indicate that the 1976 reform of the German penal law on bankruptcy was not successful. One aim of the file analysis is to evaluate the existing laws regarding bankruptcy, with particular attention to their practicability or lack thereof. Another issue to be studied is to what extent the centralization and specialization of investigations in such criminal proceedings have an effect on the length of time required to conduct the investigation and its outcome. Parallel to this file analysis, the statistical data presently available will be evaluated.

In a third phase, a survey of the police departments that deal with bankruptcy offenses will be carried out. The results of the file analysis and the statistical evaluations will be supplemented by police findings with regard to criminal proceedings of fraudulent bankruptcy, as there are some factors relevant to the study that cannot be found in the files or statistics. The results of this research project are expected to be available in 1991.

5 Prevention of Economic Crime[17]

"The more thoroughly potential victims are informed about potential economic crimes, the fewer illegal opportunities there will be for potential offenders to commit these crimes."[18] This theory gave rise to two studies aimed at finding out which law enforcement agencies and which nongovernmental organizations provide potential victims with information on economic crime and how to prevent it.

Prevention is generally understood to consist of measures aimed at avoiding, deterring, preventing, and detecting crime. For purposes of the studies, it is also meant to include all measures directed toward reducing the damages resulting from such crimes.

The studies focused on the following preventive measures:

- The provision of general information on economic crime such as descriptions of typical forms of offenses and how to prevent them
- Expert advice on how an individual can protect himself against criminal economic acts; for example, information on the reliability of certain individuals or companies and on precautionary measures in clearly defined situations
- Warnings to potential victims, for instance, in a certain area where criminals are known to be operating or if suspicious advertisements have been discovered
- Reprimanding offenders for carrying out illegal practices such as placing misleading advertisements in the newspapers or conducting unfair competition.

The two empirical surveys deal with police prevention work and with nongovernmental prevention activities. They cover all forms of preventive action with particular reference to counseling potential victims. Both studies were based on questionnaires and interviews.

5.1 Police Prevention Work

A survey conducted among police officers was designed to register all of the counseling activities the police provide on fraud and economic crime. The nature and extent of the counseling work and the factors determining it were to be analyzed. These determining factors can be divided into three groups: (1) the counseling offered, (2) the demand for counseling, and (3) external influences on the counseling work.

The quality of the counseling work is dependent on the personality and ability of the policeman doing the counseling, on the one hand, and the conditions within

[17] Aprill and Poerting 1979; Sieben and Poerting 1977.
[18] Opp 1975, p 184.

the police force on the other. During the interviews, most police expressed a rather negative assessment of counseling activity, which could be seen in approximately one-third of the answers referring to fraud in general and in almost 80% of those on economic crime.

The importance of the conditions within the police force for such counseling such as personnel, training, how much time the officers have for this work, etc., is underlined by the fact that nearly all of their suggestions for improvement pertained exclusively to such aspects.

The individual asking for help, that is, the potential victim, has considerable influence on the nature and extent of the counseling. External influences on such counseling efforts include, for example, both the existing laws governing secrecy and privacy and those prohibiting the police from giving legal advice.

5.2 Nongovernmental Activities

The BKA also initiated a research project to survey the preventive measures against economic crime taken by the various self-help facilities not connected with the government. Three topics were to be dealt with: (1) What nongovernmental organizations work in combating fraud, economic crime, and violations of civil law in business? (2) What kinds of preventive measures do they use? (3) What kinds of offenses and law violations in business are such measures aimed at?

The study revealed that there are several hundred institutions all over the Federal Republic of Germany which take active measures in preventing economic delinquency. Three large groups of institutions must be differentiated:

1. "Self-administrative bodies" of business persons (e.g., the Chambers of Commerce)
2. Federations of business enterprises and consumer associations
3. Protection organizations (mostly associations designed to combat unfair practices or to help their members protect themselves against crime).

The activities of nearly every nongovernmental organization focus on the interests of particular groups of business people or consumers. Accordingly, they tend to concentrate on the kind of action they take and/or the phenomena of economic offenses they are confronted with.

With regard to the kind of preventive measures taken, it was found, that rather than preventing the criminal acts themselves, most measures are aimed at preventing the damage resulting from such crimes. In other words, action is taken after the offenses have been committed. At most, crime fighting programs are successful, if at all, in deterring offenders from repeating such crimes. Moreover, crime prevention organizations are more apt to take action as a response to a complaint about economic crime. Thus, they usually deal with individual cases rather than systematically fighting certain types of crime.

In examining the question as to what kinds of offenses these institutions deal with it was found that they consider only a small number of crimes as being relevant. As would be expected, they are mostly interested in unfair competition or certain types of fraud, while other offenses are of secondary importance. Civil law violations constitute another large portion of behavior combated by the institutions, with unfair competition being first and foremost and penal law offenses being of lesser importance. This is consistent with the statements made by the respondents regarding their cooperation partners. Police and public prosecutors were rarely mentioned. Civil law action was preferred over either administrative or penal law intervention, and taking the law into one's own hands was rejected. In particular, reprimand proved to be an effective tool.

5.3 Results of the Two Studies on Prevention

Consumers for the most part took advantage of police counseling services. Business persons rarely came to the police for advice. In contrast, companies and business persons usually referred to nongovernmental organizations for advice, whereas consumers rarely did. Despite the high number of consumer frauds, consumer protection agencies were very rarely called on.

An interesting finding was that very few persons seek advice before a business transaction is made; that is, before a potential offense can be committed. Most advice is sought after a transaction has been finalized when one of the partners has become doubtful about the other's business ethics.

There was no conclusive information as to what specific economic crimes the nongovernmental institutions deal with. Ordinarily, these organizations take action only after the offense has been committed and a complaint has been made by the victim. Their measures are directed at avoiding any further offenses and/or damages, not at preventing the original crime itself. The reason for this is that the victims usually report the offense too late, if at all, not knowing which agency could have helped them.

All of the preventive activities examined constitute ad hoc action as a reaction to the requests and complaints made by crime victims.

One of the major reasons for unsatisfactory crime prevention is that the police and other crime fighting agencies are inadequately staffed and equipped. Also, there are legal obstacles to police work, which among other things obstruct effective cooperation of state authorities and nongovernmental institutions. The results obtained in the two studies on the information provided for victims of fraud and economic crime show that victims must cooperate and take initiative. This is indicated by the fact that of all the preventive measures discussed in the interviews, counseling was the one given most attention. Counseling requires cooperation and initiative on the part of the victims. If they do not take the advice available to them, preventive action will not have a chance to succeed. Unfortunately, it often appears that people almost want to be cheated, which makes helping them extremely difficult.

References

Aprill R, Poerting P (1979) Kriminalpolizeiliche Beratung als Instrument zur Prävention der Betrugs- und Wirtschaftskriminalität. Wiesbaden (BKA-Forschungsreihe. Special volume)

Berckhauer FH (1975) Kriminologie der Wirtschaftsdelinquenz. In: Jung H (ed) Fälle zum Wahlfach Kriminologie, Jugendstrafrecht, Strafvollzug mit einer Einführung in das Studium dieser Wahlfachgruppe. München, pp 136–145 (Schriftenreihe der Juristischen Schulung, no 31)

Geis G, Stotland E (1980) Introduction. In: Geis G, Stotland E (eds) White collar crime. Theory and research. Beverly Hills, London , pp 7–13 (Sage Criminal Justice System Annuals, vol 13)

KES-Sicherheitsenquête (1986) KES. Zeitschrift für Kommunikations- und EDV-Sicherheit 2:49–54

Knecht H (1971) Instruktive Fälle von Wirtschaftskriminalität. Kriminalistik 25:400–405, 466–473

Liebl K (1984) Erscheinungsformen und beispielhafte Fälle. In: Zimmerli E, Liebl K (eds) Computermißbrauch, Computersicherheit. Ingelheim, pp 25–81

OECD (ed) (1984) Ad hoc meeting on computer-related criminality. Paris

Opp K-D (1975) Soziologie der Wirtschaftskriminalität. München

Poerting P (1983) Begriff und Besonderheiten der Wirtschaftskriminalität aus kriminalpolizeilicher Sicht. In: Poerting P (ed) Wirtschaftskriminalität, Part 1. Wiesbaden, pp 9–49 (BKA-Schriftenreihe, vol 53)

Poerting P (1985) Polizeiliche Bekämpfung von Wirtschaftskriminalität. Wiesbaden (BKA-Forschungsreihe. Special volume)

Poerting P, Pott EG (1986) Computerkriminalität – Ausmaß, Bedrohungspotential, Abwehrmöglichkeiten. Wiesbaden (Berichte des Kriminalistischen Instituts)

Programm für die Innere Sicherheit in der Bundesrepublik Deutschland (1974) Gemeinsames Ministerialblatt 25, Supplement to no 9

Sieben G, Poerting P (1977) Präventive Bekämpfung von Wirtschaftsdelikten durch Selbstverwaltungsorgane, Selbstschutzeinrichtungen und Verbände der Wirtschaftsteilnehmer. Wiesbaden (BKA-Forschungsreihe. Special volume)

Sieben G, Matschke MJ, Neuhäuser H-J (1974) Bilanzdelikte. Wiesbaden (BKA-Forschungsreihe, vol 1)

Sieber U (1977) Computerkriminalität und Strafrecht. Köln Berlin Bonn München

Volk K (1982) Strafrecht und Wirtschaftskriminalität. Kriminalpolitische Probleme und dogmatische Schwierigkeiten. Juristenzeitung 37:85–92

Von zur Mühlen RAH (1973) Computerkriminalität. Gefahren und Abwehrmaßnahmen. Neuwied Berlin

CHAPTER 14

Organized Crime in the Federal Republic of Germany

E. Rebscher and W. Vahlenkamp

Contents

1 Introduction

Within the West German police forces, there has been little agreement concerning the magnitude and the structure of organized crime. The fact that estimates of this phenomenon range from exaggeration to denial of its existence has been a source of irritation for both police and policymakers. In 1982, a committee made up of leaders of both the federal and state police worked out a definition of organized crime: Several persons working together on a regular basis for the purpose of engaging in criminal activities, frequently taking advantage of modern infrastructures, with the aim of obtaining fast, easy, and large profits. There is still some controversy over this definition. Many police practitioners feel it is too general. However, for the design of any program to combat organized crime there must be a clear understanding of what this type of criminal behavior constitutes.

In 1985, the Research and Training Institute of the *Bundeskriminalamt* (BKA) conducted an empirical study on the current state of organized crime in the Federal Republic of Germany. The goals were to determine how practitioners define organized crime, to obtain a reliable picture of organized crime, to assess its devel-

Kube/Störzer (Eds.)
Police Research in the Federal Republic of Germany

opment and growth, and to make recommendations for more intensive and effective approaches to controlling it. (The study did not consider terrorist groups because of their special political motives.)

2 Method

The data were obtained in interviews with 66 federal and state investigators who had had practical experience with organized crime investigations. The interviews were held, analyzed, and evaluated by police officials from the research group. The results of the study are based on qualitative statements. Attempts to measure the scope of organized crime failed at the very beginning stages of the inquiry.

3 Findings

3.1 Organization

There is thought to be no one structure for all areas and branches of organized crime. Two basic types are assumed to exist in the Federal Republic of Germany: (1) autonomous groups and (2) criminal networks.

An autonomous group is characterized by an internal group structure with relatively permanent membership and a rather strong hierarchy. This form is frequently found among foreign offenders. These groups either consist of residents of Germany or exert their influence from outside the country.

Criminal networks, the most common form, are made up of a variety of individuals who work together as creators of organized crime, predominantly in the metropolitan areas of the Federal Republic of Germany. In these networks temporary groups can be formed for a particular purpose. Unlike that of the autonomous groups, the structure is relatively loose and extends over a very wide area.

Both types work according to the same rules of business. Generally speaking, the Federal Republic of Germany can be seen as an area of operation in which all the regions of the country are more or less developed through personal, business, and criminally useful connections. These connection networks often transcend the boundaries of Western Europe.

3.2 Leadership and Cohesion

The autonomous groups generally have stricter leadership than the networks. In some cases the style of leadership is very authoritarian. This particularly applies to foreign groups.

Within the criminal networks, there are certain persons or teams who stand out because of their financial or logistic resources. The style of leadership can be considered loose. Only in certain groups of foreign-born criminals does the leader tend to be more authoritarian. German organized criminals have no "bosses" like those found in the Mafia.

The motto followed in German criminal circles is "money is power." Wealthy patrons and clients are almost automatically recognized as leaders, as they personify the source and driving force of organized crime. They are thus of particular interest to the police.

Cohesion in the criminal networks, with their loose structure, is based on mutual interests and mutual gains. The leaders recognize that working together would save them a great deal of expense, guarantee them more profit, and provide stronger resistance to law enforcement. Idealistic or ideological motives are rarely involved. Only members of some ethnic groups and motorcycle gangs have a strong sense of unity due to kinship and national ties.

Personal advantage is primarily what attracts persons to careers in crime on an organized scale. Each one of the participants would rather remain independent and chooses to work with partners only if it is absolutely necessary or if it promises to be more lucrative. This has a considerable effect on the stability of the cooperation. Thus it must be assumed that the cooperation between individuals fluctuates and that very often temporary groups are formed for a particular purpose. The necessity of special knowledge and skills or sophisticated logistics for this purpose can gradually turn the ad hoc group into a lasting alliance. Among German criminals the general feeling seems to be that there is no reason to get "tied down" in a group as long as the system functions well in a laissez-faire manner. Many foreign criminals living in the Federal Republic of Germany have also come to follow this line of thinking.

Nonetheless, tried and tested connections form the real basis for business. The quality of usable connections is measured according to how much and how certain the profits are.

3.3 Violence

Police estimates of the degree of violence used often do not reflect the true picture. This is because most of the law enforcement officials responsible for such estimates base their figures on experience with particular cases involving authoritarian and violent (usually foreign) leaders. However, these spectacular cases are few and far between and personal violence cannot be considered typical for organized crime in the Federal Republic of Germany.

Moreover, violence appears to have decreased since the beginning of the 1980s. This indicates that there is growing agreement and understanding among the criminals and more sophisticated organization.

A more typical characteristic of organized crime is its aim to assume a monopoly position by smothering outside competition. This is achieved by pressure and intimidation or by threats of violence. Generally, however, such conflicts are avoided, as they may draw the attention of the public and the police.

3.4 Conspiracy

The hierarchical separation of members in the networks or in the autonomous groups is not enforced as rigidly as was once thought. Most of the members of the organized crime scene in a metropolitan area know each other personally, as do the leaders from the various parts of the country. Even the police know for the most part who are the persons in key positions. This does not mean that opportunities, interesting and lucrative offers, and requests are not kept secret from outsiders and potential competitors. An indiscreet businessman runs the risk of doing himself out of the deal and out of any future ones. Many of the persons interviewed expressed it in roughly the following words: Everyone knows everyone. Everyone knows what deals are being carried out at any given time, but only a few know who is working on what deal.

Persons are often insulated for the purpose of minimizing risks in cases in which the identity of and contact with such persons are not crucial for the operation and when an unnecessary risk is avoided by eliminating personal contact. This is the case, for example, when outsiders are used to perform jobs such as smuggling drugs or transporting stolen goods.

Personal insulation practices were and are chiefly recorded in the central law enforcement agencies in the German states (apart from the three city-states). In many interviews, however, it became clear that the insulation – something the criminal had not even considered – apparently only existed in the opinion of the nonlocal investigators in central departments who often kept coming across new and unknown criminals. Apparently, "well-insulated organizers" are known to the local police agencies involved in organized crime enforcement. The sudden appearance of a leader completely unknown to the police is a rare occurrence.

The secrecy referred to above does not mark the general behavior of organized criminals. Conspiratorial activities in all feasible forms are characteristic of how such criminals deal with the police and business competitors. Otherwise, in their leisure time, for instance, the behavior is usually very open.

3.5 Illegal Business

There is no one kind of organized crime nor is organized crime restricted to certain offenses. Organized criminals tend to prefer crimes that ensure them a fast, large profit with a low risk. Low risk means that there is no victim involved (selling narcotics, fencing) or that the victim is not prepared to report the offense (unlawful gambling, certain types of economic crime). It follows that there must be an extremely high number of unreported crimes in the field of organized crime.

It is not always easy for foreign criminals to make use of German connections, particularly for the sale of illegal goods. Certain groups therefore confine themselves either to crime areas in which they are not dependent on German channels (e.g., robberies of financial institutes, racketeering), or they concentrate on businesses in which they directly control the process from the beginning to the end. The latter, however, is an exception.

Major criminal business operations are usually divided up into individual stages, which requires a division of labor. Either each member is allocated a certain task or, and this is usually the case, the division of labor is not worked out and each person or group of persons is left to discover a gap and fill it on his or their own. It is reasonable to assume that a major illegal transaction is not handled completely by one person or group, but that autonomous groups, ad hoc alliances, and individual persons cover the individual steps of the deal in continually changing roles. In this context it becomes clear that a criminological classification of criminals as lone offenders, gangs, or members of criminal associations or criminal organizations is of only secondary importance for police control of organized crime.

Legal and illegal business deals can be efficiently linked together. By running a legal business, organized criminals are able to establish fronts for their other activities, to find a way to launder illegal profits, and to secure their existence.

3.6 Investing Illegal Profits

Illegally acquired profits are usually put to economically efficient use. They are invested in real estate, either at home or abroad, or in legitimate businesses (trade, services). Often, the criminals open bank accounts or invest the money in bonds or in valuables such as jewelry or antiques. Front men are hired, a practice which is carried out primarily to enable the investment of substantial amounts of money without the tax office having access to the identity of the investor. The police are usually able to see through this practice of hiring front men but are not in the position to prove it.

The many points at which organized crime overlaps with legal business life furnish the breeding ground for organized crime. In addition, it can be safely maintained that organized crime thrives on making use of legitimate economic branches and money channels.

3.7 Expected Trends

As a result of the increasing experience of the perpetrators, on the one hand, and the rise of new legal and illegal markets, on the other, a constant increase in organized crime is expected to take place in the near future. The extent of organized crime will increase at a rate that is highly out of proportion with the general development of crime. More crucial, however, will be the qualitative changes; that is to say, organized crime will be perfected. With the increasing number of leaders, more talent and skill will come onto the scene and broaden the scope of action. Furthermore, more flexibility on the part of the criminals is predicted. New markets will be included such as the illegal disposal of refuse. Economic crime is expected to infiltrate legitimate areas of the economic and social system. Particularly with regard to influence on authorities. However, there is no long-term or short-term prediction of Mafia-type activities in the Federal Republic of Germany.

Organized crime in the Federal Republic of Germany is closely related to the economy. The danger lies in the fact that organized crime is as diverse and flexible as the nation's economy and that it can profit just as much as legitimate business from the freedoms and opportunities that are available.

It is almost impossible for the general public to assess this danger without being educated by the police and the criminal justice officials. Only experts can recognize and judge the extent and consequences of such usually victimless criminal activities: organized crime that can be detected is, in the view of the perpetrator, poorly organized crime.

3.8 Controlling Organized Crime

In the opinion of the experts questioned in the interviews, police control of organized crime can be intensified by improvements made in the areas of organization, tactics, training, the law, and development of public awareness.

To deal with the two basic forms of organized crime stated above, the control of organized crime should accordingly be divided into two groups: (1) offender-oriented, local police units that investigate *criminal networks* in the local or regional "milieu" of metropolitan areas. (2) Specialized, case-oriented, central and local police units that investigate *autonomous groups* and those temporary groups concentrating on special types of crime. The existing specialized departments for crimes frequently committed by organized criminals (such as involving drugs, counterfeit money, economic crimes, etc.) should be incorporated into this control system. By setting up special committees made up of a few, highly motivated detectives, a powerful combination of various types of departments, depending on the case, can be created.

The reciprocal flow of information between the various departments dealing with organized crime must be intensified. The electronic file "organized crime" (APOK) that has been in national use since July 1, 1987 must be built up to form the core of this information exchange. Moreover, the flow of information from the entire police base to the departments working with organized crime must be improved. This can be achieved above all by setting up appropriate education and training programs.

The fight against organized crime requires efficient cooperation between the various law enforcement agencies. International cooperation, particularly in urgent cases, should be improved by making the mutual support (ICPO–Interpol) more effective and by bilateral and multilateral agreements. Cooperation with public prosecutors can be made more intensive by setting up additional prosecuting offices specializing in organized crime. These departments can increase their knowledge by working directly with the police and by taking part in police training programs. Furthermore, cooperation with the administrative authorities (tax, trade, employment offices) is of major importance, especially in view of the overlapping of legal and illegal activities.

The high flexibility of organized crime requires fast reaction on the part of the police. Organized crime cannot be curbed if bureaucratic delays continue to hold up the police response. Well-worn practices must be reconsidered.

The units involved in organized crime enforcement should be physically separated from the rest of the police because of the attempts of infiltration associated with organized crime.

It is not easy to statistically establish the scope of organized crime. Police working statistics, used to date for the allocation of personnel and budgetary funds, including combating organized crime, are insufficient to estimate its size. The necessarily long and far-reaching investigations required in cases of organized crime can also hardly be evaluated statistically. Their success often lies in merely disquieting the scene. Thus, only a qualitative evaluation of the investigation work of organized crime can be reached.

It is not enough to just collect and record minute facts and suspicious actions as evidence of crimes. Active efforts are required in searching and establishing such evidence. The illegal activities of organized crime groups are conspiratorial, making the work of undercover agents and informants indispensable. Improvement is also necessary in this respect, in terms of providing better security equipment for undercover agents and increasing funds for informants.

The police should use special measures – even unconventional ones – to shake up and put pressure on the scene. Such measures include showing up at offender meetings, spot checks, observation, telephone surveillance, starting and spreading false rumors, or even just announcing such measures. Such methods prevent further consolidation and cause criminals to figure out ways to evade such measures, which in turn can provide tips for the investigative work.

The fight against organized crime should concentrate on persons in key positions. It would seem important to keep current lists of the most important leaders in the respective metropolitan areas. These lists should be distributed to all police units investigating organized crime in the entire country.

As was already mentioned, members of the organized crime scene are bound by mutual interests and benefits. Thus, the seizure of criminal assets is an extremely valuable tool in the fight against this type of crime.

The training and education of law enforcement officials dealing with organized crime is an essential means of its control. Training programs must be structured to cover all the various aspects relevant to this type of crime, including the behavior and know-how typical of organized criminals, covert investigations, and the behavior of law enforcement officials as witnesses. Every police officer should be made aware of the extent and danger of organized crime.

Those questioned in the interviews called for several revisions in the penal statutes regarding organized crime. They recommended that both the penal code and the code of criminal procedure be restructured to accommodate the requirements of effective control. Those interviewed, however, did not deem it necessary to introduce a special criminal offense for "organized crime."

In the area of criminal procedure, clear regulations for establishing covert investigations are mandatory. The use of false identity papers and the setting up of dummy firms by the police must be legally permitted.

The right to undertake eavesdropping measures (wiretapping) must be broadened to encompass eavesdropping on face-to-face conversations outside the private sphere. The list of crimes for which wiretapping can be used should include organized fencing. Other demands include:

- Ensuring the confidentiality of information starting from the point when the initial contact is made with an informant
- Extending the legal means of tracking down and seizing criminal assets
- Improving the law with regard to the protection of witnesses
- Introducing far-reaching regulations on chief witnesses
- Providing the possibility for witnesses (especially informants) to be questioned in court without their identity being known to the defendant and the defense
- More legal possibilities to question police officers as witnesses by hearsay
- Insulation of leading members of the organized crime scene from their confidants during pretrial detention and while in prison.

While preventive measures, in the form of informing the public on the methods of organized criminals, and the available security techniques will have little direct impact on organized crime, such efforts can support the continuing fight against it.

Public understanding and public rejection of organized crime as a special threat to the community should be promoted. Active efforts against crime on the part of the citizens, such as disclosing information and reporting criminal activity, are limited by the dangerous and covert nature of organized crime.

4 Conclusions

The study produced many insights which should be of theoretical and practical importance to the police and to policymakers. It is generally agreed that organized crime in the Federal Republic of Germany has already reached an advanced stage. Although it is impossible to permanently and completely eradicate this type of crime, it should be recognized that its structure and scope can be tremendously influenced if the appropriate measures are taken. If organized crime is not effectively fought, there will be a serious risk of its developing into an almost uncontrollable phenomenon, as has already happened in parts of the USA.

References

Bundeskriminalamt (ed) (1987) Macht sich Kriminalität bezahlt? Aufspüren und Abschöpfen von Verbrechensgewinnen. Arbeitstagung des Bundeskriminalamtes Wiesbaden vom 10.–13. November 1986. Wiesbaden (BKA-Vortragsreihe, vol 32)

Daoust L (1979) Organized crime. A bibliography. Ottawa (manuscript)

Doleschal E, Newton A, Hickey W (1981) A guide to the literature on organized crime. An annoted bibliography covering the years 1967–81. Hackensack, N.J.

Kelly RJ (ed) (1986) Organized crime. A global perspective. Totowa, N.J.
President's Commission on Organized Crime (1986a) The cash connection: organized crime, financial institutions and money laundering. Interim report to the president and the attorney general. Washington
President's Commission on Organized Crime (1986b) The impact: organized crime today. Report to the president and the attorney general. Washington
Schaefer C (1987) Polizeiarbeit auf schwankendem Grund. Ist organisierte Kriminalität mit dem geltenden Recht wirksam zu bekämpfen? Kriminalistik 41:230–235
Schwind H-D, Steinhilper G, Kube E (eds) (1987) Organisierte Kriminalität. Beiträge zu einer Fachtagung der Deutschen Kriminologischen Gesellschaft und zur Verleihung der Beccaria-Medaille 1986. Heidelberg (Kriminologische Schriftenreihe, vol 93)
Störzer HU (1987) „Organisierte Kriminalität". Eine Auswahlbibliographie. In: Schwind H-D, Steinhilper G, Kube E (eds) Organisierte Kriminalität. Beiträge zu einer Fachtagung der Deutschen Kriminologischen Gesellschaft und zur Verleihung der Beccaria-Medaille 1986. Heidelberg, pp 111–132 (Kriminologische Schriftenreihe, vol 93)
Weschke E (1986) „Netzstruktur-Kriminalität" – Eine spezifische Form des Intensivtäterverhaltens. Kriminalistik 40:297–317

CHAPTER 15

Environmental Crime: Present Status and Future Trends

M. Wulff-Nienhüser and N. Seitz

Contents

1 Development of Environmental Awareness

Over the years, environmental protection has become one of the top priorities of the politically responsible, ranking second to the task of securing peace.[1] People are increasingly measuring the quality of life by the successes of environmental policy. The preservation of a world in which life is possible has finally attained its

[1] Spranger 1985, p 361.

Kube/Störzer (Eds.)
Police Research in the Federal Republic of Germany

rightful position, both among the general public and policymakers.[2] Furthermore, responsibility mandates that an intact environment worth living in be preserved for future generations. Thus, advance precautions are called for such that environmental damage is checked right at the source and that harm to the environment is permitted only to the degree that it simply cannot be avoided. This is the primary objective of environmental policy.[3]

The principle of taking advanced precautions has its legislative counterpart, for example, in Paragraph 1a of the Law on Water Resource Management, which prohibits any deliberate interference in the management of water resources. If this law is not complied with, or if permits, regulations, or bans are not observed by authorized water resources managers then the law enforcement agencies may investigate the possibility of a criminal violation.

Until the 18th criminal law amendment – a law for combating environmental crime – came into force on July1, 1980[4], the penalty clauses were usually contained in special laws. They essentially served the protection of the environment (e.g., Law on Water Economy, Waste Disposal Law) and merely sought to state the penalty for punishable behavior. In 1974, in a decision made by the *Bundesrat* (upper house of parliament), the federal government requested that the penalty clauses concerning protection of the environment be adapted to current needs and findings and that the most important regulations be entered into the penal code.[5]

In 1973, before this "rearrangement" of criminal environmental law had taken place, 2321 "violations and criminal offenses against the environment" had been recorded in the police crime statistics.[6] In 1986, there were 14 853 cases entered in the police crime statistics under the heading "Crimes Against the Environment."[7,8] An increase of 20.7% was recorded for the year 1987.[9] The main reasons for the striking increases, in comparison with other types of crimes, were considered to be the intensified control efforts on the part of concerned institutions and greater awareness by the general public.[10] Citizens' growing awareness of possible harm to their environment and their increased willingness to supply information on violations they may have observed have made environmental offenses more "criminal." It is not that more environmental offenses are actually being committed; rather, it is that past environmental criminal behavior is being recognized and judged as

[2] Rat von Sachverständigen für Umweltfragen 1987, p 7.

[3] Spranger 1985, p 361; Peine 1986, p 250.

[4] Bundesgesetzblatt I, p 373.

[5] Sack 1986, p 375.

[6] Bundeskriminalamt 1974, Table appendix, p 19.

[7] Bundeskriminalamt 1987, p 160.

[8] As concerns the criteria used for the police criminal statistics note that the illegal actions dealt with by the police are only registered if the files have been submitted to a prosecutor or a court after completion of the investigations. See Bundeskriminalamt 1987, p 5.

[9] Bundeskriminalamt 1988, p 23.

[10] Rüther 1985, p 2.

such.[11] Through the most important enforcement body, the police[12], it is now being punished with stricter sanctions.

It was against this background that the Research and Training Institute of the *Bundeskriminalamt* (BKA) initiated an empirical study on the causes and development of environmental crime, the main findings of which are summarized below.[13]

2 The Delphi Questionnaire

The Delphi questionnaire is a written questionnaire constructed from a series of discussion sessions, in which those taking part in the discussions remain anonymous to one another. The participants are given a summary of the results of each previous session, which forms the basis for each further round of questioning.

In a questionnaire mailed in two stages, nearly 100 experts from industry, government, and the media were asked for their opinion about environmental crime. The questionnaire resulted in many "diagnostic" statements, ideas for possible changes, and predictions of trends in environmental crime and its control.

2.1 The Perpetrators of Environmental Crime

It is not possible to identify a set of typical characteristics of the perpetrators of environmental crime. Furthermore, it is necessary to differentiate according to the severity of the crimes and as to whether the perpetrator acted negligently or deliberately. Furthermore, it is necessary to distinguish the sectors in which the crimes are committed (e.g., industry, private, etc.).

When a perpetrator acts deliberately, his relevant considerations are economic ones, that is, he wants to avoid costs or make profit. A perpetrator's acting out of negligence is usually caused by a lack of knowledge and a lack of sensitivity to the environment. Environmental crimes often occur, however, because perpetrators do their jobs as they have always done, but due to changing laws these acts are now considered criminal. The perpetrator seldom thinks about consequences such as detection and condemnation when he performs a criminal act against the environment, and he does not have to be afraid of social condemnation because society does not usually blame such criminals.

---

[11] From the Bundestag 1988, p 79.

[12] Rüther 1985, p 2.

[13] Wittkämper and Wulff-Nienhüser 1987, p 38.

2.2 Informers and Complainants

Developments in environmental crime are strongly influenced by the behavior of citizens and the authorities. Someone who feels personally affected by problems of the environment, who is well-informed about such problems, and who is sensitive to what is happening to the environment is more likely to report environmental crimes to the authorities.

The experts believe, however, that administrators should not be obliged to inform the police about every environmental crime that comes to their attention. Such an obligation seems advisable only in cases of serious crimes. However, the experts believe that responsible administrators should be held liable if they act too slowly or if they tolerate criminal pollution of the environment.

This increase in the reporting of crimes conceals many dangers. Criminals will do more to camouflage the crimes, investigations will be blown out of proportion, and the authorities will not be able to keep up with all the cases.

2.3 Action Taken by the Authorities

Administrators in charge of environmental protection have been criticized by the experts for their lack of knowledge about environmental problems and a lack of sensitivity to the issues. The police and criminal justice system are ill-informed about relevant technology and science, and their equipment is inadequate and out of date.

Environmental administrations, on the one hand, and the police and the courts, on the other, are not cooperating efficiently. Although experts have criticized the current behavior of the police, they think that their role in the prosecution of environmental crimes is very important. They also feel that the police play too small a role in its prevention.

2.4 Social Attitudes Towards Environmental Crime

Environmental crimes and perpetrators are judged less negatively by society than many other criminal acts and offenders. This is due to the fact that private property is valued more highly than public property and is also due to limited public concern with environmental problems. Apart from the media and the environmental movement, industrial associations and leaders are considered to have the most influence on social attitudes towards environmental crime and its perpetrators. Nonetheless, due to increasing public concern about environmental problems, experts expect that society will condemn environmental crime more strongly in the future.

2.5 Environmental Awareness and Knowledge

Private individuals and employees of small and medium-sized companies know little about environmental criminal law. By contrast, employees of large companies and members of the different administrations assigned with the protection of the environment are well-informed. The necessity for environmental protection is widely recognized in large industries and to a great extent determines their work. Industry and government are highly motivated to invest in the protection of the environment. By contrast, private persons are not willing to spend money for such purposes.

The experts consider education to be the most effective means of providing more knowledge about environmental crime. Advanced training courses offered in companies and joint training for company employees and members of different government agencies are valuable ways to inform and instruct.

The experts predict that within the next 10 years ignorance will no longer be the cause of environmental crime. Environmental crime will also decrease because public concern about environmental protection will result in an increased social condemnation of these offenses.

2.6 Environmental Law

Environmental criminal law is accepted as one instrument of environmental policy, although it suffers many deficiencies. The most important of these include the large number of constantly changing regulations, a lack of clarity of definitions, the difficulties associated with determining guilt, and the fact that environmental criminal law becomes ineffective in the face of other environmental regulations. Such deficiencies impede recognition of both the criminal character of much environmental pollution and the increase in knowledge about environmental regulations.

2.7 Environmental Policy

The experts consider the following aims of environmental policy to be important:

1. The large number of regulations must be reduced and the constant change in regulations stopped to keep environmental law simple. This would help people to understand and obey the law.
2. Political action must be taken to provide economic incentives.
3. Existing policies of constraints and instructions should be maintained.
4. Politicians should promote the development of technology and engineering.

2.8 Environmental Crime: Present Status

Most environmental offenses are not very serious and in most cases the offender acts out of negligence. However, the number of crimes committed deliberately is considerable.

The majority of environmental crimes occur in industry, but many crimes are also committed by private citizens. By contrast, there is little environmental crime in the public sector.

There are considerable problems associated with detecting and proving environmental crimes which to some extent are due to their nature (that is, these crimes are often invisible). To solve such problems, the knowledge, qualifications, and technology of agencies fighting environmental crime must be improved.

2.9 Predicted Trends in Environmental Crime

The Delphi participants were requested to make predictions about environmental crime. These predictions are contingent upon the aforementioned weaknesses being eliminated and on their suggestions for improvement being implemented. Only in this context will the following statements have any meaning.

The quantity and quality of detected offenses increase more than the quantity and quality of the committed offenses. This holds true for every environmental medium, especially, however, for *Altlasten* (old waste), which had previously been disposed of and whose pollutant effects are not yet known.

Many of the experts predict that there will be a moderate increase in the quantity and quality of crimes involving land, while for the other environmental media only a slight increase is expected.

The clearance of petty offenses will increase slightly or moderately, while the majority of the respondents predict a large increase in the number of serious crimes solved.

A large majority of the experts rate insight and knowledge as prerequisites – even the only prerequisites – for a solution to the problem of environmental crime. A majority of participants name the establishment of norms and the social condemnation of environmental crime as necessary conditions.

Further prerequisites for containing environmental crime include a change in environmental policy, a change in the behavior of the authorities, and, to a somewhat lesser extent, a change in environmental law.

3 Survey of Industrial Employees

As part of the project, industrial employees were questioned regarding their awareness of environmental problems. These persons were selected because they could be considered as having a double role: that of a co-worker in an industry and that of a private citizen. The sample was to comprise persons from industrial enterprises of various sizes, holding different positions in their companies, and representing different levels in society.

More than 100 enterprises were contacted, of which 43 expressed their willingness to cooperate in the survey. These were sent 570 questionnaires, which were distributed by the personnel departments in accordance with the specified criteria. Of the questionnaires sent, 210 (36.8%) were filled out and returned, which can be regarded as a success given the very sensitive issue of environmental awareness. The 210 respondents also fulfilled the aforementioned requirements for the sample composition.

The questionnaire mainly addressed the problem of environmental awareness and the respondent's readiness to inform the authorities about possible environmental crimes. The results are described here.

3.1 Strong Agreement on the Value of Environmental Protection

The respondents expressed a high degree of sensitivity to environmental problems. This was especially true of those who felt personally concerned about environmental matters, who considered themselves possibly responsible for pollution, who were informed about environmental crime, who changed their behavior as a result of their awareness of environmental problems, and who mistrusted the environmental protection authorities.

3.2 Concern About the Environment

The respondents felt that the serious problems were pollution of the environment caused by traffic noise, leaded gas, industrial refuse in the water, and industrial air pollution. However, only a few believed that they were personally affected by environmental pollution. Most of those questioned felt affected only by traffic noise and the air pollution caused by automobiles.

3.3 Responsibility for Air Pollution

The respondents considered the large number of automobiles, industrial practices, and the industry of neighboring countries as being largely responsible for air pollution. Almost 40% also blamed politicians. Only 20% of the respondents, however, believed that they themselves might have been responsible for air pollution.

3.4 Sensitivity to Environmental Problems and Everyday Behavior

Verbal support of environmental protection does not necessarily imply appropriate action. The number of respondents whose everyday behavior is actually consistent with environmental concern is much lower than the number of those expressing such concern. Nevertheless, concern with environmental problems does have an effect on everyday life, as those who are concerned and who acknowledge their responsibility for environmental pollution are more likely to take measures to protect their natural environment.

3.5 Knowledge Regarding Environmental Crime

Only few of the respondents knew whether particular acts constitute criminal pollution of the environment. This was especially true of those who showed no awareness of environmental problems, who did not feel responsible for environmental pollution, and who did not act to protect the natural environment. Similarly, most respondents did not know the penalties for environmental crime. Only a few of those questioned knew that environmental offenders may be sentenced to prison. Even fewer were aware that the longest possible period of imprisonment for this kind of crime is 10 years. Only those active in environmental protection knew the penalties for environmental crime.

3.6 Readiness to Report Environmental Crime

Whether the police or the different administrations handling problems of the environment are informed about a possible environmental crime or not depends to a great extent on the social context. An environmental crime committed in the industrial sector is seldom reported by employees, but if the observed criminal act has been committed in the private sector, people are more likely to inform the police or other authorities. If people are personally affected by an environmental crime, they are more likely to inform the police. This is especially true where a person suffers physical injuries caused by the environmental crime. People will inform the appropriate government agency before they will talk to the police. Those people who show personal concern with problems of the environment, those who know much about pollution and protection of the environment, and those acting to protect the environment in everyday life are more likely to report environmental crimes.

4 Recommendations

4.1 General Recommendations

Crucial for an effective campaign against environmental crime is developing an awareness among the population of the fact that they are directly affected by such crimes and that they have rights that are legally protected. Therefore, it is recommended that all means of communication, including educational institutions, environmental organizations, and the media, as well as political parties, government departments, and police authorities work to develop the public's sense of awareness.

Efforts should be made through general education and professional training to describe the possible consequences of environmental offenses on the population and to disseminate information about legally protected environmental rights and the ways in which environmental crimes can be committed.

An understanding of legal culpability is obstructed by a number of ambiguities and lack of specificity with respect to legal rights. Section 28 of the penal code should therefore undergo major reform on the basis of the critical literature pertaining to environmental crime. A particular problem needing to be dealt with is overdependence on criminal law.

4.2 Specific Recommendations

Special police units to combat environmental crime should be set up. These must be supported by:

1. Representatives at the local police level who are responsible for information and communication with the public.
2. Study groups on environmental crime who are responsible for coordination and cooperation with official agencies and with industry.
3. Project groups on environmental crime who are responsible for solving operational problems such as the provision of in-service training.

Police working in these units should have backgrounds in technology, natural science, economics, and ecology. Furthermore, they must be able to understand the connections between these different areas of knowledge. In this respect, the knowledge of the staff in the environmental police unit must be up-to-date. Training for police and administrators in the environmental protection agencies should be integrated so as to reduce the problems of cooperation and communication.

It is also important that the police are motivated to prosecute environmental offenders since the role of the police in the area of environmental crime is not clearly defined. If cooperation within and between the police and within the different environmental protection agencies, the media, ecological associations, and industry could be intensified, the preventive effectiveness of police work would increase. Finally, because of the growing importance of organized crime in this area, a special "organized environmental crime" department, responsible for the necessary international cooperation, should be established.

4.3 Phase Model for Trends in Environmental Crime

Findings with regard to the predicted trends in environmental crime can be summarized in a phase model. For this model it is assumed that the foregoing recommendations are accepted and implemented. Three phases are assumed, each of them lasting 3 years:

Phase 1: A further increase in detected and solved environmental crimes in direct proportion to the degree that recommendations are implemented.

Phase 2: An increasing concentration of premeditated organized crimes, but in other areas a decrease of premeditated crimes and a predominance of negligent crimes.

Phase 3: A further reduction of premeditated and negligent crimes and a further concentration of premeditated offenses in the area of national and transnational organized crime.

References

Aus dem Bundestag (1988) Umweltkriminalität. Zeitschrift für Rechtspolitik 21:79

Bundeskriminalamt (ed) (1974) Polizeiliche Kriminalstatistik 1973. Wiesbaden

Bundeskriminalamt (ed) (1987) Polizeiliche Kriminalstatistik 1986. Wiesbaden

Bundeskriminalamt (ed) (1988) Polizeiliche Kriminalstatistik 1987. Wiesbaden

Peine FJ (1986) Die Kompetenzen der Polizei im Umweltstrafrecht. Die Polizei 77:249–255

Rat von Sachverständigen für Umweltfragen (1987) Kurzfassung des Umweltgutachtens. Bonn 1987 (Der Bundesminister für Umwelt, Naturschutz und Reaktorsicherheit informiert)

Rüther W (1985) Ermittlung der Ursachen für den Anstieg der polizeilich festgestellten Umweltschutzdelikte – Kurzfassung des Schlußberichts. Berlin (unpublished)

Sack HJ (1986) Das neue Umweltstrafrecht – Bewährung in der Praxis. In: Schulze G, Lotz H (eds) Polizei und Umwelt. Teil 1. Wiesbaden, pp 375–404 (BKA-Schriftenreihe, vol 54)

Spranger CD (1985) Politische Zielsetzungen im Umweltschutz aus der Sicht der Bundesregierung. Die Polizei 76:361–365

Wittkämper GW, Wulff-Nienhüser M (1987) Umweltkriminalität – heute und morgen. Eine empirische Untersuchung mit Prognose und Empfehlungen für die Praxis. Wiesbaden (BKA-Forschungsreihe, vol 20)

CHAPTER 16

The Escape Behavior of Bank Robbers and Circular Blockade Operations by the Police

H. Büchler and H. Leineweber

Contents

1 Introduction

Bank robbery has been the subject of numerous criminological investigations which have focused on characteristics of the crime and the offender. What has been neglected in criminological research, however, is the escape behavior of criminals after robberies. This is of particular importance to the police, who expend considerable resources including the deployment of many patrolmen, in order to apprehend fleeing robbers. In particular, a special police tactic involving a circular blockade around the crime site (*Ringalarmfahndung*) is now routinely activated.

To aid in the planning of circular blockade operations after a robbery, it would be useful to have answers to the following questions:

- What kind of getaway vehicle do robbers use?
- Where do they leave their getaway vehicle?
- At what distance from the scene of the crime do the offenders switch vehicles and how do they continue their escape?
- Do they try to get as far away as possible from the crime scene or do they stay close by?
- What routes of escape do they prefer?
- What is their escape destination?

Other important considerations are whether the crime is committed by one person or by a group and whether the institution robbed is located in an industrial or in a rural area.

Kube/Störzer (Eds.)
Police Research in the Federal Republic of Germany

2 Summary of the Main Findings Concerning the Escape Behavior of Bank Robbers[1]

The foregoing questions were investigated on the basis of a nationwide analysis of police files relating to a total of 351 solved robberies that had been committed in the Federal Republic of Germany between 1977 and 1978. Only solved cases were included in the study to ensure that information obtained would cover the entire course of the escape.

The large number of cases of bank robbery included in the survey and the fact that the questions addressed only objective data contributed to the validity and reliability of the results. With regard to the course of the escape, however, an unexpectedly high number of respondents gave insufficient and vague descriptions. This suggests that during investigations there is a lack of attention to this phase of the crime event. Nevertheless, there were sufficient thorough and detailed escape descriptions to make it possible to draw some firm conclusions.

Since approximately three-fourths of the bank robbers in the survey had initially been able to successfully complete their escape (even though they were eventually identified and arrested), in this respect they are on a par with robbers who were not apprehended.

Robberies of banks are, almost exclusively, planned criminal offenses, but the thoroughness of planning and the factors taken into account vary tremendously. However, the quality of planning is important for the success or failure of the robbery.

The high percentage of planned escapes (84.8%) is consistent with the figure established in the 1986 study published by Büchler and Leineweber on *Preventing Bank Robbery*. Out of the 963 robberies analyzed, 864 were clearly classified as planned crimes. Only Servay and Rehm, in their study *Bank Robbery from the View of the Robber*, reported a lower percentage (75%) of planned bank robberies. This difference could be due to the more restricted definition of "plan" used in the Servay and Rehm study.

In planning a robbery, every robber is mainly concerned with figuring out a way to avoid apprehension once the robbery is completed. However, not all robbers go to the same trouble to work out detailed escape plans. It was found that escape plans are more important to robbers who have accomplices than robbers working alone. The lone robber usually does not have the means and the time to do the same kind of extensive research that a team of offenders can do.

In planning their escape, robbers pay special attention to escape routes and escape vehicles, or to the need to switch escape vehicles at some point when they might have to split up, and finally, where their escape is going to end. Less important to the escape plan are the time of the crime, the number of persons held up, and the internal security equipment of the target institution. These latter factors are of greater importance in planning the actual robbery.

[1] Based on the 1983 study on *Täterfluchtverhalten nach Raubüberfällen auf Geldinstitute* by U. Behder.

The location of the bank seems to have overriding importance for the escape. The study found that when the robbery is committed in an urban area the robbers tend to stay nearby, whereas robbers of banks located in a mixed urban-rural or rural area try to get as far away as possible from the crime scene.

The facts of the escape that can be objectively established such as the use of ready-and-waiting transfer vehicles, the escape routes, and the escape destinations indicate that robbers keep to their original escape plan. Only in cases where they are followed by witnesses or victims or when they feel they have been seen do they seem to deviate from their plan.

In organizing escape vehicles the offenders take into account whether the vehicle will be needed for the initial getaway or for the continuation of the escape in one of the subsequent phases. Since they usually assume that they will be seen as they are leaving the scene of the crime, groups of robbers usually use stolen cars equipped with stolen license plates to avoid being identified. Lone offenders, provided they use a car at all for the first phase of the escape, use their own car or a borrowed one, sometimes disguising the license plates by covering over or changing numbers. In comparison with group offenders they seldom use stolen license plates. Lone offenders also use bicycles or rented automobiles for the initial escape phase. Both single and group robbers have their getaway cars ready and waiting no further than 50 m from the scene of the crime (Table 1).

Table 1. Escape (1st phase)

Escape by	Single robbers (*n*)	Group robbers (*n*)	Total robberies (*n*)
Foot	118	27	145 (41.3%)
Bicycle	21	2	23 (6.6%)
Motorcycle	6	7	13 (3.7%)
Car	58	98	156 (44.4%)
Taxi	2	–	2 (0.6%)
Unknown	10	2	12 (3.4%)
Total	215	136	351 (100.0%)

For the subsequent phases of the escape the robbers almost always use their own cars with official license plates. The transfer cars for the second escape phase are usually kept no more than 2000 m away from the crime in cities and no more than 5000 m from the crime in more rural areas. They are usually kept ready on a public road.

Among the robbers who had committed two or more robberies it was clear that they tended to follow the same pattern of escape. Thus, it would appear that the mode of escape contains information which can help relate unsolved robberies to known robbers.

The risk of being apprehended during the actual robbery is not a matter of concern for bank robbers. Extreme measures such as taking hostages or tying and locking up witnesses rarely occurred. In most cases they merely instructed the victims to keep quiet and calm. This behavior underlines the fact that the most important thing for the robber is to get away as fast as possible before the police arrive. The time element is of utmost importance both in terms of the crime itself and the escape.

The first escape phase usually lasted no more than 5 min (Table 2). Upon beginning their search, the police frequently only had information on the vehicle used in the first phase of the escape. By that time, however, the robbers had switched to a different vehicle. The group offenders in the majority of cases began their getaway in one automobile and usually remained together throughout the entire escape. This is an important finding as it means that, during the search, vehicles should be sought in which the number of passengers matches the number of robbers reported.

Table 2. Duration of escape

Duration	By single robbers (%)	By group robbers (%)
0– 3 min	50.0	53.5
4– 5 min	18.0	18.2
6–10 min	9.0	11.0
11–15 min	4.0	7.1
16–20 min	4.0	4.0
21–30 min	4.9	3.0
31–40 min	2.5	–
About 40 min	7.4	3.0

Over half of the offenders included in the study had begun a second escape phase. Robbers operating alone prefer to continue their escape in an automobile after having carried out the first phase on foot or by bicycle (Table 3). It is therefore important for the police to concentrate on the immediate vicinity of the robbed bank, as the fleeing robbers usually switch getaway cars parked in nearby streets.

Table 3. Escape (2nd phase)

Escape by	Single robbers (*n*)	Group robbers (*n*)
Foot	14	35
Bicycle	2	–
Motorcycle	1	–
Car	31	127
Bus/tram	7	11
Subway/train	7	13
Unknown	2	37

Although none of the offenders used public transportation in the first phase of their escape, some did so in the second phase. The train, in particular, was used for distant escape destinations. It is thus advisable to include the railway police in the search. Other means of transportation such as airplanes or ships were not used by the offenders included in this study.

Only a very few of the robbers who committed the crime in urban areas took advantage of the possibilities for a quick disappearance near the crime scene. The most frequent escape destination of the final phase of the escape was the offender's own home or the home of someone else. Although more than half the robbers had carried a handgun during the robbery, only a very small number of them used them against persons who followed them.

The foregoing findings regarding escape patterns of bank robbers also apply to criminals who hold up couriers. It should be noted, however, that these criminals used much more brutal methods than bank robbers.

3 Implications for Circular Blockade Operations[2]

A circular blockade operation is a special police tactic for apprehending fleeing criminals. Essentially, police patrol cars form a ring around the area in which a serious crime has been reported, blocking off all exit routes. The most relevant factors determining the formation of the ring are where and when the crime was committed and how far the criminal has managed to flee in the meantime. At the beginning of 1974, circular blockade was introduced nationally into the *Polizeidienstvorschrift* (PDV; Police Service Regulations) No. 384.1.

Unlike general apprehension methods, circular blockade is precisely timed and the steps which are to be followed for immediate deployment of police manpower are listed and defined in a catalogue of police tactics. A fast and organized response on the part of the police reduces the head start of the criminal, which in turn increases his risk of being caught.

Crimes occurring in heavily populated areas pose a problem for implementing a circular blockade. Experience has shown that, whereas the criminal in lightly populated areas tries to get as far away from the crime scene as fast as possible, criminals in cities remain in the vicinity. Accordingly, the PDV were revised to stipulate that instead of one blockade encircling the entire city, the police should divide up into teams and surround smaller sections of the area.

Circular blockade is reserved for special incidents that pose a threat to public safety. According to Behder's survey[3], 63.4% of the 845 circular blockades in 1978 were executed after robbery attacks on financial institutions, post offices, stores, armored cars, and courier services.

The purpose of the study described below was to examine the interaction between the escape behavior of the offender after the bank robbery and the formation

[2] Based on the 1984 study on *Ringalarmfahndung* by L. Schuster.

[3] See Behder 1983.

of the circular blockade. It takes an average of 26.7 min to form a circular blockade. In an experiment carried out in Stuttgart, however, policemen simulated escapes from three different locations and in all three cases the escape vehicle had passed the control point before the police were able to get there.

The success rate of circular blockade operations, measured up to 1978, varied considerably throughout the country. In Bavaria 19.6% of the circular blockade operations were successful, in Lower Saxony 17.6%, in Rhineland-Palatinate 16.0%, in Hesse 14.7%, in Baden-Württemberg 12.4%, and in Schleswig-Holstein only 3.8%. These figures are consistent with findings of the present study. Of the 248 circular blockades included in the study, 44 were successful, i.e., the offender was apprehended in the course of the operation.

The comparatively limited success of circular blockade seemed to be out of proportion to the enormous technical and organizational expense. Apprehension measures were therefore analyzed under the following heading:

- The percentage of false alarms
- Time between the occurrence of the crime and triggering of the alarm
- Control points of the blockade (when occupied, number, manpower)
- Expansion or displacement of the ring
- Type of controls
- Quality of the search information
- Extent of the area barricaded
- Success of the blockade and the quality of the written reports
- Termination of the blockade.

The criminal's escape behavior – in terms of both the timing and location of his movements – determines what measures the police take in response to the crime. In heavily populated areas, the offender usually stays within the city limits. The same holds true for crimes committed in mixed rural-urban areas, whereas in more rural areas the tendency is to get further away from the crime scene. The timing of the escape corresponds to these locational factors: in urban areas the first phase[4] of the escape is usually over within 5 min after the occurrence of the crime. The first escape destination is within a radius of 5 km (usually 2 km) from the scene of the crime. Consequently, the initial witness reports of the crime quickly become irrelevant and cannot be used as the basis for the search and blockade. Only in rural areas does the first phase of escape last longer than 10 min, with the second phase usually following immediately and sometimes lasting longer than 30 min. This second phase of escape is the same for rural and mixed urban-rural regions in terms of both timing and geographical factors, whereas in urban areas it is much shorter and the criminal does not flee as far.

These findings have general relevance for circular blockade operations. The fact that criminals – particularly in urban, densely populated areas, but also in mixed

[4] The first escape phase begins when the offender leaves the scene of the crime and ends as soon as the offender changes his first escape behavior such as switching the escape vehicle or spending a considerable length of time in a hiding place.

urban-rural regions – tend to stay closer to the scene of the crime for a longer time demands that apprehension plans confined to the close vicinity of the scene of the crime should be given priority. For this purpose, the cities of Hamburg and Frankfurt have developed a search map.

This leads to the question of the planning and management of the circular blockade. Generally (with the exception of Hamburg and Hesse), planning takes place at the higher police levels and hence at a good distance from the actual incidents. However, the primary information concerning the crime and the offender, which determines the organization of the blockade, rests at lower levels. It would thus seem sensible to relocate the responsibility for planning. This, however, would require that a permanent reporting headquarters be set up, through which all of the information relevant to the local search would be transmitted without delay to the search management. The major functions of such headquarters would be to coordinate the planning and forming of the blockade and to direct the cross-regional flow of information. Thus, there would be two different levels of organization at which directives could be issued at the same time. The search management would be in charge of making sure that the two levels did not function independently of one another.

The setting up of the ring at some distance from the crime scene is a result of the assumption that criminals flee far and fast. The results of the survey, however, indicate that long distance escapes are the exception and not the rule. The time element involved in organizing the steps of the apprehension plan compounds the problem of where to set up the blockade. The calculations to determine where to form it are based on the time span between the escape and when the blockade order is given. This, however, leaves a substantial portion of the police response time out of account. The total time span (i.e., mean police response time) in fact extends from the time of the crime to when the circular blockade has been set up. In other words, the further the criminal has managed to flee, the larger the blockade that is necessary. However, the larger the ring, the more time required for its formation. In this time the fleeing criminal has escaped even further, and so on. The discrepancy between the timing and spatial elements of escape behavior, on the one hand, and the total amount of police response time, on the other, makes it doubtful that circular blockade, as currently being practiced, can be successful.

Given the mean police response time, the blockade would have to be made considerably larger than it has been to date. However, this is not consistent with the geographic and time aspects of escape behavior. With the possible exception of robberies in rural areas, the criminals tend to remain in the vicinity of the crime and thus police search measures must be taken accordingly. Concentrating police forces in the area close to the crime can exhaust the police capacity available. Measures must be taken to ensure that all of the available forces are deployed.

4 Recommendations

These findings give reason to reevaluate both the PDV 384.1 and the way the circular blockade is being executed:

1. The blockade has been conceived of in terms of both dynamic elements (patrolling the area) and static elements (occupation of the control points), both of which should be maintained. Search efforts, however, should be concentrated in the vicinity of the crime with more attention paid to semipublic space.

2. In cities and in mixed urban-rural areas the average fleeing distance is 5 km. Forming the blockade outside this radius is largely pointless, especially in view of the unresolvable conflict between the escape time and police mean response time. A more detailed study should be undertaken to decide whether the circular blockade as it is presently being executed should be modified, especially for urban and mixed urban-rural areas.

3. The blockade set up in the vicinity of where the crime took place should be organized by the local police department connected with the central department through an information headquarters.

4. Each and every police officer must know exactly what to do in the case of a blockade and must be able to carry out his assignment automatically. This will not only accelerate the formation of the blockade, but will also reduce the amount of communication necessary between the local and central organization levels. Proactive response of the forces deployed has led to the construction of a model of passive as opposed to active management. That means that a large number of the search activities are carried out at the level of the police force without explicit instructions having to come from the search management. Only a limited amount of feedback from the police force is necessary. The search management assumes that the police departments deployed for the search do in fact carry out their tasks. The passive model is superior to the active model in making the circular blockade a routine operation that thrives on the automatic response of the police force involved in the operation.

5. Since the first escape phase is usually very brief and in close proximity to the crime location, it is imperative that the information on the crime and the offender be kept up to date by the police operating in this area. For the search management this means that they must be especially careful that the information they transmit is still relevant.

6. Nonpolice institutions must be included more in the search measures, as is stipulated in PDV 384.1. This applies particularly to public transportation, which plays an important role after the first phase of the escape. Criminals who try to escape a large distance away may use public trains.

7. The occupation of the control points is just as problematic as it is indispensable. Problems include the number of policemen required, the considerable amount of time necessary to occupy the control points and the local geography. This applies to varying degrees to both urban and rural areas as well as to mixed urban-rural regions. Although PDV 384.1 calls for patrol cars stopping motor ve-

hicles, this also poses problems, especially in terms of safety. The results of the study demonstrate the major discrepancy between theory and practice.

8. The police make a record of vehicles and passengers that pass through each of the blockade points, checking each vehicle that passes. These lists have proved to be unreliable, not only due to heavy traffic and poor visibility, but largely as a result of errors and misjudgments on the part of the police. With respect to this point there have been a number of misunderstandings. Consequently, such control lists produce findings based more on coincidence than on a systematic analysis.

Apart from the suggestions relating to the conception of the circular blockade, some points can be made with regard to administrative aspects:

The blockade as an instrument of the police must be used sparingly to avoid the destructive effect of overuse. The operation is and must be reserved for special cases of crime so that when it is executed the police always react with the appropriate urgency. Nonetheless, police forces should receive regular training in the functions and assignments to be carried out during a blockade. More intensive training is necessary for policemen who might find themselves in the position of having to take over leadership during a blockade operation. Crucial decisions have to be made at this level and problems can arise due to a lack of experience. Training should also include the interaction between the local operation leaders on the scene and the search management at the higher level.

The police could be motivated by the successful circular blockades being reported to all of the police departments. The criteria for the success of a particular operation should be determined. It would also seem useful to distribute information about the weak points of operations carried out over a larger period of time.

In an area of modern science and technology a perfectly functioning radio communications network should be taken for granted. This is essential not only for search operations as described here, but for all routine police work. Blockades which transcend regional borders, however, seem to present communications problems so that the demand for a uniform communications channel in the case of emergency has not been fulfilled. The success of the blockade is largely determined by the information conveyed to those carrying out the operation. The technical means necessary to accomplish this must be created or developed further.

It appears necessary to inspect the individual measures and aids used in the circular blockade to make sure that they are up-to-date. This also applies to control points, which may have to be relocated for topographic infrastructural and technical reasons. The aids used in carrying out the blockade operation must be inspected for suitability and handling. The study revealed that the Hamburg search map, though logically constructed, is difficult to use. Not only is it too comprehensive and complicated, making it difficult for the police using it to get their bearings, it is seldom readily available in the case of an emergency operation. Either it has not been taken along in the police car, or it is locked in a case in the trunk of the car. The same applies to the Frankfurt search map. Those responsible for designing such material must make efforts to keep them simple to use.

References

Behder U (1983) Täterfluchtverhalten nach Raubüberfällen auf Geldinstitute. Eine Analyse für den Polizeipraktiker. Wiesbaden (BKA-Forschungsreihe. Special volume)

Büchler H, Leineweber H (1986) Bankraub und technische Prävention. Phänomenologie – Bestand und Auswirkungen der Sicherungstechnik. Wiesbaden (BKA-Forschungsreihe, vol 18)

Schuster L (1984) Die Ringalarmfahndung. Eine empirische Untersuchung in den Ländern Baden-Württemberg, Hamburg und Hessen. Wiesbaden (BKA-Forschungsreihe. Special volume)

Servay W, Rehm J (1986) Bankraub aus Sicht der Täter. Täterleitende Faktoren bei Raubüberfällen auf Geldinstitute. Wiesbaden (BKA-Forschungsreihe, vol 19)

CHAPTER 17

Preventing Bank Robbery: The Offense from the Robber's Perspective

H. Leineweber and H. Büchler

Contents

1 Introduction

Technology has had a role in the prevention of bank robbery in the Federal Republic of Germany for more than two decades and it seems likely to take on a greater role as a result of the increasing automatization of bank operations. According to police experts, security techniques have had a major effect on crime, although there have been no detailed empirical studies of the nature of this effect. The BKA therefore conducted two studies to elucidate the empirical connections between technical prevention and the commission of crime.[1] These studies employed analysis of police files and interviews with convicted bank robbers.

The research produced information on the present standard of security systems in banks and about the possible connection between very different security techniques and the increase or decrease in the incidence of bank robberies. In addition, the effects of preventive measures on the behavior of the robber and persons involved in the crime (bank employees, customers) were established.

2 Trends in Bank Robbery in the Federal Republic of Germany

Bank robbers often employ different modes of operation at the same time. In the following, the term "bank robbery" will be used to refer to all robberies without regard for the particular kind of operation. However, a necessary distinction must be

[1] Büchler/Leineweber 1986, Servay/Rehm 1986. See also Büchler/Leineweber 1985.

Kube/Störzer (Eds.)
Police Research in the Federal Republic of Germany

made between "classical" and other types of bank robbery. Classical bank robbery is committed at the cash points of a bank and during regular banking hours. It may involve hostage-taking during the course of the crime. The other forms of bank robbery include breaking into the bank after hours, waiting for bank employees to leave the bank to take them hostage, or taking bank personnel hostages in their homes or somewhere else outside the bank.

Robberies of banks and post offices have been recorded in the police crime statistics since 1971. The statistics reveal that the number of these robberies in West Germany increased by more than threefold, from 297 in 1971 to 981 in 1986. In contrast to other types of robbery that show a more continuous increase, the incidence of bank robbery showed two peaks in 1977 and 1982. Especially striking is the decrease in robberies from 639 in 1977 to 411 in 1980 (a decrease of 55%). This reduction can be explained by the increased use of bank security measures during this period. The dip in bank robberies in 1983 parallels the start of equipping banks with optical surveillance systems at the beginning of the 1980s (Fig. 1).

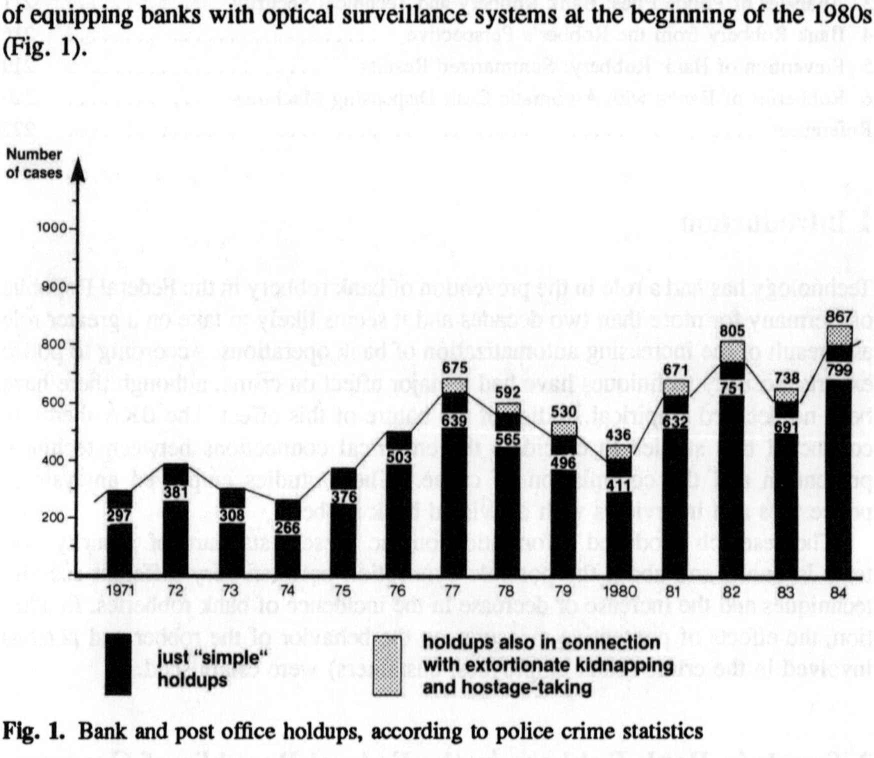

Fig. 1. Bank and post office holdups, according to police crime statistics

With the introduction of the automatic teller (cash dispensing) machines for bank staff operation at the beginning of the 1980s (see Sect. 6), a further decrease of robberies was predicted – an expectation that has not yet been fulfilled. The police crime statistics only began to include bank robberies involving kidnapping and hostage-taking in 1977. As was already mentioned, the trend of these robberies runs about parallel to that of classical robberies.

Although the incidence of bank robbery underwent an increase in past years (from 436 in 1980 to 867 in 1984), it did not rise nearly as much as that of holdups of armored cars and money couriers (from 192 in 1980 to 639 in 1984). This suggests that bank security systems have been effective in deterring bank robbery.

3 Analyses of Police Files: Bank Robbery and Technical Security

Police files were analyzed to obtain information on the extent and standard of technical security equipment in banks, along with information on the offender and the stages of the crime. Beyond that, an attempt was made to establish a relationship between the introduction of various security systems and the pattern of robberies. A further topic of study was the relationship between security measures and the behavior of robbers and bank employees.

Police records of 963 cases of bank robbery from the period between January 1, 1981 and June 30, 1983 were analyzed. The study was supplemented by an evaluation of the robberies involving cash dispensing machines. Comparisons were made with the results obtained in earlier studies conducted by the *Bundeskriminalamt* (BKA): (1) an unpublished report of the BKA from 1978 on the study of robberies of banks, cashiers' offices, postal and railway agencies, and couriers[2]; (2) a study on the *Escape Behavior of Bank Robbers* published as a special volume of the BKA research series in 1983.[3] The first study comprised 677 robberies that had occurred all over the Federal Republic of Germany in the years 1974 and 1975. The second study evaluated 351 completed and solved robberies of banks, post offices, and money couriers which had occurred nationwide in the years 1977 and 1978.

To get a better idea of where robberies take place, communities were divided into categories (Fig. 2). It is striking that communities with up to 5000 inhabitants (category 1), as well as the suburbs of the metropolitan areas with more than 100000 inhabitants (category 7) have a high number of robberies.

A comparison with the aforementioned studies of 1978 and 1983[4] reveals that there is a marked decrease of robberies in the cities (category 6) and an increase in the suburbs of large cities and in the independent communities within metropolitan areas (categories 7 and 8). On a nationwide basis more robberies take place in typically urban areas (categories 3, 4, 6, 7) (Fig. 3).

With regard to the German States (excluding the three city-states, Berlin, Bremen, and Hamburg, and the state of North Rhine-Westphalia), a high percentage of robberies occur in typically rural areas (categories 1, 2, 5, 8).

[2] Bundeskriminalamt 1978.

[3] Behder 1983.

[4] See footnotes 2 and 3.

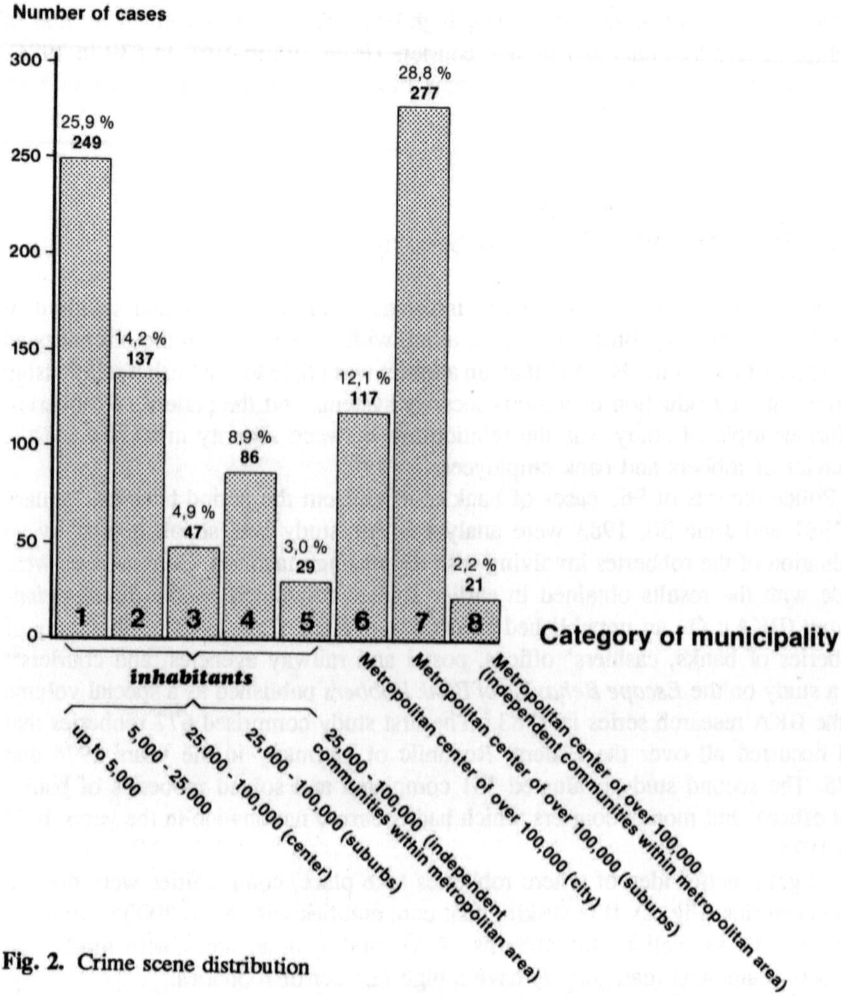

Fig. 2. Crime scene distribution

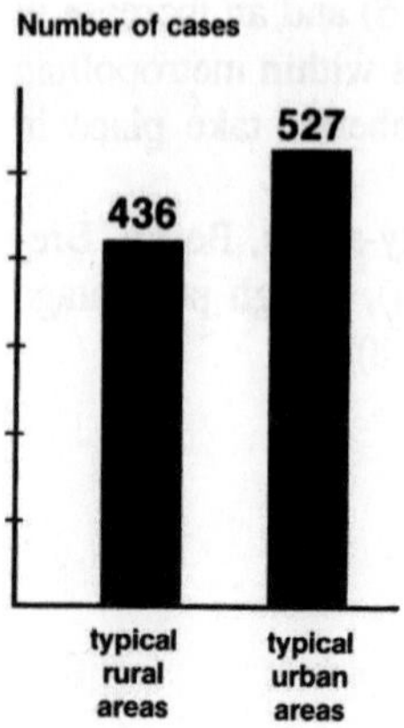

Fig. 3. Area structure

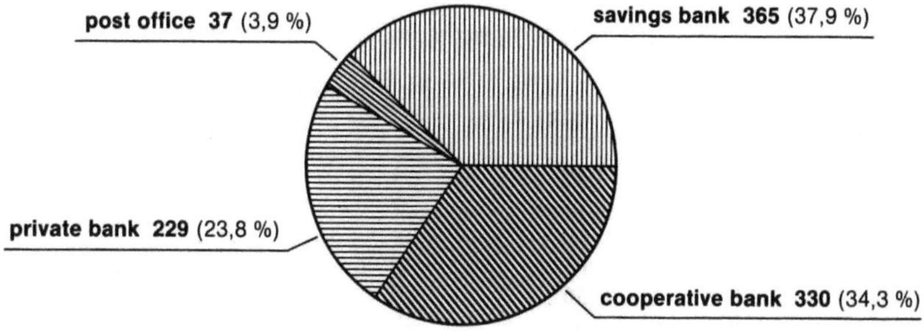

Fig. 4. Types of banks

The banks in Germany are divided into savings banks (about 17 000), cooperative banks (about 19 000), private banks (about 6200), and branches of the German post office (about 10 800). Considered in the absolute, savings banks were victimized more than the other types of financial institutions (Fig. 4; in two cases the type of bank held up was not known). In relation to the number of existing banks and post offices, robberies were carried out in 3.7% of the private banks, 2.15% of the savings banks, 1.74% of the cooperative banks, and 0.34% of the post offices. With regard to the distribution of robberies among the categories of communities, the highest rates were observed in communities of less than 5000 inhabitants (category 1), among savings banks (117 robberies) and cooperative banks (122 robberies), and in the suburbs of metropolitan centers of over 100 000 inhabitants (category 7), among private banks (116 robberies). The highest robbery rates were found during the winter months (December and February) and on Thursdays and Fridays. Most crimes were committed at opening and closing times, with the highest rates being on Thursday between 5 and 6 pm (the banks in Germany are open later on Thursday than on other days of the week; Tables 1, 2).

While the BKA study of 1978 found Friday to be the day on which most robberies are committed, Behder, in 1983, found that most bank robberies take place on Thursday.

Table 1. Daily rate

	Number of cases				
	1981	1982	First half of 1983	Total	%
Monday	51	72	32	155	16.1
Tuesday	76	67	39	182	18.9
Wednesday	57	73	27	157	16.3
Thursday	102	88	51	241	25.0
Friday	74	104	42	220	22.9
Saturday	3	5	–	8	0.8
Total	363	409	191	963	100.0

Table 2. Monthly rate

	Number of cases				
	1981	1982	Total 1981–1982	First 6 months of 1983	Total
January	26	39	65	35	100
February	39	37	76	27	103
March	32	27	59	39	98
April	29	33	62	28	90
May	25	31	56	28	84
June	19	33	52	31	83
Subtotal	170	200		188	
July	34	36	70		
August	24	35	59		
September	31	26	57		
October	27	35	62		
November	31	34	65		
December	46	46	92		
Total	363	412			

In 87.3% of the robberies (840 cases), the robbery took up to 3 min. Of these cases, 18.7% never got past the attempt stage. Most of these crimes were committed by lone offenders. The duration of the crime was dependent on the modus operandi. In comparison with the results of the earlier studies[5], the number of robberies committed within 3 min has more than doubled.

Of the banks that were robbed, 85.1% were equipped with bullet-resistant barriers. In 40.3% of the robberies studied the bank employees were not behind bullet-resistant barriers at the time of the hold up and in 25.8% they were not shielded by any kind of protective structure.

A strong relationship was determined between the interruption of the crime and the bullet-proof protection of the personnel, which indicates that the success of the crime is also dependent upon the physical characteristics of the bank.

In 39.4% of the cases the banks were equipped with an alarm system that was hooked up directly to the police. In 15.3% there was only an audiovisual alarm system and in 4.8% there was no alarm system at all (according to the BKA report of 1978, 16% of the banks do not have an alarm system). In 54.9% of the robberies the alarm went off during the holdup, which is a major increase in comparison with the earlier studies (BKA 1978: 29.6%; Behder 1983: 28.8%). More than 75% of the alarm systems with direct hookup to the police were used during the holdup. In 64.1% of the cases the police were notified first, in 17.5% someone else was contacted first. The alarm system failed in 3.3% (34 cases).

Of the banks and post offices that were robbed, 74.6% (718 cases) were equipped with cameras (BKA 1978: 2.3%), which were only triggered off in 68.2% (490 cases) before and after the robbery. Usable pictures of the holdup were ob-

[5] See footnotes 2 and 3.

tained in 31.8% of the cases examined (306). The main reasons for the inadequacy of the pictures included defective installation, inadequate maintenance of the system, and poor photographic quality.

In 49.2% of the cases the employees followed the instructions given by the robber. In another 49.2% the personnel did not cooperate. In the latter case the rate of robberies that did not get past the attempt stage was markedly higher. Resistance was usually manifested by hesitation or refusal to hand over the money (passive resistance).

Resistance on the part of the employees had an impact on the course and the success of the crime. Inappropriate behavior, and in particular, aggressive acts of resistance, often resulted in aggravating the crime, thus causing danger for those involved (Table 3).

Table 3. Categories of resistance

Category	Behavior	Number of cases	Attempted robberies
1	Passive resistance	153	41 (26.8%)
2	Other resistance	95	25 (26.3%)
3	Resistance by using serucity system	30	8 (26.7%)
4	Aggressive resistance	25	13 (52%)
		303	87 (28.7%)

In 233 cases (24.2%) the robber tried to interfere with the security equipment. In 152 cases the offender took hostages during the holdup. These persons were usually held at gun point only until the offender was handed over the money. In 114 cases hostages were taken immediately, in 34 cases not until events escalating the offense had occurred. There was no evidence of an increase in cases in which hostages were taken immediately as a reaction to the security equipment.

In 91.1% of the cases the offender only "threatened" with a gun. Only in 1.3% of the cases was the gun used against persons. These findings were consistent with those of the 1978 and 1983 studies.[6] The hypothesis that technical security measures cause an increased use of firearms was not supported.

The number of persons injured or killed in the 963 cases of robbery examined was very small and there was little evidence of increasing brutality by bank robbers.

The number of cases where the "haul" was more than DM 100 000 rose in comparison with rates found in the earlier studies of 1978 and 1983.[7] A total of DM 28 840 000 was taken in the 963 cases examined. Among the successful robberies, an average of DM 38 000 was stolen. The largest haul in a single robbery was more than DM 1 million.

[6] See footnotes 2 and 3.

[7] See footnotes 2 and 3.

In 63.7% of the cases (480) the robbers took cash from the cash register. In 150 cases the money taken was from several sources. Marked money was handed over in 470 cases.

Only in 28 cases (5.1%) did the police appear at the scene of the crime during the holdup. In 56.2% the police showed up within the first 5 min after the alarm sounded; in a total of 83.1% the appeared within 10 min.

Of the 963 cases 573 (59.5%) were solved. The rate of robberies solved on the day of the crime was a remarkably high 30.5% (294 cases). This corresponded to 51.3% of all solved cases. Behder in 1983 determined a rate of 46.2%.

In 58 cases the photographs provided by the bank cameras assisted in the solution. In 88 cases the alarm went off in time for the robbers to be apprehended.

4 Bank Robbery from the Robber's Perspective

The survey of robbers, commissioned by the BKA and carried out by Irle and colleagues at the University of Mannheim (Servay and Rehm 1986) was conceived as a subsequent project to the analysis of police records. The study focused on the following:

- The decisions made by the offender (target selection, perception of risk)
- Planning and execution of the crime
- Planning and execution of the escape.

In the initial phase of the study, 152 imprisoned bank robbers were interviewed. A further 107 offenders were included in a second experimental phase which centered on testing the hypotheses derived from the results of the survey and finding out which factors made a particular bank attractive to the robber.

For the robber, there are several reasons for the appeal of bank robbery. Everyone has free access to banks. No special knowledge or skills are required for planning and preparing the robbery (particularly the "classical" robbery). Once the offender is over his nervousness, the execution of the crime is relatively simple and calls for neither extraordinary physical strength nor special tools and techniques. Bank robbery can be committed with weapons that are generally easy to obtain (for example, toy guns, blank guns, gas guns). The positive subjective assessment of the success-to-risk ratio associated with bank robbery is another factor contributing to its appeal.

The interviews with the convicted criminals revealed several common motivations and thinking processes among bank robbers. Most have an urgent need of large sums of cash. They possess minimal skills and have no access to licit or illicit alternatives of acquiring money. The robber has relatively high expectations of the reward, hoping it to be a large amount of usable cash. Thus, his calculations in terms of cost and effect are very favorable. The bank robber relies on the predictable nature of the victims, both the bank and the employees. This reduces the amount of preparation needed.

Very few of the offenders committing "classical" robberies reported doing any substantial planning. In fact, as many as 11% committed "spur of the moment" robberies; that is, they had not started out with any intent to carry out a robbery.

Preparation included procuring masks and suitable weapons or dummies, "casing" the bank premises and possible escape routes, and organizing the escape. In this respect the greatest differences were shown between lone and group offenders; group offenders generally made more thorough preparations.

From the data obtained in the interview, a distinction could be made between "amateurs" and "professionals." The amateur is defined as a one-time bank robber who has no clear plan of the actual commission of the crime or of what he will do in the event of something unforeseen happening during the act. The typical professional is an habitual offender who has a detailed plan for the crime and a plan of reaction to any unexpected events.

The different kinds of bank robbers also differ in terms of target selection. Amateurs chose the bank according to the possibilities for escape, the size of the bank, and the location. The interior of the bank and thus the security devices did not seem to play a role in the selection.

Hiding places in the vicinity of the bank constituted a major selection criterion for the professionals. This was about the only common denominator among this group. Some of them also considered factors such as the distance from the nearest police station, the interior of the bank, and the specific security equipment.

Only 75% of all offenders planned how they would proceed once in the bank. Most of them confined their preparation to the planning of single steps and largely took a wait-and-see approach. This was evident in the planning of such things as the criteria for interrupting the robbery, the exact time of the crime, and opening the safe.

About two-thirds of the offenders had worked out a plan for an intermediate or final escape plan. The most common getaway vehicle was a car. Although in most cases the plan had flaws, it was seldom altered and the bank robbers regarded it as being extremely important for the holdup.

While devising their plans, most of the robbers experienced doubt about whether or not they would be successful. They were extremely nervous before and during the holdup. For more than a third of the offenders questioned, the bank robbery was the most exciting event they had ever experienced. The most commonly used tranquilizer was alcohol. These findings do not support the common image of bank robbery as a cold-blooded act of violence. Only a small percentage of the robbers reported that the robbery had gone smoothly. Most of the unexpected situations arose while the money was being handed over. Either the offenders did not react at all to such incidents or they did so with threats. Violence seldom occurred.

Other findings can be summarized as follows:

- In 17.4% of the cases the robber took hostages, usually upon entering the bank. Only rarely were hostages taken by the fleeing bank robber after the police had arrived and this was rarely planned by the offenders.
- Some 15% of the offenders broke off the robbery.

- Approximately 72% of the robbers were masked because they had presumed the existence of a camera.
- Active measures to damage or block the security equipment were rare. Of those questioned, 69% noticed that the alarm had gone off.
- In 44% the robbers reported deviating from their robbery plan. Nevertheless, the majority believed they had the situation under control. In this respect the single and group offenders differ, for the single offenders had more trouble getting a view of the entire situation.
- While about 20% of those questioned remained in the vicinity of the scene of the crime, most of the criminals tried to reach their destination by changing vehicles.
- Some 29% were arrested before they could reach their destination.
- The plan of escape went as expected for less than a third of the criminals questioned. About 30% had unexpected problems with the police or bank employees, which the criminals considered to be responsible for their arrest.
- Some 10% of the robbers had no escape plans.
- Betrayal on the part of their accomplices was named by 25% of the criminals as the reason for their arrest. Another 11% said mistakes made by their accomplices were responsible. Mistakes were thought to be the reason for arrest just as frequently as tips from the public (14% and 12%, respectively). According to 14%, the arrest was a result of police measures, including the circular blockade operation (see Chap. 16) and the study of photographs from the security camera. Such arrests were made within one day after the robbery in more than half of the cases.
- Approximately 50% were unaware of the penalty prior to the crime. For the majority of those who did know what penalty awaited them, this was inconsequential. No criminal expects to be arrested and punished.

Most of the respondents made accurate estimates of the percentage of cleared bank robberies. However, they were also of the opinion that bank robbery, if thoroughly and well planned, has a low clearance rate. Most of the criminals considered their own actions to be responsible for the success or failure (i.e., arrest) of their robbery.

The survey reveals that in devising preventive measures against bank robbery it should be assumed that most bank robbers are relatively unprofessional. An important preventive measure suggested was that the coverage of bank robberies in the media be geared to deterring such crimes. Depending on how the media informs the public about penalties, the chance of apprehension, and the haul, the potential bank robber may come to think that robbing a bank just might not be worth it.

5 Prevention of Bank Robbery: Summarized Results

The results of the foregoing research as well as those of the studies conducted in the last 20 years confirm that the measures taken in the area of technical prevention of bank robbery have been effective in keeping robbery under a certain degree of control. The effect of the security equipment on the success or failure of a robbery and on the clearance rate is further proof of this.

The results of the studies reveal that technical prevention in the area of bank robbery has "neutralizing" effects. That means that, having discovered the security devices, the offender shifts his criminal energy to unprotected targets (known as the displacement effect) or tries to adapt his modus operandi to the new situation (for instance, the offender may threaten the life of bank employees and customers, known as the escalation effect). However, the fact that the offender is able to adapt to the new situation does not cast doubt on the value of technical prevention. In contrast to the view that, at worst, nothing can be done in terms of preventing bank robbery in general; there is always the hope that in the individual case positive results can be achieved, as has been demonstrated here.

In judging the effectiveness of technical prevention of bank robbery it must also be considered to what extent the positive or neutralizing effects of security measures are accompanied by negative effects and how important these effects are.

One risk is escalation. Hostage-taking during a bank robbery is a sign of such escalation and is one of the negative consequences of increased security. The number of bank robberies involving hostage-taking has increaseed since security measures were introduced, although in the last 10 years there has been a slight decrease.

A look at the phenomenology of bank robbery over the course of time reveals that it has not undergone any basic change since the introduction of bank security measures. There is not one, but many types of bank robbery, which have different characteristics. The feared changes have not taken place.

Figures on the use of weapons and injuries or deaths give no indication that bank robbery has become more brutal. The number of violent robberies has never reached unsettling proportions and has stagnated for over 10 years. Moreover, such events usually only involve short-term hostage-taking (that is, briefly taking someone under control in order to reinforce a demand for money – something which is not legally regarded as hostage-taking).

The results call for a revision of the widespread view that increased bank security measures have possibly dangerous consequences with regard to the use of violence in robbery. The physical characteristics of the bank have considerable importance for crime prevention. There seems to be a relationship between permanently installed security devices and the success of a robbery. The survey showed that bank employees behaved differently depending on whether they were behind bullet-resistant shielding or whether or not customers were present. Passive resistance, particularly when protected by built-in security measures, seems to be a necessary though not a sufficient condition for the failure of a robbery attempt. Rash, exaggerated, and aggressive resistance, on the other hand, can result in an escalation of the event and thus pose a threat to the lives of bank employees and customers.

It goes without saying that even the best security is doomed to failure if it is not properly installed, maintained, and operated. The results show that the implementation of security measures varies considerably.

6 Robberies of Banks with Automatic Cash Dispensing Machines

Automatic cash dispensing machines for bank staff operation were first installed inside German banks at the beginning of the 1980s. Intended primarily to increase efficiency, these machines were also meant to serve as security devices, as the money is stored under lock and is dispensed only to bank employees. At the same time as these machines were introduced, many of the other security devices such as bullet-proof screens were removed. Police warnings about the inevitable dangers that would accompany the use of such machines were unfortunately ignored.

The first known robberies of banks with cash dispensing machines occurred in 1984. An analysis of the cases that have become known through the criminal intelligence system is presented below:

1. In 1984, seven cases were registered. Four cases were attempted robberies in which the offenders gave up their plan after bank employees had pointed out that time delay systems were built into the machines which prohibited large sums of money from being paid out quickly.

In one case the cash dispensing machine was opened with a key and DM 62 190 were handed over after the offender had threatened to use force. In the second completed robbery the robber was given DM 10 665 from the cash register. His demand for more money was averted by reference to the machine. In a third case the offenders were not diverted by the existence of the cash dispensing machine and managed to take DM 359 600 from the vault and the cashier counter.

2. In 1985, 16 cases were registered, 5 of which were attempts. In 6 of the 11 perpetrated robberies the offenders took the money from cash dispensing machines. In three spectacular cases the robbers boldly waited out the full 10-min delay before the cash dispensing machine paid out the cash. In one case the two robbers were so nonchalant that no one even noticed the attack and normal business proceeded as usual.

In the other five completed robberies the money was taken from the cashier counters and from the daily cash receipts safes. In the five cases of attempted robbery the offenders gave up after having been shown the cash dispensing machines.

3. In 1986, 16 cases were registered, 2 of which were attempts (offense aborted after the offender found out about the time delay mechanism).

In five cases the robbers received cash from cash dispensing machines in amounts of DM 3000–5000. In six other cases the robbers were not diverted by the existence of the cash machines and simply took money from cash registers and safety vaults. In two cases cash was handed over to the offenders after the cash machine was opened. In both cases the time delay was not working at the time of the attack so that they had direct access to the storage chests inside the cash dispensing machines.

These cases show that the money machines present a completely new, unexpected situation for both the bank employees and the robber, a situation for which they are not prepared. Those who tried and failed to commit a robbery unanimously agreed that the cause of the failure was the sudden and unexpected situation: instead of finding the familiar bank teller who the offender knows has some kind of safety device, the robber is now confronted with a strange gadget and, not knowing how it works, he thus sees the situation as being out of his control and his effort therefore futile. It can be assumed that the offender's view of bank personnel walking around unprotected may have also intensified their sense of futility. The bank employees in all these cases reacted in the same way. They first pointed out the existence of the automatic teller machines and then explained the delay function of the devices. Some of the offenders were so surprised that they interrupted the act and did not even attempt to gain access to other sources of money.

The attacks that were completed showed that bank employees are unprepared for the new and potentially more dangerous situations. This was made particularly clear in the three cases in which the robbers walked around the cashier area to monitor the behavior of the employees to that the latter were no longer able to set off the alarm or camera. These cases confirm the importance of having an alarm or camera somewhere in the cashier area where it can be activated by other employees. The results of being directly confronted with the offender with no protection are manifest in the extreme nervousness of many of the employees: too upset to operate the cash machine properly, they referred the robber to other sources of cash in order to steer his attention away from them.

The evaluated cases also demonstrate how the delay function of the cash dispensing machine, which represents a greater risk for the robber, can contribute to escalation of the act. The robber becomes more nervous, his reaction to the new, unexpected situation becomes more unpredictable. As the attack is taking longer he may have to invest more criminal energy to prevent failure. The successful attacks, however, also demonstrate the ability of the robbers to learn and adapt quickly. In those cases in which the robbery took at least 10 min it can be seen that the robber counted on having to wait 10 min for the money. In the other cases the offenders seem to have taken other sources of money (such as cash register, vault, drawers) into consideration right from the start. This is seen in some spectacular cases, other than the ones evaluated in this study, in which the robbed bank was equipped with cash dispensing machines but the robber demanded money from other receptables. The fact that bank robbers have unhindered access to other money receptacles is the result of the lack of built-in safety devices that have accompanied the introduction of the cash dispensing machine.

References

Behder U (1983) Täterfluchtverhalten nach Raubüberfällen auf Geldinstitute. Eine Analyse für den Polizeipraktiker. Wiesbaden (BKA-Forschungsreihe. Special volume)

Büchler H, Leineweber H (1985) Bankraub und Sicherungstechnik. Sicherungstechnische Einrichtungen und ihre Auswirkungen auf das Täterverhalten bei Raubüberfällen auf Geldinstitute. Wiesbaden (Berichte des Kriminalistischen Instituts)

Büchler H, Leineweber H (1986) Bankraub und technische Prävention. Phänomenologie – Bestand und Auswirkungen der Sicherungstechnik. Wiesbaden (BKA-Forschungsreihe, vol 18)

Bundeskriminalamt (1978) Bericht über die Untersuchung von Raubüberfällen auf Geldinstitute, öffentliche Kassen, Dienststellen der Bahn und Post und auf deren Geldboten. Wiesbaden (unpublished)

Servay W, Rehm J (1986) Bankraub aus Sicht der Täter. Täterleitende Faktoren bei Raubüberfällen auf Geldinstitute. Wiesbaden (BKA-Forschungsreihe, vol 19)

Part V
Enhancing Effectiveness of Detection and Criminal Investigation

CHAPTER 18

Investigation of Economic Crime

P. Poerting

Contents

1 Introduction

Police and other investigative bodies dealing with economic crimes need special knowledge of economics, business administration, and the tactical methods employed by perpetrators of economic crimes to be able to establish and assess the evidence necessary for securing a conviction. The criminal police have tried to meet these requirements through the following organizational measures by:

- Setting up specialized police units with central areas of jurisdiction
- Setting up an exchange of news and information on economic crime between the criminal authorities
- Providing initial and in-service training for police dealing with economic crime
- Hiring auditors and other experts with business training.

In the absence of a valid analysis of the effectiveness of such measures, the Research Unit on Criminology and Criminal Investigation of the *Bundeskriminalamt* (BKA), in 1984, took on the task of establishing an accurate picture of police action in dealing with economic crime. The results were to describe the work of the criminal police on the basis of empirical data and to provide objective decision

Kube/Störzer (Eds.)
Police Research in the Federal Republic of Germany

making aids. Particular attention was paid to the effect of the centralization and specialization of the areas of investigation.[1]

The data were gathered from all of the criminal police units dealing with economic crime. Given the number of units and their distribution all over the Federal Republic of Germany, the use of questionnaires was the only feasible procedure.

The questionnaire was drawn up with the help of representatives from the criminal police departments of every German state to ensure that all questions important for criminal investigation work were included.[2] Most of the approximately 100 questions were formulated in such a way that the answers could be coded and processed by computer. This allowed for a multidimensional evaluation. The answers from 147 units were included in the evaluation. In one state not all of the relevant departments were questioned but only those that specialized exclusively in economic crime. In another state, some questions were excluded from the questionnaire.

An initial objective of the study was to find suitable and measurable operational criteria for the factors of centralization and specialization. The following criteria were used:

- The level of organization, that is, the position of the department in the organizational hierarchy of the state police
- Personnel
- The specific crimes dealt with
- The percentage of personnel allocated to economic crime proceedings.

The first two criteria provide information on the degree of centralization, the last two relate to specialization. For both groups the first variables are of a more formal and qualitative nature, while the second two represent a more quantitative measure. These structural variables reveal several conditions under which the criminal investigation work in economic crime is done. The state in which the individual department is located must also be included among the factors determining the structure; Germany is a federal republic, and the influence of the state is often just as strong as that of the aforementioned variables.

2 Levels of Organization

The police jurisdiction in the states of the Federal Republic of Germany is divided into very different organizational structures. This makes it difficult to carry out a systematic comparison. For research purposes, a cross-state categorization with six levels of organization was drawn up:

---

[1] Poerting, Peter (1985) Polizeiliche Bekämpfung von Wirtschaftskriminalität. Wiesbaden (BKA-Forschungsreihe. Special volume).

[2] Each state has a state criminal police office (*Landeskriminalamt*) as a central criminal police facility.

Level A: State criminal police offices and BKA
Level B: Regional police departments (only in states that are not city-states)
Level C: Departments of local police authorities who have regional jurisdiction
Level D: Police departments of large cities
Level E: Departments of other police authorities
Level F: Detached units

The departments which responded to the questionnaire are distributed across these levels as shown in Table 1.[3]

Table 1. Levels of organization of the responding departments

Level of organization	Number of responding departments	%
A	12	8.2
B	11	7.5
C	12	8.2
D	32	21.8
E	72	49.0
F	8	5.4
Total	147	100.0

Table 2. Levels of organization in the states and the BKA

State	Levels of organization A	B	C	D	E	F
Baden-Württemberg	1	5	–	7	22	–
Bavaria	1	–	–	8	22	6
Berlin	1	–	–	1	–	–
Bremen	1	–	–	2	–	–
Hamburg	1	–	–	2	–	–
Hesse	1	2	–	5	15	–
Lower Saxony	1	–	–	7	13	2
North Rhine-Westphalia	1	–	4	–	–	–
Rhineland-Palatinate	1	–	8	–	–	–
Saarland	1	–	–	–	–	–
Schleswig-Holstein	1	4	–	–	–	–
BKA	1	–	–	–	–	–

The distribution of the departments across the levels of organization in the various states (Table 2) is an indication of the degree of centralization of the investigations in matters of economic crime.

The degree of centralization is particularly high in the city-states (Berlin, Bremen, Hamburg) and in the small states (Rhineland-Palatinate, Saarland, Schleswig-

[3] Since in one of the states not all of the departments answered the questionnaire, the number of city police authorities (level D) is misleading. There are 23 city police authorities that are missing.

Holstein). It is striking that the large states of Bavaria and Lower Saxony have no central departments for economic crime. Baden-Württemberg and Hesse are the only two states with departments having jurisdiction over the entire upper level of integration (*Regierungspräsidium*, Regional Commissioner).

3 Size of the Departments

The number of officers in the departments questioned ranged from 1 to 76. Most of the departments had three to seven officers (Table 3). Four groups of departments were distinguished for the study: (1) small departments with up to five officers: (2) medium-sized departments with six to ten officers; (3) large departments with 11–20 officers; (4) very large departments with more than 20 officers. More than two-fifths of the departments questioned fall into the first category, almost one-third into the second, one-fifth into the third, and only some 7% into the last category.

Table 3. Size of departments (number of criminal police officers)

Number of officers per department	Number of departments	%	Cumulated number of officers	%
1– 5	46	41.8	180	17.0
6–10	33	30.0	250	23.6
11–20	23	20.9	343	32.4
> 20	8	7.3	286	27.0
Total	110	100.0	1059	100.0

Bremen, Lower Saxony, and Rhineland-Palatinate have more than an average number of small departments. Hesse and Schleswig-Holstein have more than an average number of medium-sized departments (none of the departments in Schleswig-Holstein were larger). Hesse has an above-average number of large departments. Only three states, two of which are city-states, and the BKA have very large departments.

With regard to the levels of organization, the number of large and very large departments increases with the hierarchy of organization. Conversely, the number of medium-sized and small departments is larger, the lower the level of organization. In addition, there seems to be a tendency for the departments to be small, the less specialized they are and vice versa.

4 Specialization

To be able to assess the degree of specialization, information was obtained concerning what crimes the departments actually deal with. These include: exclusively economic crime; economic crime and other crimes of fraud; and economic crime, other crimes of fraud, and miscellaneous crimes (Table 4).

Table 4. Jurisdiction of the departments

Jurisdiction	All departments	Levels of organization A	B, C	D, E, F
Exclusively economic crime	14.4%	54.5%	47.8%	3.6%
Economic crime and other crimes of fraud	8.2%	18.2%	8.7%	7.1%
Economic crime, other crimes of fraud, and miscellaneous crimes	77.4%	27.3%	43.5%	89.3%

Less than one quarter of the departments questioned specialized in "exclusively economic crime" or "economic crime and other crimes of fraud." A comparison of the 11 states shows that the large states have a smaller percentage of highly specialized departments than either the small states or the city-states. The degree of specialization was greater, the higher the level of organization of the particular department, which is certainly not surprising. What is surprising, however, is that the percentage of departments specializing exclusively in economic crime at the levels A, B, and C is only 36%–60%. In addition, the percentage of the departments concerned with economic crime and other crimes of fraud is just as low. Thus, the present degree of specialization must be regarded as being relatively low.

A further measure of the degree of specialization of the departments questioned is the percentage of the total personnel assigned to investigate economic crimes. The results of this question also fall into the three categories: city-states, small states, and large states. Whereas the small states show the highest percentages (average 86.9%), the city-states have moderate (average 62.7%), and the large states only low percentages (average 48.8%) (Table 5).

There seems to be a relationship between the degree of specialization and the degree of centralization. This becomes evident when the percentage of personnel in the departments is put in relation to the respective level of organization. This percentage increases with the level of organization.

Table 5. Average percentage of personnel dealing with economic crime by state

State	Average %
Schleswig-Holstein	89.0
Rhineland-Palatinate	85.7
Saarland	85.0
Berlin	77.5
Bremen	64.5
Baden-Württemberg	62.7
Hamburg	51.6
Hesse	49.9
Lower Saxony	42.9
Bavaria	40.7

In general, it appears that the conditions in the individual states, especially the degree of centralization, are largely responsible for the degree of specialization.

5 Extent of Centralization and Specialization

The following conclusions can be drawn with respect to the structural variables:

1. The states of the Federal Republic of Germany can be divided into three groups: city-states, small states, and large states. This division is closely related to centralization, since the police in the city-states are always centrally organized and most of those in the small states are more centrally organized than in the large states.

2. The degree of centralization of investigations in the area of econonomic crime in terms of the work done by police departments at higher organizational levels with a large number of personnel is still relatively low. Only 23.9% of the respondents belonged to A, B, and C level departments; only 28,2% to large and very large departments (with more than 10 officers).

3. The degree of specialization is also very low. Only 14.4% of the responding departments specialize exclusively in economic crime and only another 8.2% in economic crime and property crimes. Even among the central departments (levels A, B, and C) no more than 45%–55% deal exclusively with economic crime. The same applies to the percentage of the total personnel assigned to economic crimes, which on the average is 55%. In this respect, however, the upper organizational levels show higher percentages. That means that although the departments at these levels are not officially specialized in economic crime, most of the actual investigative work is in this area of crime. Conversely, only a very low percentage of the personnel in the level D, E, and F departments deal with economic crime. In terms of numbers, central departments generally show a higher degree of specialization than others.

6 Impact of Centralization and Specialization on Investigative Work

At this point it is not possible to present the abundance of data in detail. Rather, a few factors will be singled out and presented with examples.

6.1 Personnel Structure

In West Germany, government posts and salary levels are grouped into categories: superior, higher, and middle service levels. Of the responding departments, 107 provided data regarding which categories their members belonged to. Of a total of 991 officers, 16 belonged to the superior level (1.6%), 599 to the higher level

(60.5%), and 376 to the middle level (37.9%). Leaving the BKA out of consideration, since its special personnel structure somewhat distorts the total picture, the following percentages result: superior, 0.9%; higher, 58.0%; and middle 41.1%.

The structure of the categories among those working in economic crime is not relevant in itself, but only in comparison with the structure of the entire criminal investigation service among the law enforcement authorities. For this purpose the ratio of the number of officers at the higher level to those at the middle level has been calculated for the departments dealing with economic crime and for the entire criminal police department. Whereas this quotient reaches 1.14 for the entire criminal service of all of the responding authorities, the departments working in economic crime attain a value of 1.41. Thus, based on the average of all of the respondents, the departments responsible for economic crime have a better personnel structure in terms of the proportion of higher level officers. Considerable differences can be found among the various states, at the various levels of organization, and among the different areas of jurisdiction.

With respect to organizational levels, departments working in economic crime at the lower levels D and E reach only a below average quotient. Departments at level A achieve a considerably higher quotient.

The experience of police officers is determined by their age, length of time in criminal police work, and how long they have been a member of their present department. The results of the questionnaire showed that the "average department head" is 47 years old, that he has been with the criminal police for 26 years. The "average" officer is 37 years old, has been with the criminal police for almost 17 years, and with his present department for 6 years. Considerable differences exist among the various states.

A look at the different areas of jurisdiction reveals that the officers in specialized units are older than those in nonspecialized units.

With respect to the levels of organization it was established that the central departments below the state criminal police offices (levels B and C) have above average values; level D has below average values.

Of the officers in the departments questioned, 494 had taken a special training course in economic crime. In 67 of the 104 responding departments (64.4%) at least one of the department heads had completed a special course.

A total of 109 departments provided data on training courses for their members. The percentage of departments in which more than half of the members had taken a course in economic crime was 40.9%. Levels B and C had higher values (50.0%), followed by level A. Central departments (at the state or national level) have an above average percentage of specially trained officers.

Not all of the officers specially trained in economic crime remain in the field. As compared with the total number of 494 officers, who at the time of the survey had completed a special training course in economic crime, 109 officers who had taken such a course were no longer working in economic crime. The average rate of those who leave the area of economic crime is 18.1%. Thus, more than one in six officers is no longer working in the area for which he was trained. The more highly specialized a department is, the higher the percentage of officers who leave.

6.2 Initiating Investigations

138 departments (93.9%) answered the question concerning the initiation of investigations. Criminal police investigations of economic crimes are usually initiated by reports made by the public, including anonymous calls to the police department (24.3%) and investigations at the request of the public prosecutor (66.6%). Only 9.1% of investigations are initiated on the basis of information obtained by the police departments themselves. Differences exist among the individual states, at the various levels of organization, and among the different areas of jurisdiction.

The higher the organizational level, the lower the percentage of proceedings resulting from complaints made to the police and the larger the number of investigations done at the request of the public prosecutor and due to police information. There are similar connections between the initiation of proceedings and areas of jurisdiction. The less specialized the department, the higher the percentage of proceedings based on reports made to the police.

6.3 Length of Investigation

It proved to be extremely difficult to obtain data on the average length of criminal police investigations in cases of economic crime. Many of the departments questioned indicated that the length of the individual proceedings varies greatly. Nevertheless, 87 departments presented usable data concerning the average values. The (nonweighted) average was 30 weeks (7 months), the mean value and the most frequent value (as further statistical values describing central tendencies) were both 26 weeks (6 months).

A comparison of the average length of investigation at the various levels of organization and among the different areas of jurisdiction – taking into account all three values – shows that the length of investigation increases with the level of organization and with the concentration of the jurisdiction. This suggests that particularly complicated and involved investigations are carried out by highly specialized departments.

6.4 Kinds of Economic Crime Investigated

The form of economic crime named most frequently (95 times) by the responding departments was bankruptcy-related crime. This form of crime was mentioned by 69.9% of the departments who answered this question (136), thus accounting for 24.1% of all answers. Bankruptcy crimes become even more significant when violations against the law concerning private limited companies are included, in which case bankruptcy crimes were named 117 times. There were 101 departments (74.3% of all respondents) that mentioned at least one of the two types of crime.

Other important kinds of economic crime are credit fraud (mentioned 46 times), crimes in connection with illegal work (44 times), and investment fraud (27 times). It can be seen that bankruptcy crimes were mentioned as often as the three other groups together. The abovementioned economic crimes accounted for 59.4% of the answers (234 out of 394); the remaining answers were distributed over a number of other types of economic crimes.

As was expected, level A mentioned bankruptcy crime only rarely. In contrast, it was mentioned by all of the departments at levels B and C and by all but one of the departments at level D. It is rather surprising that only 75.4% of the departments at level E mentioned this type of crime.

Investment fraud, embezzlement, and subsidy fraud are a matter for the central departments (levels A, B, and C). Copyright violations are mentioned very often by departments in large cities (levels C and D). Surprisingly, general fraud is mentioned only rarely by lower level departments.

6.5 Support of Investigations by Auditors

The hiring of bookkeepers or auditors to assist the criminal police has long been considered necessary in the area of economic crime. In the 1960s, such teams were employed by the criminal police and later by the public prosecutors dealing in economic crime. Despite positive results, these auditing services have not been further developed.

Of the departments questioned, 18 have specialists in bookkeeping and accounting. Saarland and Schleswig-Holstein have no such qualified employees. In North Rhine-Westphalia only bookkeepers are employed.

Auditors or bookkeepers exist only at levels A, B, C, and D. Most of them (14; 77.8%) are in the central departments at the state level (A) or at the level of the regional commissioner (B).

The 18 departments have 82 coworkers in auditing: These include: 14 experts in 5 departments, 18 auditors in 7 departments, 38 experts for auditing in 8 departments, and 12 bookkeepers in 7 departments. In 13 out of 18 departments, bookkeepers are employed to assist in auditing for a particular investigation. Only in three departments is their main duty to deliver expert opinions.

There were 11 departments that provided useful information on the question concerning the areas of crime in which the auditor should be used. The answers show that bankruptcy crimes are the most frequent (10), followed by acts of embezzlement (6).

7 Conclusions

The federal structure plays a major role in the present criminal police fight against economic crime. The survey showed considerable differences among the answers depending on which state the particular department belonged to. This has an influence not only on organization and personnel which determine the activity of the criminal police, but also on how the investigations are conducted, relations with the justice system, and the exchange of information concerning economic offenses among the criminal police.

The degree of centralization is a more significant factor than the size of the department, although it is not as important as state affiliation. Central departments generally seem to be better equipped to handle economic crime than decentralized departments. To a lesser degree the same applies to large and very large departments, as opposed to small and medium-sized departments.

The degree of specialization of a department, more so than the degree of centralization, has an effect on what persons are assigned to work in such a department. The influence of specialization on investigative work and relations with the justice system is less pronounced.

To sum up, it can be said that centralization and specialization provide far better conditions for investigative units in the area of economic crime. This does not mean to say that decentralized and less specialized units do inferior criminal work. It means only that their work is based on a smaller foundation. Centralization and specialization could represent a major contribution to making the work of the criminal police services in the area of economic crime more efficient and more effective.

CHAPTER 19

Technical Support of Drug Detection

W. Bach

Contents

1 Introduction

For a number of years the customs service and police forces have been demanding the provision of better technical means for detecting and identifying narcotics. The objective of improved detection methods is not so much to reduce availability, but to increase the risk for the illegal drug dealer. The proportion of drug seizures based on the estimated total annual consumption appears to be very low.[1] An estimate of the total annual consumption and the percentage of drugs seized is difficult to make, since factors such as the total number of drug addicts, the average daily demand, the stretching of the quality of the drug from the "wholesaler" to the addict, and the true amount of drugs in transit (as opposed to the amount of narcotics brought back into the country) have to be taken into account.[2] Although the percentage of seizures is very low, it is nevertheless a basis for assessing the effectiveness of improved interdiction methods. Even a minimal increase in this percentage could drastically raise the risk associated with trafficking narcotics. Moreover, the police might receive additional information on the hidden, complex supply system of the drug trade and, in turn, could draw up measures for more effective prosecution.

[1] The average amount of heroin seized from 1978 to 1987 was approximately 217 kg (source: records of cases of drug-related crimes).

[2] See Kreuzer, Gebhardt, Maassen, and Stein-Hilbers 1981, pp 218–221.

Kube/Störzer (Eds.)
Police Research in the Federal Republic of Germany

2 The Research Program at the Bundeskriminalamt

The development and testing of better methods for detecting and identifying drugs constitutes one way of improving the technical equipment of the police, customs authorities, and federal border police within a comprehensive strategy to combat the illicit drug trade and smuggling.[3] The outcome of this strategy was a program of action developed by the government of the Federal Republic of Germany in 1980.[4]

In its beginning stages, the research program had virtually no procedure that could be used to guide further technical developments. It is technically very difficult to locate, recognize, and identify narcotics hidden behind the shield of a suitcase, bag, or box. Not only are there many different chemical compositions for a given drug, but there are also various ways of physically shielding drugs. Moreover, the smuggler's imagination and creativity in finding ways to camouflage the merchandise do not make the job any easier.

In 1981, the *Bundeskriminalamt* (BKA) established a research program to examine the following technical detection methods:

- Dielectrical procedures
- Sonographic detection of intracorporally smuggled narcotics
- X-ray technology
- Mobile mass spectrometer.

At present, a simulation program is being carried out in which these procedures are being successively tested. The development and testing of further methods, along with testing of the sensitivity of smell of drug detecting dogs, are in their planning stages.

2.1 Dielectrical Procedures

The dielectrical method, which was developed by a German company, measures the magnetic and dielectric properties of materials. A trial prototype, BG-1, was made to detect letter bombs and narcotics. A 4 week field test yielded only unsatisfactory results. The false positive rate was high and the machine was only able to detect 45% of the letters containing narcotics.

[3] See Brugger 1983, pp 281–295.

[4] See Bundesminister für Jugend, Familie und Gesundheit 1980.

2.2 Sonographic Detection of Intracorporally Smuggled Narcotics

The number of "swallowers" has increased in the Federal Republic of Germany in the last few years. Up to now, medical X-ray examination has been the only available method for detecting intracorporal drug smuggling. Within the scope of a research project conducted by the BKA, doctors at the Technical College of Aachen were able to detect narcotics dummies in the intestinal tract of dogs by means of ultrasound.[5] In the opinion of the researchers, it should not be too difficult to detect swallowed narcotics in humans, although the method is not expected to replace the X-ray technique in the near future.

Experiments were also carried out using nuclear magnetic resonance imaging (NMR). Drug dummies fed to animals could also be detected by this method.

2.3 X-Ray Technology

The search for narcotics in airports used to be limited to spot checks. In 1985, the BKA introduced an X-ray scanner to establish how effective such a device could be in detecting narcotics in airfreight and baggage: After the test had shown promising results, the technique was used at German airports to examine cargo. So far, 200 kg of narcotics have been discovered by this method. The use of modern X-ray machines with so-called false color representation, enhancement functions, and HI-CAT image improvement systems facilitates detection of low-contrast materials, such as drug hiding places, even when they have been worked into strongly absorbing materials such as metal.

Experience has shown, however, that modern X-ray technology alone does not guarantee success. The operating staff must be properly trained and motivated, fully acquainted with the various smuggling methods, and know how to interpret the X-ray-images correctly. Only then will the X-ray technique be an effective tool for examining mail, baggage, and cargo for the presence of drugs.

2.4 Mobile Mass Spectrometer

The mobile mass spectrometer developed by the BKA is used to detect narcotics contained in baggage, cars, and cargo containers, for example, by means of gas or microparticle analysis. An almost fully automatic mass spectrometer system has been installed in a van. The vehicle is equipped with batteries which ensure 6–8 h of operation independent of the main battery. The equipment can also be used outside the van. To date, it has been programmed and optimized to automatically detect heroin, cocaine, and cannabis products. Comprehensive field tests have shown that in suspicious cases a reliable and rapid analysis can be performed on the scene

[5] See Alzen, Banning, and Günther 1987, pp 544–547.

within a few seconds. For this purpose drug particles in the range of just a few nanograms are sufficient.

The system is now in operation with high selectivity and low false positive rates. Further investigations focus on preconcentration of drug vapors inside shipping and airfreight cargo containers. The preconcentrated samples are to be analyzed by a mobile gas chromatograph and mass spectrometer (GC-MS) system.

Apart from drug detection research, a program is presently being followed up which would extend the use of the system to other target chemicals such as explosives (post-explosion detection) and environmental pollutants. Preliminary field tests in crime scene work have already been carried out. The GC-MS system will also be programmed to detect more than 40000 environmental pollutants, in soil, water, and atmosphere, in situ.

3 Suggestions for Making Research and Equipment Planning More Effective[6]

Industry recognizes a short-term market for sophisticated detection and prevention measures to be used against explosives and weapons; for instance, as part of the package of security measures used at airports. This market justifies individual initiative and investment. In the area of drug detection, however, the high costs of technical development along with an uncertain profit require that the government make concrete efforts at promoting research. To make research and equipment planning more effective, the following points should be taken into account:

- Exchange of information and cooperation at the national level between police, customs authorities, and research institutes
- Improvement of materials equipment, and staffing of state-run research facilities which deal with developing and testing drug detection methods
- Promotion and coordination of research at a national and international level.

References

Alzen G, Banning S, Günther R (1987) Sonographische Nachweisbarkeit von Betäubungsmittelbehältnissen im Gastrointestinaltrakt. Experimentelle Untersuchung beim Hund. In: Fortschritte auf dem Gebiete der Röntgenstrahlen und der Nuklearmedizin 146:544–547

Brugger S (1983) Strategische Planung als polizeiliches Instrument am Beispiel der Drogendelinquenz. In: Kube E, Störzer HU, Brugger S (eds) Wissenschaftliche Kriminalistik. Grundlagen und Perspektiven. Teilband 1. Wiesbaden, pp 281–295 (BKA-Forschungsreihe, vol 16/1)

Bundesminister für Jugend, Familie und Gesundheit (1980) Aktionsprogramm der Bundesregierung zur Bekämpfung des Drogen- und Rauschmittelmißbrauchs. Bonn 1980 (unpublished paper from Nov. 16, 1980)

[6] See Council of Europe, 1986, pp 15–16.

Kreuzer A, Gebhardt C, Maassen M, Stein-Hilbers M (1981) Drogenabhängigkeit und Kontrolle. Kriminologische Untersuchung über Phänomenologie des Heroinkonsums und polizeiliche Drogenkontrolle. Wiesbaden (BKA-Forschungsreihe, vol 14)

Council of Europe – Cooperation Group to Combat Drug Abuse and Illicit Trafficking in Drugs (Pompidou Group) (1986) Means of detection and working methods to fight drug trafficking by air. "Technical and scientific means". Report given at the Seminar on control services in major European airports (Paris, March 6–7, 1986) Strasbourg (P-PG(86)22)

CHAPTER 20

Police Information Retrieval Systems and the Role of Electronic Data Processing

E. Rebscher and F. Rohrer

Contents

1 Introduction

The general criminal investigation notification system of the entire police force in the Federal Republic of Germany is built around the concept of a habitual offender who commits offenses of an identical or related type, always in a similar manner. An example of this would be a burglar who always breaks into apartments by prying open the balcony door, having previously rung at the front door to make sure that no one was at home. This kind of information system was introduced for the first time in England in 1907.[1]

The fact that an offender sticks to a particular type of crime and modus operandi can be attributed to a lack of sophistication. This makes it possible to identify an initially unknown offender by his or her particular work (series detection) and also means that further, as yet unsolved cases can be attributed to an offender once he or she is finally caught. The chief aim pursued by the crime notification system is thus to match crime with crime and crime with offender.

This matching takes on even greater importance in this day and age of rapid transportation and social mobility, surpassing the boundaries of different police authorities and, indeed, of different federal states. It is thus essential for crime

[1] Schuster 1985, p 12.

Kube/Störzer (Eds.)
Police Research in the Federal Republic of Germany

notification records to be administered by central police departments, i.e., the *Bundeskriminalamt* (BKA), the state criminal police offices, and (in a number of states) specific regional departments.

Notification for the information retrieval system is required for crimes that are listed in a catalogue entitled *A Basic Classification of Offenses*, which has been updated several times. Printed forms were initially used for this notification, although these increasingly came to be supplemented and, to an even greater extent, replaced by telex messages. Work has recently commenced on incorporating the notification system into an electronically administered file system, with the ultimate aim of providing an automatic search facility.

Certain areas of crime with particular information requirements (drugs, arms, counterfeit currency, state security, terrorism, economic offenses) were taken out of the general crime notification system and given separate notification channels and forms.

Complaints were soon voiced within the police force that compiling the notification reports took up a great deal of time, which was not matched by any corresponding benefit since the information retrieval departments provided relevant information in only a very few cases.

The information retrieval departments, for their part, criticized the poor quality of the incoming notification reports, which did not provide a suitable basis for analysis. As the level of recorded crime grew, the problem of quantity also became increasingly critical. In cases where the central departments were, indeed, able to provide information on a presumed series or a specific offender or offenders, they only rarely received any feedback from the local police units as to the success of their work.

Increasing doubts have thus been voiced as to the effectiveness and efficiency of the crime notification system over the past 10 years. Added to this were the results of a regional study[2], according to which repeat offenders tended, on the one hand, to operate more on a local and regional level and, on the other hand, to perpetrate a wide range of crimes.

Before the crime notification system was integrated into an electronic data processing system – a move demanding a not insignificant investment – a study was conducted of the underlying theoretical principles governing the crime notification system and the actual practices employed.

A preliminary expert opinion[3] on the significance of the modus operandi was drawn up by Professor Ulrich Oevermann, a social scientist from the Johann Wolfgang Goethe University in Frankfurt am Main, who is well-known for his concept of structural and objective hermeneutics (key factors of which are a generalization of structures and the reconstruction of sense). This expert opinion was based on both theoretical considerations and actual police files. It concluded that there is indeed an "offender's hallmark," although this is not reflected in the current notification system, which is based on superficial, external categories instead of

[2] Steffen 1982, p 17.

[3] Oevermann and Simm 1985.

underlying dimensions. In the final instance, every act, unless it is the product of neurosis, boils down to the expression of an individual personality structure within a concrete framework of space and time – something which does not lend itself to the standardization required for electronic data processing. Oevermann divides the offender's action into two phases: the commission and the cover-up, though it is possible for the two phases to run into each other. The action committed leaves clues at the scene of the crime and on the persons involved, which, taken together, make up the clue text.

It is the job of the criminal investigation department officer to "read" this clue text. During the initial phase of the investigation the officer must mentally run through all the possible ways in which the act may have been performed and establish who could be the potential perpetrator. This phase calls for intuition, unimpeded by preconceived ideas.

If investigations have led to suspicion hardening against a particular person, then, in the second phase, a precise check must be carried out to establish whether the accumulated findings do indeed tally with this person, his modus operandi, and his motive.

2 Data and Methods

By way of follow-up to the study described above, Oevermann was commissioned to carry out an empirical study of the practical procedures employed in the crime notification system and to put forward proposals for its improvement. The entire field operations and the full organizational structure of the criminal investigation department and the police were to be analyzed in terms of logic, problems, and internal consistency. This was to be done by following concrete cases through all levels of the hierarchy involved in the investigation.

A rural police headquarters in southern Germany and a city police headquarters in the Rhine-Main conurbation (representing different states with different police data processing systems) were selected for the 3 week study. The information obtained from examinations of local files, observations of the initial investigation, and interviews with the police officers deployed was compared with the written report submitted by the local and all higher ranking levels. This then constituted Part A of the study (Fig. 1).

In Part B, a study of cases was conducted of selected types of crime, which had given rise to an attempted analysis or to the supply of information to local police departments, at the central offices. The analysts a the central offices were questioned as to the criteria and strategies they employed (Fig. 2).

The survey phase of the research project employed four scientists and took 2 1/2 years. The wealth of written material involved (all radio conversations were recorded and logged at the local police stations, for instance), which is very difficult to analyze in hermeneutical terms, has resulted in a delay in the final report, which is planned to be published in the BKA research series in 1990.

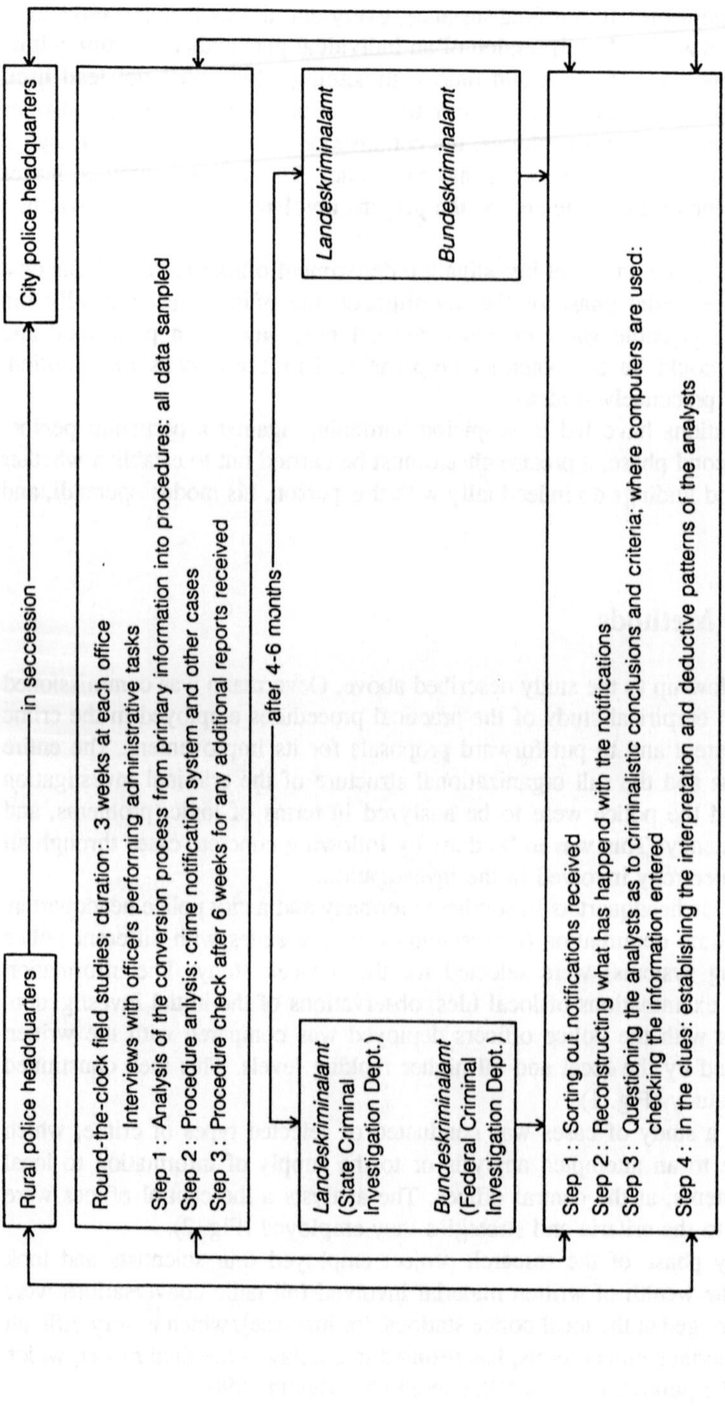

Fig. 1. Research project on the police information retrieval system (Part A)

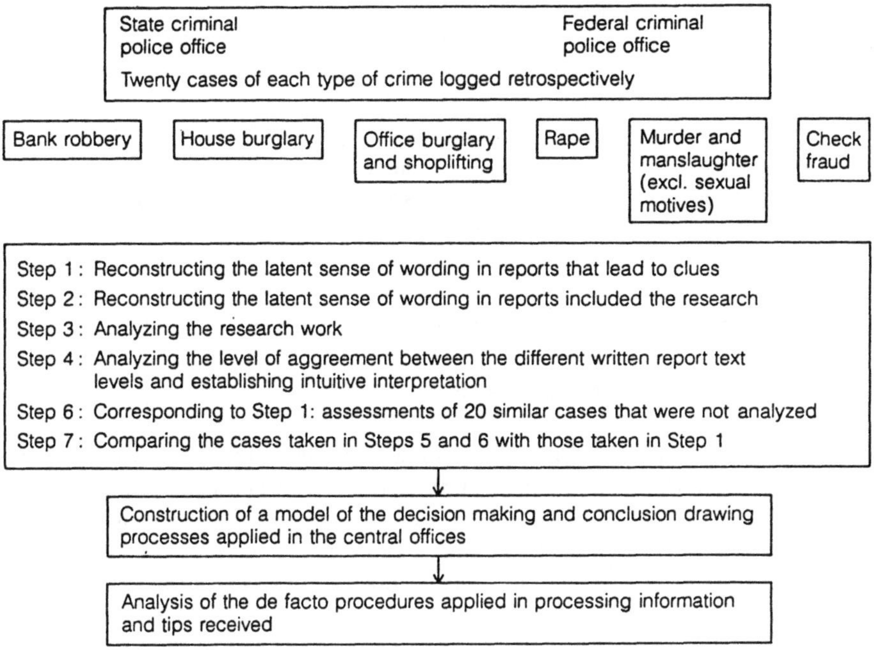

Fig. 2. Research project on the police information retrieval system (Part *B*)

3 Findings

3.1 The Researchers' Views of the Police

The researchers stressed the local competence of the police, and drew attention to the versatility, complexity, and independence of practical decision making performed by police officers on patrol duty and on criminal watch. The major part of police action is neither documented nor capable of being documented. Criminal investigation work does not lend itself to quantification or classification, nor does the work of police officers receive the recognition that it deserves, either from the public or from within the police force. This results in a lack of support for the police in their investigations.

The individual police officer represents the functional unit of the criminal investigation department and, at the same time, the source of the situation report. His written report often does not fully reflect his assessment of the situation (see below). This then leads to feedback from the upper echelons of the police to the police officer involved which he does not feel he can act upon. A motivation conflict can then result.

Active investigation takes second place to bureaucratic duties, which are highly formalized. The chances of investigations being successful are determined by the nature of the initial investigation employed and this, in turn, is based on criminal policy assessments (including anticipated media reaction).

When conducting intensive investigations, a police officer can only sensibly deal with two to three cases at a time. In order to fulfil his daily quota of work, he develops probability considerations for assessing the chances of success. These are fundamentally unrelated to the seriousness of the crime.

3.2 Practical Procedures Adopted in Crime Notification

3.2.1 The Problems of Wording Reports

The wording of the initial report is decisive in determining the prospects of follow-up investigations. The term "report" is used here to cover all methods of documentation which are intended to convey the vital facts of the case, or some of these, to third parties, i.e., it includes photographs and captions to photographs.

The wording used is based on standard models employed in telex correspondence and electronic data processing. An effort is made to achieve precise formulations to reflect the legal facts of the case. This can lead to stereotyping with a danger of the very details and particulars that are of relevance for solving the crime being omitted. The procedure involved in processing a case threatens to become independent of the detective investigations. The written "procedure" frequently provides a basis for control and assessment systems, which are linked to administrative or manpower planning goals.

The reason for potential distortions in the initial formulation is not any incapacity on the part of the officer processing the case. These officers are generally well-trained and possess a surprisingly high level of precision in their verbal expression. Oevermann suggests that the reason is much more likely to be a type of "premature obedience," whereby allegedly "objective" depictions ("which can be used in the courts") are forced into excessively rigid categories drawn up to fit in with criminal law.

Specific items of information, such as a precise knowledge of the milieu, can never be passed on in their entirety in the form of a written report. This represents an important barrier for computer-aided file systems (see below).

3.2.2 The Criminal Watch

Shortcomings in the written report will have particularly serious consequences in cases in which the work at the scene of the crime and the "administrative work" are carried out separately. This is frequently the case in big cities, where special police units are on duty round-the-clock to respond to calls and carry out scene-of-the-crime work (criminal watch) while the investigations are taken over by a specialist unit.

For the officer on criminal watch there is little prospect of any success in the investigations being directly delegated to him. This can prompt him to busy himself with swift processing of a maximum number of cases. The inevitably poor quality of the reports made at the scene of the crime, recorded on forms suitable for computer processing (see below), has a devastating effect on the follow-up investigations conducted by the specialist unit, which rarely visits the scene of the crime or, if it does, then only too late in the process. The overall lack of success in investigations, in turn, encourages further superficial work on the part of the criminal watch.

Oevermann found, contrary to common prejudices, considerable investigatory competence and a wide range of skills among a number of police officers in the central offices and also in the criminal watch units. Nevertheless, the idea of the criminal watch being a school for up-and-coming detectives remains theoretical. The lack of an adequate number of such experienced officers capable of teaching in the criminal watch scarcely permits the necessary on-the-job training.

3.2.3 Scope for Assessment

The simple rewording of reports at different levels of the notification system can produce a change in the classification awarded to a crime under criminal law. Either a dramatization (particularly in rural areas) or a downplaying of the crime can result, due to policy or professional considerations. One of the main guiding principles here would seem to be the anticipated media response.

Assessments including "interregional" criminal, "professional" criminal, "particular modus operandi," and "organized criminal behavior" are of considerable importance when it comes to detecting and evaluating series of crimes, highly active criminals, or criminal groups. A fixation on scientifically supported material evidence tends to be more of a hindrance when it comes to initially spotting a series of crimes or group of offenders. The officer's intuition plays a decisive role here. Detection of a series of crimes or a group of offenders is an important factor when it comes to handing over investigations to central, specially trained, and specially equipped units.

3.2.4 Evaluation Potential

The officer remote from a case (at the central office) who is responsible for analyzing it will only have a point of departure on which to establish the identity of the unknown offender if unique features of the suspect have been recorded or if precise information has been given on particularly striking facts of the case. Cases of this type can occur in all crime groups.

Rather than classifying all crimes on the basis of the most frequent characteristics, which may blur important distinctions, it is better to classify only cases where there are truly distinguishing features, which may lead to the identification of a particular offender or the establishment of a series of crimes.

Since it is this (virtually) unique nature that determines the capacity of a crime for analysis, there is little point in specifying *types of crime* for mandatory notification. This simply leads to an unmanageable flood of notification reports, which cannot be offset by an increase in the number of police officers deployed. If there are too many analysts, then there is a risk of information being lost due to a deficit in communication. This does not in any way affect requiremens for mandatory notification which are based on considerations other than the solving of a case. A lesser amount of information would then be required on a regular basis, and could therefore be called up from statistics or via reference numbers.

3.3 Evaluation and the Computer

The problems outlined above have become even more critical with the increasing use of computers. The predominantly administrative advantages of a central data processing system are set against a number of key drawbacks: above all, the need to place everything in categories, which leads to significant details being lost. This is followed by a lack of information on potential acts that the offender failed to carry out (to take a trivial example: the valuables that he did not take) and, finally, by the separation that exists between the officer responsible for investigating the case (detective) and the computer terminal operator, which can develop to a level where the data processing takes on an identity in its own right. If the computer operator makes inappropriate "improvements" to a report drawn up by the detective on the basis of investigative criteria, adapting it to meet data processing constraints, then there is a danger of specific information of relevance to the assessment becoming lost – specific information which has perhaps only survived in distorted form in a written report by the investigator.

Administrative criminal investigation staff often complain that they have the impression of being "slaves to computer forms" and constantly have to "petition the data processing system."

Even in cases where the officers doing administrative work operate the computer terminals themselves (which is always the ideal), difficulties will arise when officers conducting research, i.e., performing analyses and searching for relationships, have to share their terminal with an officer who is performing urgent operational tasks (such as requesting car registration numbers, checking wanted persons, etc.). The officers performing research are then frequently regarded as causing trouble and holding things up and are tempted to fall into line, that is, to perform their research work only superficially and not to use the potential of the system to the full.

It is of vital importance that the (subconscious) intelligent eye of the criminal investigation specialist should not be forgotten when telexes and notification forms come to be scrapped in the wake of the increasing move towards automation and computerization (a move which is to be strongly welcomed in that it relieves staff of office work and allows them to concentrate on the actual investigations). The right solution here is to have automatically prompted screen messages and automatic printers. The texts displayed should be kept as free as possible of the typical computer abbreviations.

4 Conclusions

4.1 The Basis of the Crime Notification System

Before embarking on any reorganization of the notification channels, measures should be taken to reinforce case-oriented, on-the-spot, criminal investigation work. Such measures would include the provision of relief from routine work and the improved design of reports. Reports should outline potential scenarios construed by the investigating officers (these being labeled "subjective" facts) and not be simply confined to purportedly "objective" (precise) facts. The best way for a beginner to learn investigative methodology is by reenacting true (solved) cases and receiving on-the-job training from experienced detectives.

Since a written report can never convey the information in its entirety (like the famous "I smell a rat" feeling of the officer at the scene where the dead body is found), care must be taken to ensure that there is steady, intensive (and informal) flow of communication both horizontally and vertically. When a different police unit takes over investigations, the original officer in charge of the case should be transferred as well, at least for a limited period of time.

4.2 The Computerized Crime Notification System

The first stage is to clarify the main aim to be pursued: either centralized evaluation (organized on the basis of criminal strategy) or decentralized research (organized on a case solving basis). With the latter, cases are to be recorded in the system only as a function of their prospects of success and not because they are listed in crime catalogues. The prospects of success are measured on the basis of highly significant information in the "clue text" relating to the description of the offender, search data for the goods involved, particular instruments used to commit the crime, and particular modus operandi. The data should be entered into the computer system once only and then by the officer in charge. Exceptions could be made for special stolen goods, such as works of art.

The computer programs should be constructed in such a way that entries can be freely worded and the screen masks frequently employed in computing avoided. In the majority of cases it will be sufficient to have small, local computers with locally managed files. It would seem wise to provide limited facilities for inquiries from outside. This could be performed on the basis of key concepts, which would simply serve to check the existence of a case. This would then create an interface for the automatic compilation of statistics and for "situation reports" to police offices.

National computerized case data files may prove necessary for certain important categories of crime, such as terrorism or drug-related crimes, not so much for investigative purposes, but for the development of criminal policy.

4.3 Central Crime Notification Offices

The institutionalized, formalized crime notification and information retrieval system should be replaced by the collection of all the information necessary and appropriate for fulfillment of the tasks to be performed. Instead of incoming case descriptions being "mechanically" checked against comparable cases in the file, investigations should be coordinated by an experienced and capable criminal investigation officer, supported as necessary by the computer.

In the framework of the assessment, special focus should be placed on a "criminal strategy" analysis, drawing on the teachings of social science. By this, Oevermann means the recognition of interlinked crimes (crime networks, organized crime) committed by specialized offenders or relating to specific objects, the establishment of correlations with social developments (e.g., new professions with scope for criminal action), and the recognition of the impact of a de facto failure to follow up petty offenses, for instance, on the population's general awareness of the law. Current practice, by contrast, would still seem to be oriented towards the individual "predatory offender" or "spontaneous offender" who tends to hold less damage potential for society as a whole.

If, contrary to the project recommendations, the central offices still insist on the notification of certain crimes, then Oevermann recommends concentrating on the following crimes (motives), bearing in mind the mission and the criminal policy considerations of the BKA:

- Check frauds
- Crimes involving more than one country
- Offenses committed by itinerant offenders, i.e., fraud associated with rented accommodations and thefts in hotels
- Economic crime extending over more than one state and so-called organized crime
- Crimes involving unidentified bodies and missing persons
- Searches for high value goods without a serial number to enter in computer search files.

There will be a wish to maintain the practice for manslaughter and murder for presentational reasons, even though a central notification system is not necessary to solve crimes of this type (and the existing system is scarcely used).

In the interests of "strategic" analysis, it is important for local police units to be made more aware of the "commonplace" concomitant circumstances that appear in the course of their work. This should take place in lengthy consultations between the local and central offices. Shared training and continued training facilities would also be an advantage, as would an exchange of personnel. Information on the tasks, modes of operation, and capabilities (and hence also the limits) of the other offices involved – the willingness to cooperate aside – constitutes a basic condition for worthwhile cooperation.

References

Oevermann U, Simm A (1985) Zum Problem der Perseveranz in Delikttyp und modus operandi. Spurentext-Auslegung, Tätertyp-Rekonstruktion und die Strukturlogik kriminalistischer Ermittlungspraxis. Zugleich eine Umformung der Perseverenz-Hypothese aus soziologisch-strukturanalytischer Sicht. In: Oevermann U, Schuster L, Simm A (eds) Zum Problem der Perseveranz in Delikttyp und modus operandi. Wiesbaden, pp 129–433 (BKA-Forschungsreihe, vol 17)

Schuster L (1985) Perseveranz und Kriminalpolizeilicher Meldedienst. In: Oevermann U, Schuster L, Simm A (eds) Zum Problem der Perseveranz in Delikttyp und modus operandi. Wiesbaden, pp 7–127 (BKA-Forschungsreihe, vol 17)

Steffen W (1982) Untersuchung der Möglichkeiten des datenmäßigen Abgleichs von Täterbegehungsmerkmalen zur Fallzusammenführung. Zusammenfassung. München (Publication of the criminological research group of the Bavarian Police, Bayerisches Landeskriminalamt)

CHAPTER 21

The Role of Pattern Recognition in Forensic Science: An Introduction to Methods

E. Bunge

Contents

1 Introduction

Technology today plays an important role in solving and fighting crime, which will continue to increase in the future. Although the layperson may be impressed with what the conventional methods of forensic science can achieve, it is unsettling for the insider to realize how uncertain the effects of most classical procedures can be. The same is true of both collecting huge quantities of information for data processing and any of the possibilities involved in the identification of persons. In order to ensure the efficiency of police work for both the present and the future, the *Bundeskriminalamt* (BKA) decided approximately 10 years ago to establish a Research Unit on Technological Development, which would analyze those police problems that were technically soluble. The research unit set itself three major tasks:

1. *Development of new procedures* to establish objective measurement, formulation, and analysis of person-related and object-related evidence (for example, voices and photographs) which would provide additional clues for the police working in forensic science, the criminal identification department, and the police records department

Kube/Störzer (Eds.)
Police Research in the Federal Republic of Germany

2. *Optimizing established procedures* in order to increase measurement accuracy (handwriting) and to improve the quality of evidence, such as blurred, infocused surveillance photographs, photographs of the scene, low-contrast fingerprints, and noisy and distorted tape recordings
3. *Utilization of the latest data processing techniques* to rationalize and increase the efficiency of solving and fighting crimes wherever similar problems appear, for example, in computer-aided handwriting analysis, and comparison of traces left by firearms and tools.

In order to meet all three objectives, new technical disciplines have been introduced which thus far have had limited application in forensic science. These include: methods of automatic pattern recognition and artificial intelligence; information theory; and cybernetics.

Process control, photo and signal data processing, and word processing are applied within these basic subject areas. The individual research projects include:

- Computer-aided identification of persons on the basis of their handwriting
- Computer-aided identification of persons on the basis of their voices
- Computer-aided comparison of traces left by weapons and tools
- Computer-aided linguistic style analysis of texts
- Computer-aided image restoration
- Computer-aided identification of persons on the basis of their photographs
- Computer-aided comparisons of the morphology of microscopic and macroscopic samples (e.g., comparisons of hair and fibers)
- Studies of computer crimes.

A computing system has been developed which is capable of processing voices, photographs, and data obtained with devices used in criminal technology. As a result, analyses can be undertaken which produce objective findings to replace the subjective, unreproducible results obtained up to now.

The processors currently being used are those of the PDP-VAX family, VAX 785, VAX 780, VAX 750, VAX 730 PDP 11–700, as well as the array processor AP 120 for accelerating vector and matrix operations.

Analogue-digital converters, as well as digital-analogue converters with a computer controlled preamplifier and filter system are used to process signals.

The input of pictures is achieved with a high resolution video camera with stable image geometry. The image processing systems RAMTEK (1024 × 1024), GRINELL (512 × 512), and VTE (512 × 512) are employed for pictorial processing and representation. All of the hardware, which is complemented by a wide range of mostly "home-made" software, represents a new, universally employable system.

The system is connected to its environment by "eyes" in the form of video cameras, "ears" in the form of a microphone and tape recording unit, and by very different data converters. With the appropriate programming, it can carry out the most diverse analyses, comparisons, and identifications, producing fast, objective, and reproducible results.

The mathematical procedures used by the processor to recognize new information coming from digitalized images, signals, and other measurement data are drawn from the fields of mathematical statistics, decision theory, and pattern recognition.

Since pattern recognition will become one of the essential interdisciplinary activities in modern technology, an attempt will be made to give a brief introduction to the method. Application of pattern recognition will be illustrated by the research projects currently being carried out on both computer-aided voice identification and handwriting identification.

2 Principles of Pattern Recognition

2.1 Human Pattern Recognition

Humans possess excellent pattern recognition capabilities. They perceive their surroundings with the receptors of their five senses and process this input information or "input pattern" according to learned rules to form new decisions. They are able to sort particular information patterns into prescribed categories and to recognize things such as cars by their form, people by their voices, and flowers by their scents.

The principle underlying all human recognition is the same. The physical reality which is to be recognized is transformed into electrical potential signals by means of data transformers (the human sensory organs). The signal sequences are first analyzed by the brain according to rules which are not yet understood and then compared with previously stored patterns. They are either classified in certain categories (recognition) or they are used to learn the characteristics of a newly defined category. Essential for accurate recognition is that the characteristics of the category to be recognized have been derived from as many examples (test patterns) as possible.

That which the human learns is called "experience" and differs from person to person, since the rules of information processing in humans are the individual result of previous stimulus processing. The subjectivity of recognition results in the fact that several people, receiving the same input patterns, can come to very different conclusions, which may even be opposite in character. Forensic science, however, is concerned with objective recognition and descriptions, which when given the same input patterns supply objective and reproducible fundamental decisions. Therefore, it is the purpose of future research to bridge the gap between the still common practice of subjective recognition and evaluation of evidence, on the one hand, and the objectivity desired by the administration of justice, on the other. Application of computer-aided identification methods and statistical evaluation procedures is an important development in this area.

The specific difficulties in criminal pattern recognition – as opposed to industrial pattern recognition – are due to the fact that there are no standard patterns for processing. The patterns are concealed by a large number of unwanted side effects.

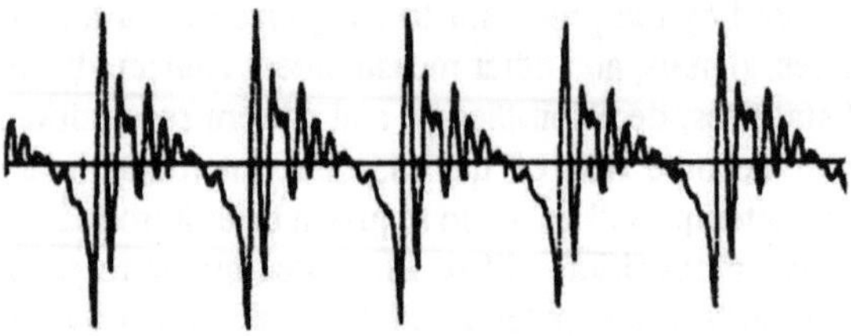

Fig. 1. Amplitude-time function of the spoken sound "ah"

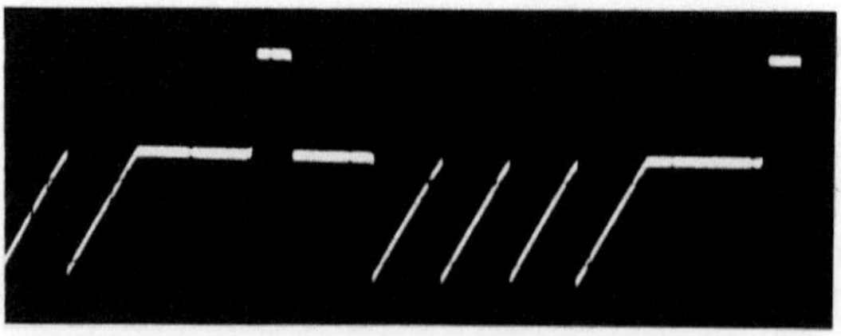

Fig. 2. Brightness-voltage curve of a scanned line

2.2 Pattern Recognition Using Computerized and Technical Systems

Pattern recognition involves the following steps: data conversion, digitization, preprocessing, feature extraction, feature assessment, feature selection, a learning phase, a recognition phase, classification, a test phase, and, finally, determination of recognition accuracy.

2.2.1 Data Conversion/Digitization

Sound and speech are converted into electrical signals by means of a microphone. Pictorial data are scanned line by line and point by point with a special camera and the brightness of each point is converted into electric voltage. Figure 1 shows the amplitude-time function of the spoken vowel "a" as an example for speech; Fig. 2 illustrates the brightness-voltage curve of a scanned line.

The digital conversion of voltage curves using an analogue-digital converter results in huge amounts of data: speech signals are displayed by 20 000 scanning results per second, whereas the digitization of an image containing 1024 points per line and 1024 lines per picture results in 1 048 576 digits. Since many seconds of speech and numerous pictures have to be processed, bottlenecks will arise during the processing and storage of this flood of data. This problem can be alleviated by employing rapid process computers, array processors, and mass storage units.

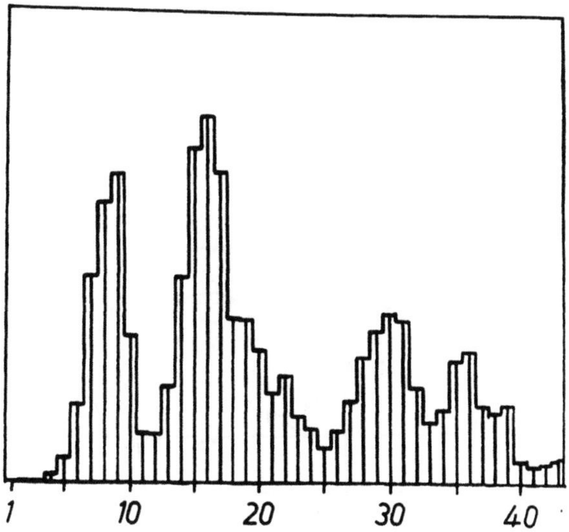

Fig. 3. Long-term spectrum of a speaker

2.2.2 Pattern Preprocessing/Feature Extraction

The large amount of scanning data retrieved for voices and pictures contains redundancies which have to be eliminated before the material can be applied to a specific identification task. In other words, the relevant information has to be calculated from the total amount of information by a series of linear and nonlinear transformations in the form of individual and specific feature vectors. Calculation of features can be considered a special form of data compression.

A 10 s speech sample, for instance, contains all the necessary information regarding the contents, the speaker, his emotional state, and any background noise. It is displayed as 200 000 instantaneous values. To characterize the speaker, a feature vector typical for the speaker and containing approximately 100 individual components suffices. This vector describes the sound of the voice, for example, using spectral coefficients and changes in vocal chord fundamental frequency by means of pitch statistics. The compression factor for this example is 2000:1. Figure 3 shows the course of a speaker-typical feature vector, "sound", and its mean spectral components. To calculate this, a 10 s vocal sample was divided into 500 segments and a spectral analysis was carried out for each segment. The 500 spectra were combined to determine their mean value.

When identifying persons on the basis of photographs, a matrix containing 1024 × 1024 digits is used as redundant input information, describing the intensity of the photograph point by point. For identification, however, one feature vector with merely 20 components suffices, which describes the facial geometry by the distances from the eyes, mouth, nose, chin, and outlines of the head (Fig. 4). In order for the feature vectors of different sized photographs to produce the same values, the individual measurements are normalized by dividing them by each other.

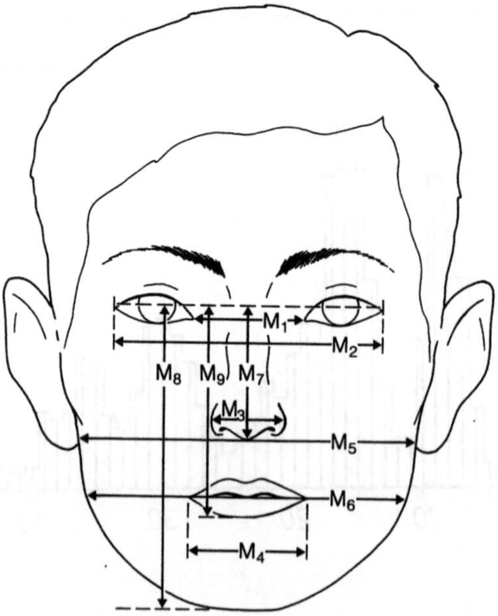

Fig. 4. Facial geometry

A very high data compression factor of 1024 × 1024: 20 = 1:52 248 results for this example of feature extraction.

To identify persons on the basis of their handwriting, geometrically described features are calculated from the digital matrix of the scanned handwriting samples and are combined to form one typical individual feature vector. This includes the angles of the slant of linear script elements, the radii of the curvature of the rounded elements, and the size relationships of lengths above and below the writing line. Several features are text-related and work on a letter basis (for example, in signatures). Others are independent of the text contents and statistically describe general structures of an entire written text.

Feature extraction is the most important step within the pattern recognition system. Since there is no systematic way to define "good" features, feature definition is usually carried out by means of a heuristic trial and error procedure.

2.2.3 Feature Assessment/Feature Selection

Since it is not possible to ascertain a priori whether a particular feature vector is suitable for characterizing defined classes, in this case persons, or for differentiating them from one another, it is necessary to statistically examine its selection effect.

The characteristics of a good feature include:

- Reproducibility of the measurement for a particular classs (person), i.e., low *intraclass* variance

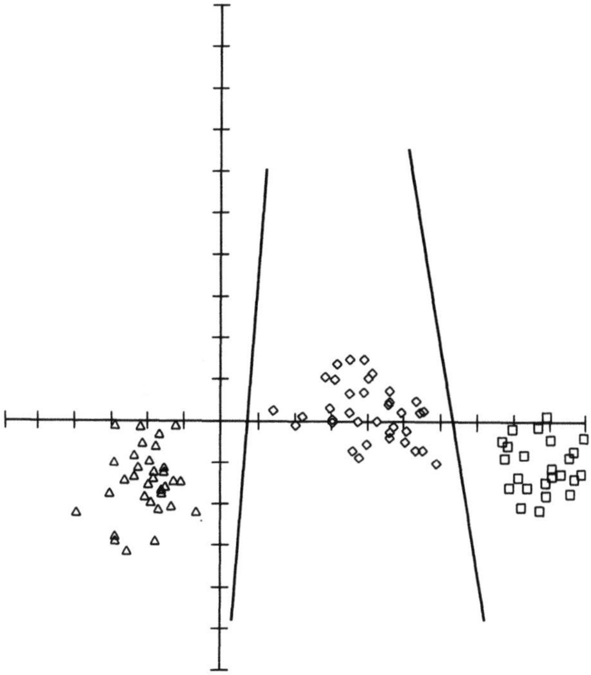

Fig. 5. Distribution of three groups of "good" features

- Large differences between classes (persons), i.e., high *interclass* variance
- Presentation of feature vectors with as few individual components as possible, i.e., small vector dimensionality
- Robustness of the sampler, i.e., insensitivity to such factors as voice and handwriting deformation.

To examine the quality of features, a quality criterion has been defined which combines the characteristics listed above. For identification purposes, only the best features are taken. Figure 5 shows an example: 50 written samples from three different writers were analyzed and described by two good features. The three writers can easily be distinguished from one another by the boundaries plotted. In Fig. 6 the same written samples are described by two "bad" features. The samples are so mixed up that a difference between the three writers cannot be made on the basis of these features.

2.2.4 The Learning Phase

One of the fundamental problems concerning pattern recognition is the nonreproducibility of patterns. For example, no human is capable of reproducing a sentence in exactly the same way twice, either in speech or writing. For this reason it is necessary, on the basis of various written and spoken samples of a person, to learn what these samples have in common and then to calculate this similarity

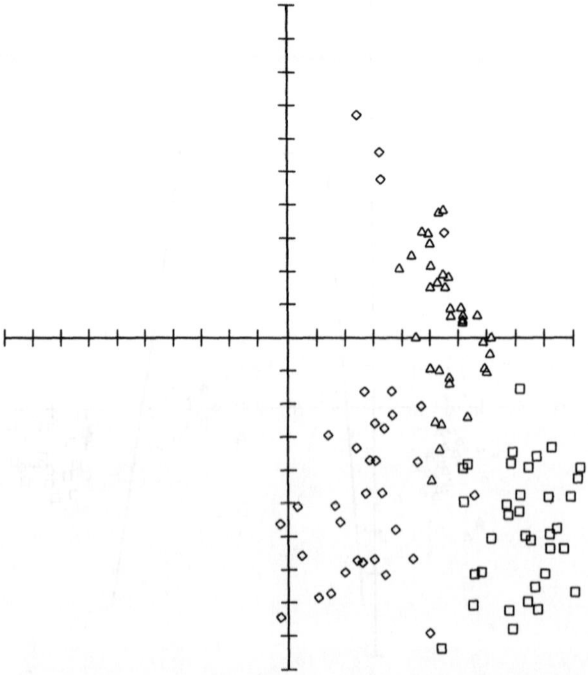

Fig. 6. Distribution of three groups of "bad" features

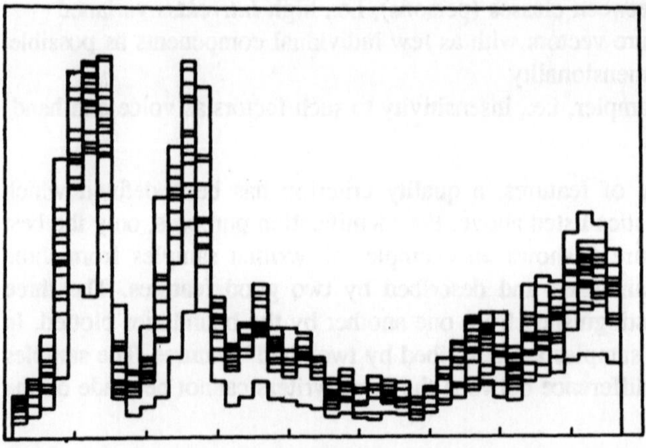

Fig. 7. An example of the nonreproducibility of speech is shown by 15 long-term spectra

as a person-specific reference pattern. This occurs during the learning phase. The learned data are statistically analyzed, isolated from their correlations by a series of transformations, and described by their mean vectors or ranges of variance. The procedures used here have been described in detail in the literature.

A simplified illustration of this phase is given in Figs. 7, 8, and 9, which were produced during speech identification procedures. A speaker spoke the same

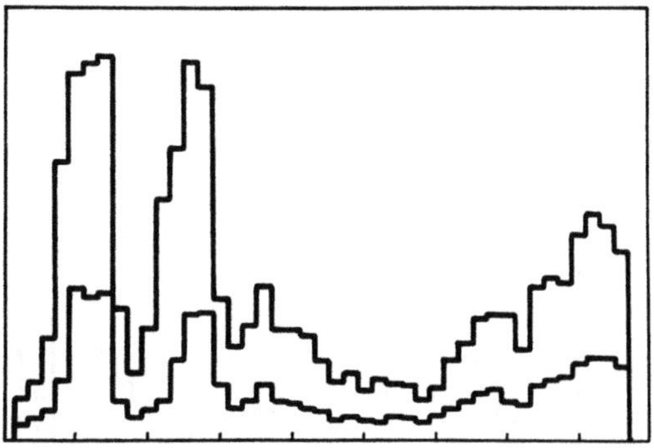

Fig. 8. Learned pattern

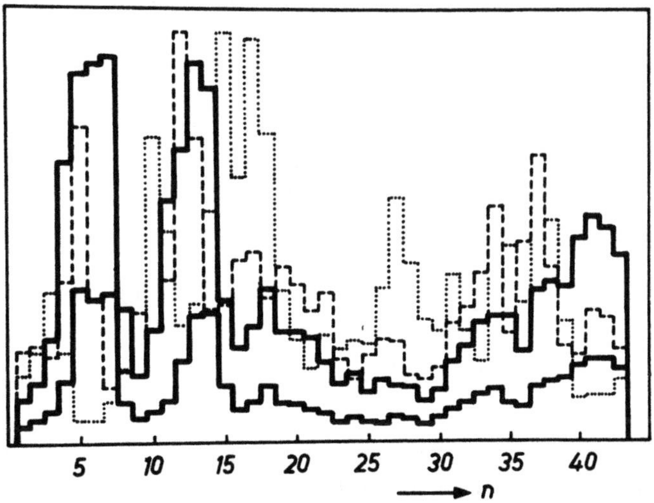

Fig. 9. Speech of original speaker (*solid lines*) and two "imitators" (*dashed and dotted lines*) who were rejected

text 15 times. Each time, the mean spectrum, which describes the sound of voice, was calculated as the feature vector. Figure 7 clearly demonstrates the effect of nonreproducibility: Although the same speaker repeated the same text, a different curve resulted from each of the 15 repetitions. All the curves are typical for the speaker.

The similarity of the 15 feature curves, which have to be calculated during one learning phase, is that all the curves lie within one range, which is characterized by the upper and lower boundary lines. This range is presented in Fig. 8 in the form of a pattern. This pattern can be considered a learned reference pattern of this speaker in the following identification attempt: Figure 9 shows that two speakers, who tried to imitate the voice of the original speaker, are not recognized by this small "system" and are consequently rejected, since their feature vectors are not

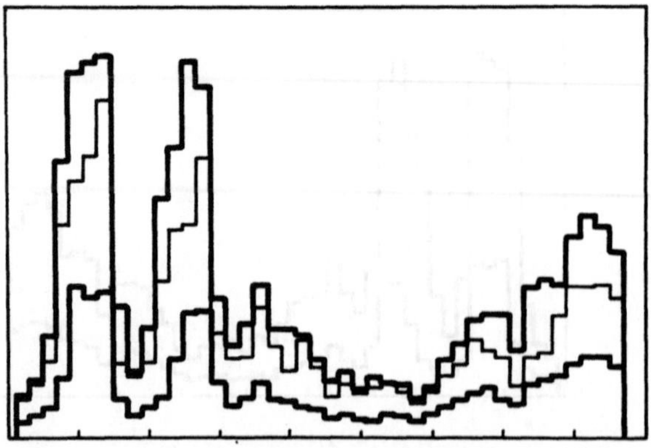

Fig. 10. The original speaker is recognized; his spectrum curve runs within the pattern

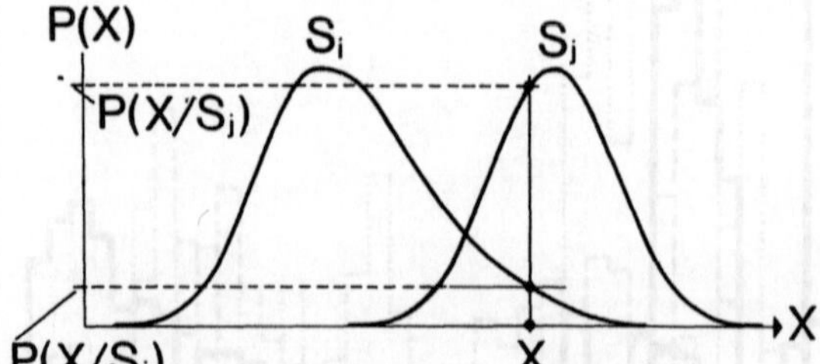

Fig. 11. The principle of the Bayes classifier

within the pattern. The curve of the original speaker, who repeated the text several days later, runs within the learned pattern and is thus recognized by the system (Fig. 10).

2.2.5 The Recognition Phase/Classification

During the recognition phase, it is the duty of the classifier to put an unknown feature vector into an already learned category. The basic principle is the Bayes-classifier, from which most other procedures have been derived. The simplified ordering rule states:

$$P(X/S_j) > P(X/Si) \Rightarrow X \rightarrow S_j$$

An unknown feature vector X is assigned to class S_j, for which S_i is the largest of all possible classes for the a priori joint probability $P(X/S_j)$. Figure 11 demonstrates this principle.

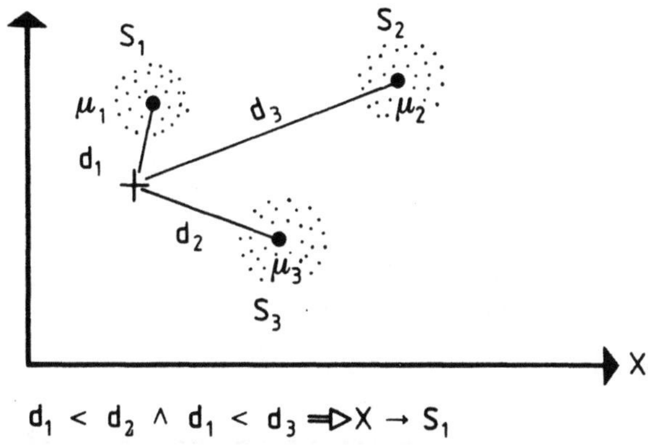

Fig. 12. Principle of the minimum distance classifier

During the learning phase, the probability densities $P(X/S)$ have been determined for the classes S_i and S_j. If an unknown pattern with the value X appears, the probability (as an example) with which X originates from the classes S_i and S_j is read from the curves. Since, in this example, $P(X/S_j)$ is larger than $P(X/S_i)$, X is assigned to the class S_j, according to the Bayes rule.

For this type of user system it is necessary to construct the distribution densities of the feature vectors for each class during the learning phase. It is easy to understand that classification results improve, the more test samples (written or spoken) are available for the system to learn. By means of a series of simplified assumptions, distance classifications can be derived from the Bayes classifier.

Figure 12 shows the function of the "minimum distance" classifier. Every feature vector acquired from the learning phase can be represented as a point in an n-dimensional space. In a diagram, of course, only a two-dimensional representation is possible.

The vectors of the individual defined classes, S_1, S_2, S_3, create scatter diagrams which scatter within a characteristic range. During the learning phase the scatter diagrams are characterized by their respective centroid points μ_1, μ_2, μ_3. If an unknown pattern x is to be assigned to one of these classes, point X is calculated from the distances, d_1, d_2, d_3 to the class centroid points y_1, y_2, y_3. X is then assigned to classs S_1, which is the smallest distance away from, in this case, class S_1.

Should the data of the learning phase exhibit such irregular scatter that it no longer makes sense to calculate a mean centroid point, the "nearest neighbor" classifier can be applied, the function of which is shown in Fig. 13. The feature vector points of the learning phase are not combined according to centroid points, rather they remain as class-specific individual points.

In order to assign the unknown pattern X to one of several defined classes, S_1, S_2, S_3, the distances from X to each individual point are calculated. X is then assigned to the "nearest neighbor."

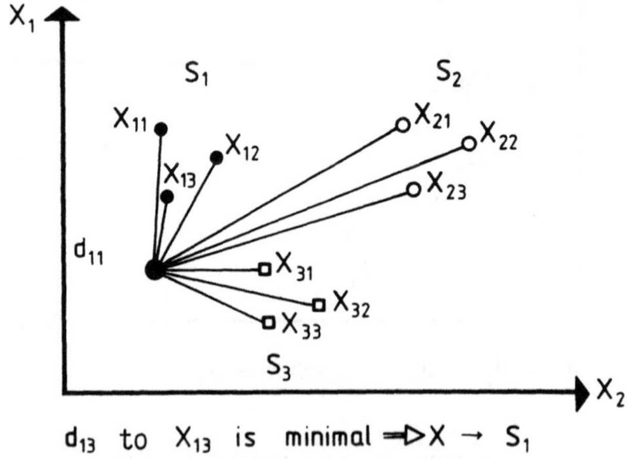

Fig. 13. Principle of the nearest neighbor classifier

2.2.6 Test Phase/Determining Recognition Accuracy

The test phase follows the learning phase, in which a series of known patterns that were not contained in the learning phase are automatically classified. The relation of the correct to the incorrect classification yields the typical recognition rate.

3 Practical Application

All of the steps described here are carried out during each application of a pattern recognition system: pictures and sound are transformed into electrical signals and subsequently into digital chains or matrices. Low dimensional feature vectors are calculated from these higher dimensional input patterns. In the learning phase the reference pattern for individual patterns are calculated on the basis of samples belonging to known classes. Reference patterns can be either centroid point vectors or pattern structures, as shown in the examples. After the learning phase, tests are carried out and the recognition accuracy is determined.

The types of procedures described are typical for pattern recognition systems which have already been applied commercially (automatic speech identification, handwriting analysis). In forensic science, however, pattern recognition methods are essentially used for research purposes. Fully automated person identification is limited by the large variation in external parameters, such as voice and handwriting deformations and distorted photographs and recordings. This system can thus be used to prescreen in order to reduce the number of possibilities that ultimately have to be evaluated by a human expert. For example, the computer can print out a "suggestion list" of the 10 most similar candidates and then supply a decision making aid in the form of an interactive measurement and evaluation system for the final identification.

References

Bunge E (1983) Technisch-wissenschaftliche Datenverarbeitung und Forschung im BKA. In: Bundeskriminalamt (ed) Polizeiliche Datenverarbeitung. Arbeitstagung des Bundeskriminalamtes Wiesbaden November 2–5, 1982. Wiesbaden, pp 213–219 (BKA-Vortragsreihe, vol 28)

Duda RO, Hart PE (1973) Pattern classification and scene analysis. New York etc.

Fukunaga K (1972) Introduction to statistical pattern recognition. New York, London

Klement V (1984) Rechnergestützter Handschriftenvergleich als Beispiel für die Anwendung der digitalen Bildverarbeitung und Mustererkennung in der Kriminaltechnik. In: Kube E, Störzer HU, Brugger S (eds) Wissenschaftliche Kriminalistik. Grundlagen und Perspektiven. Teilband 2: Theorie, Lehre und Weiterentwicklung. Wiesbaden, pp 171–200 (BKA-Forschungsreihe, vol 16/2)

Niemann H (1974) Methoden der Mustererkennung. Frankfurt am Main (Informationsverarbeitung in technischen, biologischen und ökonomischen Systemen, vol 2)

CHAPTER 22

Computer-Aided Identification of Handwriting

W. Kuckuck

Contents

1 Introduction

The *Bundeskriminalamt* (BKA) has for some time had a handwriting identification unit to assist it with identifying criminals. The handwriting samples collected for this purpose are presently being studied manually by means of the MALLY system, a classification system developed by the unit. This is a formidable task in terms of final visual comparison. The FISH system (Forensic Information System for Handwriting) was developed to facilitate handling of the constantly growing collection. FISH[1] is used for all of the tasks that accrue in the handwriting identification unit. The quality of processing is dependent on high speed and an improved selection of handwriting features.

The handwriting samples differ in terms of the amount of graphics, so that various different methods described below have been developed for processing them. All of the methods derive the handwriting features directly from the digitized image of the handwriting. A handwriting sample to identify a person is first digitized in FISH and features are then extracted which are text-insensitive, text-related, and interactively measured. Finally, a comparison is made between the type of feature and the stored handwriting features in the collection. A list of handwriting samples grouped according to similarity is then compiled and inspected by the handwriting examiner, who makes a visual comparison. If no sample for the given person is found, the procedure is repeated using other features. The efficient selection of features depends on the amount of text and the type of handwriting and requires a certain amount of experience on the part of the examiner.

[1] Described in detail by Klement 1984.

Kube/Störzer (Eds.)
Police Research in the Federal Republic of Germany

In the FISH system the process of digitizing handwriting yields a matrix of pixels (512 × 512), which can be either 0 (white background) or 1 (black text). The size of one pixel or image point is about 0.1 mm. These digitizing settings constitute a technical compromise between the accuracy of the image detail and the volume of the data to be processed. Higher resolution would considerably increase the computing effort required for feature extraction. One script image, for instance, requires 32 Kilobyte (KB) storage capacity.

To obtain writer-specific features, algorithms had to be developed which could operate on such matrices and which could consequently yield numerical data that characterize the handwriting. The discrepancy here is that, while the aim is to arrive at an overall result, the analysis itself is based on particulars in the form of pixel values.

2 Text-Insensitive Methods

To ensure comparability of the handwriting samples in the collection, extraction methods must be chosen which are not dependent on the individual text. To save time the process must be fully automatic. Characteristic shapes of individual letters cannot be analyzed by such a method, as this would require that the process be able to read the handwriting. However, these automatically identified features obviously have to depend to some extent on the specific text and so the "independence" criterion must be modifed: The features to be determined should be insensitive to text variation. That means that the given text must be of a certain length. Under these conditions specific graphics do not have much of an effect on the features.

The following method yields a measure of the width of the writing: *The length of white pixel chains between two black segments is determined along the lines of the image matrix. A frequency histogram is compiled on the lengths found.*

The histogram always shows a clear peak. The position of the peak corresponds to the typical horizontal distance between two black strokes and is therefore a measure of the width of the writing. The length does not necessarily correspond to a width measurement performed on the letters m, n, and u. The important point is that this measurement is typical for the particular writer and is subject to little variation.

Other features besides the width can be derived from the histogram. The range of deviation from the peak is characteristic for a given writer. Caution must be taken in interpreting this parameter, for example, as a measure of the width constancy. As the parameter includes rounded structures, loop sizes, and thread-like segments, it would be best to avoid interpreting it graphically. The usefulness of the parameter, however, becomes evident when the handwriting of several writers is statistically examined.

The above method of compiling frequency statistics based on white pixel chains is conducive to generalization. Such frequency distributions can be determined for different directions. In FISH, eight directions are used, which differ from each other by 22.5°. The same process can also be applied to black pixel chains. The

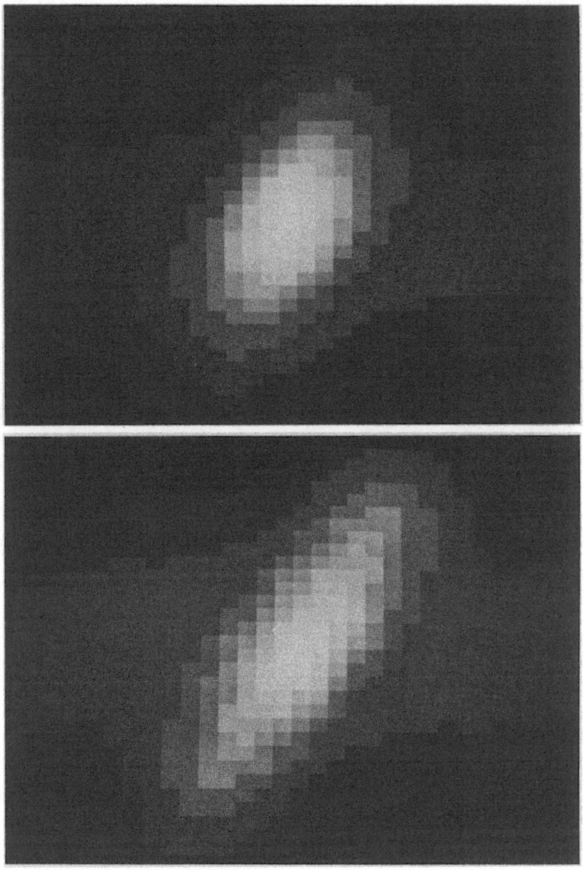

Fig. 1. Autocorrelation functions of handwriting images

shape of the histograms is recorded in terms of a parametric description, which has a smoothing effect. This simple algorithm has proved to be very efficient. It yields highly selective features and requires little computing effort.[2]

Another approach to extracting text-insensitive features is the analysis of the autocorrelation function of a handwriting image (Fig. 1). For binary images the process can be described as follows: *An imaginary copy of the digital handwriting image is displaced a certain distance in a certain direction and is superimposed on the original. The points in which there is a black pixel in both the original and the displaced copy are counted. Through this rule a function on the two-dimensional displacements is defined.*

[2] Detailed information on black pixel and white pixel statistics can be found in Steinke 1981.

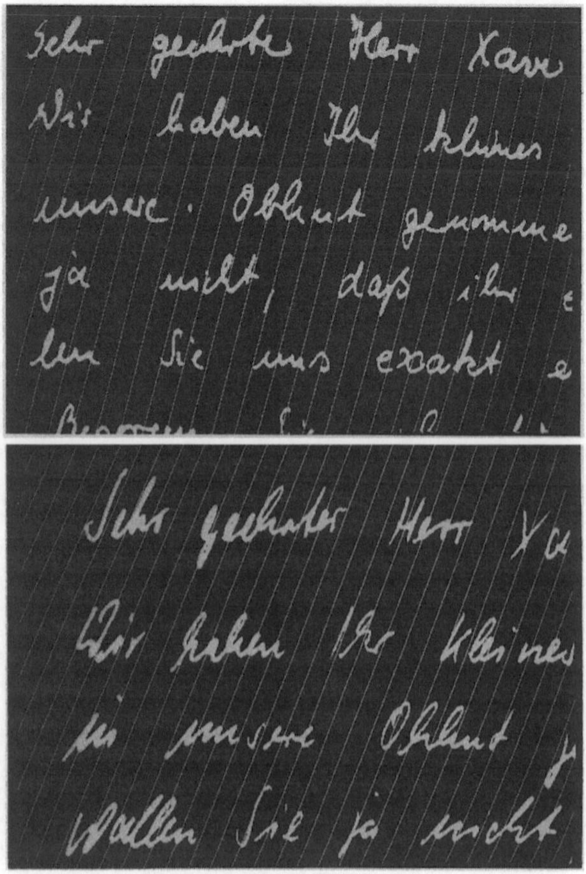

Fig. 2 Angles of the slant derived from the autocorrelation function

In this process, only values obtained for slight displacements are meaningful for the overall handwriting image, in which the function value is represented by various degrees of brightness. The striking phenomenon here is the almost elliptical position of the function values. The direction of the major axis corresponds to the slant of the handwriting. A displacement in the direction of the slant yields many coinciding text points. The function value decreases only gradually in that direction.[3]

Consequently, the angle of the slant can be determined from the correlation function. It should be pointed out that a measurement of the slant based on the downstrokes of the letters can differ from the process of measuring the width of the writing. Figure 2 shows the angles of the slant determined.

[3] A summary of the methods examined in connection with the autocorrelation function can be found in Kuckuck 1979.

Table 1. Results of several methods of handwriting analysis

Method	Recognition rate
White chain statistics	89.5%
Black chain statistics	99.0%
Autocorrelation function	95.6%

The capabilities of the foregoing methods were assessed using 40 test samples of the handwriting of 100 writers. The test was carried out under laboratory conditions (Table 1). In practical work with a CID-held collection, the recognition rates are expected to be lower. Permanent checks on this vital parameter are soon to become part of FISH.

In the course of the research project, a number of approaches other than those described here have been pursued with the aim of extracting text-insensitive features.[4]

3 Text-Related Features

The major drawback of text-insensitive methods is that they require a substantial amount of writing. This precludes the application of such processing for crimes such as check forgery, for which a method would be required that analyzes the individual letters. However, the problem here is that such writing could only be compared with samples that contain the same letters. In practice a standard must be set which restricts the freedom of selecting individual letters. Since it can be assumed that the word "hundred" will occur on a forged check, particular attention was given to the letters included in this word in lab tests. Work on individual letters always requires a degree of interaction on the part of the examiner, depending on the method used.

Analyzing letters involves reproducing the geometric aspect of the writing process. This method, however, is only suitable for letters written in one single, continuous movement. The line left by the writing instrument is roughly traced with points.

An algorithm to reconstruct the median line of the given stroke with the help of the rough tracing yields a sequence of points within the matrix representing the course taken by the center of the writing instrument. This track is approximated by a two-dimensional curve described with few parameters. It must be stressed here that this process assumes an artificial set of writing dynamics. The valuable information regarding the writing speed cannot be retrieved from the image.[5]

[4] Additional information on this subject is found in Steinke 1981, Rieger 1979, and Klement 1981.

[5] The results of a study made on the basis of this method are given in Steinke 1984.

Another approach is based on the notion that a written letter can be derived from a universal prototype by way of distortion. A prototype could be, for instance, the school standard of a letter. For practical purposes, however, a standard should be chosen which corresponds better to a general style of writing. A wide-mesh grid is placed on the written letter and on the prototype. An attempt is made to put the image contents of one grid in as close a relationship as possible to those of another within a predefined area. A local deformation of the prototype can then be determined, which yields an optimum approximation to the written letter. Figure 3 shows two examples. The displacement vectors of the grid points are a measure of the deformation applied to the prototype by the writer and can therefore be considered features typical for that writer.[6]

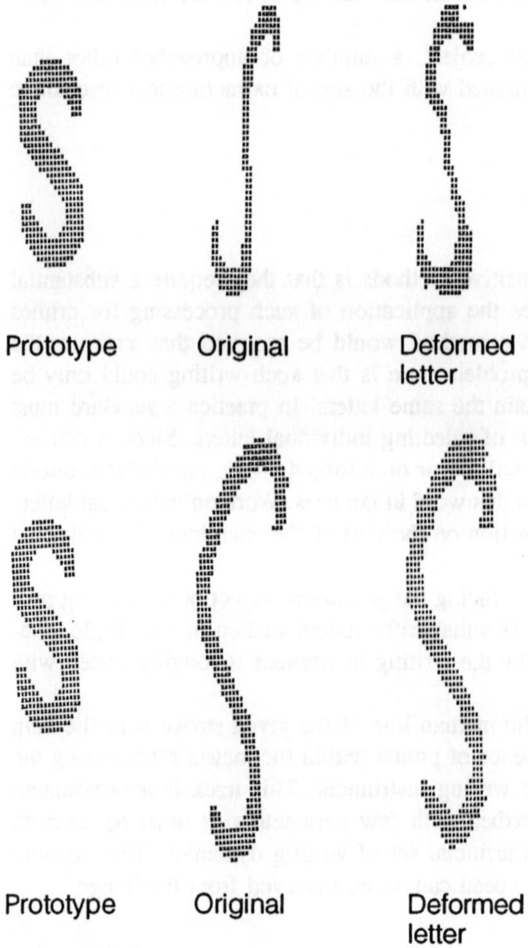

Fig. 3. Deformation of prototype letters

[6] See Naske 1983 for details on the methods and results.

Given the many different cases encountered, it would be a difficult task to try to give a uniform representation of the results. Generally speaking, however, a combination of the features of three letters yields recognition rates comparable to those obtained with text-insensitive methods.

4 Interactive Measurements

The methods described presuppose handwriting images that are free of "noise." A number of measurements are taken from the writing (height, width, slant) in order to compare the sample against the collection, should there be any heavy background print, superimposed marks, etc. These measurements are supported by image segmenting algorithms in order to keep interaction on the part of the operator to a minimum.[7] This type of feature always requires interaction by the examiner and is therefore costly to extract. Unfortunately, such an investment is mandatory for all handwriting samples if the measurements are to be used for comparing "noisy" handwriting images with the collection. Given the large number of measurements in the FISH system, it should be considered whether or not at least some of the measurements could be replaced by computed values based on text-insensitive methods.

5 State of Development

Presently, the system is undergoing a comprehensive test in which it has to prove itself, particularly in terms of its performance and efficiency in practice. A major criterion for the performance of the unit is that the system be practicable and manageable. The system user must have his work under control at all times, especially in view of the relatively complex processes and procedures. Much developmental work is invested in designing and improving the user surface.

What FISH has in common with modern fingerprint systems is that it automatically processes traces by computer. Handwriting features, which form the basis for comparison in one collection, are far more variable than features of fingerprints. The results obtained to date show, however, that the computer can be used efficiently even under such poor conditions. It is expected that in the future other police collections (ammunition used in crimes, falsified documents, etc.) will also be processed by means of modern methods.

[7] Broß 1986.

References

Broß F (1986) Projekt FISH. Untersuchungen zur Schreibererkennung mit interaktiv gemessenen graphischen Merkmalen. Wiesbaden (Bundeskriminalamt, Technischer Bericht; unpublished paper)

Klement V (1981) Forensic writer recognition. In: Simon JC, Haralick RM (eds) Digital image processing. Proceedings of the NATO Advanced Study Institute held at Bonas, France, June 23–July 4, 1980. Dordrecht, pp 519–524 (NATO Advanced Study Institutes Series. Series C, Mathematical and Physical Sciences, vol 77)

Klement V (1984) Rechnergestützter Handschriftenvergleich als Beispiel für die Anwendung der digitalen Bildverarbeitung und Mustererkennung in der Kriminaltechnik. In: Kube E, Störzer HU, Brugger S (eds) Wissenschaftliche Kriminalistik. Grundlagen und Perspektiven. Teilband 2: Theorie, Lehre und Weiterentwicklung. Wiesbaden, pp 171–200 (BKA-Forschungsreihe, vol 16/2)

Kuckuck W (1979) Schreibererkennung durch Spektralanalyse. In: Foith JP (ed) Angewandte Szenenanalyse. DAGM Symposium, Karlsruhe, October 10–12, 1979. Berlin Heidelberg New York, pp 190–196 (Informatik-Fachberichte, vol 20)

Naske R-D (1983) Verfahren zur textbezogenen Schreibererkennung aus dem Handschriftenbild von Einzelbuchstaben. Dissertation. Karlsruhe

Rieger B (1979) Skelettierungsverfahren für die automatische Schreibererkennung. In: Foith JP (ed) Angewandte Szenenalyse. DAGM Symposium, Karlsruhe, October 10–12, 1979. Berlin Heidelberg New York, pp 168–179 (Informatik-Fachberichte, vol 20)

Steinke K-H (1981) Entwicklung von Mustererkennungsverfahren zur textunabhängigen Analyse von Handschriftenbildern. Dissertation. Aachen

Steinke K (1984) Writer recognition by special characters. In: Levialdi S (ed) Digital image analysis. Marshfield, Ma., pp 364–372

CHAPTER 23

Digital Image Processing

K.-D. Brinkmann

Contents

1 Introduction

The quality of photographs, movies, video films, and fingerprints used in police work sometimes makes it impossible to recognize essential details. The reasons for such inferior quality include: overexposure or underexposure; pictures taken out of focus; smear effects produced by fast-moving objects or camera movement combined with a low shutter speed; grain structure or random noise produced by enlarging small details; and awkward camera movement when attempting both to trace the target of interest and to keep it in the middle of the screen.

Local police departments send poor quality pictorial data to the *Bundeskriminalamt* (BKA) which cannot be processed by the usual methods of photography. In keeping with the development of modern computer technology and digital signal

Kube/Störzer (Eds.)
Police Research in the Federal Republic of Germany

processing, a research and development unit for image processing has been set up at the BKA in Wiesbaden. Sponsored by the *Bundesministerium für Forschung und Technologie* (German Ministery of Science and Technology), the unit was commissioned in 1979 to design a powerful hardware and software system. A detailed description of the system is given below for the purpose of promoting an exchange of computer programs, data, and experience. Apart from using common image processing algorithms to enhance and restore poor quality images, the image processing unit also processes image sequences with VTE DataQ, a real time digitizing and processing system. The capabilities of this system are introduced and the processing tasks involved are explained.

2 Hardware Configuration

The VTE DataQ system consists of a computer, several computer terminals, graphic stations, image digitization and display systems, and a dedicated video input and processing instrumentation (Fig. 1). These components and the hardware of the special mug file retrieval system PERES, which is controlled and operated in this configuration, include:

1. Central processing unit: A modern computer (Digital Equipment Corporation, DEC) is used for imaging. In 1979, a VAX 11/780 with 1 MB main storage was installed, which was updated in 1984 to a VAX 11/785 with a floating point processor and 4 MB main storage. In 1986, the 16 K memory was replaced with a modern 256 K to expand the main storage capacity.

2. *Magnetic storage devices:* To store pictorial data and other information and to perform the common software backup activities, a magnetic tape station, TE 16; a disk, RPO7, with 516 MB storage capacity, and 2 disks, RP06, each having 176 MB storage capacity, were hooked up to the system.

3. Man-machine interaction: DEC VT 100 terminals are used to develop programs and to control image processing activities. Tektronix 4014 and VT 100 retrographics are used for graphic applications with the help of the graphic kernel system (GKS) and to input graphic information to the image processing algorithms. A VERSATEC V80 and a laser printer, LP 1200/QMS, are attached to the system to output graphic information and to print/plot the results of image processing for documentation. For program development on VAX and downloading of programs and data into the BKA mug file system PERES and to test and control the system, a DEC PROFESSIONAL 350 personal computer and a self-configurated microprocessor system for operating a digital picture retrieval system are connected to the VAX computer.

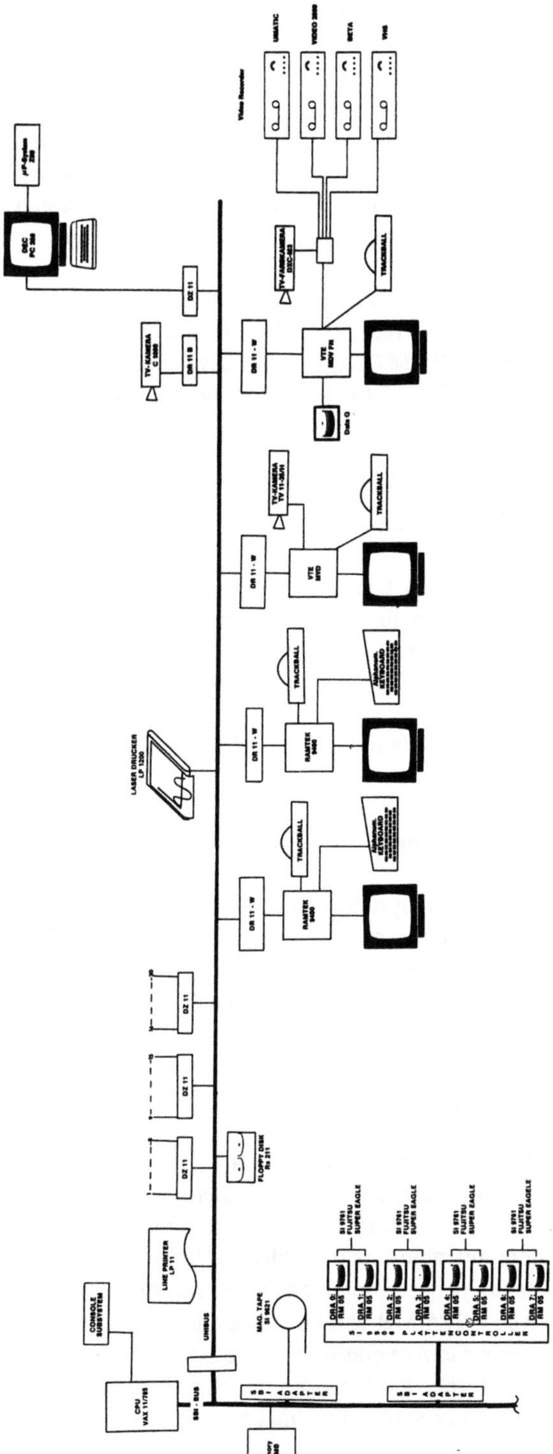

Fig. 1. BKA image processing system

3 Special Display and Image Processing Systems

3.1 RAMTEK 9400

The display size of these systems is 1280 × 1024 pixels. Ten bit data are used for every pixel to display color images or to use lookup table transformations. In the general operational mode, the systems are operated with four lookup tables containing 256 addresses to display 512 × 512 images or special windows in these pictures.

Man-machine interaction is supported by trackball and joystick units. Besides color lookup tools, the only other image processing algorithm performed with the help of the RAMTEK is interactive real time lookup processing, which allows transformation of the histogram and of the cumulative distributions function (equalization, linearization, or other user-defined distributions).

3.2 VTE MVD System

The purpose of this German System is to process black and white 512 × 512 images. To perform the image processing algorithms, the system has four input lookup tables and one output lookup table, each containing 256 addresses. With the aid of an ALU, which can be controlled by large, powerful FORTRAN software, the transformed output signals can be weighted and added to the inputs for repeated image processing. Windowing techniques are supported by trackball input.

3.3 VTE MBV System

The German MBV system is a modular color image processing system for RGB images. The image size is 512 × 512. Windowing techniques are supported by trackball input. In the BKA configuration the system is used for dedicated display of color images and for operation with the DataQ system to process image sequences.

3.4 VTE DataQ System

The purpose of the DataQ system is to digitize video signals in real time and to store them on a magnetic disk. For this difficult task the system is outfitted with a semiconductor memory to be able to store a complete 512 × 512 image. Two independent movable sets of read/write heads are used to transfer the half-pictures of the images between semiconductor memory and magnetic disk at 80 Mbit per second. About 185 MB can be stored on the disk without control information.

With the system operating in the black and white mode, 740 512 × 512 pictures with eight bit gray level can be transferred to the disk. Various operation modes are available to process color image sequences:

- RGB mode is performed using three disks in parallel to store sequences of the basic colors red, green, and blue.
- Chrominance and luminance modes are performed using two disks in parallel to store sequences of these components.
- Reduced RGB mode is performed using one disk to store 256 x 256 RGB components in one 512 x 512 frame.

In the BKA configuration the DataQ system is operated in the reduced RGB mode or in the black and white mode. There are no immediate plans to expand the system. We do plan, however, to track the 512 x 512 black and white videos to determine a sequence of coordinates of 256 x 256 windows for the purpose of storing interesting parts of a color sequence to be processed. With help of these sequences, 256 x 256 windows in different positions in each frame will be digitized in the reduced RBG mode. Transfer of the sequence from the DataQ to the MBV display system is controlled by FORTRAN subroutines, which allow slow motion and thus generate other display sequences and repetition of sequences.

3.5 Image Digitizer

Two cameras are connected to the system to input the images to be processed. With the aid of additional optical instrumentation for various enlargements and solutions, a SONY color TV camera DXC-M3 and a HAMAMATSU C1000 are used to digitize images. In the future, a digital scanner will be added to complete the image digitizing facilities.

To input videos, a powerful video signal processing unit is implemented to format and synchronize the video standards UMATIC, VIDEO 2000, BETA, and VHS.[1] These different signals are transformed to signals of "TV studio quality" by controlling, formatting, and/or adding synchronization signals to the inputs and using 5 MHz bandwidth. Besides the four standard inputs, nearly every other video system can be routed to the video signal processing unit to digitalize or to copy other video norms.

4 BVS Image Processing Software Package

The image processing hardware is operated and controlled by the general image processing package BVS[2], which enables the user to interact with these systems and different processing algorithms by a collection of more than 100 dedicated commands.

---

[1] UMATIC, VIDEO 2000, BETA, and VHS: international norms.

[2] Name of BKA software product.

4.1 Design Rule

The program package is designed to be machine-independent and portable. The standard program language is FORTRAN 77. Therefore, no VAX/VMS specific commands and program tools are used if there is no equivalent FORTRAN simulation program. For internal use and to speed up some algorithms, VAX assembler programs are available (provided a portable FORTRAN simulation program exists).

4.2 Man-Machine Interface

To design a modular program system which can be easily expanded and updated, every BVS command is carried out by a FORTRAN subroutine or one call to a collection of subroutines. Using top-down design and software engineering techniques, it is very easy to add new commands without recompiling existing program units.

The BVS commands are checked for syntax rules and interpreted by a powerful command string interpreter (CSI). The command syntax is similar to DEC RSX command language:

COMM/Cm_Quali OUTPUT < INPUT/In_Qual

CSI is able to process 500 alphanumerical characters per BVS command. With the aid of the continuation symbol "&", more than one line can be used to input commands to BVS. COMM is an abbreviation of the BVS commands with maximum length of four characters. Cm_Quali and In_Quali are qualifiers to select different operation modes or to provide the program with numeric or boolean information. OUTPUT is determined by file, device name, or specific BVS image, which resides in the main storage of the VMS operating system. These images are characterized by the character B (Bild, image) and a storage area descriptor A or B. BVS image types are characterized by the abbreviation B1 for byte, I2 for INTEGER*2, I4, R4, R8, or C8 for integer, real, or complex images of specified length. Addressing a specific image of the selected type is performed by an image number: An image (b) in the storage area A (A) of the type byte (B1) with number 3 is addressed by the name BAB13.

The actual version of CSI is capable of processing up to three outputs and/or inputs. Each input can be controlled by different input qualifiers:

DISP/HISTO/STATISTIC VERS<BAB11/NEG,BB121/BIN=8,DATAQ100

The command DISPlay transfers the byte image 1 of area A to the VERSatec printer-plotter. The input qualifier NEGative determines the way the image is printed. The integer*2 image 1 of storage area B has to be transformed to a BINary image in such a way that gray levels greater than the given threshold 8 are displayed in white. Gray levels less than or equal to threshold 8 are displayed in black. The 100th image of a sequence stored on the DataQ has to be displayed with default values of input qualifiers. The equivalent command qualifiers are used to print a HISTOgram and a STATISTIC.

CSI supports macro definition and execution by transporting actual values to local macroparameters and skipping commands dependent on the values of the BVS status registers.

4.3 Help Facility

Each BVS is documented in detail in a separate help file so that users familiar with image processing techniques can operate BCS without reading extensive manuals. These files are organized and interpreted by means of different key words to ensure interactive and selective information and support at any state of BVS processing. BVS commands illustrating the capabilities of BVS, without explaining the commands in detail, are listed in the chapter appendix. For a detailed description of these commands, the interested reader can request the German BVS manual from the BKA.

4.4 Image Restoration

The two examples of image processing (Figs. 2, 3) show the effect BVS can have on police work. Such results can be achieved by filtering in the frequency domain (see Appendix, no. 4).

5 Image Sequence Processing

5.1 Image Sequence Repositioning

The police usually record actions such as a violent demonstration against nuclear power plants by conventional film or video. The recording is generally done to document the course of the action, but not to identify individuals. That means that while the camera is taking in entire scenes, single persons or areas of interest may be moving at various speeds in different directions from one part of the screen to the other.

Due to the superimposition of the movement of the camera and the movement of persons it may be difficult to examine the details of a specific action. To equalize this superimposition of various movements, specific techniques and algorithms have been developed to reposition regions of interest into the center of the display screen.

The RAMTEX system is able to sequentially display different windows in different TV frames. To generate a film of different pictures, for example, the system must be programmed in such a way that the first picture is displayed in TV frame 1, the second in TV frame 2, and so on. To reposition pictures it is possible

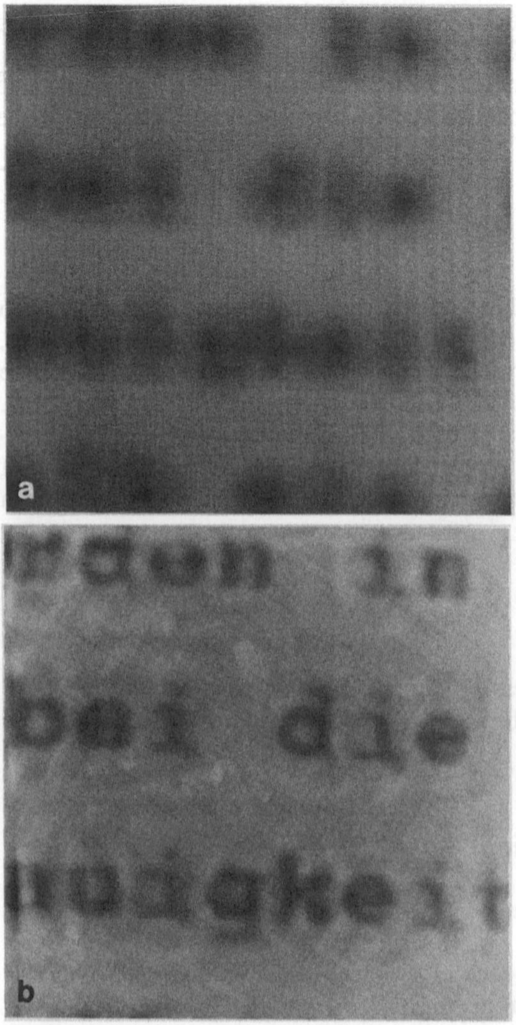

Fig. 2a,b. Picture out of focus. **a** Original; **b** results of restoration with different filter parameters

to program the system so that every picture can be moved relative to a determined picture and all of the pictures can be displayed as a film.

In general, pictures of the original scene will be displayed as a film. If the camera moves during the recording, the interesting details will move within the film. To fix the window of interest in the center of the display this region must be positioned to the desired coordinates by moving it in the opposite direction of the motion.

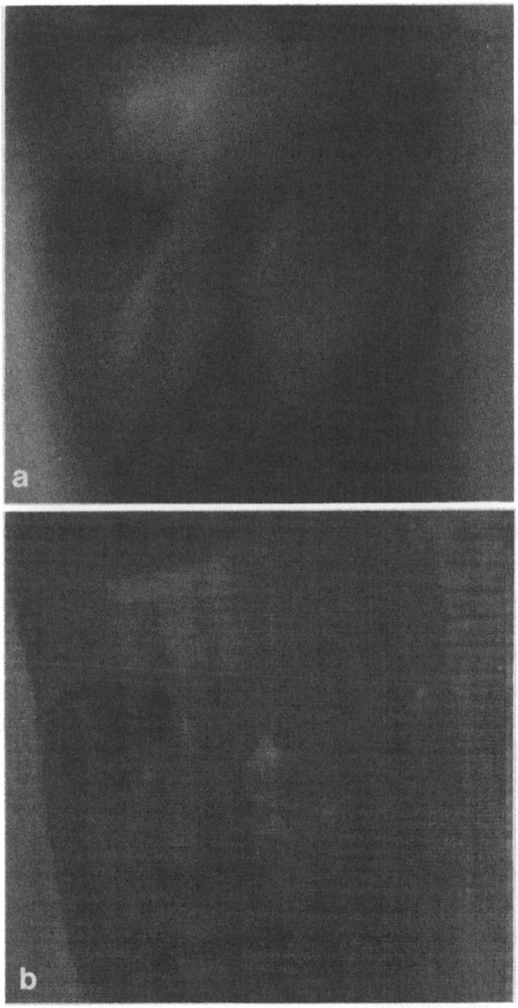

Fig. 3a,b. Blurred picture. **a** Original; **b** results of restoration with different filter parameters

The position of a determined geometric structure within the pictures of a sequence is computed with the help of a correlation algorithm. The difference of the position of the tracked structure in adjacent frames results in a displacement vector which describes the movement of the objects.

Automatic shift into the negative direction of this vector and display as a sequence will result in a new film without any movement of the region of interest. Using a modified tool, structures that change even slightly from frame to frame can be tracked.

5.2 Constrained Image Addition

In the case of violent action it may be necessary to identify the offenders by their appearance, figure, or clothes. Possibilities for enlarging single pictures in a film sequence may be limited by grain noise. Reducing the influence of grain noise in order to recognize a detail may be performed by adding several time adjacent pictures on the sequence with respect to a fixed geometric position of this detail. For this it is necessary to reposition the pictures of the sequence. Repositioning may be done interactively or automatically.

Adding these repositioned pictures will result in one part of the scene becoming blurred and another part being enhanced. In other words, specific local details of interest will be enhanced, while the overall quality of the image is reduced.

6 Conclusions

The image processing unit within the Research and Training Institute of the BKA was created in 1979 for the purpose of researching and developing image processing tools. To control the powerful image processing hardware, the software package BVS has been developed, which offers about 100 dedicated commands to apply powerful image processing algorithms. Besides the common image enhancement and restoration algorithms, new techniques for image sequence processing have been developed. Using video signal processing units the BKA is able to process different video norms. These image processing tools used for actual case work provide valuable expert opinions for the police and for the court.

Appendix: List of BVS Commands

1. Transfer of Image Data
Copy
Move window
Norm (adapt picture to given minimum and maximum)

2. Digitization and Display of Images
Deallocate
Disable cursor
Display
Display image squence
Enable VTE cursor
Erase display screens
Farbe (switch to display color or black and white)
Fiche (address image on microfiche carousel)
Keyboard (set keyboard mode on RAMTEK)
Plot

Read
Store image sequence
Video look up tables
Interactive operation of VTE systems
Zoom

3. Transformation Between Space and Frequency Domain
Discrete cosinus transformation
Fast Fourier transformation
Fast gradient operators
Slant transformation
Walsh-Hadamard transformation

4. Modifications in the Frequency Domain
Image restauration
Define filter matrix
Define transfer matrix
Execute filter algorithm
Maximum entropy method
Multiplication of spectrum
Pack spectrum
Video

5. Modifications in the Space Domain
Add constant
Block truncation coding
Calculate
Contour
Correlation
Differences
Enhancement
Fast restoration system
Geometric distortions
Histogram modification
Hybrid coding
Interpolation
KIRSCH operator
Grain noise
Transformation of coordinates
Line extraction
Mathematical operations
Median filter
Multiplication by constant
Ranking filter
Region growing
Retuschiere (painting and interactive pixel correction)

Skeletonize
Simple picture manipulation programs

6. Feature Extraction for Classification
Interactive feature extraction

7. Interface to Database Systems
Enter database system

8. Internal BVS Tools

Clear	(image store areas A and B)
DCL	(interface to DEC's command language DLC)
Define macros	
Deposit constant	(in pixel, line, or area of an image)
Define register	
Define vector	
Dump	(pixel, line or area of an image to printer)
Examine	(pixel, line or area of an image to printer)
Exit	
Execute macro	
Help	
Histogram	
Increment register	
List macros	
Load macro file	
Multiply register by constant	
Multiply vector by constant	
Projection statistics	(with respect to given thresholds)
Restore	
Save	
Set parameters or operation mode	
Show parameters	
Skip command	
Text	(white text to file, image, or display screen)
Tracking	
Wait	(process synchronization tool)

Appendix: Scientific Publications of the BKA

H.U. Störzer

Contents

1 Book Series

The Research and Training Institute acts as editor of numerous publications. The *BKA-Vortragsreihe* (BKA Series of Conference Lectures) contains the papers and discussions derived from the annual BKA conferences on practice-oriented topics.

The *BKA-Schriftenreihe* (BKA Monograph Series) deals with the personal training and advanced training of the CID officer.

Mainly final reports of in-house or external projects of the Research Unit on Criminology and Criminal Investigation are published in the *BKA-Forschungsreihe* (BKA Research Series). Only selected final reports appear as regular, consecutively numbered volumes; the remaining reports, other scientific monographs, and the proceedings of symposia held at irregular intervals on basic matters of crime and its control are edited as special volumes within this series.

The series *BKA-Technische Forschung* (BKA Technical Research) presents the results of research and development which have been obtained by BKA divisions involved in technical matters.

In order to translate the findings of research work into practical police use, the Research and Training Institute also publishes the series *Berichte des Kriminalistischen Instituts* (Reports of the Research and Training Institute) and the newsletter *Forschung und Entwicklung* (Research and Development), which appears at least twice a year as a supplement to the *Bundeskriminalblatt* (the BKA's Federal Law Enforcement Bulletin). In addition, the *Berichte des Kriminalistischen Instituts* also contain smaller-scale studies.

Every year, the *Polizeiliche Kriminalstatistik* (Police Crime Statistics) compile all figures available on police crime control activities at the federal and state levels.

The great wealth of criminal science literature is dealt with in the *BKA-Bibliographienreihe* (BKA Bibliography Series) featuring compilations of literature

Kube/Störzer (Eds.)
Police Research in the Federal Republic of Germany

on certain subjects and in the volumes of the *COD-Literatur-Reihe* (COD Literature Series) published for each BKA Conference and containing the appropriate references of the BKA *Co*mputer-aided *D*ocumentation System (COD) for police literature.

With the exception of the volumes belonging to the *BKA-Schriftenreihe*, the foregoing publications are distributed free of charge.

English speaking readers can find an English summary in each edition of the *Polizeiliche Kriminalstatistik* (e.g., 1987 p 219–225; 1988 p 219–223, see also p 3); the two series of bibliographies are confined to German literature. For scientists researching criminology, criminal justice, criminal investigation, and the like, the most interesting and most relevant of the other publications are the *BKA-Forschungsreihe*, the series *BKA-Technische Forschung* and, in some cases, the series *Berichte des Kriminalistischen Instituts;* a special note is added if one of the listed volumes of these series contains an English summary or abstract or any English contributions.

2 BKA-Forschungsreihe (BKA Research Series)

2.1 Regular Volumes

Volume 1: Sieben, Günter, Manfred Jürgen Matschke und Hans-Jürgen Neuhäuser: Bilanzdelikte/Unter Mitarbeit von Rainer Schmid. Wiesbaden 1974

Volume 2: Schwind, Hans-Dieter, Wilfried Ahlborn, Hans Jürgen Eger, Ulrich Jany, Volker Pudel und Rüdiger Weiß: Dunkelfeldforschung in Göttingen 1973/74. Eine Opferbefragung zur Aufhellung des Dunkelfeldes und zur Erforschung der Bestimmungsgründe für die Unterlassung von Strafanzeigen/Unter Mitarbeit von Herbert Gallus und Gernot Steinhilper. Wiesbaden 1975. (English summary pp 259–266)

Volume 3: Stephan, Egon: Die Stuttgarter Opferbefragung. Eine kriminologisch-viktimologische Analyse zur Erforschung des Dunkelfeldes unter besonderer Berücksichtigung der Einstellung der Bevölkerung zur Kriminalität/Mit einem Geleitwort von Günther Kaiser. Wiesbaden 1976. (English summary pp 353–366)

Volume 4: Steffen, Wiebke: Analyse polizeilicher Ermittlungstätigkeit aus der Sicht des späteren Strafverfahrens/Mit einem Geleitwort von Günther Kaiser und einer Einführung von Erhard Blankenburg. Wiesbaden 1976. (English summary pp 309–312)

Volume 5: Deusinger, Ingrid M. und Henning Haase: Psychologische Probleme der Personenbeschreibung. Zur Aufnahme und Beurteilung von Zeugenaussagen/Unter Mitarbeit von Monika Plate. Wiesbaden 1977. (English summary pp 159–162)

Volume 6: Schmitz, H. Walter: Tatortbesichtigung und Tathergang. Untersuchungen zum Erschließen, Beschreiben und Melden des modus operandi/Mit einer Analyse der Dokumentationssprache der Straftaten-/Straftäterdatei von Winfried Lenders und einem Geleitwort von Gerold Ungeheuer. Wiesbaden 1977. (English summary pp 475–482)

Volume 7: Banscherus, Jürgen: Polizeiliche Vernehmung: Formen, Verhalten, Protokollierung. Eine empirische Untersuchung aus kommunikationswissenschaftlicher Sicht/Mit einer Einleitung von Edwin Kube. Wiesbaden 1977. (English summary pp 261–267)

Volume 8: Schwind, Hans-Dieter, Wilfried Ahlborn und Rüdiger Weiß: Empirische Kriminalgeographie. Bestandsaufnahme und Weiterführung am Beispiel von Bochum ("Kriminalitätsatlas Bochum"). Wiesbaden 1978. (English summary pp 381–390)

Volume 9: Schmitz, H. Walter: Tatgeschehen, Zeugen und Polizei. Zur Rekonstruktion und Beschreibung des Tathergangs in polizeilichen Zeugenvernehmungen/Mit Beiträgen von Winfried Lenders und Elfriede Reents. Wiesbaden 1978. (English summary pp 557–568)

Volume 10: Salewski, Wolfgang D. und Kurt Schaefer: Geiselnahme und erpresserischer Menschenraub. Eine interaktionsanalytische und motivationspsychologische Studie für den Polizeipraktiker. Wiesbaden 1979. (English summary pp 299–307)

Volume 11: Kerner, Hans-Jürgen: Kriminalitätseinschätzung und Innere Sicherheit. Eine Untersuchung über die Beurteilung der Sicherheitslage und über das Sicherheitsgefühl in der Bundesrepublik Deutschland, mit vergleichenden Betrachtungen zur Situation im Ausland. Wiesbaden 1980. (English summary pp 395–414)

Volume 12: Sessar, Klaus, Ulrich Baumann und Josef Müller: Polizeibeamte als Opfer vorsätzlicher Tötung – Eine Studie zur Eigensicherung. Wiesbaden 1980. (English summary pp 292–301)

Volume 13: Rolinski, Klaus: Wohnhausarchitektur und Kriminalität/Unter Mitarbeit von Wilfried Ahlborn, Rudolf Heger, Peter Höhmann und Marianne Schwabe-Höllein und mit einem Ausblick von Edwin Kube. Wiesbaden 1980. (English summary p 217)

Volume 14: Kreuzer, Arthur, Christoph Gebhardt, Marcel Maassen und Marlene Stein-Hilbers: Drogenabhängigkeit und Kontrolle. Kriminologische Untersuchung über Phänomenologie des Heroinkonsums und polizeiliche Drogenkontrolle. Wiesbaden 1981. (English summary pp 413–420)

Volume 15: Baurmann, Michael C.: Sexualität, Gewalt und psychische Folgen. Eine Längsschnittuntersuchung bei Opfern sexueller Gewalt und sexuellen Normverletzungen anhand von angezeigten Sexualkontakten. Wiesbaden 1983. (English summary pp 523–533)

Volume 16/1: Kube, Edwin, Hans Udo Störzer und Siegfried Brugger (eds): Wissenschaftliche Kriminalistik. Grundlagen und Perspektiven. Part 1: Systematik und Bestandsaufnahme. Wiesbaden 1983. (English contribution pp 69–95)

Volume 16/2: Kube, Edwin, Hans Udo Störzer und Siegfried Brugger (eds): Wissenschaftliche Kriminalistik. Grundlagen und Perspektiven. Part 2: Theorie, Lehre und Weiterentwicklung. Wiesbaden 1984

Volume 17: Oevermann, Ulrich, Leo Schuster und Andreas Simm: Zum Problem der Perseveranz in Delikttyp und modus operandi. Spurentext-Auslegung, Tätertyp-Rekonstruktion und die Strukturlogik kriminalistischer Ermittlungspraxis. Zugleich eine Umformung der Perseveranzhypothese aus soziologisch-strukturanalytischer Sicht. Wiesbaden 1985

Volume 18: Büchler, Heinz und Heinz Leineweber: Bankraub und technische Prävention. Phänomenologie – Bestand und Auswirkungen der Sicherungstechnik/Unter Mitarbeit von Guido Scherer und Rüdiger Weiß. Wiesbaden 1986. (English summary pp 150–153)

Volume 19: Servay, Wolfgang und Jürgen Rehm: Bankraub aus Sicht der Täter. Täterleitende Faktoren bei Raubüberfällen auf Geldinstitute. Wiesbaden 1986. (English summary pp 181–185)

Volume 20: Wittkämper, Gerhard W. und Marianne Wulff-Nienhüser: Umweltkriminalität – heute und morgen. Eine empirische Untersuchung mit Prognose und Empfehlungen für die Praxis/Unter Mitarbeit von Ludger Vielemeier und Heinz Becker. Wiesbaden 1987. (English summary pp 38–49)

Volume 21: Schwind, Hans-Dieter, Wilfried Ahlborn und Rüdiger Weiß: Dunkelfeldforschung in Bochum 1986/87 – Eine Replikationsstudie. Wiesbaden 1989. (English summary pp 290–314)

2.2 Special Volumes

1977

Bundeskriminalamt (ed): Straftatenklassifizierung und -gewichtung sowie ihre praktische Anwendung/Offence Classification and Rating, and Practical Applications Thereof. Papers from the international symposium organized at the Bundeskriminalamt, Wiesbaden, February 16–18, 1977/Tagungsleiter: Edwin Kube. Wiesbaden 1977. (German papers with English abstracts/English papers with German abstracts)

Sieben, Günter und Peter Poerting: Präventive Bekämpfung von Wirtschaftsdelikten durch Selbstverwaltungsorgane, Selbstschutzeinrichtungen und Verbände der Wirtschaftsteilnehmer – Eine Bestandsaufnahme. Wiesbaden 1977.

Silbermann, Alphons: Untersuchung und Gutachten zum Projekt "Medienfahndung", zugleich zum Verhältnis Polizei – Presse – Öffentlichkeitsarbeit/Unter Mitarbeit von Albin Hänseroth, Herbert A. Sallen und Klaus Hang. Wiesbaden 1977

1978

Martens, Ulrich: Wirtschaftliche Krise, Arbeitslosigkeit und Kriminalitätsbewegung. Eine empirische Studie über die Auswirkungen der wirtschaftlichen Rezession auf das sozialabweichende Verhalten der Bevölkerung der Stadt Mannheim/Mit einer Vorbemerkung von Gernot Steinhilper. Wiesbaden 1978. (English summary pp 190–191)

1979

Aprill, Rainer und Peter Poerting: Kriminalpolizeiliche Beratung als Instrument zur Prävention der Betrugs- und Wirtschaftskriminalität. Bericht über die Ergebnisse einer Befragung. Wiesbaden 1979

Bundeskriminalamt (ed): Städtebau und Kriminalität/Urban Planning and Crime. Papers from the international symposium organized at the Bundeskriminalamt, Wiesbaden, December 11–13, 1978/Tagungsleiter: Edwin Kube. Wiesbaden 1979. (German papers, English papers)

Kühne, Hans Heiner und Koichi Miyazawa: Kriminalität und Kriminalitätsbekämpfung in Japan. Versuch einer soziokulturell-kriminologischen Analyse/Mit einer Vorbemerkung zum internationalen Kriminalitätsvergleich von Uwe Dörmann. Wiesbaden 1979

1980

Aprill, Rainer, Monika Plate und Rüdiger Weiß: Probleme der Personenbeschreibung in der polizeilichen Praxis – Eine Studie zur Erprobung eines Beschreibungsverfahrens anhand vorgegebener Merkmale. Wiesbaden 1980

1981

Hamburger, Franz, Lydia Seus und Otto Wolter: Zur Delinquenz ausländischer Jugendlicher – Bedingungen der Entstehung und Prozesse der Verfestigung. Wiesbaden 1981

1982

Knuf, Joachim: Polizeibeamte als Zeugen vor Gericht. Eine kommunikationswissenschaftliche Untersuchung/Mit Beiträgen von Gerold Ungeheuer, H. Walter Schmitz, Sibylle Berner und Angelika Regh-Birker. Wiesbaden 1982. (English summary pp 273–277)

1983

Behder, Uwe: Täterfluchtverhalten nach Raubüberfällen auf Geldinstitute. Eine Analyse für den Polizeipraktiker/Unter Mitarbeit von Rüdiger Weiß, Leo Schuster und Doris Hammen. Wiesbaden 1983

Bundeskriminalamt (ed): Symposium: Wissenschaftliche Kriminalistik. Referate und Diskussionsbeiträge am 23. und 24. Juni 1983 im Bundeskriminalamt/Tagungsleiter: Edwin Kube. Wiesbaden 1983

1984

Bundeskriminalamt (ed): Symposium: Perseveranz und kriminalpolizeilicher Meldedienst. Referate und Zusammenfassungen der Diskussionsbeiträge am 29. und 30. Mai 1984 im Bundeskriminalamt/Tagungsleitung: Leo Schuster und Hans-Jürgen Eyrich. Wiesbaden 1984

Schuster, Leo: Die Ringalarmfahndung. Eine empirische Untersuchung in den Ländern Baden-Württemberg, Hamburg und Hessen/Unter Mitarbeit von Uwe Behder, Rüdiger Weiß und Doris Hammen. Wiesbaden 1984

1985

Ahlf, Ernst-Heinrich: Das Bundeskriminalamt als Zentralstelle. Wiesbaden 1985

Bundeskriminalamt (ed): Zweites Symposium: Wissenschaftliche Kriminalistik – "Kriminalitätsprognose" und "Zusammenarbeit von Wissenschaft und Praxis". Referate und Diskussionsbeiträge am 2. und 3. Oktober 1984 im Bundeskriminalamt/Tagungsleiter: Hans Udo Störzer. Wiesbaden 1985

Herbertz, Claus-Walter und Wolfgang D. Salewski: Gewalttätige Jugendliche und soziale Kontrolle. Wiesbaden 1985

Plate, Monika, Ulrich Schwinges und Rüdiger Weiß: Strukturen der Kriminalität in Solingen. Eine Untersuchung zu Zusammenhängen zwischen baulichen und sozialen Merkmalen und dem Kriminalitätsaufkommen. Wiesbaden 1985. (English summary pp 196–203)

Poerting, Peter: Polizeiliche Bekämpfung von Wirtschaftskriminalität. Wiesbaden 1985

1986

Bundeskriminalamt (ed): Symposium: Nutzung der Sicht des Täters und des Täterwissens für die Verbrechensbekämpfung. Referate und Diskussionsbeiträge am 26. und 27. November 1985 im Bundeskriminalamt/Tagungsleiter: Erich Rebscher. Wiesbaden 1986

Bundeskriminalamt (ed): Was ist Gewalt? Auseinandersetzungen mit einem Begriff. Vol 1: Volker Krey: Zum Gewaltbegriff im Strafrecht. Part 1/Unter Mitarbeit von Norbert Arenz und Klaus Freudenberg; Friedhelm Neidhardt: Gewalt – Soziale Bedeutungen und sozialwissenschaftliche Bestimmungen des Begriffs. Wiesbaden 1986

Fehrmann, Hans, Klaus Jakobs, Rolf Junker und Claus Warnke: Das Mißtrauen gegen vergewaltigte Frauen. Erfahrungen von Vergewaltigungsopfern mit Polizei und Justiz. Eine Untersuchung von Polizeibeamten an der Hochschule für öffentliche Verwaltung in Bremen/Redaktion: Michael C. Baurmann. Wiesbaden 1986

Kreuzer, Arthur und Rainer Oberheim: Praxistauglichkeit des Hehlereistraftatbestands. Die Reform der §§ 259 bis 262 StGB und ihre Auswirkungen in der Strafverfolgungspraxis. Wiesbaden 1986

Kube, Edwin: Systematische Kriminalprävention – Mit praktischen Hinweisen. Wiesbaden 1986

1987

Dölling, Dieter: Polizeiliche Ermittlungstätigkeit und Legalitätsprinzip. Eine empirische und juristische Analyse des Ermittlungsverfahrens unter besonderer Berücksichtigung der Aufklärungs- und Verurteilungswahrscheinlichkeit. Part 1: Textteil und Verzeichnisse. Wiesbaden 1987. (English summary pp 314–316). Part 2: Tabellenteil und Materialien. Wiesbaden 1987

Kube, Edwin: Systematische Kriminalprävention. Ein strategisches Konzept mit praktischen Beispielen. 2nd edn. Wiesbaden 1987

1988

Ahlf, Ernst-Heinrich: Polizeiliche Kriminalakten (KpS). Wiesbaden 1988

Bundeskriminalamt (ed): Symposium: Der polizeiliche Erfolg. Referate und Diskussionsbeiträge am 15. und 16. Oktober 1986 im Bundeskriminalamt/Tagungsleiter: Hans Udo Störzer. Wiesbaden 1988

Bundeskriminalamt (ed): Was ist Gewalt? Auseinandersetzungen mit einem Begriff. Vol 2: Volker Krey: Zum Gewaltbegriff im Strafrecht. Part 2/Unter Mitarbeit von Martina Weber-Linn, Klaus Freudenberg, Bastian Endrulat und Helmut Konrad; Michael C. Baurmann, Monika Plate und Hans Udo Störzer: Polizeirelevante Aspekte bei der Auseinandersetzung mit dem Gewaltbegriff. Wiesbaden 1988

Krainz, Klaus W.: Prävention von Hauseinbrüchen. Ergebnisse einer Täterbefragung/Mit einer Einführung von Hans Udo Störzer. Wiesbaden 1988. (English summary pp 366–373)

Rebscher, Erich und Werner Vahlenkamp: Organisierte Kriminalität in der Bundesrepublik Deutschland. Bestandsaufnahme, Entwicklungstendenzen und Bekämpfung aus der Sicht der Polizeipraxis. Wiesbaden 1988

1989

Bundeskriminalamt (ed): Was ist Gewalt? Auseinandersetzungen mit einem Begriff. Vol 3: Bundeskriminalamt (ed): Symposium: Polizei und Gewalt. Erfahrungen im Umgang mit Gewalt und Folgerungen für künftiges Handeln. Referate und Diskussionsbeiträge. 30. Juni und 1. Juli 1988 im Bundeskriminalamt/Tagungsleitung: Hans Udo Störzer, Michael C. Baurmann und Monika Plate. Wiesbaden 1989

Fiedler, Joachim, Rolf Hoppe, Peter Berninghaus und Aleksandar Lenhart: Anhalterwesen und Anhaltergefahren unter besonderer Berücksichtigung des "Kurztrampens". Wiesbaden 1989

Leineweber, Heinz, Heinz Büchler und Karl-Heinz Dufner: Falschalarme – Ursachen und Auswirkungen. Wiesbaden 1989

Meyer, Jürgen, Axel Dessecker und Jürgen Rüdiger Smettan (eds): Gewinnabschöpfung bei Betäubungsmitteldelikten. Rechtsvergleichende und kriminologische Untersuchung. Wiesbaden 1989. (English summary pp 491–517)

Plate, Monika und Hans Schneider: Schwereeinschätzung von Gewalthandlungen. Ergebnisse zweier repräsentativer Bevölkerungsbefragungen. Wiesbaden 1989

Rehm, Jürgen und Wolfgang Servay: Wohnungseinbruch aus Sicht der Täter/Unter Mitarbeit von Susanne Bisson. Wiesbaden 1989. (English summary pp 154–160)

3 BKA-Technische Forschung (BKA Technical Research Series)

Volume 1: Deinet, Werner, Michael J. Linke und Bernd Rieger: Analyse der Schreibdynamik. Projekt-Bericht. Wiesbaden 1987

Volume 2: Bundeskriminalamt (ed): Symposium: Forensischer linguistischer Textvergleich. Referate und Zusammenfassungen der Diskussionsbeiträge am 8. und 9. Dezember 1988 im Bundeskriminalamt/Tagungsleitung: Rudolf Atzbach. Wiesbaden 1989

4 Berichte des Kriminalistischen Instituts/Auswahl (Series of Reports of the Research and Training Institute/Selection)

1981

Kriminalistisch-kriminologische Forschungsgruppe des BKA: Einbrüche in Wohnungen – Eine Pilotstudie. Wiesbaden 1980

1982

Kriminalistisch-kriminologische Forschungsgruppe des BKA: Einbrüche in Wohnungen – Eine Pilotstudie. 2nd edn. Wiesbaden 1982

Poerting, Peter: Polizeiliche Jugendarbeit. Ein Diskussionsbeitrag/Mit Beiträgen von Uwe Dörmann und Horst Grimminger. 1st and 2nd edn. Wiesbaden 1982

1983

Kube, Edwin und Leo Schuster: Vandalismus – Erkenntnisstand und Bekämpfungsansätze. 1st and 2nd edn. Wiesbaden 1983

1984

Kube, Edwin: Prävention von Wirtschaftskriminalität – Möglichkeiten und Grenzen. Wiesbaden 1984

1985

Kube, Edwin: Prävention von Wirtschaftskriminalität (unter Berücksichtigung der Umweltkriminalität) – Möglichkeiten und Grenzen. 2nd edn./Unter Mitwirkung von Franz Rohrer. Wiesbaden 1985

Kube, Edwin und Leo Schuster: Vandalismus – Erkenntnisstand und Bekämpfungsansätze. 3rd edn. Wiesbaden 1985

Schuster, Leo: Opferschutz und Opferberatung – eine Bestandsaufnahme. Wiesbaden 1985

1986

Poerting, Peter und Ernst G. Pott: Computerkriminalität. Ausmaß, Bedrohungspotential, Abwehrmöglichkeiten. Wiesbaden 1986

1988

Koch, Karl-Friedrich: Überregionale Kriminalitätslagebilder. Ergebnisse einer Expertenbefragung und Modell einer kriminologischen Regionalanalyse. Wiesbaden 1988

1989

Meyer, Jürgen: Gewinnabschöpfung bei Betäubungsmitteldelikten. Rechtsvergleichender Querschnitt und rechtspolitische Empfehlungen. Wiesbaden 1989. (German/English)

Vahlenkamp, Werner: Kriminalitätsvorbeugung auf kommunaler Ebene. Ergebnisse einer Städteumfrage des Bundeskriminalamtes mit Unterstützung des Deutschen Städtetages. Wiesbaden 1989

1991

Struth, Rainer, Eberhard Bode und Heinz Büchler: Diebstahlsdelikte als Ergebnis von Tatgelegenheiten. Ergebnisse einer Täterbefragung im Rahmen erweiterter Beschuldigtenvernehmungen. Wiesbaden 1991

Name Index

Subject Index

MIX
Papier aus verantwortungsvollen Quellen
Paper from responsible sources
FSC® C105338

If you have any concerns about our products,
you can contact us on
ProductSafety@springernature.com

In case Publisher is established outside the EU,
the EU authorized representative is:
Springer Nature Customer Service Center GmbH
Europaplatz 3, 69115 Heidelberg, Germany

Printed by Libri Plureos GmbH
in Hamburg, Germany